The Panic of 2008

The Panic of 2008

Causes, Consequences and Implications for Reform

Edited by

Lawrence E. Mitchell

Theodore Rinehart Professor of Business Law, The George Washington University Law School, USA

Arthur E. Wilmarth, Jr.

Professor of Law, The George Washington University Law School, USA

Edward Elgar

Cheltenham, UK • Northampton, MA, USA

Published by
Edward Elgar Publishing Limited
The Lypiatts
15 Lansdown Road
Cheltenham
Glos GL50 2JA
UK

Edward Elgar Publishing, Inc.
William Pratt House
9 Dewey Court
Northampton
Massachusetts 01060
USA

A catalogue record for this book
is available from the British Library

Library of Congress Control Number: 2010922145

FSC
Mixed Sources
Product group from well-managed
forests and other controlled sources
www.fsc.org Cert no. SA-COC-1565
© 1996 Forest Stewardship Council

ISBN 978 1 84980 261 1

Printed and bound by MPG Books Group, UK

Contents

Acknowledgements

The editors would like to thank the following people for their help in preparing the manuscript for this book: Tonietta Foncette and Winifred Hercules of The George Washington University Law School support staff, and Adele P. Maloney and Christopher Scott Pollock of The George Washington University Law School Class of 2010.

Contributors

Edward I. Altman, Max L. Heine Professor of Finance, New York University Stern School of Business.

James Fanto, Professor of Law, Brooklyn Law School.

Tamar Frankel, Professor of Law, Boston University School of Law.

Theresa A. Gabaldon, Lyle T. Alverson Professor of Law, The George Washington University.

William C. Handorf, Professor of Finance, The George Washington University School of Business.

Brenda J. Karlin, Research Associate, Salomon Center at New York University.

Maury Klein, Professor Emeritus of History, University of Rhode Island.

Edward Labaton, Senior Partner, Labaton Sucharow LLP.

Patricia A. McCoy, George J. & Helen M. England Professor of Law, University of Connecticut Law School.

Frank Partnoy, Professor of Law, University of San Diego School of Law.

Steven L. Schwarcz, Stanley A. Star Professor of Law & Business, Duke University School of Law.

Kenneth A. Snowden, Jr., Associate Professor, Department of Economics, The University of North Carolina, Greensboro.

Michael W. Stocker, Of Counsel, Labaton Sucharow LLP.

Arthur E. Wilmarth, Jr., Professor of Law, The George Washington University Law School.

Introduction

Thirty years of substantial deregulation based largely on neoliberal free market philosophies unleashed a regime of finance capitalism in America. Many American industrial corporations began to increase their reliance on debt in the 1980s. By the 1990s, commercial and investment banks had turned the invention of new financial derivatives into a major business, and generated huge profits from dealing and trading in them. They also discovered that profits from derivatives rose considerably as the instruments and underlying assets were increasingly leveraged. The mantra of 'risk management' provided a tempting rationale for speculation that often assumed reckless dimensions. The American economy reached a point toward which it had aimed for a century – the dominance of finance over industry, as many of the best minds from the academy and the most talented from business were drawn to Wall Street.

As early as the 1950s, insightful thinkers like Peter Drucker predicted a shift in the American economy from manufacturing to service. Less clearly anticipated was a more dramatic, and ultimately more significant, transformation from production to finance. The prolonged (if inconstant) bull market that began in the 1980s and resumed after the 1987 market crash made this shift look both inevitable and infinitely sustainable. By the late 1990s, there was widespread acceptance of the view that a new era in finance had come, that the old rules no longer applied and that virtually limitless wealth was available to those who invested in old and new forms of securities and relied on the inexhaustible ingenuity of American enterprise. After all, hadn't old Junius Morgan himself instructed his son never to sell America short? A new era was at hand.

The phrase 'New Era' was used both at the turn of the twentieth century and in the late 1920s to describe the apparent repeal of the business cycle. The financial and economic ends of both exuberant eras were devastating. Yet the federal government at the turn of the twenty-first century serially dismantled many of the most important protections that resulted from the sad learning of the earlier period. Perhaps most significantly, the venerable Glass-Steagall Act, which from its enactment in 1933 had helped to prevent the kind of systemic banking panics that had repeatedly occurred in America during the previous century, was repealed. In the Gramm-Leach-Bliley Act of 1999 (GLBA), the federal government for the first time gave its explicit blessing to the nation's most significant financial institutions – those responsible for sustaining and protecting credit supply and systemic financial integrity – to speculate in securities. Commercial banks blended with investment banks and the resulting 'universal banks', together with the remaining securities firms, increasingly leveraged their equity to generate higher profits. A compliant Securities and Exchange Commission, charged with ensuring the safety of American securities markets, stood back in the face of apparently increasing prosperity and, perhaps, based on some degree of misplaced faith in the integrity of market actors.

The bursting of the dot.com bubble in the earliest years of the twenty-first century did little to dampen spirited speculation. Instead, the Federal Reserve's accommodating monetary policy helped to spread the fever from stock markets to housing markets. A housing boom empowered homeowners to finance record levels of consumption by borrowing against the illusory growth in home values. Rising consumption produced a sharp increase in corporate earnings. Analysts, traders, and investors celebrated record corporate profits while failing to see that, during the preceding three decades, internal equity had fallen sharply and had been replaced by debt. A new wave of leveraged buyouts swept through the economy as private equity firms repeated, with new variations, the takeover strategies Michael Milken pioneered during the 1980s. To protect themselves against such buyouts, incumbent managers borrowed heavily to 'enhance shareholder value', either by engaging in debt-laden internal restructurings to return capital to shareholders or by financing large share buybacks. The overleveraging of American industry proceeded in tandem with overleveraging of American housing. The proliferation of complex derivatives and a dramatic increase in off-balance sheet financing helped to mask the truth. American industrial corporations, financial institutions, and investors assumed, and exposed the American economy to, dangerous levels of credit risk, liquidity risk and market risk.

The triumph of the financial sector in America inspired imitators in the United Kingdom and Europe. UK and European universal banks followed similar strategies of underwriting speculative securities, dealing in complex derivatives, and promoting housing booms. As in the US, housing bubbles in UK and European markets were inflated by dramatic increases in housing prices and reckless extensions of mortgage credit to borrowers who could not afford to pay for homes they had purchased. In the United States, mortgage lending reached unprecedented levels, thanks to the willingness of mortgage lenders to create subprime and 'Alt-A' mortgages with low initial borrowing costs, as well as the Federal Reserve's policy of maintaining historically low interest rates. Mortgage originators sold these risky mortgages to universal banks and investment banks, which repackaged them into mortgage-backed securities and collateralized debt obligations. Credit rating agencies gave their stamp of approval, and the volume of mortgage-related securities skyrocketed along with the steady rise in housing prices.

After reaching record highs, housing prices stopped rising in 2006 and began to decline sharply in 2007, as interest rates edged upwards and monthly payments on subprime loans increased according to their contractual terms. With the puncturing of the housing bubble, investors became concerned about the security of any investments related to the housing market. In a manner eerily reminiscent of the Panic of 1907, gradually increasing fear among financial institutions and investors created disturbances in American and international credit markets during the late summer and early autumn of 2007. The Federal Reserve and its UK and European central bank counterparts responded by injecting liquidity into the financial markets, but their efforts proved ephemeral. Liquidity in interbank lending markets evaporated, major financial institutions reported large losses, and securitization markets shut down.

Stronger financial institutions acquired weaker ones beginning in March 2008, when JP Morgan Chase announced its fire-sale acquisition of one of the world's storied investment banks, Bear Stearns. The deal, supported by the Federal Reserve Board and Treasury Department and backed by government financial guarantees, recalled John Pierpont Morgan's famous rescue of the Trust Company of America during the Panic of 1907. A brief period of calm ensued during the early summer of 2008, and then the American economy appeared to tear apart at the seams.

During the late summer and fall of 2008, the following massive firms, from every major sector of the financial services industry, either failed, were merged into stronger competitors with federal assistance, or were seized and placed under federal oversight: (1) investment banking: Lehman Brothers and Merrill Lynch; (2) commercial banking: IndyMac, Wachovia and Washington Mutual; (3) insurance: American International Group; (4) mortgage finance: Countrywide, Fannie Mae and Freddie Mac. Despite $90 billion of capital support and $400 billion of asset guarantees provided by the federal government, two giants of commercial banking, Bank of America and Citigroup, were severely damaged and were obliged to accept close oversight by federal regulators. In addition, the last two titans of investment banking, Goldman Sachs and Morgan Stanley, were forced to convert from investment banks into bank holding companies.

Confronted with an imminent collapse of the stock market, Congress approved a $700 billion Troubled Assets Relief Program (TARP), urged by Treasury Secretary Henry Paulson as a tool to enable government buy-outs of devalued derivative securities. The program's limited early successes led the Treasury Secretary quickly to shift TARP's purpose extensively into a program of government debt and equity financing for a cascade of failing financial institutions numbering in the hundreds or thousands. In a demonstration of the financial crisis' far-reaching impact on the real economy, the Bush administration also opted to use TARP funds to provide capital to the country's automotive manufacturing sector, lending $14 billion to Chrysler and General Motors (GM) to avert their immediate bankruptcies.

Despite unprecedented federal government financial intervention, the nation's economy collapsed into the worst recession since the Great Depression of the 1930s. Many analysts argued that 'depression' was a more accurate description of the US economy in early 2009. The Obama administration took office and quickly persuaded Congress to approve an $800 billion stimulus package. The new administration also engineered comprehensive restructurings of Chrysler and GM through accelerated bankruptcy proceedings that required $40 billion of additional financing from the federal government. However, despite occasional signs and pronouncements of the beginning of a much-anticipated recovery, the US economy continued to languish in the summer and autumn of 2009. Many corporations that previously relied heavily on debt financing no longer had sufficient internal equity or external financing to sustain their operations. The national unemployment rate rose to nearly 10 per cent, a level not seen since the early 1970s, and home foreclosures reached levels unmatched since the 1930s. The long-term consequences of the financial crisis for the American economy remained uncertain in late 2009, as large-scale defaults on commercial real estate loans and other corporate obligations loomed on the horizon.

Since the beginning of the financial crisis in August 2007, investment professionals, participants in the financial services industry, policymakers, members of Congress, academics, and the media have sought to identify and understand the causes of the crisis, assess its continuing extent, and develop ways both to clean up the fallout and to prevent future panics or at least mitigate their magnitude. It was in this environment, and to meet this need, that a conference entitled 'The Panic of 2008: Causes, Consequences and Proposals for Reform' – upon which this volume is based – was held at The George Washington University Law School on April 3–4, 2009.

The following speakers presented their views on various aspect of the panic at the conference: Robert Ahdieh, Edward Altman, Dennis Berman, William W. Bratton, Robert Bruner, Sean Carr, Rodgin Cohen, James D. Cox, Rob Cox, Lawrence A. Cunningham, Jesse Eisenger, Lisa M. Fairfax,

James A. Fanto, Tamar Frankel, Theresa A. Gabaldon, Charles Geisst, Anna Gelpern, Harvey Goldschmid, Daniel Gross, William C. Handorf, Henry T.C. Hu, Susan L. Karamanian, Maury Klein, Edward Labaton, Donald C. Langevoort, Gregory E. Maggs, Joseph McCahery, Patricia McCoy, Floyd Norris, Frank Partnoy, Irving M. Pollack, Jay R. Ritter, Jeffrey Rosen, Heidi Schooner, Steven L. Schwarcz, David Skeel, Heather Slavkin, Ken Snowden, Stanley Sporkin, Richard Sylla, Michael Waibel, Peter J. Wallison, Arthur E. Wilmarth, Jr., and David Zaring. The conference was organized by a committee of faculty members specializing in business and financial law at The George Washington University Law School, chaired by Lawrence E. Mitchell.

The chapters in this volume, a subset of the papers presented at the conference, cover a wide range of issues and both explain and, in their diversity, illustrate, the extent of the crisis. The first part of the book turns to history in order to situate this particular economic collapse within the broader scope of what Charles Kindleberger, in his classic book, describes as manias, panics, and crashes. Maury Klein leads off with a wonderful piece of historiography, explaining how history can and cannot help us understand what happened. Unfortunately, history is limited in its ability to guide us because, as Klein observes, life is messy and people are messy. So while historical patterns may exist, based on evidently enduring human impulses and imperfections, passions and predilections, the lessons of one panic will never fully explain the causes of another crisis, still less enable us to solve it or prevent it. Simply put, context matters, and the social, economic, regulatory and political context of the current decade is so different from, for example, the context of the late 1920s, that despite the obvious parallels, the differences are equally compelling.

As important, no serious historian can tell us very much about the causes and consequences of the panic of 2008 because it remains an ongoing event. Just as Klein points out that historians continue to disagree about the causes of the 1929 crash and the Great Depression, contemporary thinkers have only begun to explore the surface of the problems that brought on the current crisis, even as they live through it and try to cope with its fallout. Time alone will tell how similar or different this panic is to others of the past, whether the current great recession will mimic the patterns of the Great Depression, or whether the distinctive features of the present crisis will require us to classify it as an entirely different kind of economic event. Nonetheless, Klein deftly provides us with a fascinating comparative overview of the two most significant US financial crises in living memory.

Ken Snowden's chapter explores a critically important aspect of the possible historical analogy between the Great Depression and our contemporary situation: namely, the residential mortgage crisis of the 1930s. As he describes it, the crisis and its long-term effects originated in a series of four major events; (i) the dramatic growth of residential mortgage debt in the 1920s, facilitated by high leverage, easy credit, the innovation of private mortgage insurance, and securitization of some mortgages; (ii) the liquidation during the 1930s of many of the financial intermediaries that had created the financial innovations that stimulated the mortgage boom; (iii) federally-backed efforts to strengthen portfolio lenders (including commercial banks, life insurance companies, savings & loan associations (S&Ls), which grew out of the failed building & loan associations (B&Ls), and mutual savings banks); (iv) the federal government's creation of the Home Owners Loan Corporation, a 'bad bank' designed to purchase defaulted mortgages; (v) regulatory changes that created a dominant position for portfolio lenders; and (vi) the success of the Federal Housing Authority's loan program combined with the failure of efforts to create a government-sponsored program for securitizing mortgages. The failure of securitization in the 1930s shaped the residential mortgage market for the next 40 years.

The New Deal's transformation of mortgage lending produced an institutionalization of the residential mortgage business. Snowden notes that in the 1920s, more than 40 per cent of residential mortgages were held by individual investors in a population that consisted primarily of renters. Mortgages were made conservatively, typically for no more than the value of the property, and ran for what by modern standards were very short terms. But while financial institutions were the minority of lenders, they grew rapidly in significance during the 1920s. B&Ls expanded aggressively, as residential builders used them to finance new housing projects. Institutional lenders began to offer second mortgages as a way to provide higher loan-to-value mortgage financing. At the same time, individual mortgage investors found ways to diversify their investments and obtain liquidity by participating in the new methods of securitization offered by mortgage guaranty companies and real estate bond houses. Mortgage guaranty companies also began to offer private mortgage insurance and participation certificates on mortgage collateral.

Due to the massive increase in housing credit and homeowner indebtedness produced by these innovations, crisis was at hand. Defaults began to reach alarming rates in the late 1920s and continued throughout most of the 1930s, affecting primarily the lightly-regulated B&Ls, thousands of which were liquidated in the early and mid-1930s. Mortgage guaranty companies, which were more closely regulated, initially escaped that fate despite financial difficulty, although significant liquidations were to occur by 1933. Approximately 80 per cent of real estate bonds, issued by unregulated bond houses, were in default in 1935.

Snowden describes the regulatory responses of the Hoover and Roosevelt administrations, in which the federal government allowed many B&Ls, mortgage guaranty companies, and real estate bond houses to fail, while working to save most of the commercial banks and insurance companies, as well as a subset of the B&Ls which were the most professionally and soundly managed and which eventually came under the auspices of the newly-created Federal Home Loan Bank Board. Mortgage relief to homeowners was provided by the Home Owner's Loan Corporation, which, as Snowden describes, was a 'publicly-financed "bad bank" for home mortgage lenders'. The emergency New Deal measures attained greater permanence after the immediate crisis was addressed. Many B&Ls converted to regulated S&Ls, and the Federal Savings and Loan Insurance Corporation, created in 1934, provided new measures of financial security, including a deposit insurance scheme for S&Ls. The National Housing Act of that year also authorized the creation of Fannie Mae and Freddie Mac to buy and sell Federal Housing Administration loans from the local mortgage companies that originated them.

Snowden concludes with a discussion of the system of residential mortgage lending that was created by the New Deal's reforms. Portfolio lenders dominated the mortgage industry for four decades, backed by federal regulation and deposit insurance. However, the stability of porfolio lenders was ultimately destroyed by the great inflation of the 1970s and early 1980s. After portfolio lenders failed or abandoned the mortgage lending business, a new form of mortgage securitization arose. In turn, the new securitization scheme helped to sow the seeds of the present crisis.

Part II of the book addresses the causes of the panic and proposals for reform. We begin with James Fanto's analysis of how misguided risk management practices contributed to the crisis. Risk management is designed to assess and monitor the risks a financial institution undertakes, assure the availability of resources to deal with them, provide adequate risk information to senior managers, and to devise ways of dealing with risk. Risk management has increasingly come to rely on quantitative financial modeling. However, as Fanto explains, stress testing (which assesses the strength of an institution to meet financial adversity) and scenario analysis (which analyzes the ways in which adverse events might occur and the consequences if they do) also remain centrally important components of risk analysis. It is these latter components of risk analysis – stress testing and scenario analysis – that Fanto claims failed in the face of the oncoming crisis.

The risks incurred by a financial institution determine the amount of capital that the institution must hold to protect itself from failure. Not surprisingly, minimum capital requirements have long been an important feature of financial regulation. Changes in the business models of financial institutions, facilitated by the enactment of GLBA in 1999, led traditional lending institutions increasingly to engage in securities trading and other capital markets activities. Thus, one of the first changes in risk management Fanto describes is a regulatory shift from capital requirements based primarily upon credit risk – namely, the risk of default in a financial institution's loan portfolio – to capital requirements based on market risks inherent in the lines of business engaged in by the institution, including interest rate risk and systematic risk from general market conditions. As financial professionals developed their own quantitative risk models for pricing securities, regulators agreed to a form of quasi-self-regulation, in which regulators permitted financial institutions to use their own internal risk models as long as they complied with certain conditions.

Fanto focuses primarily on two adjuncts to risk assessment based on quantitative models – namely, stress testing and scenario analysis. Stress testing and scenario analysis are financial analogues to military contingency planning. While quantitative in part, these forms of risk management also involve significant qualitative factors and are grounded in human judgment as much as they are in mathematics. Stress testing and scenario analysis take into account not only the cultures and businesses of specific financial institutions but also their interrelatedness with other participants in the market, as well as risk managers' assessment of the anticipated behavior of other financial institutions. The quality and reliability of an institution's stress testing and scenario analysis are factors evaluated by regulators in determining capital requirements.

Despite the importance of stress testing and scenario analysis for anticipating and responding to a financial crisis, Fanto argues that these methods of risk management failed, and that their failure was a significant contributing cause of the crisis. Financial institutions relied too heavily on quantitative analysis, which typically assumed a very low probability of serious adversity. To the extent such analysis was performed, it was not done well. Risk managers, perhaps made unduly confident by superior recent performance, failed to take a long view of a financial history peppered with crises and did not plan accordingly. Moreover, risk management typically occurred at a divisional level, and there was a noted failure to aggregate the separate results into a firm-wide risk profile. Risk managers failed to consider the interrelatedness of different sectors of the financial system and the possibility that failure in one segment might infect others, or financial markets more generally. Senior managers and boards were unduly complacent. And regulators were insufficiently rigorous in demanding that financial firms use adequately adverse scenarios in their evaluations.

Based on these failures, Fanto calls for a thorough reform of the stress testing and scenario analysis procedures. Notwithstanding the good sense of his proposals, he recognizes that serious obstacles exist to implementing them, not the least of which are the extraordinary complexity of business lines and relationships both within and among financial institutions. This complexity poses a danger that managers will be lulled into a false sense of security by reassuring results from stress tests that are incapable of fully capturing an institution's risk. It is also reasonable to expect that managers will not fully act on even reliable risk assessments because of the human tendency to underestimate the risk of loss and the unwillingness of profit-oriented executives to manage an institution based on concerns about worst-case outcomes. Fanto concludes with a plan of action to more forcefully address these problems and ensure that risk management properly serves its critical functions.

Steven Schwarcz's chapter moves us from financial institutions to financial markets. He reconceives the financial regulatory safety net to address modern conditions, moving from the moral hazard of protecting financial institutions that have grown too big to fail to broader protection of financial markets which have become the dominant suppliers of credit within developed economies. Schwarcz importantly begins with a recognition that has been all-too absent in contemporary regulatory debates – namely, the reliance of the real economy on funding from the capital markets in order to produce the essential goods and services and the acquisition by consumers of houses and durable goods on which we rely. Treating the panic as a market story rather than a banking story, Schwarcz's focus reflects Willie Sutton's answer as to why he robbed banks; that's where the money is. And, in Schwarcz's view, it is important to recognize and protect the transformation from bank-based finance to market-based finance because disintermediation – the process of moving the funding of enterprises from financial intermediaries to capital markets – has the potential to increase financial efficiency significantly.

Schwarcz contends that the efficiency of securitization enables borrowers to obtain capital from capital markets more cheaply than from financial intermediaries whose own administrative costs, capital requirements, and costly acquisition of information are reflected in their credit pricing. Securitization also permits institutional loans to be packaged and sold in return for additional cash to be loaned for real economic purposes. Schwarcz acknowledges the moral hazard created by the originate-to-distribute model of securitized lending that developed in the years preceding the crisis, the conflicts of interest in servicing, and the potential (and, in the current crisis, realized) problems created by unjustified reliance on quantitative risk modeling. Nevertheless, Schwarcz believes that the potential benefits of securitization are sufficient to outweigh its potential risks. Indeed, Schwarcz tells us that although the abuses created by securitization of mortgages and its related products, like ABS CDOs, may have precipitated the crisis, 'securitization can also help get us out of it'.

While Schwarcz has elsewhere proposed prescriptive regulation to help prevent systemic financial crises, he acknowledges that market developments can easily outpace regulation. As a consequence, he proposes the development of a regulatory facility that can serve as a safety net when regulation fails, a facility that he calls 'a market liquidity provider of last resort'. Schwarcz contends that a liquidity provider of last resort should perform for financial markets a service similar to that which the Federal Reserve's discount window provides to banks. While such a facility would not be expected to function in normal markets, it would intervene to prevent a market disruption from degenerating into a full-blown crisis in which panicked investors produced a generalized collapse of prices by continuing to sell assets into falling markets.

The liquidity provider could stabilize markets by purchasing securities at prices that reflect deep discounts, both from their recent market prices and also from their intrinsic values, but are higher than an anticipated panic-induced level. Alternatively, the liquidity provider could provide hedging for the falling securities. Among other advantages of such a system, Schwarcz suggests that the liquidity provider would address the too-big-to-fail problem because its purchases or hedging would protect large financial institutions whose solvency might otherwise be threatened by a market collapse.

Schwarcz shows how such a liquidity provider might have acted in the current crisis, comparing the actual relief efforts provided by government authorities to the assistance that a liquidity provider of last resort might provide. He then goes on to address practical issues, as well as to extend his vision to international markets to show how his proposed liquidity facility might help to prevent the globalization of a financial catastrophe, or at least to mitigate its effects.

Financial markets, especially the credit markets, have long relied upon the rating agencies to ensure the marketability of bonds and other debt securities, among other instruments. Frank Partnoy lays much of the blame for the crisis directly at the feet of the ratings agencies, and argues that both regulators and investors should substantially lessen their dependence on those agencies in order to prevent another crisis.

Ratings agencies arose as a means of correcting information asymmetries between sellers of securities, which possess information that is difficult and costly to convey credibly, and investors. As Partnoy explains, credit rating agencies fulfilled this informational intermediary role from their creation in the nineteenth century until the mid-1970s, a time when the SEC began relying upon the agencies for regulatory purposes and also when the agencies shifted from an 'investor pays' business model to one in which the issuer paid the agency in order for their securities to be rated. In Partnoy's felicitous phrasing, ratings agencies changed from informational intermediaries to sellers of 'regulatory licenses'. As financial innovation proceeded and the earliest forms of CDOs were created, issuers consulted with ratings agencies in order to structure deals in ways that would achieve the desired ratings, and the agencies were happy to collect handsome fees for their consulting work. Partnoy tells the story of how the combination of the 'issuer pays' business model and the proliferation of new types of structured rated securities led to significant downgrades in the quality of ratings analysis, as illustrated by the 1994–1995 bond market crisis.

Partnoy's cogent tale of the move from first level to second level securitizations, which took advantage of the apparent mispricing of highly-rated mortgage-backed securities, inexorably leads us deeper into the complexity and deceit of the recent credit bubble, in which the ratings agencies were prime players. Synthetic CDOs and SIVs depended for their marketability on their credit ratings. Even if investors had wanted to examine the underlying assets, those assets were frequently unidentifiable and subject to rapid and unpredictable turnover based on banker-determined investment parameters. Credit rating agencies willingly acquiesced in providing high ratings for complex tranches of opaque CDOs, using risk models that relied on outdated assumptions and other flawed inputs to produce the desired results.

In the absence of overreliance by regulators and investors on the rating agencies, Partnoy suggests that the crisis might not have occurred because the toxic financial instruments that precipitated the crisis could not have been marketed and sold. Accordingly, one solution is to combat this over-reliance. How is this to be done? Partnoy suggests that regulators should cease to rely on credit ratings. Regulatory reliance is not only a problem in the US. As he points out, the Basel II capital accord drafted by the Basel Committee on Banking Supervision allows banks to use credit ratings to determine their net capital requirements. Partnoy's recommendation is to substitute market-based risk measures for credit ratings. He also suggests the administration of 'shock therapy' to investors to wean them from over-reliance on ratings agencies. He particularly notes the differences in meaning between ratings on corporate bonds and those on exotic structured financial instruments such as CDOs and SIVs, which require far deeper and more nuanced analysis than the ratings agencies provided during the past decade. Improved disclosure to investors by issuers is also important. Partnoy concludes with a discussion of how market measures and asset prices can facilitate better risk analysis than can the ratings agencies.

Thus, in explaining the causes of the financial crisis, Fanto tells a story of failed risk management, Schwarcz offers a tale of dysfunctional capital markets, and Partnoy provides an account of overreliance by government officials and private investors on highly conflicted ratings agencies. For her part, Patricia McCoy tells a story of regulatory competition and agency capture to support her conclusion that effective consumer financial protection is urgently needed to protect our economy from a repetition of the widespread predatory lending that helped to promote the housing bubble and ultimately led to massive defaults on subprime and Alt-A mortgages. The dispersal of lending regulation within the federal government and among states created a fragmentation in which lenders were able to choose the most lax regulatory regime, regulators became compliant because of the competition among regulators for business, and bank profitability rather than consumer protection became the primary goal of regulatory agencies.

In terms of contributing to the crisis, the high degree of dispersion among lenders produced results contrary to what one would expect in an industry characterized by vigorous competition. Instead of reducing their prices to consumers, mortgage lenders increased their market share by introducing new and risky products that were superficially attractive to borrowers who were not equipped to assess the risks of such products. Loan-to-value ratios increased and banks relaxed their underwriting standards in order to generate higher volumes of mortgages for securitization. The riskiest borrowers turned to, and were readily granted, the riskiest loans. Moreover, the riskiest loans were concentrated in regions with expensive housing markets. The availability of mortgage credit expanded with the influx of new financing from Wall Street investment banks, causing housing markets to become sellers' markets in many areas. Consequently, home prices rose to unsustainable levels.

Low interest rates following the 2001 recession started the housing bubble, but as interest rates began to rise and demand for prime mortgages fell, lenders responded by creating new types of subprime mortgage products with introductory 'teaser rates' that made borrowing seem initially affordable to those priced out of the prime mortgage market. However, the longer-term costs of subprime mortgages, and thus their true risks to borrowers, were masked by complex terms, the difficulty of obtaining loan commitments early enough to allow borrowers to comparison shop, and the hidden yield spread in commissions paid to mortgage brokers. The perverse dynamics of the subprime mortgage market, McCoy reports, made 'informed consumer choice impossible'.

Lenders' ability to hide risks in the fine print allowed the purveyors of these dangerous mortgage products to win market share from traditional lenders offering 30-year, fixed-rate prime loans. Federal regulators allowed this to happen. Federal regulators failed to exercise their powers to ensure the safety of loan products and enforce regulations against lenders that ignored them. In addition, regulators failed to prevent banks from investing in risky mortgage-backed securities and CDOs, and they allowed banks both to hold dangerously risky assets on their balance sheets and to 'park' such assets in off-balance-sheet conduits the banks sponsored. The core cause of all of this hazardous behavior, McCoy tells us, was fragmented regulation, and she explains in detail the nature and consequences of that fragmentation.

Notwithstanding the problem of supervisory fragmentation, regulatory control could still have been asserted. The Federal Reserve Board (FRB) could have prohibited toxic mortgages by adopting comprehensive federal anti-predatory lending rules. Largely because of former FRB Chairman Alan Greenspan's commitment to deregulation, the FRB failed to adopt such rules, leaving the market at best under-regulated and, at worst, unregulated entirely. Interestingly, McCoy points out, state regulators began to act more aggressively under their own consumer protection legislation than did federal regulators. But this was of no avail in the case of national banks and federal savings associations, because those institutions – which included many of the largest originators and funders of subprime and Alt-A mortgages – were shielded from state law by preemptive regulations adopted by their regulators. The Office of Thrift Supervision (OTS) and the Office of the Comptroller of the Currency (OCC) had ample financial incentives to adopt preemptive rules to immunize their regulated constituents from state regulation, because both agencies depended on fees paid by their constituents to fund their budgets. Granting preemptive immunity discouraged lending institutions from defecting to other federal regulatory regimes, and also had the potential to persuade state-chartered lenders to shift to federal charters.

Federal regulators could have, but failed to, tighten their regulation and enforcement. Instead, as McCoy puts it, 'federally regulated lenders – as well as all lenders operating in states with weak regulation – were given *carte blanche* to loosen their lending standards free from meaningful regulatory intervention'.

The results of such regulatory failure are now painfully obvious, and McCoy highlights the 'inextricable' link between consumer protection and systemic stability. Her solution, which as of her writing is consistent with the Obama administration's proposals, is to (i) adopt federal uniform consumer protection standards for all consumer financial service providers;

(ii) vest the authority to administer and enforce these laws in one federal agency created for the purpose of consumer protection, (iii) allow states to adopt supplemental consumer protection laws; and (iv) provide 'parallel enforcement authority to federal banking regulators and the states and allow consumers to bring private causes of action to recover for injuries they sustain'.[1] McCoy concludes by evaluating the Obama administration's plan in light of her analysis, and she supports the plan's proposal for a unified and independent federal consumer protection agency with authority to regulate federally-chartered and state-chartered providers of financial products.

William Handorf, approaching the problem from the perspectives of a banker, a bank regulator and an academic, sees plenty of blame to go around, but he understands the crisis as resulting largely from regulatory failures. Unfortunately, he sees little evidence in the regulatory responses to the current crisis to give us comfort that we can prevent future systemic failures, noting that banking panics occur roughly every 15 years. The nations of origin and particular catalysts may change, but the pattern of financial crisis remains roughly the same, arising out of inadequate bank capital, inadequate liquidity reserves, inappropriate pricing, risky investment, concentrations of risk, reckless origination of loans, and aggressive distribution of investment products in order to produce fees and promote a rapid growth of bank profits. The economic environment also is important, particularly when widespread bank failures accompany a recession or, as in the current crisis, precipitate a recession, which increases bank losses by causing defaults by borrowers and depriving consumers and businesses of necessary credit. Finally, failure occurs because bank management becomes complacent, failing to identify and properly monitor and control risk. As Handorf notes, these factors all correlate with lax monitoring and enforcement of prudential requirements by regulators. Additional factors, present in the current crisis, include overleveraging and bank reliance on less-expensive, short-term funding to increase return on assets (thereby increasing bank liquidity risk), and investing in poor quality assets.

Handorf moves quickly from the causes of the present crisis to the lessons to be drawn from it, which nicely summarize the arguments of the previous chapters. Handorf's lessons include (i) the Federal Reserve's maintenance of interest rates that were too low for too long, thereby encouraging speculation with cheap money, (ii) managerial inattention to risk management, and (iii) regulatory failures to assert control over dangerous consumer loan products. In addition, as Hahndorf puts it, 'credit rating agencies failed miserably', and investment banks pursued an 'originate-to-distribute' business strategy, which reduced due diligence and created conflicts of interest at each step of the lending and securitization process. Meanwhile, the predominance of unregulated loan brokers helped to promote a nationwide proliferation of toxic mortgage products, and the federal government pushed too hard to expand homeownership by encouraging the extension of credit to borrowers who simply could not afford to pay the mortgages on their homes.

His clear insights into the causes of the current crisis lead Hahndorf to conclude on a pessimistic note: 'Unfortunately, history suggests similar problems discussed in this conference will resurface in approximately 15 years.'

The consequences of the credit crisis are all too graphically presented by Edward Altman. Surveying the wreckage in the high-yield bond market, Altman's study shows that distressed and defaulted high-yield debt rose to $3.59 trillion in 2008 from only $867 billion a year earlier. Although Altman's default rate forecast of 4.64 per cent was slightly higher than the actual default rate of 4.60 per cent in 2008, the predictions for 2009 are horrifying, with a consensus average rate of 13.63 per cent (and a range of 7.98 per cent to 18.23 per cent). The first quarter of 2009 was well on target to achieve this result. The average recovery rate on defaulted high-yield debt in 2008 was only 42.5 per cent, and Altman's projections indicate that the average recovery rate will fall to 24 per cent or less in 2009. These data are just the tip of the iceberg. Altman presents his characteristically thorough and detailed analysis of a junk bond market that has yet to show any significant recovery from the financial crisis, and can be characterized as little short of devastated. Indeed, Altman predicts that '[w]ith the current recession likely to continue through the entirety of 2009 (or beyond), it is quite likely that the high-yield default rate will continue to rise in 2009, and possibly in 2010'.

Although many of the preceding chapters conclude with reform suggestions, the remaining chapters move more directly to reform than diagnosis. Tamar Frankel's interesting chapter considers the way we think about regulating our financial markets. As she notes, we traditionally engage in two core forms of regulation; disclosure by issuers of essential financial and business information, and self-regulation by financial intermediaries, all based on the underlying policies of monitoring the costs and benefits of regulation, protecting financial innovation, and enforcing the law after it is broken (in contrast to rigorous *ex ante* monitoring).

The existing regulatory structure clearly failed to prevent the present crisis. While Frankel continues to support mandatory disclosure, her core answer to the question of how we prevent future crises is that we should set up regulatory mechanisms that monitor markets continuously in order to detect bubbles. As Frankel aptly puts it, market regulators should perform examination functions similar to those of bank regulators, paying special attention to the largest institutions and those that have received regulatory exemption. But Frankel is cautious; this kind of continuous monitoring has the potential to chill financial innovation. Therefore, the new market regulators should not be charged with altering the economic incentives of those forces that appear to be driving prices to bubble levels but rather should be limited to detecting and prosecuting legal violations, as well as addressing behavior that, while not technically illegal, appears to violate the 'spirit of the law'. While admittedly an expensive way to regulate, Frankel believes that the cost of enhanced monitoring by financial regulators is undoubtedly far less than the costs imposed on the economic system and society by market crashes and panics.

Frankel makes the important point that the intensity of regulation by examination should be countercyclical rather than the procyclical regulation that characterized oversight prior to the panic. In other words, regulation should be more intensive when times appear to be good rather than bad. For it is in the good times, the frothy, bubbly times, that fraud and illegality are most likely to flourish and are most difficult to detect. Naturally, the most intensive examinations should be performed on the largest, most highly leveraged, institutions, as well as those who have received legal exemptions, and regulators should be especially suspicious of those whose share prices appear to rise steadily and without significant fluctuations. Frankel closes with an evaluation of other, failed, regulatory approaches, and concludes that the bank regulatory model is likely best to serve us in protecting economic and financial stability.

Theresa Gabaldon tells a sad tale of collateral damage that teaches important lessons for reformers while explaining that one of the most significant forms of damage created by the crisis is lost trust. And she trenchantly tells the tale in the form of a case study involving the sewer bonds of Jefferson County, Alabama.

Finance is inherently about what will happen in the future. That is, of course, no reason to disregard the lessons of the past. Gabaldon plumbs a single, but impressive, failure of modern finance, the sewer bonds issued by Jefferson County. This story provides an opportunity to examine how the subprime mortgage crisis roiled the waters of finance, swamping with debt service issuers of securities that had nothing to do with subprime lending. As a morality tale, that same story unhappily cautions against trust at the same time that it teaches that trust of a sort is an inevitable precondition for modern finance.

One of the most important lessons of the Jefferson County sewer debacle is that disclosure, as presently practiced, is plainly inadequate as a method of avoiding financial harm. For instance, Gabaldon's examination of the actual prospectuses used in connection with the Jefferson County debacle demonstrates that, in complicated financings, the wrong entities are called upon to make public disclosures. Even with revamping, however, she concludes that disclosure is unlikely to provide the protection that many of the participants in modern securities markets arguably need. In some instances, it appears that the only realistic course of action for those participants is to resort to trust.

Trust, however, can be neither justified nor sustained without significant attention to its conditions. Those conditions include both the intentions and the abilities of trusted actors to perform. Although the law has at least some capability to deal with problems of intention, it deals awkwardly, at best, with problems presented by a lack of ability to perform one's commitments. Gabaldon's solution is to buttress the conditions of trust with a full-cry demand that certain actors 'speak the truth' or suffer significant legal consequences. Although this appears to circle back to a requirement of full disclosure, the 'duty of truth' is different, because it calls upon an actor to be right and not just forthcoming. Thus, Gabaldon argues, the statements of actors critical to financial systems should be required, in the rearview mirror, to be completely correct on what effectively is a strict liability basis.

Trust has been breached in another way as well. Long before the crisis, executive compensation had become a major issue of public and scholarly debate. While some analysts question the extent to which the dramatic rise in executive compensation in recent years, especially in the financial industry, had much to do with the causes of the panic, others see a direct link. At the very least, there appears to be general revulsion at the continuation of extraordinary bonuses paid by financial institutions that were leading participants in the crisis and also received federal bailout money, not the least of which include AIG, Goldman Sachs, and JP Morgan Chase, the latter two of whom reported record profits and plans for large bonus payments in the third quarter of 2009, even as the crisis continued.

Edward Labaton and Michael Stocker see executive compensation and its metatastic growth as clearly playing some role in the reckless assumption of leverage and risk that led to the panic. Even if that role is indirect, we agree that the atmosphere created by excessive executive compensation leads both to short-term performance incentives and a concomitant willingness of top executives either to ignore excessive risk or affirmatively to embrace it.

A major problem in restraining executive compensation, which at least for the moment remains largely an issue of state law, lies in legal restrictions on the ability of plaintiff shareholders to bring derivative litigation on behalf of their corporation. As Labaton and Stocker nicely illustrate, the rules requiring shareholder demand on the company's board of directors, and the concomitant principles governing demand excusal or futility, have effectively shut most shareholders out of the possibility of getting past the dismissal stage of a derivative suit, making the process of very limited utility.

Related to limitations on derivative suits is the traditionally high burden of proof for establishing corporate waste, the cause of action most often relevant to executive compensation. Indeed it is safe to say that, until recently, waste was an almost impossible cause of action to sustain, even assuming one got past the initial procedural limitations of derivative litigation.

As Labaton and Stocker explain, the main culprit limiting derivative litigation is the power of a corporate board to appoint its own special litigation committee, with all of the real (but, according to courts, not disabling) problems of structural bias that the special committee's decision-making process, and judicial deference to it, creates. Balancing the concerns of courts and policymakers that derivative litigation will be frivolously brought with the real need for shareholder enforcement, Labaton and Stocker propose amending derivative litigation rules by incorporating procedures familiar under federal class action reform. In particular, they suggest that demand rules be relaxed for significant shareholders, those holding more than 1 per cent of the corporation's stock (or $25 million of the corporation's stock in the case of small cap companies), as well as a six-month holding period prior to initiating suit. Courts can reasonably be assured that such shareholders have real interests at stake and are not acting frivolously in bringing suit.

Once past the hurdles of derivative suit procedures, plaintiffs face the formidable burden of the business judgment rule, which typically applies even to executive compensation issues. However, Labaton and Stocker see promising signs – both in the writings of several Delaware judges as well as recent Delaware case law – indicating that the law is beginning to acknowledge the problems of excessive compensation and to increase the legal opportunities for redressing those problems through strengthened prohibitions against corporate waste. Together with reform in the derivative litigation process, Labaton and Stocker see new hope for the possibility of restraining executive compensation that bears little relationship to performance or rationality.

In the final chapter in this volume, Arthur Wilmarth examines the Supreme Court's recent decision in *Cuomo v. Clearing House, L.L.C.*, and he contends that the decision can best be understood as the Court's response to the subprime financial crisis. In *Cuomo*, the Court held that the Office of the Comptroller of the Currency (OCC) exceeded its authority when it adopted a regulation in 2004 that barred state officials from filing lawsuits to enforce applicable state laws against national banks. *Cuomo* arose out of an attempt by the New York Attorney General (NYAG) to enforce New York's fair lending laws against several large national banks that were heavily engaged in nonprime mortgage lending. By affirming the NYAG's authority to enforce state mortgage lending laws through the courts, the Supreme Court exhibited a perspective on banking regulation that sharply contrasted with the Court's approach two years earlier in *Watters v. Wachovia Bank, N.A.*

In *Watters*, the Court upheld another OCC regulation, which preempted the application of state laws to nonbank mortgage lending subsidiaries of national banks. As Wilmarth explains, *Watters* took a broad view of the preemptive reach of the National Banking Act and indicated that national banks would not benefit from any supplemental regulation by the states. In *Cuomo*, however, the Court took great pains to limit the precedential force of *Watters*. Moreover, *Cuomo* indicated a renewed appreciation for the historic role of the states in regulating financial institutions and protecting consumers. Three members of the Supreme Court (Justices Ginsburg, Breyer, and Souter) switched from supporting the OCC in *Watters* to opposing the OCC in *Cuomo*. Wilmarth believes that their positions changed because they modified their views about the merits of the OCC's preemptive regime and the value of state regulation between April 2007, when *Watters* was decided, and June 2009, when *Cuomo* was issued.

Wilmarth suggests that the most plausible explanation for the three Justices' change in perspective is that they were influenced by the outbreak of the subprime financial crisis in August 2007 and subsequent federal bailouts of several major national banks that were deeply involved in nonprime lending. Amicus briefs filed in support of the NYAG included numerous references to the financial crisis. In addition, the briefs sharply criticized the OCC for its sweeping preemption of state laws and for its weak record of protecting consumers from abusive lending practices. Statements made by Justices Ginsburg and Souter during oral argument in *Cuomo*, and also by Justice Stevens in his dissenting opinion in *Watters*, indicate that the Court was aware of the mortgage crisis and the growing controversy over the OCC's preemptive actions.

In Wilmarth's view, *Cuomo* represents a much-needed affirmation of (i) the principles of regulatory federalism inherent in the dual banking system and (ii) the central importance of consumer protection in preserving financial stability. In addition, *Cuomo* supports current legislative proposals by the Obama administration, which seek to preserve the states' longstanding role in protecting consumers of financial services. Like Patricia McCoy's earlier chapter, Wilmarth's chapter shows that, during the past decade, the states have been far more proactive than the OCC and other federal agencies in enacting laws and bringing enforcement proceedings to protect consumers against predatory lending and other abusive financial practices. The subprime financial crisis has demonstrated that effective consumer protection (including the prevention of predatory lending) is closely linked to the safety and soundness of financial institutions. Wilmarth argues that the states' positive record of legislation and enforcement over the past decade has confirmed the wisdom of preserving a federalist system of financial regulation, which includes not only a federal component but also a supplemental state role in enacting and enforcing consumer protection laws.

Wilmarth suggests that the only disappointing aspect of *Cuomo* for the states is that the Supreme Court failed to resolve a recurring issue about the appropriate level of judicial deference that federal agencies should receive when they claim authority to preempt state law. *Cuomo* did not follow a relatively demanding, four-part framework for judicial review of agency preemption claims that Justice Stevens developed in his opinion for the Court in *Wyeth v. Levine*. Instead, *Cuomo* left open the possibility that future preemption claims by federal agencies may receive a more accommodating level of judicial deference known as '*Chevron* deference'. However, the Court in *Cuomo* refused to defer to the OCC's preemptive regulation, based on the Court's conclusion that Congress did not delegate the preemptive authority asserted by the OCC. *Cuomo* indicates that, even if the Supreme Court chooses to apply *Chevron* in future cases involving agency preemption claims, the Court may apply an enhanced level of scrutiny with regard to the issue of whether Congress actually delegated the preemptive power claimed by the agency. While *Cuomo* does not resolve this important question, the broader context of the decision reveals that the policies of all three branches of the federal government, and those of many state governments as well, have been deeply influenced by the ongoing financial crisis.

As we noted above, it is far too early to understand all of the causes of the current crisis, and it would be presumptuous to offer any comprehensive analysis of the direct and indirect effects of the crisis or the best remedies for the problems we presently confront. If the history of the Great Depression is any guide, our descendants will continue to debate these issues 80 years from now. Despite the limitations of trying to understand interesting times while living through them, the essays in this volume present, we hope, a useful first step in understanding not only the causes of the Panic of 2008 but also its consequences and implications for reform.

Lawrence E. Mitchell
Arthur E. Wilmarth, Jr.
1 November 2009

NOTE

1. As we write this introduction, the Obama administration has been forced to concede one aspect of its consumer protection plan, including the proposal that financial services companies should be required to offer straightforward 'plain vanilla' products like 30-year, fixed-rate mortgages and low-interest, low-fee credit cards. Stephen Labaton, 'White House Pares Its Financial Reform', www.nyt.com, 23 September 2009. Whether these concessions are bellweathers for other problems the plan will encounter will only be revealed over the course of time.

Chronology of the panic of 2008

1997

- The Asian Financial Crisis led to slumping currencies, devalued stock markets and other asset prices, and a rise in private debt. In response, the International Monetary Fund ('IMF') developed country bailout programs that were conditional upon the participating country making reforms such as cutting back on government spending to reduce deficits, allowing insolvent banks and financial institutions to fail, and aggressively raising interest rates. The rising savings rates increased cash flow to United States capital markets and in turn into funding real property markets.

1999

- 30 September – Fannie Mae eased credit requirements to increase home ownership rates for low-income consumers.
- 12 November – President Clinton signed into law the Gramm-Leach-Bliley Act, which, in part, repealed the provisions of the Glass Steagall Act that separated commercial and investment bank activities.

2000

- 10 March – The dot-com bubble numerically burst when the NASDAQ Composite index peaked at 5048.62; more than double its value just a year before. The burst continued into 2002 and resulted in a decline of almost 80 per cent of the NASDAQ index and about 60 per cent in the S&P 500 index. In response, the US Federal Reserve Board eased its monetary policy.
- 21 December – President Clinton signed into law the Commodities Futures Modernization Act of 2000 that changed the jurisdiction, requirements, and procedures of the Commodities Futures Trading Commission ('CFTC'). First, the Act repealed an earlier

ban on single-stock futures contracts. Second, the Act narrowed the CFTC's jurisdiction by providing that products offered by banking institutions (including derivatives) were not to be considered futures contracts and explicitly exempted energy trades and trading on electronic energy commodity markets from the Act (also referred as the Enron loophole).

2001

- 11 September – Terrorist attacks targeted the United States. Terrorists hijacked four planes and crashed them into the World Trade Center in New York, the Pentagon in Washington D.C., and a field in Pennsylvania killing thousands and causing extensive economic and political havoc.
- Post 11 September – Concerned about economic deterioration from the terrorist attacks, the Federal Reserve Board maintained an eased monetary policy by targeting low interest rates and providing additional credit to sustain real property markets.

2004

- 24 April – The US Securities and Exchange Commission ('SEC') unanimously voted to exempt investment banks with assets over $5 billion from its net capital rules that required brokerages to hold capital reserves as a buffer against investment losses and economic trouble. The exemption allowed investment banks to release millions of dollars from reserves and to use the released funds in other investments such as credit derivatives and mortgage-backed securities.

2006

- The US housing bubble began to collapse as home prices decreased in value.

2007

- Increasingly widespread fear over the security of investments led to disturbances in American credit markets.

- 27 February – Freddie Mac announced that it would no longer buy the most risky subprime mortgages and mortgage-related securities.
- 4 March – HSBC wrote-off $11 billion to cover its escalating losses resulting from thousands of low-income families unable to repay loans.
- 5 March – New Century Financial Corp., a California lender specializing in mortgages to people with poor credit records or heavy debt burdens, filed for bankruptcy.
- 16 July – Bear Stearns disclosed its two subprime hedge funds (Bear Stearns High-Grade Structured Credit Fund and Bear Stearns High-Grade Structured Credit Enhanced Leveraged Fund) that invested in collateralized debt obligations ('CDOs') had lost most of their value due to the decline in the market for subprime mortgages.
- 31 July – Bear Stearns liquidated the two hedge funds that invested in various types of mortgage-backed securities.
- August – Liquidity in the Interbank lending markets began to decrease.
- 8 August – American Home, one of the largest independent home loan providers in the US, filed for bankruptcy after being unable to fund its mortgages.
- 9 August – BNP Paribas froze funds because of its loan losses.
- 23 August – The Federal Reserve loaned $2.5 billion each to Citibank, Bank of America, JP Morgan Chase & Co., and Wachovia to ease credit problems.
- 14 September – Northern Rock received liquidity support from the Bank of England due to problems in raising funds in the money market to replace maturing money market borrowings. After customers heard the news, there was a run on the bank when approximately 5 per cent of Northern Rock's total bank deposits were withdrawn.
- 18 September – The Federal Reserve cut interest rates 50 basis points from 5.25 per cent to 4.75 per cent.
- 9 October – The Dow Jones industrial average ('Dow Jones') reached an all time high of 14 164.53.
- 31 October – The Federal Reserve cut interest rates 25 basis points to 4.5 per cent.
- December – Liquidity in the interbank lending markets continued to decrease.
- 12 December – The Federal Reserve announced the creation of a Term Auction Facility ('TAF') in which fixed amounts of term funds would be auctioned to depository institutions against a wide variety of collateral.

2008

- 22 January – The Federal Reserve cut interest rates 75 basis points to 3.5 per cent, its biggest cut in 25 years.
- 30 January – The Federal Reserve cut interest rates 50 basis points to 3 per cent.
- 13 February – President Bush signed into law the Economic Stimulus Act of 2008.
- 22 February – The UK nationalized Northern Rock, the UK's fifth-largest mortgage lender, after two unsuccessful bids by private banks.
- 3 March – US Treasury Secretary Paulson proposed the broadest overhaul of US financial regulation since the Great Depression.
- 11 March – The Federal Reserve, the European Central Bank, and central banks in the UK, Canada, and Switzerland injected $200 billion of liquidity into markets.
- 14 March – JP Morgan Chase & Co. announced its fire-sale acquisition of Bear Stearns, as part of a bailout engineered by the Federal Reserve and aided by the US Department of the Treasury ('U.S. Treasury').
- 18 March – The Federal Reserve cut interest rates 75 basis points to 2.25 per cent.
- 30 April – The Federal Reserve cut interest rates 25 basis points to 2 per cent.
- 19 May – Banks and securities firms, including Citigroup, Merrill Lynch, HSBC, Deutsche Bank, Washington Mutual, and ING, failed to report $35 billion of write-downs on their income statements.
- 2 June – Standard & Poor's lowered Morgan Stanley, Merrill Lynch, and Lehman Brothers' credit ratings because of continued weakness in the investment banking business and the potential for more write-offs of devalued assets.
- 25 June – California and Illinois sued Countrywide Financial Company for deceptive trade practices and claimed the mortgage lender misled borrowers into taking risky loans that they could not afford.
- 11 July – US regulators seized IndyMac Bancorp Inc. after a run by depositors had left the California mortgage lender short on cash.
- 15 July – The SEC issued an emergency order that temporarily prohibited short selling in the securities of Fannie Mae, Freddie Mac, and primary dealers at commercial and investment banks.
- 30 July – President Bush signed into law the Housing and Economic Recovery Act ('HERA').

- 8 August – In settlements related to auction-rate securities, Citigroup, Merrill Lynch, and UBS bought back auction-rate securities from clients valued at $7.3 billion, $10 billion, and $19.4 billion respectively. Citigroup also agreed to pay a $100 million fine to settle charges that it fraudulently misled investors about the debt's risk.
- September 7 –The US Federal Housing Finance Agency ('FHFA'), which was created by HERA, seized control of Fannie Mae and Freddie Mac when it placed the two government-sponsored enterprises into an FHFA conservatorship that replaced chief executives, eliminated dividends, and allowed the US Treasury to purchase up to $100 billion of stock in each.
- September 15 –
  - Lehman Brothers filed for bankruptcy after the US Treasury and the Federal Reserve refused to provide financing for a rescue plan.
  - Bank of America announced its acquisition of Merrill Lynch.
- 16 September – To save AIG from insolvency, the US Treasury agreed to loan up to $85 billion to AIG in exchange for a 79.9 per cent equity interest and the right to suspend dividends.
- 19 September –
  - The US Treasury offered temporary insurance to money market funds.
  - The SEC issued a temporary emergency ban on short sales of financial stocks.
- 21 September – Goldman Sachs and Morgan Stanley converted into bank holding companies.
- 25 September – US Federal Deposit Insurance Co ('FDIC') seized Washington Mutual and sold its branches and assets to JP Morgan Chase & Co.
- 29 September –
  - Following Congress' failure to pass the first version of the Bush administration's bailout plan, the Dow Jones had its largest single day point loss when it dropped 777 points to 10 365.45.
  - The UK took control of Bradford & Bingley and its £50 billion ($100 billion) worth of mortgages and loans.
  - The Icelandic government took control of the country's third-largest bank when it bought a 75 per cent stake in the bank for €600 million ($860 million).
- 30 September –
  - The London Interbank Offered Rate (Libor) overnight rate,

which reflects the rate at which banks lend to each other, increased from 2.58 per cent to 6.88 per cent.

- The Irish government announced a two-year guarantee arrangement to safeguard all deposits, covered bonds, senior debt, and subordinated debt of six Irish banks.

- 3 October –
  - President Bush signed the Emergency Economic Stabilization Act. The Act created the Troubled Asset Relief Program ('TARP') that authorized the Treasury Secretary to spend $700 billion to purchase distressed assets and to inject capital into banks. The Act also expanded bank deposit guarantees, included $100 billion in tax breaks, and allowed the Federal Reserve to pay the interest on the excess reserve balances from banks.
  - The governments of Holland, Belgium, and Luxembourg each bought a stake in Fortis for a total of €11.2billion ($16 billion).
- 6 October –
  - The SEC terminated the exemptions for investment banks from their net capital rules.
  - The Dow Jones dropped more than 700 points and fell below 10000 for the first time since 2004. That week the Dow Jones closed lower at each session and had its worst weekly decline ever with an 18 per cent drop and falling over 1784 points.
  - Markets around the world also dropped, Britain's FTSE 100 Index dropped 7.9 per cent, Germany's DAX dropped 7.1 per cent, France's CAC 40 dropped 9 per cent, and Russia's RTS stock index dropped more than 20 per cent. In Iceland, trading in six banks stocks was halted to allow the government time to draft a crisis plan.
- 7 October –
  - The Federal Reserve announced the formation of a Commercial Paper Funding Facility to facilitate the issuance of term commercial paper.
  - The UK announced a rescue plan for banks to put up to £250 billion ($500 billion) into the banking system.
- 8 October –
  - The Federal Reserve cut interest rates 50 basis points to 1.5 per cent.
  - The European Central Bank, Bank of England, Bank of Canada, Swedish Riksbank, and Swiss National Bank

announced interest rate cuts of 50 basis points simultaneously with the Federal Reserve.
  - The Federal Reserve loaned AIG an additional $37.8 billion.
- 9 October – One year after reaching an all time high, the Dow Jones fell below 9000 for the first time since 2003.
- 10 October –
  - Within an hour of trading, and again when Wall Street opened, London, Paris, and Frankfurt stock markets all dropped 10 per cent.
  - Within minutes of opening, the Dow Jones dropped 697 points when it fell below 7900. The Dow Jones finished the day only down 128 points and closed at 8451. The Dow Jones finished the week down 1874 points, or 18 per cent, and 40 per cent down from the record high on 9 October 2007.
  - The Federal Reserve decided to lend directly to corporations.
- 11–12 October – The G7 nations met in Washington and pledged to support financial institutions and prevent their failure.
- 11 October – The US Treasury announced its rescue efforts would focus on the recapitalization of banks in exchange for preferred equity instead of the purchase of illiquid assets.
- 12 October – European countries announced a rescue plan for Europe's Banks totaling €1 trillion.
- 13 October – The Dow Jones closed at 9387, an 11 per cent increase.
- 14 October – The US government announced that it planned to purchase $250 billion of preferred stock in Goldman Sachs, Morgan Stanley, JP Morgan, Bank of America, Merrill Lynch, Citigroup, Wells Fargo, Bank of New York Mellon, and State Street.
- 15 October – The Dow Jones fell 733 points.
- Week of 19 October – The Dow Jones experienced extreme volatility with violent price swings.
- 27 October –
  - The US Treasury purchased $38 billion of preferred stock in 22 banks, including BB&T, Capital One, SunTrust Banks, City National Bank, Comerica, First Niagara Bank, Huntington Bancshares, Northern Trust, State Street Corporation, UCBH Holdings, First Horizon National Corporation, PNC Financial Services, Regions Financial Corporation, Valley National Bancorp KeyBank, and Washington Federal Savings.
  - The Hong Kong stock market crashed losing more than 12 per cent.

- 28 October – In anticipation of rate cuts, the Dow Jones rose 10.8 per cent and closed at over 9000.
- 29 October –
  - The IMF announced the creation of a short-term liquidity facility for market-access countries.
  - The Federal Reserve cut interest rates 50 basis point to 1 per cent.
- 31 October –
  - The Dow Jones closed up for the week.
  - Citigroup announced losses of $1.4 billion on securitizations.
- 6 November – Wells Fargo sold $11 billion of common stock to fund its purchase of Wachovia.
- 7 November – The US Labor Department released employment reports that showed about 500 000 jobs were lost in the US during September and October 2008 with unemployment reaching 6.5 per cent.
- 10 November –
  - The Federal Reserve granted American Express' request to become a bank holding company.
  - Fannie Mae lost $29 billion on write-downs.
  - The US Treasury announced another investment of $40 billion in preferred stock of AIG.
- 12 November –
  - US Treasury Secretary Paulson announced the remaining portion of the TARP budget would be used to relieve pressure on consumer credit and would not be used to purchase illiquid mortgage-related assets from financial institutions.
  - General Electric secured the temporary backing of the FDIC for up to $139 billion of the debt of its finance arm.
  - American Express sought $3.5 billion from the US Treasury.
  - ING posted its first-ever quarterly loss.
- 15 November – Washington D.C. hosted the initial session of the Summit on Financial Markets and the World Economy with the leaders of the G-20.
- 18 November – Executives of Ford, General Motors, and Chrysler testified before Congress, requesting access to the TARP for federal loans.
- 23 November – The US Treasury, Federal Reserve, and FDIC announced a rescue plan for Citigroup, which provided for an additional purchase of $20 billion of Citigroup's preferred stock and an arrangement to limit Citigroup's exposure to losses on loans

and securities in exchange for Citigroup's agreement to suspend dividend payments.

- 24 November – The Dow Jones had its biggest two-session gain of 891.10 points, or 11.8 per cent, since 1987.
- 25 November – The Federal Reserve Board announced the creation of the Term Asset-Backed Securities Lending Facility ('TALF'), under which the Federal Reserve Bank of New York would lend up to $200 billion on a non-recourse basis to holders of AAA-rated asset-backed securities and recently originated consumer and small business loans. The US Treasury also provided $20 billion of TARP money for credit protection.
- 28 November – Goldman Sachs received approval for a New York State banking license that allowed it to transform into a bank holding company and take deposits.
- 1 December –
  - The National Bureau of Economic Research officially declared that the US economy had entered a recession.
  - The US Labor Department announced 533 000 jobs were lost in November 2008, raising the unemployment rate from 6.5 per cent to 6.7 per cent.
- 3 December –
  - The US Government Accountability Office announced TARP lacked oversight.
  - The SEC approved measures to increase transparency and accountability at credit rating agencies and thereby ensure that firms provide more meaningful ratings and greater disclosure to investors.
- 11 December – The FBI announced the arrest of Bernard Madoff for his involvement in a Ponzi scheme totaling about $50 billion and affecting American and European banks, individuals, and charities.
- 16 December – AIG sold $39.3 billion of assets to a fund established by the Federal Reserve Bank of New York.
- 19 December – The US Treasury authorized loans of up to $13.4 billion for General Motors and $4.0 billion for Chrysler from the TARP budget.
- 24 December – GMAC, the financing arm of General Motors, became a bank holding company.
- 30 December – GMAC received a $5 billion cash infusion from the US Treasury in exchange for shares of preferred stock.

2009

- 5 January – The Federal Reserve Bank of New York began to purchase fixed-rate mortgage-backed securities guaranteed by Fannie Mae and Freddie Mac.
- 9 January – The Congressional Oversight Panel issued its second monthly report on the expenditures of the TARP.
- 12 January –
  - The FDIC issued a letter to FDIC-supervised institutions calling on them to implement a process to monitor their use of capital injections, liquidity support, and/or financing guarantees obtained through Treasury, FDIC, and Federal Reserve financial stability programs.
  - At the request of President-Elect Obama, President Bush submitted a request to Congress for the remaining $350 billion in TARP funding for use by the incoming administration.
- 16 January –
  - The US Treasury, Federal Reserve, and FDIC announced a package of guarantees, liquidity access, and capital for Bank of America. The Treasury and the FDIC planned to enter a loss-sharing arrangement with Bank of America on a $118 billion portfolio of loans, securities, and other assets in exchange for preferred shares. In addition, and if necessary, the Federal Reserve agreed to provide a non-recourse loan to back-stop residual risk in the portfolio. Seperately, the Treasury arranged to invest $20 billion in Bank of American from the TARP in exchange for preferred stock.
  - The US Treasury, Federal Reserve, and FDIC finalized terms of their guarantee agreement with Citigroup.
  - The US Treasury announced that it would lend $1.5 billion from the TARP to a special purpose entity created by Chrysler Financial to finance the extension of new consumer auto loans.
- 20 January –
  - President Obama was inaugurated as the 44th President of the United States.
  - The Italian automaker Fiat agreed to take a 35 per cent stake in the American auto company Chrysler.
- 28 January –
  - The National Credit Union Administration (NCUA) Board announced that the NCUA would guarantee uninsured shares at all corporate credit unions through February 2009

and established a voluntary guarantee program for uninsured shares of credit unions through December 2010.
  - The Board also approved a $1 billion capital purchase in the US Central Corporate Federal Credit Union that provides financing, check clearing, and other services to retail credit unions.
  - The IMF announced world economic growth would likely fall to 0.5 per cent in 2009, its lowest rate since World War II.
- 30 January – The Federal Reserve Board announced a policy to avoid preventable foreclosures on certain residential mortgage assets held, controlled, or owned by the Federal Reserve Bank. The policy was developed pursuant to section 110 of the Emergency Economic Stabilization Act.
- 3 February – The Federal Reserve announced the extension, through 20 October 2009, of the liquidity programs scheduled to expire on 30 April 2009.
- 6 February –
  - The Federal Reserve Board released additional terms and conditions of the TALF. Under the TALF, the Federal Reserve planned to lend up to $200 billion to eligible owners of certain AAA-rated asset-backed securities backed by newly and recently originated auto loans, credit card loans, student loans, and SBA-guaranteed small business loans.
  - The Congressional Oversight Panel announced the government overpaid for distressed financial assets and shares in 2008.
- 10 February –
  - US Treasury Secretary Timothy Geithner announced a Financial Stability Plan that included Treasury purchases of convertible preferred stock in eligible banks, the creation of a Public-Private Investment Fund to acquire troubled loans and other assets from financial institutions, expansion of the TALF, and new initiatives to stem residential mortgage foreclosures and to support small business lending.
  - The Federal Reserve announced that it was prepared to expand the TALF to as much as $1 trillion and broaden the eligible collateral to include AAA-rated commercial mortgage-backed securities, private-label residential mortgage-backed securities, and other asset-backed securities. An expansion of the TALF would be supported by $100 billion from the TARP.
- 17 February – President Obama signed into law the American Recovery and Reinvestment Act of 2009, which provided for a $787 billion stimulus package.

- 18 February –
  - President Obama announced The Homeowner Affordability and Stability Plan. The plan included a program to permit the refinancing of conforming home mortgages owned or guaranteed by Fannie Mae or Freddie Mac that currently exceed 80 per cent of the value of the underlying home. The plan also created a $75 billion Homeowner Stability Initiative to modify the terms of eligible home loans to reduce monthly loan payments.
  - The US Treasury announced plans to increase its preferred stock agreements with Fannie Mae and Freddie Mac to $200 billion and to increase the limits on the size of Fannie Mae and Freddie Mac's portfolios to $900 billion.
  - The US carmakers GM and Chrysler asked the US government for another $21.6 billion in support.
- 19 February – The Dow Jones closed at 7466, its lowest level since 9 October 2002.
- 25 February – The Federal Reserve, FDIC, Office of the Comptroller of the Currency, and Office of Thrift Supervision announced that they would conduct forward-looking economic assessments or 'stress tests' of eligible US bank holding companies with assets exceeding $100 billion. Supervisors would work with the firms to estimate the range of possible future losses and the resources necessary to absorb such losses over a two-year period. The assessment process was projected to continue through the end of April 2009.
- 2 March –
  - The Dow Jones had dropped more than 5 per cent since its summer 2008 peak.
  - The US Treasury and Federal Reserve launched the TALF, under which the Federal Reserve Bank of New York would lend up to $200 billion to eligible owner of certain AAA-rated asset-backed securities.
- 2 March – AIG announced losses of $61.7 billion, the largest quarterly loss of any company in US history. The US Treasury and Federal Reserve announced a restructuring of AIG, under which AIG would receive as much as $30 billion in additional TARP funds.
- 5 March –
  - The Mortgage Bankers Association reported that 12 per cent of Americans holding a mortgage were behind on payments or in foreclosures at the end of 2008.
  - The Dow Jones closed at 6594.44, its lowest since 1997.

- 6 March –
  - The US Labor Department announced the unemployment rate reached 8.1 per cent, the nation's highest in more than 25 years.
  - The Bank of England announced up to 150 billion pounds of quantitative easing, which would increase the risk of inflation.
- 10 March – Stephen Schwarzman, Blackstone CEO, announced that up to 45 per cent of the world's wealth had been destroyed by the global credit crisis.
- 16 March – President Obama instructed Treasury Secretary Geithner to block AIG from spending $165 million on executive bonuses.
- 19 March –
  - The US Treasury announced the Auto Supplier Support Program, which would provide up to $5 billion in financing to the automotive industry.
  - The FDIC completed the sale of IndyMac Federal Bank to OneWest Bank
- 23 March – The US Treasury announced the Public-Private Investment Program. The Program would include a partnership between the government and private investors that would purchase toxic assets from struggling banks in an effort to increase lending.
- 24 March – Treasury Secretary Geithner asked Congress to grant the government authority to take over failing financial institutions.
- 26 March – The US Treasury outlined a framework for comprehensive regulatory reform that focused on containing systemic risk.
- 30 March – President Obama gave General Motors 60 days to restructure and instructed Chrysler and Fiat to complete an alliance within 30 days.
- March 31 –
  - The General Accounting Office released a report on the status of efforts to addresses transparency and accountability issues for the TARP.
  - The US Treasury Department extended its temporary Money Market Funds Guarantee Program through 18 September 2009.
- 2 April – The G-20 nations met in London and pledged to triple funding for the IMF and improve international regulation of financial flows.
- 6 April – The Federal Reserve announced reciprocal currency agreements with foreign central banks that would enable the provision

of foreign currency liquidity by the Federal Reserve to US financial institutions.

- 24 April – The Federal Reserve published a white paper describing the process and methodologies employed by federal supervising authorities in their stress tests of large US bank holding companies.
- 7 May – The Federal Reserve released the results of the stress tests. The assessment found that the 19 firms could lose up to $600 billion during 2009 and 2010.
- 7 May – President Obama issued plans to trim $17 billion, or half a per cent, from the 2010 budget by reducing or eliminating 121 federal programs.
- 12 May – Freddie Mac reported a net worth deficit of $6.0 billion as of 31 March 2009. The Director of the Federal Housing Finance Agency, as conservator of Freddie Mac, submitted a request for $6.1 billion in funding to the US Treasury.
- 13 May – The US Treasury proposed amendments to the Commodity Exchange Act and securities laws to enhance government regulation of over-the-counter derivatives markets.
- 20 May – President Obama signed the Helping Families Save Their Homes Act of 2009, which temporarily raised FDIC deposit insurance coverage from $100 000 per depositor to $250 000 per depositor.
- 1 June – General Motors Corp. filed for bankruptcy. President Obama detailed a company restructuring plan that called for an additional $30 billion in aid and would grant the government a 60 per cent stake in the automaker. New York Bankruptcy court approved the sale transaction of Chrysler to Fiat.
- 17 June – The US Treasury released its proposal for reforming the financial system. The plan called for giving additional oversight power to the Federal Reserve aimed at improving risk monitoring, higher capital and liquidity requirements for banks, increased reporting requirements for issuers of asset-backed securities, and the creation of a Financial Services Oversight Council to coordinate the different existing regulators.
- 22 June – The World Bank projected that global production for 2009 would fall for the first time since World War II by 2.9 per cent.

Prepared by Adele P. Maloney
George Washington University Law School 2010

PART I

Historical antecedents

1. The panic of 2008: something old and something new

Maury Klein

History is often regarded as something between a balm and an oracle, replete with a variety of signs that must be interpreted by those who think they have special insight into what they mean. The story is never a complete or fully satisfying one because the variables are so maddingly elusive. Have we chosen the best set of quivering entrails to examine? Do we have all the relevant facts? Do we have them accurately? What if anything do they tell us about the present situation?

Every major crisis sends us scurrying to our past for clues to what is going on. We ransack it relentlessly but never to our complete satisfaction because it is so crowded and contradictory in its contents. Most people would like very much to believe that history repeats itself. It would help make sense of the present and offer reliable guidelines for the future. Above all it would give the hopelessly cluttered closet of the past a sense of order and meaning by offering simple and convenient explanations for complex events that otherwise defy clear understanding.

Unfortunately history never repeats itself, but historical patterns do. They are constants that arise from the timeless fundamentals of human behavior. It is through these most basic elements of human nature – love, hate, greed, sacrifice, fear, ambition and the like – that we find the clearest and most satisfying understanding of the past. Although it is true that the past is a foreign country where they do things differently, we recognize and identify with many aspects of it precisely because they contain these enduring behavioral traits. The problem is that these familiar patterns of behavior occur in radically changed contexts down through the ages, giving them a frustrating blend of the familiar and the strange. The difficulty becomes one of trying to square the patterns with the ever changing contexts in which they appear.

Consider baseball as a simple example. Jacques Barzun once said that anyone who wished to understand America had to know baseball. He meant in part that the game itself reflected many of the powerful forces of change that were driving the nation. Anyone who is a fan today would recognize the game as played a century ago, at least in its basics, yet it would also seem an alien experience in many respects because the contexts are so different. The professional game underwent major changes every decade or so for the same reasons that the larger society did, including social pressures, economic forces and technological innovations. Every era had its own context that defined how the game was played, who its players were, where they came from and what it meant to society. The essentials of the game are still the same, but is it really the same game? An argument can be made either way.

So too with economic and financial history. Since the dawn of the industrial era the American economy has undergone a series of cycles that have been studied in microscopic detail by both economists and economic historians. Elaborate theories and interpretations have been put forth to explain their nature, cause, structure and influence. So familiar has this pattern of economic activity become that it has long been woven into the popular culture as the 'boom-bust' cycle. Explanations of it range from complex mathematical formulas to stern moral dictums to the common sense notion that what goes up must come down. The pattern has been consistently recurrent in American history, yet each episode occurred in a context quite different from those before or after it.

We would like to believe that every market crash and/or depression – they do not by any means always occur as partners – has something to tell us that might help to prevent a recurrence. Unfortunately even the best minds have not been able to find connections that offer explanations on which we can all agree. In my book *Rainbow's End* I described the relationship between the crash of 1929 and the ensuing depression as

> . . . the product of an unlikely and unpredictable sequence of events – the random coming together of a confluence of unfortunate forces. The accumulated effect of these forces not only created the crisis but prolonged and deepened it, much like the strengthening of a routine storm into a killer hurricane or blizzard, when a variety of unfavorable factors, each one unpleasant but not lethal in itself, combine on rare occasions to forge the worst-case scenario. In short, the crash and its aftermath was the perfect storm.[1]

Several critics took me to task for not providing a more specific and satisfying explanation of the causes behind both events and their relationship. They wanted answers. However the desire for clear explanations does not mean that they can be conjured up. The fact remains that nearly 80 years later scholars still cannot agree on any cause-and-effect linkage between the crash and the depression. Nor have they found a persuasive explanation for why the crash or the depression occurred.

Economists and historians approach the problem in very different ways.

The economist seeks to discover the answer within the framework of a theoretical construct while historians try to understand events within the context of their particulars. Even a cursory list of explanations suggests the wide variety of approaches fashioned by both camps. The Chicago school of monetarists concluded that monetary policy was too tight; the Austrian school thought it was too easy. Joseph Schumpeter believed the root of the problem lay in under-consumption, while John Maynard Keynes found it in a contraction of investment. Charles Kindleberger fastened on a decline in foreign trade, Barry Eichengreen on the international gold standard. John Kenneth Galbraith stressed institutional dysfunction; others pointed to the Smoot-Hawley tariff or other specific events as a prime trigger if not cause. Despite all their efforts and ingenuity, the Great Crash and depression remain an unsolved puzzle.[2]

None of this would matter all that much except that the crash and the decade of depression that followed it remain national traumas that left deep and enduring scars on American life. Every financial crisis since the 1930s has sent people harking back to this benchmark experience in search of portents as to whether it heralds the onset of another depression that might be as deep or prolonged as the Great Depression. The Panic of 2008 is no exception. Media of every stripe have gorged themselves on comparisons to 1929 and its sequel. Alleged pundits, myself included, have been asked for their opinion as to whether the present mess is déjà vu all over again. The obvious answer is that it is far too early to tell; the current situation is still a crisis in progress. This fact will not stop the issuing of prophecies ranging from sweet salvation to dire catastrophe. As long as there are quivering entrails to interpret and an audience to receive the oracle's words, there will be savants eager to provide answers.

No historian worth his or her salt deals in prophecies. We are far more comfortable in the realm of what has been, and claim no special insight into that of what might be. Even so our predicament is simply this: If we do not yet understand what exactly brought on the crash or the depression or the relationship between the two events, how can we be expected to find in it reliable guidelines or clues for handling the present situation? As Maggie Mahar observed, 'History is ambiguous, and every financial mania is unique, the product of the peculiar folly of its time.' Yet if we cannot construct confident analogies from experience, neither can we afford to sit on our hands and ignore whatever lessons the past might have to offer.[3]

The heart of the matter lies in this uncertainty over the relationship between the crash and the depression. The one does not automatically lead to the other, and on several occasions in American history has not done so. While there have been numerous other panics and recessions, the most severe and prolonged linkages of the two events have occurred four times

– in 1837, 1873, 1893 and 1929. The ensuing depressions lasted seven, six, four and ten years respectively. Each of them became more severe than the last because the industrial economy grew larger, more complex, and more interconnected, thereby affecting more people directly. None of the earlier depressions rival that of the 1930s in any of these categories. However it is helpful to remember that the Great Depression did not actually start for nearly a year after the market crash.

If the question on the floor is the elusive comparison between the experience following 1929 and that of today, then the historian can suggest some important similarities and differences between the contexts of that earlier era and the present. The basic contours of the earlier experience are drearily familiar. The Dow Jones average fell 39 per cent between 23 October and 13 November 1929. Between December 1929 and March 1930 it regained 74 per cent of its loss before commencing a downward spiral that did not touch bottom until 8 July 1932. It did not again reach the level of September 1929 for a quarter of a century. The depression that settled in during the fall of 1930 lasted for a decade, during which time unemployment averaged 14 per cent a year and hit a high of 25 per cent in 1932. It ended not because of the New Deal but because of an increase in military spending that commenced in May 1940.

Time does not permit a full discussion of the similarities and differences between the economy and the stock market of the 1920s and 1990s. Here at least is a starter kit for each case.

STOCK MARKET SIMILARITIES

Both markets started inconspicuously and gained momentum over time, much like a rocket gathering thrust as it pushes upward. In their final phase they reached unprecedented heights no one thought possible, yet many people believed they would continue to rise despite periodic drops. Both drew in large numbers of new investors who knew little about investing and less about the vagaries of the market. The overwhelming majority of these innocents – or 'minnows' as the pros called them – belonged to the rapidly expanding middle class. Both markets were driven by a variety of new investment instruments only vaguely understood by investors, such as the investment trust (an early version of the modern mutual fund) in the 1920s and the cafeteria of new vehicles devised between 1985 and 2005. In both cases the market lost touch with reality as speculative buying overwhelmed investment purchases. Price/earnings ratios, for example, reached all-time highs of 32.6 in September 1929 and 44.3 in January 2000.[4]

The Dow Jones Industrial Average took 76 years to reach 1000 in

November 1972. It did not pass 2000 until January 1987. Four years later it crossed 3000; it took another four years to February 1995 before it reached 4000. It touched 6000 in October 1996 and 8000 in July 1997. When it topped 10 000 in March 1999, Thomas Frank described it as 'a figure so incomprehensibly great that it was anyone's guess what it signified'. The same observations were made of the market during its meteoric climb in the summer of 1929. In both cases most of the buying centered on a narrow group of favored stocks known as market leaders while a significant portion of the overall list languished. Nevertheless in both eras rabid bulls predicted that the average would soar much, much higher. James Glassman of the *Washington Post*, for example, insisted that the Dow should reach 36 000.[5]

Both markets featured a reckless expansion of credit, and both went their merry ways unfettered by regulatory restraints. In 1929 the New York Stock Exchange was entirely self-regulated; federal regulation did not occur until 1933. Although the market was regulated in the 1990s, several of the restraints had been removed while others were simply ignored by lax regulators. The result in both cases was a growing atmosphere of loose practices that produced a steady parade of scandals ranging from the original 1919 scheme of Charles Ponzi and his successors like the immortal Bernie Madoff to stock pools, corners, scams and a wave of embezzlements that usually came to light after the market crashed. In addition, as Maggie Mahar observed, 'the market's spiral not only pushed share prices to unsustainable heights, it also fostered a corrupt corporate culture hooked on high growth.' Between 1997 and 2002 nearly a thousand companies were forced to admit that earnings they had reported earlier were not accurate.[6]

During both eras the available media did much to promote the market and push it to the center of the culture. Pundits of every stripe staked out positions as instant experts, often shoving aside more learned and experienced financial authorities who took a more cautious view of what was happening. The higher the two markets rose, the more shrill grew the voices of their apostles and the harsher their condemnation of anyone who said anything even mildly negative about the runaway bull. Once this irrational exuberance took hold and a mood of giddy optimism prevailed, the markets and their advocates literally lost touch with reality and became a world unto themselves. They may be viewed simply as a classic bubble but they are something more, as will be discussed later.

STOCK MARKET DIFFERENCES

The most obvious difference between the two markets is that of sheer scale. The modern bull market was vastly larger in terms of volume, prices, number of listings and types of securities that could be bought and sold. The technology of financial dealing in the 1990s completely overwhelmed that of the 1920s. The electronic revolution made possible trading at unheard of speeds from innumerable locations (including one's own home) for longer periods of time on a scale never before imagined. The 16.4 million shares traded on Black Tuesday in October 1929 dwarfed any volume that had gone before; by the 1990s that figure seemed miniscule. The stock market had become global in nature and operated on what amounted to a 24-hour basis.

One major source of that increased volume, institutional buying, scarcely existed in the 1920s. As noted earlier the financial instruments available for purchase had grown much more numerous, varied and complex. During the summer of 1929 investment trusts, still new instruments on Wall Street, increased at a rate of one a day. By 1982, the starting point for the bull market of the 1990s, the nation had 340 mutual funds; in 1998 the number reached 3513, a higher figure than the number of stocks listed on the New York Stock Exchange. In 1988 some 22.2 million American households owned mutual funds; by 1999 that figure had more than doubled to 48.4 million.[7]

Technology, especially the advent of cable television and the internet, radically increased the amount of media attention to the market and the number of pundits devoted to explaining its mysteries to rapt audiences. Through these mediums they reached investors more often and more directly than ever before. There is no way to measure or calculate the influence on investors of this instant and incessant analysis, but it was always there for the taking.

SIMILARITIES IN THE ECONOMIES

One striking similarity binds the two eras together in frustration and despair. The Great Depression and the current panic created want in the midst of plenty. Neither involved the effort of a poor country to keep its economic head above water. People went hungry when there was food to waste, did without warm clothing when stores and warehouses bulged with garments, lacked shelter when houses and apartments stood empty. The irony of the world's richest country failing to feed, clothe, house and care for so many of its people became a perverse indictment of the system itself as well as its values. The modern era has not yet begun to reach the depths and breadth of misery witnessed in the 1930s, but it has started down that dangerous road.

Both economies were deeply rooted in consumer goods. The 1920s marked the beginning of this domination, which in our own time has reached a point where consumer spending constitutes 73 per cent of economic activity. This dependence required new financial tools to sustain it, and both eras proved ingenious in providing them. Advertising first emerged as a big business in the 1920s and became a vital instrument in coaxing people to spend rather than save. This amounted to a historic reversal of national values. New forms of media, most notably movies and radio, introduced people throughout the nation to every kind of product. Manufacturing output increased dramatically, thanks in large part to increased use of electricity, and created the flow of goods needed to sustain the new ethos of the 'good life', which was based on the possession of more and better material goods.

The good life in both eras devolved into a culture of self-indulgence and crassly material values. The astonishing flow of new goods became a siren's song to consumers, who soon learned the new rules of mass-market fashion and planned obsolescence. In 1928 banker Paul Mazur described the spectacle in terms that ring true 80 years later:

> Bathtubs appear in stylish shades. Dishpans no longer are plain Cinderellas of fire and ashes; following a wave of the hand by the fairy godmother – style – they now appear resplendent in blues and pinks. It is the vogue to have tinted linen – this year green and peach; next year, the sales manager hopes, beige and blue. Automobiles change with the calendar. Last year's offerings are made social pariahs, only this year's model is desirable until it, in turn, is made out of fashion by next year's style. Furniture, clothing, radios, phonographs, tumble from the fertile minds of scientists and designers and . . . drown the sales possibilities of products that already stagger with infirmity at the age of one year.[8]

New forms of credit were devised to help people buy even when they did not have cash in hand. Installment buying made its debut; as early as 1925 some 75 per cent of all automobile sales were financed this way. Charles Mitchell of National City Bank led the banks into a new era in 1928 by establishing a Personal Loan Department that enabled ordinary people to borrow as much as $1000 without collateral. 'Installment credit', said Mitchell, 'is beginning to do for the consumer what the gradual development of the commercial banking system has done for the producer.'[9]

All of this is familiar fare to the modern era, which is in many respects the product of these same forces writ large. New technologies propelled the consumer economies of both eras. The automobile emerged as the central staple of the American economy in the 1920s and continued that role. The 1920s also saw the advent of electrical appliances, radio and movies, which played similar roles to that of the computer, the internet, television and electronics in the 1990s. Their influence penetrated far beyond the economy to the basic values and lifestyles of Americans, and accelerated the role of change in American society.

Both periods witnessed a large increase in the unequal distribution of wealth and income in society, and both endured weak banking systems that ultimately spearheaded the economic collapse. Maldistribution of wealth and income became especially important because then, as now, a consumer economy needed lots of consumers with money to spend and a willingness to spend it. During the 1920s more people had more money than ever before, but the upper 5 per cent controlled about a third of total wealth and income. In 1978 the top 0.1 per cent claimed 2.7 per cent of all income; by 2006 that figure had soared to 11.6 per cent. This top 0.1 per cent included 148 361 taxpayers who took home at least $1.9 million each.[10]

Both periods also experienced a rapid growth and consolidation of corporations as sector after sector of the economy grew more concentrated. Holding companies appeared that were so complicated in their structure that hardly anyone could fathom their inner relationships. A powerful pro-business ideology came to dominate American society as well as politics, and business leaders stepped cheerfully into the role of cultural heroes along with entertainment and sports figures. In both cases they rode this role to the heights of fame and then to the depths of shame when economic collapse coupled with scandals turned them into pariahs. Congressional investigations soon followed.

The two eras produced eerily similar mythologies to explain their spectacular economic growth. The first major similarity between them is the belief that they had somehow reached a new economic plateau in which the old rules no longer applied. More specifically they imagined that they had burst the chains of the old boom and bust cycle that prosperity would endure and not crumble as it had so many times before. The 1920s called it the 'New Era', while the 1990s hailed it as the 'New Economy'. Both became grand illusions that ultimately extended far beyond the economy to pervade almost every area of American life. Both phrases embodied the same notion that change was inevitable and nearly always for the best; today improved on yesterday and tomorrow would be better still.

This euphoria was rooted deep in the dominant political rhetoric of each period. The three Republican presidents of the 1920s were quick to take credit for what Frederick Lewis Allen called the 'seven fat years', and to attribute them to Republican pro-business policies. During their reign business moved to the center of the culture as never before. When Calvin Coolidge proclaimed in 1925 that 'the chief business of the American people is business', he echoed his predecessor. 'The business of America is the business of everybody in America', declared Warren G. Harding. 'This is essentially a business country . . . We must get back to the methods of business.' Herbert Hoover carried this credo one step further by attempting to make government itself a business conducted on sound business principles. Inherent in their approach was the conviction that the economy performed best in the hands of the private sector with as little government interference as possible.[11]

Although the Republicans did not control the presidency during the 1990s, they dominated Congress and did much to feed the prevailing mantra that prosperity depended above all else on markets unfettered by government regulation. One element of this market arrogance was the concerted attack on some provisions of the Glass-Steagall Act, the landmark legislation passed in 1933 to reform a financial system that lay in ruins. One of the leaders in that crusade was Walter Wriston, who occupied Charley Mitchell's old chair at the top of what had become Citibank.[12]

During both eras the conservative wing of the Republican party gained control and used its dominance to advance its own ideology and an agenda based on it. In both cases the ideology was strongly pro-business and anti-government, promising an era of prosperity without end. The buzz phrase for the 1920s was 'laissez faire', that of the 1990s 'free markets'. Both worked vigorously to discredit liberals, radicals, and policies that favored the less fortunate in society. Both eras, for example, passed tax legislation that reduced taxes for the wealthy. In the end both approaches ultimately ran to extremes and crashed in flames.

DIFFERENCES BETWEEN THE TWO ERAS

Here, too, many of the differences between the two eras derive directly from the steps taken after the traumatic experience of the 1930s. The most obvious one is the vastly enlarged role of the federal government in the economy and American life in general. It was the need to do something about the depression that brought big government into existence – a development that Herbert Hoover tried desperately to avoid. The financial system underwent profound changes. Both Wall Street and the banking system were made subject to federal regulation, although as noted earlier, some of this was stripped away during the heady 1990s. The Federal Reserve Board, which was a weak entity during the 1920s, became much more centralized and active in its role. The tax system also underwent major changes between the two eras.

The New Deal began the task of creating a safety net of social welfare programs that did not exist prior to 1932. These include social security, unemployment insurance and a host of programs that have come into existence since the 1930s. The depression generation had none of these cushions to soften the blow of a collapsed economy. Relief came from private charities, which were overwhelmed by the magnitude of the crisis. States did little more than the federal government; New York and Illinois were virtually alone in having any sort of welfare programs. The Hooverian philosophy of rugged individualism stoutly resisted any form of social welfare program in the belief that it would sap the character and vitality of the recipients, who would ultimately become dependent on the dole, as it was called.

The two eras also differed widely in the spirit of the people. Many Americans in the 1930s blamed themselves for their plight and were crushed by the experience of failing to find work and support their families. They became a haunted generation whose pain and bewilderment was etched in their faces. As the depression wore on, their sense of hopelessness and raw fear deepened. While it is too early to read the modern response to the crisis, this attitude seems light years away from that of the entitled generation that has long taken for granted its privileges and opportunities.

In many respects the 1920s marks the beginning of the modern era, and similarities between it and the current era extend beyond financial and economic matters deep into the social and cultural milieu. This does not mean that we are reliving the 1920s but only that familiar patterns exist that may provide some insight into the current crisis. Put another way, the key element is not the crash itself or even the financial milieu that produced it. Rather it is the social, cultural and political context in which it evolved and which set the stage for the depression that followed. In the same manner the present crisis did not arise overnight. It was in many respects the logical, even predictable result of forces that have been accumulating since the 1990s.

Seen in this context, the panic of 2008 is at once something old and something new. It is at bottom the product of some of the oldest and most drearily familiar human behaviors operating in a context with so many new elements that we have yet to digest their impact and implications. The modern economy is far larger, more complex, more varied, and global in nature than in the 1920s, and it operates at much faster speeds. It provides a radically different context than that of the 1920s, yet it has fallen into some very familiar pitfalls and excesses.

Perhaps there are at least one or two clear lessons to be learned from this historical record. First, the American economy, like every other area of American life, is far too varied, complex and dynamic to be stuffed into the straightjacket of any ideology. In addition the past has much to tell us if we could only figure out what it is saying. Those who today rail against government interference in the economy, for example, tend to ignore the fact that the government got deeply involved in the economy precisely because the private sector made such a complete mess of things in the 1920s. Regulation came into being because lack of it had created unacceptable conditions in so many sectors of American life.

Another lesson might be the need to pay closer attention to the banking system as a barometer of both financial and economic health. It is a major irony of American history that the growth of the world's largest and most productive industrial system was accompanied by a weak and often erratic banking system. Every financial panic and depression brought a host of failures, but so did good times. Between 1921 and 1928, the seven fat years, no less than 5055 banks failed, an average of 632 a year. During the four years between 1929 and 1932 a total of 5761 banks suspended, an average of 1440 a year. Last year only 25 banks failed, but that number exceeded the total for the previous five years. Given this history and the enormous size and influence of modern banks, it is hardly surprising that the government has poured billions into the major institutions in an effort to stabilize them. In many respects they are, and long have been, the canary in the mine.[13]

Finally it is worth remembering the vital if not dominant role played by psychology in economic as well as other affairs. Financial markets have always danced to its tune. We talk today of consumer confidence and investor confidence and their importance. For all the clever charts, graphs and polls we have devised, these factors are still more to be sensed than measured. Franklin Roosevelt was exactly right when he declared that the only thing the American people had to fear was fear itself. In the end the most crucial factor in trying to divine when recovery might come may prove to be the extent to which people view the glass as half empty or half full.

NOTES

1. Klein, Maury (2001), p. xx.
2. Ibid., p. xii-xiii.
3. Mahar, Maggie (2003), p. 6.
4. Shiller, Robert (2000), p. 8.
5. Frank, Thomas (2000), pp. 88, 128, 154–55; Mahar (2003), pp. 121, 300–1.
6. Mahar (2003), p. 270.
7. Shiller (2000), p. 35; Frank (2000), p. 120.
8. Quoted in Klein (2001), p. 124.
9. Ibid., p. 112.
10. *Newsweek*, 2 March 2009, 30.
11. Allen, Frederick Lewis (1935), p. 222; Klein (2001), p. 67.
12. Frank (2000), pp. 54–55.
13. U.S. Bureau of the Census (1975), 1038.

REFERENCES

Allen, Frederick Lewis (1935), *The Lords of Creation*, New York: Harper and Brothers.

Frank, Thomas (2000), *One Market Under God*, New York: Doubleday.

Klein, Maury (2001), *Rainbow's End: The Crash of 1929*, New York: Oxford University Press.

Mahar, Maggie (2003), *Bull!: A History of the Boom, 1982–1999*, New York: Harper Business.

Shiller, Robert (2000), *Irrational Exuberance*, Princeton: Princeton University Press.

US Bureau of the Census (1975), *Historical Statistics of the United States, Colonial Times to 1970*, Washington.

2. The anatomy of a residential mortgage crisis: a look back to the 1930s

Kenneth A. Snowden, Jr.

INTRODUCTION

The residential mortgage crisis that triggered the Panic of 2008 is more severe, in terms of rates of foreclosure and decreases in home prices and residential wealth, than any since the Great Depression. We should look back to the 1930s for more than benchmarks of misery, however, since it provides an opportunity to examine the origins, impacts and consequences of one severe mortgage crisis as we live through another. In this chapter I identify four elements that shaped the 1930s crisis and define its long-run impact on the nation's mortgage market:

1. The crisis was preceded by a decade during which the nation's residential mortgage debt grew at an unusually rapid pace while financial innovation reshaped the mortgage market itself. Three innovations of the 1920s figure prominently – high-leverage, affordable home mortgage loans, private mortgage insurance and two early forms of securitization.
2. Each of the intermediaries that brought innovations to the market in the 1920s suffered prolonged liquidations during the 1930s. These complex processes were publicly-managed but not publicly-financed.
3. Federal emergency measures, including a publicly-financed 'bad bank' (the HOLC), strengthened institutional portfolio lenders while the innovators of the 1920s were liquidating. Additional regulatory change created institutional structures within which these portfolio lenders dominated the residential mortgage debt for the next four decades.
4. Proposals were offered to incorporate each of the innovations of the 1920s into new federal programs. One effort – for high-leverage, insured mortgages – succeeded in the form of the FHA loan program;

> the other – for a publicly-sponsored securitization structure – did not. As a result securitization in the residential market was delayed for four decades and then took on a fundamentally different institutional structure.

The chapter focuses on how innovation, institutional disruptions and policy responses combined to shape events between 1920 and 1940, but these details raise broader questions concerning the causes and consequences of mortgage crises. These issues are examined in the conclusion of the chapter where events in the 1930s are connected to developments in the mortgage market after 1950. In anticipation of that discussion, as well as to provide context for the discussion of this historical episode, Figures 2.1 and 2.2 provide a long view of the magnitude and impacts of the mortgage crisis of the 1930s.

The 1930s episode was the worst in a series of booms and busts that shaped the development of the mortgage market in the US during the nineteenth and early twentieth centuries.[1] The 1930s crisis was also the last crisis in this series because policy responded in a way that favored stability over innovation. To illustrate that development, Figure 2.1 provides a century-long view of residential building starts and decadal growth rates in inflation-adjusted mortgage debt.[2] The volume of inflation-adjusted nonfarm residential tripled in nominal terms between 1921 and 1929 (from $9 to $30 billion) and also grew faster in inflation-adjusted terms than during any other decade during the twentieth century. The expansion of mortgage debt even outpaced the well-known residential construction boom of the 1920s as the ratio of debt to residential wealth doubled from 14 to nearly 30 per cent and the rate of nonfarm homeownership jumped from 41 to 46 per cent.[3] The growth in residential mortgage debt stopped suddenly in 1930 and remained virtually constant in inflation-adjusted terms across the entire 1930s. Meanwhile, the more visible manifestations of the mortgage crisis unfolded with a total collapse in homebuilding activity and a complete reversal of the gains that were made in homeownership during the 1920s.

After the disruptions of the 1930s and World War II, the residential housing sector went through an unusual two-decade period during which mortgage debt expanded nearly as rapidly as in the 1920s, rates of home ownership surged to modern levels and homebuilding activity sustained a high level with relatively low volatility, all without reversal or crisis. The landscape changed in 1970 and for the next quarter-century inflation-adjusted mortgage debt grew modestly by historical standards and homebuilding activity remained at postwar levels – although with increased volatility. After 1995, however, the residential housing sector returned to

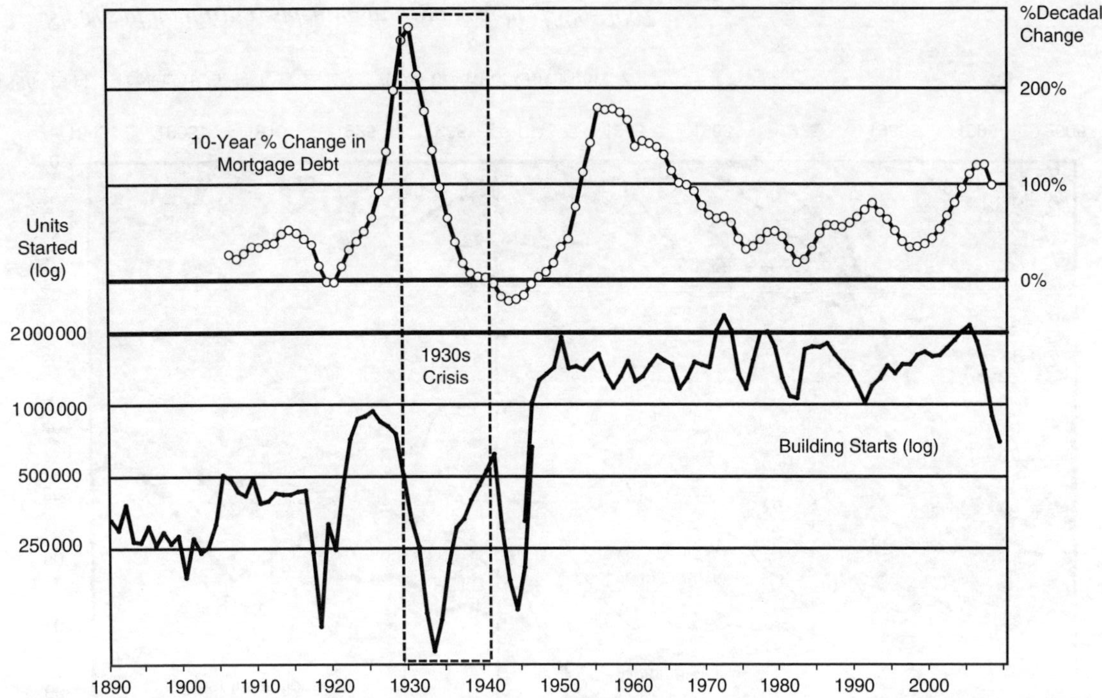

Source: Nonfarm Housing Starts: 1890–1995, Series Dc510, Dc531, Historical Statistics, 2006; 1995–2008: www.census.gov/const/ Nonfarm Residential Mortgage Debt: 1896–1948 Grebler (1956, Table L-1); 1948–2008: Board of Governonrs, L.217.

Figure 2.1 Building starts & decadal change in CPI-deflated mortgage debt, 1890–2008

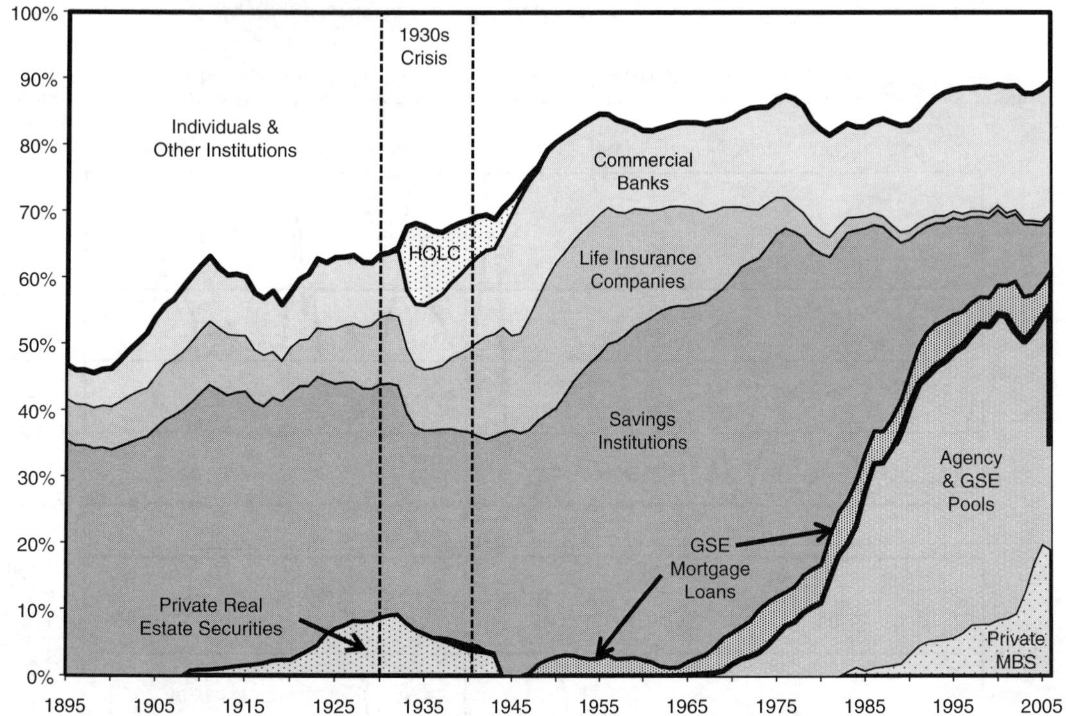

Source: 1896–1944: Grebler, 1956, N-1, N-2; 1945–2008: Board of Governors, Z-1.

Figure 2.2 Shares of nonfarm residential mortgage debt, 1896–2007

the pattern we had not seen since the 1920s and 1930s – as severe disruptions in the mortgage market and homebuilding activity that followed an unusually rapid expansion in both.[4]

Figure 2.2 provides a long-run view of changes in the institutional structure of the residential mortgage market over the same period. Non-institutional investors played an important role in the 1920s and two types of mortgage-backed securities appeared during that decade to serve this segment of the market. The 1930s crisis shows up in Figure 2.2 in two ways – the gradual but complete disappearance of private mortgage-backed securities and the large impact of the Home Owners' Loan Corporation (HOLC) that served as a publicly-sponsored 'bad bank' by buying delinquent mortgages off the balance sheets of major institutional portfolio lenders. A third important institutional development of the 1930s that plays a central role in the narrative below is hidden within the 'savings institutions' aggregate of Figure 2.2 – during the crisis the traditional Building & Loan industry was transformed into its modern Savings & Loan form.

The long-run changes in the institutional structure of the residential mortgage market that followed the crisis of the 1930s are also clearly shown in Figure 2.2. The portfolio lenders that survived the crisis – commercial banks, life insurance companies, Savings & Loans and mutual savings banks – dominated the residential mortgage market for two decades after World War II as mortgage debt, homebuilding and homeownership all increased rapidly without innovation or crisis. But fault lines began to show up after 1970 in the Depression-era mortgage structure as securitization, innovation and instability all reappeared. In the conclusion of the chapter I explain how an understanding of the 1930s mortgage crisis provides perspective on these broad institutional developments after 1950 and the mortgage crisis of 2008.

THE RESIDENTIAL MORTGAGE MARKET IN THE 1920S

Four intermediaries – commercial banks, life insurance companies, Building & Loans (B&Ls) and mutual savings banks – were the most important institutional lenders in the urban mortgage market in 1920. The first three were active in the markets for single-family, multifamily and commercial mortgages, but in different geographic areas. Mutual savings banks operated almost exclusively in New England and urban areas of the Mid-Atlantic region, while commercial banks had their largest impact in the East North Central, Mountain and Pacific regions (Morton, 1956, 42).

The headquarters of life insurance companies were geographically concentrated, but these large intermediaries lent in all regions of the country through interregional mortgage lending networks they had developed beginning in the 1870s (Snowden, 1995). B&Ls, in contrast to the others, specialized in home mortgage lending and had significant presence as local mortgage lenders in virtually all areas of the country.

Despite the presence of financial intermediaries, the residential mortgage market in 1920 was institutionally immature relative to modern standards. Non-institutional investors held more than 40 per cent of outstanding residential mortgage debt, for example, so that large segments of the market were poorly served by intermediaries. Mortgages were also not used to finance modern levels of home ownership as only 41 per cent of the nation's nonfarm housing units were owner-occupied in 1920, and only 40 per cent of these properties were mortgaged. Terms on home mortgages were also less liberal: loans were typically written for no more than 50 per cent of property value, were structured as straight or partially-amortized balloon loans, were restricted to maturities of three to five years and were typically renewed one or more times before being fully repaid (Morton, 1956, 21–2).[5] Finally local supplies of mortgage credit were constrained by mortgage lending restrictions on National Banks while interregional urban mortgage lending was undertaken by only a few, large life insurance companies and private mortgage companies.[6,7]

The institutional gaps and rigidities that were at work in both local and interregional mortgage markets in 1920 created opportunities for change and innovation during the great mortgage expansion of the 1920s. Life insurance companies, mutual savings banks and commercial banks met the challenge by more than tripling their combined holdings of residential mortgages.[8] But their combined $6.6 billion in new investment represented only one-third of the total expansion of residential mortgage debt during the 1920s – as the bulk was funded by B&Ls ($4.3 billion) and non-institutional investors (more than $8 billion). The remainder of this section examines the innovations that transformed these two components of the mortgage market.

Building & Loans

The pre-Depression Building & Loan association was a different type of intermediary than the modern Savings & Loan (S&L). The typical B&L was a small, local and undiversified mutual fund into which members contributed weekly or monthly dues; the pooled dues were then lent to members who chose to purchase new or existing homes. The interest payments and fees on these loans, net of expenses and loan losses, were returned to the members as dividends. The B&L model spread slowly for five decades after the first association was founded in the 1830s, but during the 'B&L Movement' of the 1880s more than 5000 new associations were organized and B&Ls became a significant source of local home mortgage credit in all regions and in cities of all sizes (Snowden, 1997). By 1920 B&Ls remained an elastic source of intermediated local mortgage credit and active innovators in the design of home mortgage contracts.

State law made it much easier to incorporate a new B&L than to charter a regulated depository institution (Snowden, 1997). As a result the industry grew during the 1920s not only by attracting new customers (from 4 to 12 million members) and assets (from \$2.5 to \$8 billion), but also by increasing in number – from some 8000 in 1919 to nearly 13 000 at the peak in 1927 (Bodfish, 1931, 136). The low barriers to entry allowed B&Ls to pursue two types of market opportunities during the 1920s. First, the industry responded quickly to the regional shift of population and homebuilding described earlier – associations, membership and assets grew much faster in southern and western markets than in the rest of the nation so that the relative importance of B&Ls was remarkably similar in all regions by 1930 (Snowden, 2003, 169). A second more worrisome trend during the decade was the creation of associations by developers and builders for the specific purpose of financing their own suburban residential building projects (Clark, 1925, 90; Riegel et al., 1927, 36; Herman, 1969, 820). B&Ls had always been organized and managed by networks of real estate professionals and builders, but regulators in Pennsylvania, Ohio and Wisconsin documented abuses within builder-dominated B&Ls during the 1920s that suggested conflicts of interest within the industry were becoming a greater problem (Snowden, 1997; Herman, 1969, 820).[9]

During the nineteenth century B&Ls were the only lender to write amortized, long-term mortgages and during the 1920s they were leaders in developing affordable, low-down payment loans. One of these products was called the 'Philadelphia Plan'. Under it the B&L issued a second, amortized mortgage for 30 per cent of the property's value after the borrower had secured a first loan from a bank, insurance company or mortgage company for 50 per cent of the property value (Loucks, 1929). The plan was affordable because the borrower paid interest only on the first, straight mortgage while the second loan was repaid according to the typical B&L amortization schedule – at which point the borrower could refinance the straight loan as a regular, amortized B&L mortgage loan. There was concern expressed within the industry that offering such terms placed the borrower, and the B&L, at greater risk of default and failure. But the discussion did not prevent a variant of the Philadelphia Plan – the 'split-loan' where the B&L held both the first and second mortgage – from being widely used during the 1920s (Loucks, 1929, 1–3, 50–61; Clark and Chase, 1925, 192–8).[10]

The innovations paid off for the B&Ls as they wrote more mortgage debt on one- to four-family homes by the end of the 1920s than life insurance companies, commercial banks and mutual savings banks combined (Grebler, 1956, 489). This growth was accompanied by increasing heterogeneity within the industry, however, that shaped how the industry would be affected and transformed by the impending mortgage crisis. Differences in the size, structure and mission of individual associations polarized the B&L industry into two groups: small, traditional B&Ls that were managed on a part-time basis by real estate professionals and large, permanent plan associations that B&L professionals operated as full-time businesses. The first group took the lead in introducing the innovations discussed above, while the latter group dominated the industry's trade group – the US Building & Loan League (USBLL) – and criticized the conflicts of interest and increased risks that were associated with these innovations. So although B&Ls were the nation's dominant home mortgage lenders in 1929, the B&L industry was moving in two different directions on the eve of the mortgage crisis.[11]

Guaranteed Mortgages, Participation Certificates and Real Estate Bonds

The importance of non-institutional investors made the 1920s a welcoming environment for innovations that repackaged urban mortgage loans into attractive financial instruments for individual investors. Mortgage guarantee companies and real estate bond houses – were leaders in these developments and by 1930 they had together marketed between $6 and $10 billion of the total $44 billion of outstanding nonfarm mortgage debt.[12] Most of these securities financed commercial property development, but $2.5 billion was issued against single and multifamily residential mortgages (Grebler, 1956, 446). These innovations were introduced in most major urban markets but had their greatest impact in the New York and Chicago metropolitan areas.

Mortgage guarantee companies actually brought two innovations to the market in the form of mortgage insurance and participation certificates that were issued on mortgage collateral.[13] The private mortgage insurance component first appeared in urban New York markets around the turn of the century when title insurance companies were given the authority to write policies not only against defects in land titles, but also on the payments due on bonds and mortgages (Alger, 1934). At first these companies offered policies to investors who had originated their own mortgages or who had purchased loans from independent mortgage companies. Some guarantee companies began to combine mortgage banking functions with insurance in the 1910s by originating, selling and servicing insured commercial and residential mortgage loans. By 1921 only 12 companies in New York were active in this business, but by 1930 some 50 companies in the state had written insurance on $3 billion of mortgages that they originated and marketed.

Two-thirds of these insured mortgages were sold as whole loans to investors, but by the end of the decade nearly $1 billion of the insured mortgages had been placed in trust accounts against which the companies issued collateral trust certificates of participation (Chamberlain, 1927, 455). Some certificates were issued against single large mortgages, while 'group certificates' were issued against pools of mortgage loans. In either case the certificates were pass-through securities written on the cash-flows generated by insured mortgages similar to the instruments that are widely used in the modern mortgage market.

The real estate bond movement of the 1920s used a different form of securitization to finance the construction of large commercial and multifamily residential projects in major urban centers. The organizers of these ventures invested equity in corporations that were created to own specific buildings or developments; the corporation would then use a first mortgage on the property, and a lien against its net income, to secure partially amortized bonds in denominations of $100, $500 and $1000 (Koester, 1939a, 50; Fisher, 1951, 30).[14] Single-property real estate bonds were marketed on a modest scale before and during World War I, but generally only on completed properties after bank loans had been used to finance construction. By the mid-1920s, however, real estate bonds were issued even before construction had been completed (Chamberlain and Edwards, 1927, 444–6).

The intermediary most responsible for popularizing this innovation was the specialized real estate bond house.[15] The strength and reputation of these underwriters was critical to marketability of real estate bonds even though they accepted no legal liability for the payment of interest or principal (Gray and Terborgh, 1929, 25). The houses promised, however, to repurchase at a small discount the securities they had marketed. This policy not only protected investors against credit losses, it also provided liquidity since attempts to establish an active secondary market for real estate bonds were generally unsuccessful (Miller, 1930).

The market for single-property real estate bond grew rapidly during the 1920s, but estimates of its size vary widely. The most conservative places outstanding issues at slightly more than $4 billion in 1930 which represented 14 per cent of total nonfarm mortgage debt and 11 per cent of the total corporate debt issued between 1921 and 1930 (Clark, 1933, 66; Halliburton, 1939, 45). Bonds on properties in New York and Chicago dominated the market, and one-third of all securities were issued against office buildings (Johnson, 1936b, 307). Residential properties – apartments and apartment-hotels – secured less than 20 per cent of real estate bond issues nationwide, but nearly 50 per cent of the bonds issued on Chicago property (Johnson, 1936b, 307; Koester, 1939a, 51).

Concerns about the general quality of real estate bonds were raised in 1926 after several bond issues defaulted. More telling, perhaps, were reports of rising vacancy rates and declining rents (Halliburton, 1939, 7–8). Several state governments investigated the industry and the Attorney General of New York actually issued a warning in 1927 that real estate bond houses were over-appraising properties and improperly managing their trust accounts (Gray, 1929, 36). Soon thereafter the American Construction Council, the National Association of Real Estate Boards and the National Association of Security Commissioners adopted explicit codes for issuers of real estate bonds that were embraced by all major bond houses (Gray, 1929, 43–5). The volume of new bond issues then surged in 1928 to its second highest level in the 1920s.

The View From the Residential Mortgage Market in 1929

In 1929 the Brookings Institution produced an assessment of 'First Mortgages in Urban Real Estate Finance' (Gray and Terborgh, 1929). The conclusions drawn in that report provide an interesting assessment of the performance of the nation's mortgage market on the eve of its crisis. The authors acknowledged that some risks were associated with the innovations that had appeared in the 1920s, but they expressed no general sense of alarm. The report focused, instead, on the market's failure to equalize mortgage rates across regions. The authors noted that the activities of life insurance companies, real estate bond houses and mortgage guarantee companies had all helped the situation during the 1920s, but concluded that they were unlikely on their own to solve the underlying misallocation of funds. The recommendation, therefore, was to establish a public, European-style central mortgage bank – similar to the Federal Farm Loan Bank that had been established in 1916 – that could pool urban mortgages made by local originators and place them behind mortgage-backed debentures that could trade in thick, secondary markets at low yields. This same model would be proposed a few years later at the depth of the mortgage crisis, but was ultimately rejected.

THE CRISIS OF THE 1930S: DISRUPTIONS, EMERGENCY MEASURES AND A NEW SYSTEM

> [A] tremendous surge of residential building in the [last] decade . . . was matched by an ever-increasing supply of homes sold on easy terms. The easy terms plan

> has a catch . . . [o]nly a small decline in prices was necessary to wipe out this equity. Unfortunately, deflationary processes are never satisfied with small declines in values. They feed upon themselves and produce results out of all proportion to their causes . . .. [O]ur economic system has become so complex and so finely balanced that every business transaction affects vitally many other transactions. In the field of real-estate finance, particularly, we have depended so much upon credit that our whole value structure can be thrown out of balance by relatively slight shocks. When such a delicate structure is once disorganized, it is a tremendous task to get it into a position where it can again function normally. (Hoagland, 1935)

Henry Hoagland was well-positioned in 1935 to assess the state of the mortgage market because he was a member of the Federal Home Loan Bank Board that was the lead agency overseeing nearly all of the federal programs designed to ameliorate the crisis. The timing of Hoagland's somber view is as disquieting as its content – given that he was writing eight years after the peak in housing construction, six years after the onset of recession, three years after the FHLB system had begun to supply liquidity to the home mortgage market and two years after the passage of New Deal emergency housing measures.[16] In this section we examine the dislocations which arose during the mortgage crisis and the federal government's response to it.

Rates of nonfarm mortgage foreclosure began to escalate in the late 1920s and reached the level of 1000 per day in 1933 before falling back slowly to pre-depression levels by 1940. Estimates of nonfarm residential mortgage holdings of closed commercial banks and Building & Loans show a similar trend – as each increased to $250 million by 1933 and then gradually decreased for the remainder of the decade (Grebler, 1956, 489). But the extent and timing of disruptions during a mortgage crisis are not fully captured by trends in foreclosure rates or numbers of failed institutions. Foreclosures by Massachusetts mutual savings banks, for example, also peaked in 1933 and receded slowly thereafter; but the amount of foreclosed real estate held by these institutions did not peak until 1937 and represented two-thirds of their capital surplus accounts until 1940 (Lintner, 1948, 272). As Hoagland emphasized, recovery from the mortgage crisis was complex, protracted and difficult.

The disruptions in the mortgage market began as the total nominal residential debt fell from $30.2 to $25.5 billion between 1930 and 1933 (Grebler, 1956, 466). Ninety per cent of the decrease occurred in the mortgage holdings of Building & Loans and non-institutional investors even though these two groups together held only 60 per cent of the total debt in 1930. After their poor performance in the first stage of the crisis, these innovators of the 1920s were allowed to slowly liquidate and disappear while federal policy rehabilitated other institutions.

The Demise of B&Ls, Guaranteed Mortgages and Real Estate Bonds

Traditional Building & Loan associations entered the 1930s with a unique contractual structure – called the share accumulation loan plan – that placed thousands of institutions into protracted liquidations during the crisis of the 1930s (Clark and Chase, 1925, 134–7). The B&Ls achieved loan amortization with this plan by combining two contracts – a straight mortgage loan that required only periodic interest payments and a subscription to buy, with weekly or monthly dues, association shares equal in face value to the principal of the loan. Amortization was accomplished, therefore, through a sinking fund; after 11 or 12 years the value of the member's share account grew equal to the loan balance and the debt was cancelled. These contracts caused severe problems for B&Ls during the 1930s because losses on one member's loan reduced the value of all other members' sinking fund and, therefore, increased their effective loan balances.[17]

Thousands of associations that operated under the share accumulation loan plan were forced to close in the early 1930s as defaults and foreclosures by some members encouraged others to stop making loan payments. But B&Ls were protected from involuntary liquidation because they were member-owned corporations, not depository institutions (Clark and Chase, 1925, 400–1). So when faced with large demands for withdrawals a B&L became 'frozen' and operated only to liquidate its loan portfolio and real estate account on behalf of members.[18] Thousands of associations found themselves in this condition during the 1930s. By 1933 some 2000 associations were frozen and the foreclosed real estate holdings of the industry represented 17 per cent of industry assets (or $.8 billion). Another 3000 associations closed after 1933 and real estate still represented 12 per cent of industry-wide assets in 1939. Real estate holdings were highest (22 per cent of assets) in the Mid-Atlantic region where the traditional serial associations were common. Conditions remained so weak in Philadelphia, Milwaukee, New Orleans and New Jersey, in fact, that the FSLIC undertook special Community Programs in 1936 'to bring about comprehensive rehabilitation of the savings and loan industry in certain localities where general weaknesses in . . . structure have been apparent' (*Eighth Annual Report*, FHLBB, 1940, 107–10, 227–31). More than one-half of the 12 000 B&Ls that were operating in 1929 had failed by 1941, many of them through a process of liquidation that took years to complete.

The mortgage guarantee companies that were concentrated in New York during the 1920s operated under the supervision of that state's Department of Insurance. These companies were subject to examination each year, but by 1932 not one major company had been closed. The frequency and thoroughness of examinations increased in 1931, however, after nearly all companies delayed repayment of principal to investors (Alger, 1934, 59). But even then regulators continued to exercise forbearence in the hope that the companies would recover.

Regulatory forbearance of the mortgage guaranty companies ended with the national bank holiday in March 1933 when state regulators ordered them to stop selling guarantees and distributing dividend payments. Five months later the Department of Insurance seized 18 mortgage guarantee companies for liquidation (Alger, 1934, 63). These companies together had sold $1 billion of insured whole mortgage loans and $.8 billion of participation certificates on loans that were held in trust accounts; these certificates were held by more than 200 000 investors.[19] The Department of Insurance found that $1.1 billion of guaranteed mortgages were in default and that the default rate was highest among the mortgages that had been placed behind participation certificates. The state legislature eventually passed legislation (the Shackno Act) and created a temporary Mortgage Commission to facilitate and oversee the liquidation process (Cramp, 1940, 1). At that point the disposition of $0.7 billion of guaranteed mortgages still had to be worked out and that a process that was not completed until the early 1940s.

The public investigation of the mortgage guaranty industry in New York revealed that many companies had violated their own underwriting standards, substituted bad loans for performing mortgages behind participation certificates and maintained inadequate guaranty funds to support their insurance policies. Some of these abuses were the result of gaps in the regulatory structure and poor oversight, but there was little appetite for reform or remediation. In 1937 the Joint Legislative Committee to Investigate the Guaranteed Mortgage Situation concluded 'that the business of guaranteeing mortgages should be prohibited entirely' (New York, 1937). Private mortgage insurance was not written again in the US until the 1950s (Rapkin et al., 1967).

The real estate bond houses, unlike the mortgage guarantee companies, were not publicly regulated. By 1929 market participants signaled concern about their viability, however, and the volume of newly-issued real estate bonds fell dramatically. Defaults increased in the same year and peaked on securities written on Chicago properties in 1931. By 1935, 80 per cent of all outstanding real estate bonds were in default and the rate was even higher for apartment buildings in Chicago, Detroit and Cleveland (Koester, 1939a, 54).[20] The average recoverable value on all defaulted real estate securities during the mid-1930s was estimated to be just over 50 per cent of face value.

The real estate bond houses were excoriated for the methods they used to originate bonds and sell securities, and for abusing their position as fiscal agent for the bondholders.[21] But real estate bonds earned their greatest notoriety when 10000 bondholders gathered in Chicago in April 1934 to protest the treatment they had received after their bonds had defaulted. The uproar led the US Congress, under the auspices of the Sabath Committee, to conduct an investigation in 1935 of real estate bondholders' reorganizations and to sponsor remedial legislation in amendments to the Securities and Exchange Act and the federal bankruptcy law (Halliburton, 1939, 125). These legal complications, along with the sheer size and number of defaults, led to a contentious decade of recovery after which the single property real estate mortgage bond disappeared from the US mortgage market.[22]

Emergency Measures: the FHLB System and the HOLC

The federal government implemented emergency measures to respond to the mortgage crisis as the protracted liquidations described above were unfolding. These programs did not save traditional B&Ls, guaranteed mortgage companies or real estate bond houses. The goal, instead, was to relieve distress within other major institutional mortgage lenders.

Among the institutions to be assisted was the subset of B&Ls that favored the model of a large, professionally-managed institution that their trade group, the USBLL, had been advocating for more than a decade. The mortgage crisis presented an opportunity for this segment of the industry to distance itself from the traditional B&Ls and to do so it used the new Federal Home Loan Bank system.[23] The USBLL first pressed Congress to create a federal discount bank for B&Ls in 1919, but met with little success until Hoover supported the creation of home loan banks in his 1928 campaign. The President finally made good on the pledge in 1932 over the objections of the B&Ls principal competitors – commercial banks, life insurance companies and mortgage companies. Two senior USBLL executives actually helped Congress draft the Federal Home Loan Bank Act that was enacted in summer 1932 (Ewalt, 1962, 87; Bodfish and Theobald, 1938, 290).[24]

The USBLL not only helped to draft the FHLB Act, it also supplied two League executives to the original FHLB Board and 91 out of 132 directors to the boards of the system's 12 regional banks. These facilities began to make advances to member institutions in early 1933 so that they could honor withdrawals from members and refinance the loans of distressed homeowners (Ewalt, 1962, 66).[25] The same FHLB discount facilities could have been used to assist the thousands of B&Ls that were experiencing severe distress by 1933, but only sound institutions with management and loan policies consistent with building and loan 'ideals' were accepted into the system (Snowden, 2003, 195). This entry policy became a powerful tool for reshaping the industry. There were nearly 11 000 B&Ls in 1933 – many of them already frozen. Of these only 2086 had become FHLB members by December 1933 and only 3900 (including 600 new Federal S&Ls) joined the system over the next four years. These associations became the core of the modern S&L industry and by 1950 held 92 per cent of all S&L assets.

The Home Owners' Loan Act of June 1933 represented a second federal emergency response to the mortgage crisis. The act authorized the Home Owners' Loan Corporation to offer new loans to homeowners who were delinquent on existing mortgages. HOLC accomplished the task by opening 400 offices throughout the country and employing a staff of 20 000 to process loans and appraise properties. In only three years the agency received applications from 40 per cent of all residential mortgagors and wrote new loans on ten per cent of the owner-occupied homes in the US. In doing so the HOLC implemented two underwriting standards that assisted the homeowners: (1) all HOLC loans were long-term (15-year), fully-amortized, direct reduction loans and (2) HOLC appraised each property at its 'normal' market value rather than at its current market price. After approving a loan, HOLC offered to purchase the defaulted loan from the original lender under the terms its underwriters had set. The lender could refuse to sell if the loan amount approved by HOLC did not fully extinguish the borrower's obligation, and borrowers generally did not qualify for a reduction in their loan's principal as a result of HOLC refinancing (Rose, 2010).

In less than three years HOLC exchanged $2.7 billion of its own bonds for delinquent mortgages that were held by mortgage lending institutions – more than $.7 billion each from B&Ls, commercial banks and life insurance companies, and $.5 billion from individual lenders and other intermediaries. HOLC was, in essence, a publicly-financed 'bad bank' for home mortgage lenders. The agency did not address the problems of frozen B&Ls, guaranteed mortgage companies or real estate bonds, but it restored the balance sheets of major institutional lenders that would become dominant in the post-crisis residential mortgage market. The HOLC's authority to make loans expired in 1936 after which it serviced its outstanding loan portfolio until the agency was liquidated in 1951.[26]

The New System Emerges: Federal S&Ls, FHA and FNMA

Once the FHLB discount facility and the HOLC lending program were in operation, there was opportunity to address permanent regulatory considerations. Two issues took precedence. First, how would the USBLL use its influence within the FHLB system to reshape surviving B&Ls into a modern, professionally-managed Savings & Loan industry? Second, what would become of the innovations of the 1920s – high-leverage loans, mortgage insurance, participation certificates and real estate bonds – given that the intermediaries who introduced them were all liquidating? The structure of the nation's residential mortgage market was permanently transformed as these issues were resolved.

The FHLB Board was given authority in the Home Owners' Loan Act of June 1933 to establish a system of federally-chartered Savings and Loan Associations, but the legislation provided few specific details. The USBLL recommended that the Board consider adopting its own comprehensive 'Uniform Code' that had been developed in the late 1920s, and much of it was incorporated into the FHLB guidelines (Bodfish and Theobald, 1938, 516–17, 556–7; Ewalt, 1962, 80–81). Two elements of the model ensured that members of the federal S&L industry would be structured and behave differently than traditional B&Ls. First, federal S&Ls offered new kinds of contracts: share savings accounts instead of membership dues and direct reduction loans to replace the fragile share accumulation loan plan. Second, federal charters erected new barriers to entry so that small, part-time associations would never again represent a competitive fringe.[27]

The final element of the industry's transformation – the FSLIC insurance program – was enacted in the 1934 National Housing Act. The USBLL (soon to become the US Savings and Loan League) originally opposed the creation of an insurance program because of concerns with moral hazard. But the industry ultimately became convinced that S&Ls would suffer a competitive disadvantage without share account insurance given that bank deposits were by then insured by the FDIC (Ewalt, 1962, 91–96). More than 20 per cent of B&Ls and S&Ls (1450 in number) operated under Federal charters by 1941 and together they held 35 per cent of the industry's assets. More than 800 of these institutions had entered the federal system by converting from their original state charters, the remaining 639 were new associations that organized as Federal S&Ls. These institutions, along with the state-chartered associations that joined the FHLB system, comprised the heart of the S&L industry for the next four decades.

Title I of the National Housing Act of 1934 created the Federal Housing Administration which became a counterbalance to the USBLL-dominated FHLB Board in the formulation of federal residential mortgage policy (Ewalt, 1962, 138–44). Title II of the act, moreover, created the FHA mortgage insurance program that was designed to encourage commercial banks, competitors of S&Ls, to increase their presence in the mortgage market. The FHA loan program itself was objectionable to the USBLL because it insured long-term, highly-levered, fully-amortized loans to stimulate housing demand. The USBLL saw this as a government subsidy for the same type of risky loan products that traditional B&Ls had promoted in the 1920s. S&Ls were eligible to use the FHA program, but made relatively little use of it well into the post-World War II era.

There was also criticism of specific terms on FHA loans – the loan limits and loan-to-value ceilings were initially thought to be too low and the insurance funding fee too high. Changes in these features soon attracted commercial banks, life insurance companies and, interestingly, mortgage companies to the program. FHA loans, and VA guaranteed loans in later years, came to play three important functions in the post-crisis residential market (Jones and Grebler, 1961, 40–44; Klaman, 1959). First, federally-insured and guaranteed mortgages became the dominant instrument that was used in the interregional transfer of mortgage credit. Second, these loan programs were used to finance the activities of large merchant builders because they provided advanced commitments for permanent financing during construction. Finally, FHA financing was used extensively to finance the expansion of the multifamily housing stock. Note that builder-dominated B&Ls, mortgage guarantee companies and the real estate bond houses performed the same three functions during the 1920s. So the FHA and VA mortgage programs helped life insurance companies, mutual savings banks and commercial banks to fund segments of the residential mortgage market that had previously been served by the failed innovations of the 1920s.

Title III of the National Housing Act authorized the creation of a system of privately-owned, federally-chartered National Mortgage Associations to buy and sell FHA loans from local originators. The associations were to finance their activities by issuing debenture bonds against insured loans that they held in their portfolios (Jones and Grebler 1961, 115–19). These institutions were similar in structure to the private joint-stock mortgage banks that had been created under the Federal Farm Loan Act of 1916. The idea at that time, and the intended purpose of the National Mortgage Associations, was to introduce European-style mortgage banking to the American mortgage market. The Brookings Institution advocated for a similar system in 1929, while an almost identical proposal was introduced in the New York state legislature in 1935 (Gray and Terborgh, 1929; New York, 1935). These plans, had they been adopted, would have fundamentally changed the structure of the residential mortgage market.

The New York proposal was never enacted, and by 1937 not one National Mortgage Association had been organized despite modifications to the original legislation that were designed to attract private investors (Jones and Grebler, 1961, 116). In order to demonstrate the viability of the proposed system the Federal Housing Administrator authorized the Reconstruction Finance Corporation to organize a National Mortgage Association of Washington in February 1938. It was soon renamed the Federal National Mortgage Association and its first issue of $25 million of debentures was oversubscribed by a factor of 50. Despite the success of this experiment, the FHA announced in May that it would no longer process applications and not one privately-owned mortgage association was ever chartered under the National Housing Act.[28] With the proposals for a regulated mortgage securitization system turned aside, the FNMA functioned for the next three decades as a secondary market discount facility serving institutions that originated and held federally-insured and guaranteed loans.

THE LEGACY OF THE 1930S MORTGAGE CRISIS

By 1939 a decade of crisis, emergency measures and regulatory change had created a system of institutional portfolio lenders that would dominate the residential mortgage market for the next 30 years. The new Savings & Loan industry served local mortgage markets and small-scale builders; commercial banks and mortgage companies used FHA and VA loans to finance large tract builders and multifamily projects; and life insurance companies and mutual savings banks dominated the interregional residential mortgage market through networks of dedicated mortgage companies. Within this structure depository financial institutions dominated the residential mortgage market; regulatory boundaries limited competition among lender groups; financial innovation was de-emphasized; and loan origination, servicing and credit risk management were integrated within single institution or small networks of institutions. The structure was particularly well-suited to the massive post-WWII expansion of residential mortgage debt and successfully financed a historic surge in homebuilding and home ownership without crisis or substantial instability.

By the late 1960s, however, serious problems arose within the postwar mortgage system. The problems arose because the standard home mortgage loan that had emerged during the 1930s shifted nearly all of the risks associated with changes in interest rates on the lender – borrowers enjoyed fixed-rate long-term rates when interest rates increased, but could also refinance loans without prepayment penalties when interest rates fell. During the 1950s and 1960s interest rates remained low and stable and so the portfolio lenders that dominated the residential market were shielded from the risks associated with funding their mortgage portfolios. But the situation changed markedly when the level and variability of inflation and nominal interest rates increased in the 1970s; all portfolio mortgage lenders had difficulty funding mortgages profitably and the S&Ls were particularly hard-hit by the liability-asset mismatch. As the share of residential mortgage debt held by S&Ls, life insurance companies and mutual savings banks fell in the 1970s and especially in the 1980s, securitization once again appeared in the US mortgage market but this time for different reasons and in a different form than in the 1920s.

Modern mortgage securitization in the US also took a different form than the system of federally-chartered, private mortgage banks that had been proposed in the National Housing Act of 1934. In the 1970s, instead, securitization was narrowly built on one federal agency (Ginnie Mae) and the Government Sponsored Enterprises (Fannie Mae and Freddie Mac) that were carved out in 1970 from the secondary market operations of the depression-era FNMA and FHLB system. These agencies guaranteed the credit risk on pools of mortgage loans so that their cash-flows could be passed-through as marketable securities. These mortgage-backed securities also passed-through the interest rate risk that had undone institutional portfolio lenders, so in the 1980s private agencies began to repackage GSE pass-throughs within structured, collateralized securities that offered different exposures to the funding and prepayment risk associated with changes in interest rates. The result was the surge in the share of mortgage debt financed by GSE pools between 1970 and 1990 that we have seen earlier in Figure 2.2.

In the 1990s the boundaries in mortgage securitization shifted in two important ways. First, the GSEs began to generate profits for their stockholders by retaining large volumes of whole mortgages and pass-through securities in their own portfolios and then funding these securities, and the interest rate risk they carried, at low interest rates because of their implicit federal guarantee. Second, private agencies began issuing and underwriting credit risk on their own mortgage-backed securities in order to fund loans that the GSEs would not securitize. By 1995 forces converged to generate the third great expansion of mortgage debt in the past century, the re-emergence of private-label mortgage securitization on a scale not seen since the 1920s, a relaxation of mortgage lending standards and, finally, the most severe mortgage crisis since the 1930s.

NOTES

1. Snowden (1995a, 2003, 2007) for accounts of failed innovations in the farm, commercial and residential mortgage markets in the 1870s and 1890s. Sparks (1932, Chapter VI) describes efforts by state governments to establish real estate mortgage banks before

the crisis of the 1830s. Wheelock (2008) examines the 1920s and 1930s crisis with an emphasis on federal interventions to reduce foreclosures.

2. Building starts include both single- and multi-family construction. The series for mortgage debt shows for each year the percentage change in the volume of residential mortgage relative to ten years earlier; this measures changes in the growth of the absolute size of the market.
3. Non-farm homeownership rate was 37 per cent (1890) and 41 per cent (1920). Grebler et al (1956, 168) provides estimates of mortgage debt relative to residential wealth for the pre-1950 era.
4. For purposes of comparison nominal GDP, mortgage debt and residential wealth were, respectively, \$91.2, \$30 and \$79 billion in 1930 – and \$12.4, \$10.2 and \$16.4 trillion in 2005. The ratio of mortgage debt to wealth in residential structures, therefore, was .38 in 1930 and .61 in 2005 while the debt to GDP ratio was .33 in 1930 and .81 in 2005 (Grebler et al, 1956, Table D-1 and L-6; Board of Governors (2008), Table L.217; BEA Table 1.1.5; and BEA Fixed Asset Table 5.1).
5. Morton (1956, 150–5) documents contract terms on loans written in the 1920s by different institutions. Building & Loans were an exception to the generalization – they offered loans up to two-thirds of the property's value with full amortization over an 11- or 12-year horizon.
6. National banks were allowed to hold urban mortgages in 1916, but only loans with maturities of one year or less until 1927. The size of their mortgage portfolios was also limited to one-half of time deposits (Behrens, 1952, 17–21).
7. Davis (1965) explains the development of interregional lending channels in the late nineteenth century as a response to capital market segmentation; Snowden (1987, 1988) shows the segmentation was particularly severe in the residential mortgage market. Morton (1956, 21–2) and Gray and Terborgh (1929, 14) show that regional disparity in mortgage rates persisted into the 1920s.
8. Mutual savings banks doubled their investment in residential mortgages during the 1920s but their share of residential debt decreased from 19 to 15 per cent because the mortgage market expanded even more rapidly (Lintner, 1948, 218; Grebler et al, 1956, 472). Life insurance companies and commercial banks increased market shares during the 1920s by quintupling and trebling their residential mortgage portfolio in only nine years (Saulnier, 1950, 13; Grebler et al, 1956, 466–8).
9. Piquet (1931) reports that 14 per cent of directors and 12 per cent of presidents in New Jersey B&Ls were builders.
10 Gries and Ford (1932, 88) report that in 1928 B&Ls in Philadelphia held a total of \$721 million of real estate loans of which \$455 million were second mortgages.
11. The small, serial plan B&L associations were concentrated in Pennsylvania, Illinois and New Jersey while the larger permanent plan associations were concentrated in Ohio and New York (Snowden, 2003, 179–81).
12. Goldsmith (1955, R-41) estimates that \$6.5 billion of nonfarm real estate securities were outstanding in 1931; while Halliburton (1939, 5) estimates a range between \$6 and \$10 billion.
13. Snowden (1995a) describes a similar attempt to issue mortgage-backed debentures by western farm mortgage companies in the 1880s. These programs were loosely modeled on European-style mortgage bonds, but they all failed.
14. Koester (1939a, 50) reports that small numbers of real estate securities in Chicago used leasehold bonds rather than mortgage bonds as security, and were organized as trusts.
15. Chamberlain and Edwards (1927, 443) notes that a few investment banks were also active in the market. Halliburton (1939) provides an exhaustive account of the real estate bond house. Goetzmann and Newman (2010) examine the performance of the real estate bond market in depth.
16. The FHLBB oversaw the Home Owners' Loan Corporation, a new system of federally-chartered Savings & Loan Associations, the Federal Savings & Loan Insurance Corporation and the discounting facilities of the Federal Home Loan Banks.

17. The principal on the modern direct reduction loan, in contrast, decreases each time the borrower makes a payment of principal. A minority of B&Ls employed the direct reduction contract in the 1920s, but most were required by state law to use the share accumulation contract (Bodfish, 1931, 203–5).
18. Members in a frozen B&L could wait for liquidation, reorganize their association into a 'good' and 'bad' B&L, or liquidate shares in a secondary market at a discount (Kendall, 1962, 76–7, 144; Bodfish and Theobald, 1938, 161; Ewalt, 1962, 116–18).
19. In describing the task facing the regulator the Moreland Commissioner noted (Alger, 1934, 2) that the assets of the guarantee companies represented more than 40 times the volume of all liquidations the Department of Insurance had handled since its inception in 1859.
20. Johnson (1936a, 1936b) examined the status of all real estate bonds that had been offered between 1919 and 1931 in amounts of at least $1 million – a total of 1100 separate securities with a combined face value of $2.7 billion.
21. Halliburton (1939, 43–96) provides an exhaustive account.
22. Koester (1939a, 1939b) examines the reorganization and operation of the secondary market for real estate bonds after 1935.
23. Hoover endorsed the idea of a home mortgage discounting facility at his 1931 Conference on Homebuilding and Home Ownership. The conference brought together real estate professionals, planners, architects and mortgage market participants to make recommendations regarding the construction, ownership and financing of housing.
24. Life insurance companies and savings banks were eligible to join the FHLB, but few did.
25. During the Bank Holiday of March 1933 the new FHLB advanced $40 million of currency to members B&Ls – these were the only financial institutions in the nation that offered their members cash during the bank holiday (Ewalt, 1962, 66–7).
26. Harriss (1951) provides the definitive treatment of the HOLC. Tough (1951) assesses HOLC effectiveness upon its liquidation.
27. New federal charters could be issued only if the applicant could demonstrate that its entry would not injure an existing association. The FHLB also adopted a '50-mile rule' which restricted the lending activities of chartered associations to their local markets. These provisions created local S&L monopoly markets that became a target for deregulation in the 1970s and 1980s.
28. The *New York Times*, 28 May 1938 reported that applications for new NMAs increased after FNMA's successful bond offering , but that with the FHA decision 'private interests planning to take advantage of this potential market . . . appear doomed to disappointment or at least considerable delay', p. 25. Jones and Grebler (1961, p. 115) refer to the NMA proposal as a 'frustrating episode'.

REFERENCES

Alger, George (1934), *Report on the Operation, Conduct, and Management of Title and Mortgage Guarantee Corporations*, New York.

Behrens, Carl F. (1952), *Commercial Bank Activities in Urban Mortgage Financing*, New York: National Bureau of Economic Research.

Board of Governors of the Federal Reserve System (2008), *Flow of Funds Accounts of the United States*, Federal Reserve Statistical Release *Z.1* (11 December 2008), Washington, DC.

Bodfish, H. Morton (1931), *History of Building and Loan in the United States*, Chicago: United States Building and Loan League.

Bodfish, H. Morton and A.D. Theobald (1938), *Savings and Loan Principles,* New York: Prentice Hall.
Carter, Susan B., Scott S. Gartner, Michael R. Haines, Alan L. Olmstead, Richard Sutch and Gavin Wright (eds) (2006), *Historical Statistics of the United States, Earliest Times to the Present: Millennial Edition*, New York: Cambridge University Press.
Chamberlain, Edward and G. Edwards (1927), *The Principles of Bond Investment,* New York: Henry Holt.
Clark, Evans (1933), *The Internal Debts of the United States*, New York: Macmillan and Co.
Clark, Horace and Frank A. Chase (1925), *Elements of the Modern Building and Loan Associations*, New York: Macmillan and Co.
Cramp, Ralph (1940), 'Guaranteed Mortgage Companies in Review – A program for the Future', *Contemporary Law Pamphlets*, Series 4, No. 6, NYU School of Law, 40 pp.
Davis, Lance (1965), 'The Investment Market, 1870–1914: The Evolution of a National Market', *Journal of Economic History*, **25**(2), 355–93.
Ewalt, Josephine (1962), *A Business Reborn*, Chicago: American Savings and Loan Institute.
Federal Home Loan Bank Board, Annual *Report*, Washington, DC, various years.
Fisher, Ernest M. (1951), *Urban Real Estate Markets: Characteristics and Financing,* New York: National Bureau of Economic Research.
Goetzmann, William N. and Frank Newman (2010), 'Securitization in the 1920s', National Bureau of Economic Research, Working Paper 15650.
Goldsmith, R. (1955), *A Study of Savings*, Princeton: Princeton University Press.
Gray, John H. and George W. Terbough (1929), 'First Mortgages in Urban Real Estate', *The Brookings Institute Pamphlet Series*, **1**(2).
Grebler, Leo, D. Blank and L. Winnick (1956), *Capital Formation in Residential Real Estate*, Princeton: Princeton University Press.
Gries, J.M. and J. Ford (eds) (1932), *President's Conference on Home Building and Home Ownership*, Washington, DC: National Capital Press.
Halliburton, Robert A. (1939), *The Real Estate Bond House*, Franklin, IN: Indiana University.
Harriss, Lowell (1951), *History and Policies of the Home Owners' Loan Corporation,* New York: National Bureau of Economic Research.
Herman, Edward, S. (1969), 'Conflicts in the Savings and Loan Industry', in I. Friend (ed.), *Study of the Saving and Loan Industry*. Vol. 2, Washington, DC: Government Printing Office.
Hoagland, Henry (1935), 'The Relation of the Work of the Federal Home Loan Bank Board to Home Security and Betterment', *Proceedings of the Academy of Political Science*, **16**(2), 45–52.
Johnson, Ernest A. (1936a), 'The Record of Long-term Real Estate Securities', *Journal of Land and Public Utility Economics,* **12**(1), 44–8.
Johnson, Ernest A. (1936b), 'The Record of Long-term Real Estate Securities: By Types of Property', *Journal of Land and Public Utility Economics*, **12**(3), 306–9.
Jones, Oliver and Leo Grebler (1961), *The Secondary Mortgage Market*, Los Angeles: UCLA.
Kendall, Leon T. (1962), *The Savings and Loan Business*, Englewood Cliffs, NJ: Prentice-Hall.

Klaman, Saul (1959), *The Postwar Rise of the Mortgage Company*, New York: National Bureau of Economic Research.

Koester, Genevieve (1939a), 'Chicago Real Estate Bonds, 1919–1938: I. Corporate History', *Journal of Land and Public Utility Economics*, **15**(1), 49–58.

Koester, Genevieve (1939b), 'Chicago Real Estate Bonds, 1919–1938: II. Market Behavior,' *Journal of Land and Public Utility Economics*, **15**(2), 201–11.

Lintner, John (1948), *Mutual Savings Banks in the Savings and Mortgage Markets*, Boston: Harvard University.

Loucks, William N. (1929), *The Philadelphia Plan of Home Financing*, Research Monograph No. 2, Chicago: The Institute for Research in Land Economics & Public Utilities.

Miller, Cyrus (1930), 'An Organized Real Estate Securities Exchange', *Annals of the American Academy of Political and Social Science*, **148**, 26–32.

Morton, Joseph (1956), *Urban Mortgage Lending: Comparative Markets and Experience*, Princeton: Princeton University Press.

New York State (1937), *Report of the Joint Legislative Committee to Investigate the Guaranteed Mortgage Situation*, Albany: J.B. Lyon Company.

New York State Mortgage Commission (1936), *Recommendations as to Proposed Legislation Pursuant to Subsection 21 of Section 4 of Chapter 19 of the Laws of 1935,* Albany: J.B. Lyon Company.

Piquet, Howard (1931), *Building and Loan Associations in New Jersey*, Princeton: Princeton University Press.

Rapkin, C., J. Ferrari, R. Blood and G. Milgram (1967)*, The Private Insurance of Home Mortgage*, Philadelphia: University of Pennsylvania.

Riegel, Robert and J. Russell Doubman (1927), *The Building and Loan Association*, New York: John Wiley & Sons.

Robins, Kingman, (1916), *The Farm Mortgage Handbook*, New York: Doubleday.

Rose, Jonathan (2010), 'The Incredible HOLC? Mortgage relief during the Great Depression', Working Paper.

Saulnier, Raymond (1950), *Urban Mortgage Lending by Life Insurance Companies,* New York: National Bureau of Economic Research.

Snowden, Kenneth (1987), 'Mortgage Rates and American Capital Market Development in the Late Nineteenth Century', *Journal of Economic History*, **47**(2), 671–91.

Snowden, Kenneth (1988), 'Mortgage Lending and American Urbanization, 1880–1890', *Journal of Economic History*, **48**(2), 273–85.

Snowden, Kenneth (1995a), 'Mortgage Securitization in the US: 20th Century Developments in Historical Perspective', in M. Bordo and R. Sylla (eds), *Anglo-American Financial Systems*, New York: Irwin, 261–98.

Snowden, Kenneth (1995b), 'The Evolution of Interregional Mortgage Lending, 1870–1940: The Life Insurance-Mortgage Company Connection', in N. Lamoreaux and D. Raff (eds), *Coordination and Information: Historical Perspectives on the Organization of Enterprise*, Chicago: University of Chicago, 209–47.

Snowden, Kenneth (1997), 'Building and Loan Associations in the US: The Origins of Localization in the Residential Mortgage Market,' *Research in Economics*, **51**(3), 227–50.

Snowden, Kenneth, (2003), 'The Transition from Building and Loan to Savings and Loan, 1890–1940', in S. L. Engerman, P. T. Hoffman, J. L. Rosenthal and

K. L. Sokoloff (eds), *Finance, Intermediaries, and Economic Development*, New York: Cambridge University Press.

Snowden, Kenneth A., (2007), 'Covered Farm Mortgage Bonds in the Late Nineteenth Century US', unpublished working paper.

Sparks, Earl (1932), *History and Theory of Agricultural Credit in the United States*, New York: Thomas Y. Crowell Company.

Tough, Rosalind (1951), 'The Life Cycle of the Home Owners' Loan Corporation', *Land Economics*, **27**(4), 324–31.

U.S. Bureau of Economic Analysis (2008), 'Table 1.1.5 Gross Domestic Product', available at http://www.bea.gov/ (accessed 12 February 2009).

U.S. Bureau of Economic Analysis (2008), 'Table 5.1 Current-Cost Net Stock of Residential Fixed Assets', available at http://www.bea.gov/ (accessed 12 February 2009).

Wheelock, David (2008), 'The Federal Response to Home Mortgage Distress: Lessons from the Great Depression', *Federal Reserve Bank of St. Louis Review*, **90**(3), 133–48.

PART II

Causes, consequences, and implications for reform

3. Stress testing and scenario analysis in risk management: preparing for the worst

James Fanto[1]

INTRODUCTION

The purpose of this chapter is to consider how several risk management practices, including stress testing and scenario analysis, contributed to the problems in the large financial institutions that were at the heart of the current financial crisis. The goals of risk management are to assess the risks facing a financial institution as a result of its activities and the business environment, to monitor the risks for any change, to determine whether the institution has the resources to deal with the risks, to alert senior managers and boards of directors about the risk information and to suggest courses of action for the decision makers to take to address the risks. During the past two decades, the risk management process has become increasingly dominated by the use of quantitative risk models that, for a given financial asset or class of assets, predict the probability and amount of loss for a future period at a given confidence level. However, risk management also includes stress testing and scenario analysis, which, in general, involve testing an institution against possible adverse future situations and predicting the institutional consequences of them.

My argument is that stress testing and scenario analysis in systemically important financial institutions failed, which contributed to the collapse of many large financial institutions and the meltdown of the financial system. There are a number of reasons for this failure, both those internal and external to these risk management practices. The chapter identifies the reasons and offers suggestions on how stress testing and scenario analysis can be reformed in the financial institutions. Moreover, it discusses impediments to the reforms, chiefly the complexities of the institutions that make adequate stress testing and scenario analysis difficult.

The chapter proceeds as follows. It first briefly describes the financial crisis in order to situate the problems in stress testing and scenario analysis.

It then explains risk management in financial institutions, the role of stress testing and scenario analysis and the failings of these practices as revealed by the financial crisis. The failings include (i) an overemphasis on quantitative modeling at the expense of stress testing and scenario analysis in risk management; (ii) the failure even to engage in, or to use sufficiently adverse assumptions in applying, stress testing and scenario analysis; (iii) governance problems in financial firms that impaired the effectiveness of stress testing and scenario analysis; and (iv) inadequate regulatory oversight of risk management practices. The chapter next explains how stress testing and scenario analysis can be improved so that a future crisis would be avoided. It also identifies impediments that could frustrate much-needed reforms in risk management. The chapter concludes with a proposed plan of action for financial institutions and regulators that could overcome such impediments.

THE FINANCIAL CRISIS

The financial crisis and its origins are now so familiar (and well covered by other chapters in this volume) that there is no need to spend much time on them. The crisis was triggered by the collapse of the credit markets, which was itself caused by losses in asset-backed securities, initially those backed by subprime mortgages (mortgage-backed securities or 'MBS').[2] In the years before the financial collapse, there was an enormous growth in real estate loans to borrowers with low incomes and little savings who thus had little hope of repaying them, unless real estate prices continued to rise. The home mortgage loans were pooled and interests in the pools were sold by financial institutions as differing kinds of securities to investors who sought higher returns on debt investments during this period.[3] During the years before the crisis, investment banks securitized the loans that were ineligible for the programs of home mortgage securitization operated by the government-sponsored entities, Fannie Mae and Freddie Mac.

When subprime borrowers began to default on the loans, this caused a failure of some, and a reevaluation and repricing of other, MBS backed by subprime loans. The loss of value in MBS led investors to doubt the valuation of other asset-backed securities, and they proceeded to sell off their positions and to refuse to buy new issues of these securities.[4] Many MBS and other financial assets thus became illiquid. As the value of financial assets declined because of this illiquidity, financial institutions throughout the world both incurred substantial losses and were threatened with insolvency.[5] They also became wary of doing transactions with, and particularly extending credit to, other firms, because they were unsure about the exposure of the firms to the MBS. The subprime meltdown triggered a systemic crisis in worldwide finance.

Famous financial conglomerates collapsed, had to be hastily merged with others or received government support simply to survive. In the United States, Bear Stearns was merged with JP Morgan;[6] the federal government seized Fannie Mae and Freddie Mac;[7] Lehman Brothers filed for bankruptcy (with Barclays Bank acquiring many of its operations), while at the same time Merrill Lynch agreed to be acquired by Bank of America;[8] and the federal government took over one of the largest US insurance companies, American International Group, Inc., because of its massive liabilities from writing credit default swaps on MBS.[9] Additionally, Goldman Sachs and Morgan Stanley became bank (and then financial) holding companies under the jurisdiction of the Board of Governors of the Federal Reserve System ('Federal Reserve') because that regulatory status increased the federal safeguards available to them.[10]

Major legislative and regulatory actions addressed the crisis. The Emergency Economic Stabilization Act of 2008 ('EESA')[11] was passed, which, among other things, established the Troubled Asset Relief Program ('TARP') that gave the US Treasury the authority to purchase or guarantee up to $700 billion in troubled assets held by financial institutions. Under the authority of EESA, the Treasury established the Capital Purchase Program, which allowed it to provide direct capital support to financial institutions.[12] The Obama Treasury Department continued to provide capital to major financial conglomerates that had suffered in the crisis, such as Bank of America. It also initiated a 'Financial Stability Plan', to put financial institutions and the financial system on a sound footing.[13] This Plan includes a program of providing capital to financial institutions (now renamed the 'Capital Assistance Program') and, significantly for the purposes of this chapter, to 'stress test' the largest, most systematically important financial institutions to ensure that they had enough resources to weather the crisis.

STRESS TESTING AND SCENARIO ANALYSIS, AND THEIR FAILURES

Stress Testing and Scenario Analysis

Risk management has become an essential function in financial institutions because it helps an institution to identify the risk of loss associated with its investments and activities, monitor and keep in check these risks and prepare for, and minimize, the losses associated with them.[14] An important reason for the growth in the importance of risk management is the regulation of capital. Since financial institutions are highly leveraged (they use other peoples' money to make money), their owners have always been required to invest a minimum of their own funds in an institution. This capital provides a cushion for the lenders and motivates the owners not to take excessive risks in their investments and activities. Over time, regulators have made capital primarily risk-based. This means that a financial institution must have capital in proportion to the riskiness of its assets and activities: the riskier an institution is, the more capital it must have, which means that the less borrowed funds it may use for its investments and activities.[15]

In adopting risk-based capital requirements, regulators originally focused, in a standardized way, only on credit risk (namely, the risk that a borrower would default on its payment of principal and interest) in an institution's loan portfolio and related off-balance sheet activities.[16] However, this standardized approach proved inadequate as the largest banks began to engage in securities market activities by purchasing securities (chiefly debt) for investment purposes and for trading. Accordingly, regulators revised their capital rules to take account of market risk, which is the risk of loss of value of the securities due to such factors as changes in interest rates and securities market developments.[17] These market risk rules enhanced the importance of risk management, because finance academics and professionals produced quantitatively-based methods and techniques for modeling the risks of securities in order to establish accurate pricing of the instruments.[18] Regulators allowed banks engaged in securities market investing and trading to develop and use their own market risk assessment models, provided that the models met certain standards.[19] The largest, most sophisticated banking institutions can now use their own models even in the assessment of credit risks, as well as in a new category of operational risk, which measures the risk of losses from such events as fraud (external and internal), occupational safety, failure to fulfill fiduciary obligations, system breakdowns, problems in transaction processing, terrorism and natural disasters.[20]

This chapter focuses on financial risk assessment procedures, including stress testing and scenario analysis, which are different from standardized regulatory guidelines and quantitative internal risk models. Both stress testing and scenario analysis assess a firm's risk of loss in its assets and activities by assuming the existence of seriously adverse situations or 'scenarios', and then by evaluating how the firm would be affected under a given situation and whether it would be adequately prepared, and have adequate capital, to deal with it.[21] While both of these forms of risk analysis are related, they are distinguishable. Stress testing focuses on the projected losses to an institution from a hypothetical situation. Scenario analysis, by contrast, is more dynamic insofar as it requires senior decision makers and others in a financial institution to simulate their roles in an adverse scenario and to anticipate how others, such as an institution's trading counterparties and creditors, would act in such a scenario.[22]

While quantitative risk modeling plays a role in stress testing and scenario analysis, the latter practices are also qualitative. In performing stress testing and scenario analysis, risk managers must have a historical perspective and must use their imagination to envision possible adverse events and scenarios for the testing and analysis. They must also understand the frameworks, assumptions, and results of the quantitative risk models so that they can test and challenge them appropriately. In addition, practitioners of scenario analysis must understand in detail the connections between their institution and the financial system in order to predict the reactions of counterparties in a given scenario. Since these practices have important qualitative and judgmental components, there is frequently disagreement (sometimes within the same institution) between risk managers who rely only upon quantitative risk models and their results, and those who believe that quantitative risk measures must be supplemented with stress testing and scenario analysis.[23]

Financial regulators supervise the risk management practices of financial institutions, including stress testing and scenario analysis. They must approve the adequacy of the quantitative risk models and of the qualitative practices of the institutions under their jurisdiction. For example, the Federal Reserve is required to rate bank holding companies based on their risk management practices.[24] Current capital rules emphasize that regulators are responsible for evaluating the sufficiency of risk management procedures and internal risk models used by large financial institutions to calculate their required capital.[25]

Stress Testing and Scenario Analysis Failures

The financial crisis can be attributed in large part to failures in risk management.[26] It is not entirely clear why risk management failed in financial firms because complete information about the institutions involved in the crisis has yet fully to emerge. However preliminary evidence suggests that risk management failures included serious shortcomings in stress testing and scenario analysis.

One problem is that financial firms relied too much on quantitative risk assessment models at the expense of stress testing and scenario analysis.[27] The use of the quantitative models thus took attention and resources away from qualitative risk assessment. Because the quantitative models predicted the maximum potential loss with respect to specific financial assets with a high degree of confidence on the basis of past performance, risk managers might well have seen little need to consider highly adverse but low-probability scenarios and to run costly simulations of their conduct and that of counterparties in these scenarios. Some firms simply neglected to engage in this type of testing and analysis. By contrast, firms that performed better in the crisis did not rely solely on loss predictions from quantitative models but instead used such quantitative risk measures in conjunction with other risk management methods, such as stress testing and scenario analysis.[28]

Another failure is that, when financial firms conducted stress testing and scenario analysis, they often did it poorly. As already noted, under these approaches risk managers test a firm's assets and activities under seriously adverse events, such as the failure of an important counterparty, a significant rise in interest rates, a shock in the currency markets or sustained illiquidity, and they evaluate the financial institution's likely conduct (and predict others' conduct) in the scenarios. Some financial firms used relatively 'benign' adverse scenarios for the tests and analyses.[29] For example, although respected economists had warned about the possibility that the US housing market was in a bubble, many firms did not run a stress test based upon a significant price decline in that market.[30] Risk managers thus failed to take a sufficiently long historical perspective in their stress testing and scenario analysis, and they did not consider the impact of an event comparable to the thrift and banking crises of the 1980s or the Great Depression, involving a generalized financial crisis and a loss of liquidity across a broad range of assets. Moreover, risk managers often performed stress testing and scenario analysis at a business or division level and did not aggregate results for the entire financial holding company, thereby missing the firm-wide effects of an adverse scenario.

In addition, stress testing and scenario analysis were often flawed because the risk managers conducting them did not anticipate the collateral or 'feedback' effects from adverse scenarios. This phenomenon is known as 'tail dependence', which is the risk that losses at the tail end of a probability distribution can be extreme because they produce a cascade of losses in other domains that magnify them.[31] In other words, there is a contagion effect in highly adverse scenarios, which scenario analysis is supposed to anticipate and to prepare the institution to withstand. The financial crisis has provided numerous examples of these collateral effects. For instance, widespread defaults on subprime loans that were pooled in MBS caused a loss of liquidity for other asset-backed securities and eventually all securities, which then resulted in the insolvency of major financial institutions and a general downturn in the economy as financial institutions stopped lending.[32] In turn, the shutdown in new lending cut off refinancing possibilities for subprime mortgages and reinforced the illiquidity of MBS backed by subprime loans.[33]

The failure of stress testing and scenario analysis to anticipate collateral effects in a seriously adverse scenario may be connected to the human inability to imagine low-probability catastrophic outcomes. Although his criticism is primarily directed at quantitative risk modeling, financial expert Nassim Taleb argues more generally that catastrophic events (and extraordinarily beneficial outcomes) occur in a random way that cannot be predicted. These events are always unexpected and thus unimaginable; they are in his terminology the 'black swans'.[34] In his view, risk management enhances risk because it leads people to believe that risk can be 'managed', and this mistaken belief encourages them to engage in even riskier conduct.[35] From a less extreme perspective than Taleb's, one could say that stress testing and scenario analysis were too complacent by focusing on the recent past, which was relatively benign for the securities markets, and by not being more imaginative or sensitive to new situations of risk.

There were also corporate governance failures in financial firms related to stress testing and scenario analysis. Senior executives and boards of directors of many financial firms clearly did not pay enough attention to the risk profiles of their firms, or even to risk management in general.[36] Stress testing and scenario analysis are particularly suited for executive input, since they demand the exercise of critical, imaginative thinking and judgment by experienced people who consider how an extreme situation might affect an entire institution. However senior executives frequently did not require risk managers to perform adequate stress testing and scenario analysis using suitably adverse scenarios, or to produce firm-wide risk measures for their review.[37] Executives were also reluctant to engage in the role playing and counterparty anticipation required by scenario analysis. It is similarly doubtful whether directors of financial firms fulfilled their supervisory duty over risk management by reviewing stress test outcomes and questioning test assumptions and the scenarios used.[38] Board members, and the responsible board committees, evidently were content to rely upon their firm's risk managers, and it is likely that many of them did not understand the limitations of the stress testing and scenario analysis that were conducted.[39] The passivity of senior executives and directors with respect to risk management may well have resulted from the fact that their firms were reporting record profits and thus seemed to be prepared for any eventuality.

Finally, financial regulators failed in their task of supervising the adequacy of stress testing and scenario analysis in financial firms. As discussed above, financial regulators examine and rate a financial firm on its risk management.[40] However, regulators did not ensure that firms were using suitably adverse scenarios to stress test their operations and assets.[41] Moreover, when regulators did detect problems in stress testing and scenario analysis and report them to senior executives of a firm, they did not insist that firms quickly remedy the problems and did not take more serious enforcement action against a firm if it did not do so. Instead, they relied on management's assurances that any problems would be corrected or were not serious in light of the overall profitability and adequate capital position of the institution.[42] Indeed, regulators admitted that, like firm risk managers, executives and board members, they did not think that a serious financial crisis was likely, and they therefore did not compel firms under their jurisdiction to be prepared for its eventuality.[43]

REFORMS OF STRESS TESTING, IMPEDIMENTS AND A PLAN OF ACTION

Reforms

Several reforms of stress testing and scenario analysis in financial institutions are straightforward and should be undertaken. First, the exercises should actually be performed and not neglected because of quantitative risk modeling.[44] Second, stress testing and scenario analysis needs to be emphasized and enhanced. Based on its review of failures in risk management at financial institutions, the Basel Committee on Banking Supervision has made several recommendations for improvements in stress testing and scenario analysis. It recommends, among other things, that extreme and imaginative scenarios be used in the testing and analysis, that the practices be always done from a firm-wide perspective and that senior executives, boards, and experts seriously participate in the scenario analysis.[45] It also recommends that a financial institution conduct a 'reverse' stress test or scenario analysis. Under such a 'reverse' exercise, participants assume that their financial institution is insolvent, and they then imagine ways in which this scenario could come about and try to undertake measures to prevent it from occurring.[46]

Third, senior executives and board members of a financial firm must have greater involvement in stress testing and scenario analysis.[47] Senior decision makers should supply the judgment and perspective that are necessary if these qualitative risk management practices are to work well. However, they cannot provide their insights and supervision unless they are adequately informed about, and understand the assumptions inherent in, the risk management practices followed in their firm, including why particular scenarios are used in stress testing and analysis. A financial firm should have a risk committee, which may be a committee composed of both executives and board members. The risk committee should oversee stress testing and scenario analysis, review critically the scenarios proposed to be used, ensure that the testing and scenario analysis are actually conducted firm-wide, evaluate the results and propose a course of action to prepare the institution for adverse consequences.[48] The committee should retain outside risk management experts periodically to review the firm's quantitative models and qualitative procedures.

Fourth, financial regulators must improve their supervision of stress testing and scenario analysis. They must demand that firms actually run stress tests and conduct scenario analysis with sufficiently adverse scenarios and with full support and participation by senior executives and board members. They must also penalize firms for their failures in these areas.[49] The true test of regulatory commitment to these risk management practices must be demonstrated in the good times, when financial institutions will again become complacent and will push back on regulatory efforts requiring them to prepare for adverse scenarios that are not readily foreseeable. It is ironic, but understandable, that it took a financial cataclysm for US financial regulators to force major financial conglomerates to conduct stress tests that are a 'more consistent, realistic, and forward looking assessment about the risks on [their] balance sheets'.[50] In these extraordinary circumstances, with investors and counterparties losing confidence in the ability of large financial institutions to withstand the current severe economic situation, regulators insisted that the institutions conduct the tests. Moreover, the stress tests demonstrated the proper approach that financial regulators should follow to ensure the effectiveness of stress testing. In administering the stress tests, regulators approved the benchmarks used in the tests, oversaw the performance and evaluated the results of the tests and required institutions to remedy the problems revealed by the tests.[51] The regulators must maintain this approach in the future, again particularly when financial firms are profitable and catastrophes are unimaginable.

Impediments

There are, however, significant impediments to reforming stress testing and scenario analysis. These obstacles include the fact that large financial groups have so many activities and operations that stress testing and scenario analysis on a firm-wide basis may be too complex an undertaking and thus almost impossible to do in a useful way.[52] Given the complexity of these institutions and their interconnectedness in the financial system, which produces even more complexity, it is extremely difficult to run a stress test or to engage in a scenario analysis that adequately predicts the losses that an institution may suffer from an adverse scenario, particularly those associated with feedback effects in a crisis. If, as is likely in light of their wide-ranging powers, financial institutions continue to expand their financial and other activities, stress testing and scenario analysis may have reached the limits of their utility by being unable to give the institution much guidance on likely outcomes in an adverse scenario.[53]

This complexity obstacle suggests that stress testing and scenario analysis may even be dangerous because they give senior decision makers in financial institutions and financial regulators the illusion that they have identified, and prepared for, extreme scenarios in financial institutions, when in fact the practices may be unable to do so.[54] Financial market complexities may themselves produce new risks that stress testing and scenario analysis do not even contemplate. Risk managers currently understand that they do not know when the adverse scenarios will occur, but they may believe that they have sufficient knowledge to identify the possible scenarios and understand the upper limit of their losses.[55] However, rather than being in the predicted and predictable state of affairs, financial institutions may be presented with completely unexpected situations, resulting from complexity, that stress testing and scenario analysis could not contemplate.

Even assuming that risk managers could accurately predict adverse scenarios despite the complexity of financial institutions, it may be that they, as well as executives, board members and regulators, will never take action on the basis of the predicted outcomes of the scenarios. It is questionable whether managers and regulators of financial institutions will consistently use extreme adverse scenarios and, even if such scenarios are used, whether they will allow the negative outcomes to guide their conduct, particularly when the scenarios appear to be highly unlikely and the present financial condition of the institution and the overall economy is strong. This supposition is based upon findings of behavioral psychology, which indicate that human beings are excessively optimistic, refuse properly to acknowledge the risk of loss and focus too much on present or visible problems (even if they are statistically unrepresentative).[56] In other words, people are willing to contemplate and to plan for an adverse scenario when it is already visible, such as now. But that willingness quickly fades as good times return, and people become increasingly unwilling to accept or even consider the possibility of catastrophic loss.[57]

A vivid example of the reluctance to use, and to act on, extreme adverse scenarios is the stress testing that financial regulators just conducted on the major financial institutions, which was referred to above. The regulators required the institutions to run tests under 'expected' and 'worst case' scenarios. However the 'worst case' scenario assumed over the next two years only – 4.0 per cent real GDP growth, 10.3 per cent unemployment, and an approximately 27 per cent decline in home prices.[58] Even in the middle of one of the worst financial catastrophes in decades, financial regulators arguably did not use a sufficiently extreme adverse scenario for the testing.[59] They reportedly also encountered resistance from financial institution executives, who argued that stress testing based on the 'worst case' scenario was unnecessary given the likely turnaround in the economy that they anticipated.

A Plan of Action

What should be the plan of action for improving the effectiveness of stress testing and scenario analysis, given the foregoing impediments? It may well be that the size and activities of financial institutions should be limited, and they should not be allowed to use all the inventions of finance, given the complexities and the novel scenarios that the size and inventions could generate.[60] This is unlikely to be a popular approach and may not be politically feasible. If, therefore, financial institutions continue their present expansive course, which will produce more complexity and greater uncertainty about their risks, their managers and regulators should follow a more conservative and risk-averse approach in assessing the results of stress testing and scenario analysis. Managers and regulators should require financial institutions to take protective measures sufficient to withstand highly adverse scenarios, even if the cost is significant (for example, by demanding more capital than the minimum level indicated by stress tests), in order to respond adequately to the results of stress testing and scenario analysis. This would also prepare the institution for outcomes that, due to complexity and human shortcomings, were not anticipated but could occur. In addition, financial institutions should not be allowed to engage in new market activities or to sell new financial products without 'redundant' safeguards, such as a significant capital charge, a developed market infrastructure and a regulatory framework that has been successfully used in the past for other activities and products.[61] These multiple safeguards would protect the institution from further harm generated by the additional complexities resulting from new activities and products.

Certainly all of the reforms discussed above – improving the effectiveness of stress testing, increasing the involvement of senior executives and board members and enhancing the role of regulators in risk management – should be undertaken. However, in light of the complexities of financial institutions and the financial system, the unexpected nature of financial catastrophes and the human tendency to downplay adverse scenarios, senior executives of financial institutions must recognize and address the limitations of stress testing and scenario analysis. Senior executives should ensure that risk managers who conduct the testing and analysis are specially recruited and given significant independence and authority in the institution. Risk managers should be kept close to the financial activities that they evaluate, which will help them be alert to new risks and new scenarios.[62] Although risk managers have to test the institution for scenarios modeled upon the past, they cannot allow themselves to become complacent because they have prepared for those scenarios. This complacency may prevent them from seeing a new risk challenge.

CONCLUSION

The current financial crisis has revealed serious failures in stress testing and scenario analysis in financial institutions. Those failures included the neglect of stress testing and scenario analysis in favor of quantitative risk modeling, the use of scenarios that were not sufficiently adverse, the reluctance of senior executives and directors of financial institutions to second-guess risk managers and the failure of regulators to identify flaws in risk management practices at major financial institutions. This chapter has explained how these failures could be addressed both by financial institutions and by regulators. Yet it pointed out that there are significant impediments to needed reforms, including the growing complexity of the activities and operations in financial institutions that make adequate stress testing and scenario analysis difficult to achieve. The chapter also discussed how this complexity could produce new and therefore unanticipated adverse scenarios that had not been included in the testing and analysis. The chapter concluded with suggestions of a plan of action to improve stress testing and scenario analysis in financial institutions going forward. This plan includes reducing the complexity of financial institutions, building added protections and safeguards that require institutions to prepare for overlooked or unanticipated scenarios and ensuring that risk managers involved in these practices be alert to new situations of risk.

NOTES

1. Professor of Law, Brooklyn Law School. I thank Professor Larry Mitchell and the other participants at George Washington University Law School's symposium on the *Panic of 2008* for their comments on a preliminary version of this chapter.

2. Sabry and Schopflocher (2007).
3. Joint Economic Committee (2008).
4. Caballero and Krishnamurthy (2008), p. 10.
5. Technical Committee of the International Organization of Securities Commissions (2008), pp. 16–19 (explaining difficulties of valuation of MBSs and other asset-backed securities).
6 Kelly (2008a), p. A1; Kelly (2008b), p. A1; Kelly (2008d), p. A1. See also Kelly (2008c), p. C1.
7. Hagerty (2008).
8. Mollenkamp (2008).
9. A credit default swap is a financial instrument in which, in return for a one-time payment or periodic payments, the swap writer agrees to pay the swap purchaser the value of a debt obligation if the issuer defaults in repaying that obligation.
10. Hilsenrath (2008).
11. 110th Congress 2008, H.R. 1424.
12. US Treasury (2008).
13. The initiatives under this Plan are described on the Plan's web site at http://www.financialstability.gov.
14. Rose and Hudgins (2008).
15. The risk-based capital model has been implemented pursuant to an international agreement promulgated by the Basel Committee on Banking Supervision, which is part of the Bank for International Settlements. Rose and Hudgins (2008), pp. 483–84.
16. The risk-based capital framework was later refined to take account of financial institutions' involvement in hedging activities, such as futures, interest rate and currency swaps and other hedging devices. Rose and Hudgins (2008), pp. 487–91.
17. Saunders and Cornett (2008), p. 266.
18. Saunders and Cornett (2008), pp. 268–83. The most well-known of the methods was the 'value-at-risk' ('VaR') methodology, which purports to determine, on the basis of past data, the future probability of loss for particular financial assets, or groups of assets, over a specified period with a high degree of confidence.
19. Saunders and Cornett (2008), pp. 288–90. The VAR models were required to use a 99% confidence level with respect to the probability of loss over a 10-day period. For the market risk measurement rules of the Federal Reserve for US bank holding companies, see 12 C.F.R. § 225 (Appendix D) (2009).
20. This capital regulation development is known as 'Basel II'. 'Risk-Based Capital Standards: Advanced Capital Adequacy Framework – Basel II' 2008 (guidelines of US financial regulators based on the new Basel II capital framework). In the United States, Basel II begins on a three-year transition basis in 2009. Financial regulators have adopted a 'standardized approach' for determining capital requirements under Basel II for institutions that do not have the resources to calculate their capital requirements based on internal risk models. 'Risk-Based Capital Guidelines; Capital Adequacy Guidelines; Standardized Framework' (2008).
21. For a discussion of basic principles on stress testing, see Basel Committee on Banking Supervision (2009), pp. 9–11.
22. On the relationships and differences between stress testing and scenario analysis, see Castren, Caviglia and Teixeira (2007), pp. 8–9.
23. Mikes (2008) (describing the two risk management cultures as 'calculative' and 'judgmental' and finding scenario analysis to be based more on judgmental and intuitive factors).
24. Federal Reserve Board 2005, § 4070 (discussing Bank Holding Company Rating System that includes a rating on an 'R' component, which represents risk management). Many of the largest bank holding companies are 'financial' holding companies, which are permitted to engage in a broad range of financial activities. 12 U.S.C. § 1843(k). The Federal Reserve must inspect these institutions as to their risks and their risk management systems. 12 U.S.C. § 1844(c)(2)(A).

25. Rose and Hudgins (2008), p. 493.
26. Bernanke (2009) (discussing risk management failures); Greenspan (2008) (same).
27. There were also problems in the quantitative risk models. US Government Accountability Office (2009), p. 22 (discussing how quantitative risk models used data that was not sufficiently historical or representative of the financial instruments being modeled); Senior Supervisors Group (2008), pp. 13–15 (pointing out how the models could not handle the complexities of some of the financial instruments).
28. Cf. Overbye (2009); Nocera (2009), pp. 24, 50.
29. Basel Committee on Banking Supervision (2009), pp. 4–6; US Government Accountability Office (2009), p. 23.
30. Loffler (2008) (performing stress test as of 2005 that should have been performed by financial institutions, finding that it produced a scenario of a housing decline worse than the one actually experienced in 2008, and concluding that either risk managers failed to do their job or that business managers failed to pay attention to the risk managers).
31. Basel Committee on Banking Supervision, Principles for sound stress testing practices and supervision, *supra* note 21, at 3. See also Kousky and Cooke 2009, pp. 2–3 (discussing this phenomenon in environmental catastrophes).
32. Basel Committee on Banking Supervision (2008), pp. 1–2.
33. So great was this market dislocation that the federal government has tried to finance the purchases of 'toxic' MBSs as well as new asset-backed securities. Board of Governors of the Federal Reserve System (2009).
34. Taleb (2007), pp. 274–85.
35. Taleb (2007), pp. 288–89.
36. US Government Accountability Office (2009), p. 18.
37. Senior Supervisors Group (2008), pp. 3, 7–9.
38. Under general management practice, risk management may fall under the jurisdiction of the audit committee since the latter supervises a firm's internal controls, and risk monitoring (that is, ensuring that a firm stays within designated risks) would be part of these controls. Financial firms often have a separate risk committee, which would monitor and approve a firm's risk profile. Tonello (2008), p. 4.
39. Morris (2008), p. 58 (discussing how risk management gave parties 'the illusion that the underlying risks were well understood and under control').
40. When regulators evaluate a firm with respect to other matters, risk management is often a subsidiary topic. Federal Reserve Board (2005), § 4070, pp. 15–17 (examining the financial condition of a firm from the perspective of its risk profile).
41. US Government Accountability Office (2009), pp. 18–25.
42. US Government Accountability Office (2009), pp. 21, 24.
43. US Government Accountability Office (2009), p. 24. See also Rosengren (2008), p. 7 (President of the Federal Reserve Bank of Boston observes that federal regulators did not anticipate an event where liquidity across multiple assets and markets would be so significantly disrupted).
44. Stultz (2008), pp. 18–19, 22 (emphasizing that an institution must have a risk management approach that does not rely only on statistical models, but also on evaluation the effects of catastrophe scenarios on an institution).
45. Basel Committee on Banking Supervision (2009), pp. 12–17.
46. Basel Committee on Banking Supervision (2009), p. 14. See also Basel Committee on Banking Supervision (2008), pp. 24–27 (recommending that an institution conduct stress testing related to liquidity).
47. Group of Thirty (2009), p. 41.
48. Tonello (2008), pp. 3–4. See also Basel Committee on Banking Supervision (2008), p. 33 (emphasizing the role of the board in insisting upon adequately bad scenarios for stress testing); Senior Supervisors Group (2008), pp. 6–10.
49. Basel Committee on Banking Supervision (2009), pp. 17–19; US Government Accountability Office (2009), p. 19.

50. US Treasury (2009a), p. 4. This stress test was designed to determine whether the 19 largest US financial institutions would have enough capital to survive a severe economic decline. The stress test focused on banks with assets or more than $100 billion. Those banks collectively hold two-thirds of bank holding company assets. See US Treasury (2009b), p. 2. The purpose of the tests was to estimate losses in the credit and market books in these institutions over a two-year time horizon (2009–2010) and to evaluate the adequacy of a firm's resources to deal with them.
51. Federal Reserve Board (2009a), (discussing the methodology of the stress test); Federal Reserve Board (2009b), (discussing the results of the stress test).
52. Group of Thirty (2009), pp. 26–27 (pointing out that the largest financial institutions in the United States are becoming even larger and are posing greater and more complex risks to the financial system, and questioning whether it is 'really possible, with all the complexities, risks, and potential conflicts, that even the most dedicated board of directors and top management can understand and maintain control over such a diverse and complex mix of activities').
53. Bookstaber (2007), pp. 255–60.
54. Bookstaber (2007), pp. 147–48.
55. Cooper (2008), p. 144.
56. Sunstein (2000).
57. Sunstein (2005), p. 155.
58. Federal Reserve Board (2009a), pp. 6–7.
59. The regulators claimed that, in some cases, they were using data comparable to that from the Great Depression. Federal Reserve Board (2009b), p. 7 n.5. But it is clear that they downplayed the 'worst case' by using a short two-year time horizon, which ignores the possibility that the financial downturn could extend for a much longer period. Federal Reserve Board (2009), p. 8 n.7. For an extensive critique of the methodology of the stress tests and a discussion of their limitations, see Congressional Oversight Panel (2009).
60. Bookstaber (2007), pp. 259–60. See also Krugman (2008); Bhidé (2009), pp. 7–8 (arguing for creating at least one banking system that engages only in basic finance and that is insulated from more complex financial activities).
61. Credit default swaps are a good example of the risks posed by new products that had no developed infrastructure. Kousky and Cooke (2009), p. 5 (arguing that redundancies must be built into environmental risk management systems to address tail risks and the uncertainty of outcomes).
62. See Bookstaber (2007), pp. 235–37.

REFERENCES

(n.d.). Retrieved from Financial Stability Plan: http://www.financialstability.gov
110th Congress (2008), H.R. 1424.
12 C.F.R. § 225 (Appendix D) (2009).
12 U.S.C. § 1843(k) (2008).
12 U.S.C. § 1844(c)(2)(A) (2008).
Basel Committee on Banking Supervision (2008), 'Principles for Sound Liquidity Risk Management and Supervision', http://www.bis.org/publ/bcbs144.pdf, September.
Basel Committee on Banking Supervision (2009), 'Principles for Sound Stress Testing Practices and Supervision', http://www.bis.org/publ/bcbs147.pdf, January.
Bernanke, Ben S. (2009), 'Financial Reform to Address Systemic Risk', Speech at the Council on Foreign Relations, 10 March.

Bhidé, Amar (2009), 'In Praise of More Primitive Finance', 28 January, http://www.bhide.net/financial_crisis_2008/bhide_praise_of_primitive_finance.pdf.

Board of Governors of the Federal Reserve System (2009), 'Term Asset-Backed Securities Loan Facility', http://www.federalreserve.gov/monetarypolicy/talf.htm, 2 September.

Bookstaber, Richard (2007), *A Demon of Our Own Design,* New York: John Wiley & Sons, Inc.

Caballero, Ricardo J. and A. Krishnamurthy (2008), 'Musical chairs: a comment on the credit crisis', *Financial Stability Review*, pp. 9–11.

Castren, Olli, G. Caviglia and P. G. Teixeira (2007), 'Simulating Financial Instability', *Simulating Financial Instability: Conference on Stress Testing and Financial Crisis Simulation Exercises,* Frankfurt am Main: European Central Bank, pp. 8–12.

Congressional Oversight Panel (2009), 'June Oversight Report: Stress Testing and Shoring Up Bank Capital', 9 June.

Cooper, George (2008), *The Origin of Financial Crises: Central Banks, Credit Bubbles and the Efficient Market Fallacy,* London: Harriman House.

Federal Reserve Board (2005), 'Bank Holding Company Supervision Manual'.

Federal Reserve Board (2009a), 'The Supervisory Capital Assessment Program: Design and Implementation'.

Federal Reserve Board (2009b), 'The Supervisory Capital Assessment Program: Overview of Results'.

Greenspan, Alan (2008), 'Testimony before the US House Committee of Government Oversight and Reform', 23 October.

Group of Thirty (2009), *Financial Reform: A Framework for Financial Stability*, Washington: The Group of Thirty.

Hagerty, James R., R. Simon and D. Paletta (2008), 'US Seizes Mortgage Giants', *Wall Street Journal*, 8 September, p. A1.

Hilsenrath, Jon, D. Paletta and A. Lucchetti (2008), 'Goldman, Morgan Scrap Wall Street Model, Become Banks in Bid to Ride Out Crisis', *Wall Street Journal*, 22 September, p. A1.

Joint Economic Committee (2008), 'The U.S. Housing Bubble and the Global Financial Crisis: Housing and Housing-Related Finance', May.

Kelly, Kate (2008a), 'Lost Opportunities Haunt Final Days of Bear Stearns', *Wall Street Journal*, 27 May, p. A1.

Kelly, Kate (2008b), 'Fear, Rumors Touched Off Fatal Run on Bear Stearns', *Wall Street Journal*, 28 May, p. A1.

Kelly, Kate (2008c), 'Bear's Final Moment: An Apology and No Lack of Ire', *Wall Street Journal*, 30 May, p. C1.

Kelly, Kate (2008d), 'Bear Stearns Neared Collapse Twice in Frenzied Last Days', *Wall Street Journal*, 29 May, p. A1.

Kousky, Carolyn and R. M. Cooke (2009), 'Climate Change and Risk Management: Challenges for Insurance, Adaptation, and Loss Estimation', Resources for the Future Discussion Paper No. 09–03, February.

Krugman, Paul (2008), 'Making Banking Boring', *New York Times*, 10 April, p. A23.

Loffler, Gunter (2008), 'Caught in the Housing Crash: Model Failure or Management Failure', December.

Mikes, Anette (2008), 'Risk Management at Crunch Time: Are Chief Risk Officers Compliance Champions or Business Partners?', http://www.ssrn.com.

Mollenkamp, Carrick, S. Craig, S. Ng and A. Luchetti (2008), 'Lehman Files for Bankruptcy, Merrill Sold, AIG Seeks Cash', *Wall Street Journal*, 16 September.

Morris, Charles R. (2008), *The Trillion Dollar Meltdown: Easy Money, High Rollers, and the Great Credit Crash,* New York: Public Affairs.

Nocera, Joe (2009), 'Risk Mismanagement', *New York Times Magazine*, 4 January, p. 24.

Overbye, Dennis (2009), 'They Tried to Outsmart Wall Street', *New York Times*, 10 March, p. D1.

'Risk-Based Capital Guidelines; Captial Adequacy Guidelines; Standardized Framework' (2008), *Federal Register*, 73 (146), pp. 43982–4060

'Risk-Based Capital Standards: Advanced Capital Adequacy Framework – Basel II' (2007), *Federal Register*, 72 (235), pp. 69288–445.

Rose, P. S. and S. C. Hudgins (2008), *Bank Management & Financial Services* (7th edn), New York: McGraw-Hill Irwin.

Rosengren, Eric S. (2008), 'Some Principles to Consider in Future Regulatory Reform', ICBI RiskMinds 2008 Conference: The Global Risk Regulation Summit, 8 December.

Sabry, Faten and Schopflocher, T. (2007), 'The Subprime Meltdown: A Primer', 21 June http://www.mmc.com/knowledgecenter/NERA_SEC_SubprimesSeries_Part1_June2007.pdf.

Saunders, A. and M. M. Cornett (2008), *Financial Institutions Management: A Risk Management Approach* (6th edn), New York: McGraw-Hill Irwin.

Senior Supervisors Group (2008), 'Observations on Risk Management Practices During the Recent Market Turbulence', 6 March.

Stultz, René (2008), 'Risk Management Failures: What Are They and When Do They Happen?', Dice Center Working Paper No. 2008–18, 18 October.

Sunstein, Cass R. (ed) (2000), *Behavioral Law & Economics,* New York: Cambridge University Press.

Sunstein, Cass R. (2005), *Law of Fear: Beyond the Precautionary Principle,* New York: Cambridge University Press.

Taleb, Nassim N. (2007), *The Black Swan: The Impact of the Highly Improbable,* New York: Random House.

Technical Committee of the International Organization of Securities Commissions (2008), 'Final Report of the Task Force on the Subprime Crisis', May.

Tonello, Matteo (2008), 'Overseeing Risk Management and Executive Compensation: "Pressure Points" for Corporate Directors', New York: The Conference Board Executive Action Series No. 292.

US Treasury (2008), 'Treasury Announces TARP Capital Purchase Program Description, HP-1207', http://www.ustreas.gov/press/releases/hp1207.htm, 14 October.

US Treasury (2009a), 'Secretary Geithner Introduces Financial Stability Plan', http://www.treasury.gov/press/releases/tg18.htm, 10 February.

US Treasury (2009b), 'Fact Sheet: Financial Stability Plan', http://www.financial-stability.gov/docs/fact-sheet.pdf, 10 February.

US Government Accountability Office (2009), 'Financial Regulation: Review of Regulators' Oversight of Risk Management Systems At a Limited Numer of Large, Complex Financial Institutions'.

4. Too big to fail?: recasting the financial safety net[1]

Steven L. Schwarcz[2]

Government safety nets in the United States and abroad focus anachronistically on problems of banks and other financial institutions, largely ignoring financial markets which have become major credit sources for consumers and companies. Besides failing to protect these markets, this narrow focus encourages morally hazardous behavior by large institutions, like AIG and Citigroup, that are 'too big to fail'. This chapter examines how a safety net should be recast to protect financial markets and also explains why that safety net would mitigate moral hazard and help resolve the too-big-to-fail dilemma.

The real economy relies critically on the supply of liquidity in the form of credit.[3] The subprime financial crisis, which has now devolved into a larger global financial crisis (collectively the 'subprime crisis'), 'began in the credit markets, and eventually . . . will end there'.[4] Diminished credit harms the real economy because firms need credit to operate and grow and individuals need credit to buy homes and cars and to finance other expensive purchases.

Many think that the story of the credit crunch fundamentally is a banking story.[5] Although there is now a severe lack of confidence in banks, the credit crunch predated and contributed to this lack of confidence; although the lack of confidence, in turn, is now making the credit crunch worse.

SECURITIZATION AND CREDIT

The credit crunch started with the breakdown of securitization and other financial markets for debt. Securitization is a process whereby consumer financial assets (like mortgage loans, credit card receivables and automobile loans) and corporate financial assets (like accounts receivable, lease rentals and licensing fees) are financed through the issuance of debt securities backed by the financial assets.[6] These securities – the most recognizable these days being securities backed by mortgage loans, or 'mortgage-backed securities' – are sold to institutional investors in both US and worldwide capital markets.[7] I will refer, in a broad sense, to capital markets in which securitization and other debt securities are issued and traded as 'securitization markets'.

Increasingly corporate and consumer financing is originated not from banks per se or from bank deposits but from securitization markets. This shift – known as 'disintermediation', removing banks as intermediaries of funds[8] – can be very efficient. By removing the middleman, it removes the middleman's (that is, the banks') profit mark-up.

When securitization markets broke down, however, companies and consumers were deprived of this major source of credit financing.[9] Companies had difficulty borrowing and could not purchase inventory and make capital investments. Consumers had difficulty borrowing and could not purchase homes and automobiles. The lack of credit very directly impacted the real economy.[10]

This raises two fundamental questions: Why did securitization markets break down, and how should they be protected?

WHY MARKETS BROKE DOWN

Securitization markets broke down due to a systemic cascade of failures initially triggered by the historically unanticipated depth of the fall in housing prices.[11] Mortgage loans to risky borrowers were often made with the expectation of refinancing through home appreciation. When home prices stopped appreciating, these borrowers could not refinance. In many cases, they defaulted.

These 'subprime' loan defaults in turn caused substantial amounts of low-investment-grade-rated mortgage-backed securities to default and AAA-rated securities to be downgraded. The defaults were especially large for ABS CDO securities – a class of securities backed indirectly by subprime mortgages and other assets – because of the leveraged sensitivity of these securities to underlying mortgage defaults.

That, in turn, spooked investors who believed that 'AAA' meant ironclad safety and that 'investment grade' meant relative freedom from default. Investors started losing confidence in ratings and avoiding securitization and other debt securities. Fewer investors meant that the price of these securities started falling. Falling prices meant that firms using these securities as collateral had to mark them to market and put up cash, requiring the sale of more securities, which caused market prices to plummet further downward in a death spiral. This death spiral appears to have been made worse by the high leverage of many firms. Encouraged by the earlier liquidity glut, many firms had borrowed excessively because the cost of funds was so cheap.

The refusal in mid-September 2008 of the US government to save Lehman Brothers, and Lehman's resulting bankruptcy, added to this cascade. Securitization markets became so spooked that even the highly-conservative asset-backed commercial paper segment virtually shut down. And the market prices of mortgage-backed securities collapsed substantially below the intrinsic value – essentially the present value of the expected value of the underlying cash flows[12] – of the mortgage loans backing those securities.[13]

This collapse in market prices meant that banks and other financial institutions holding mortgage-backed securities had to write down their value. That caused these institutions to appear more financially risky, in turn triggering concern over counterparty risk: afraid these institutions might default on their contractual obligations, many parties stopped dealing with them. This counterparty risk and concern over bank-asset values is what has caused the lack of confidence in banks. This lack of confidence is thus a consequence, not the cause, of the collapse in market prices.[14]

EXISTING SAFETY NETS FAILED

Existing governmental safety nets, in the US and abroad, failed to prevent this breakdown because they are structured to protect banks and other financial institutions, not financial markets per se. Indeed, until recently, the media – as well as most economists and other scholars who study systemic breakdowns – likewise have focused almost exclusively on banks. History and law help to explain this narrow focus. From an historical perspective, bank runs are the most visible symbol of the Great Depression. From a legal perspective, the Federal Reserve spearheaded US government actions over the past year to address the spreading financial crisis. But the Federal Reserve's mission is limited, under section 13(3) of the Federal Reserve Act, to act as a lender of last resort in 'unusual and exigent circumstances' to banks and other financial institutions. Other governmental central banks have similarly limited missions.[15]

Such a narrow focus worked well when banks were the primary source of consumer and company financing. But as the subprime crisis reveals, disintermediation makes this narrow focus insufficient. Greater attention needs to be paid to the securitization markets. We would not today be facing a lack of confidence in banks if their mortgage-backed and other investment securities had maintained market value reasonably corresponding to their intrinsic value.[16]

How, therefore, can securitization markets be protected? Inherent in this question is the threshold normative question of whether securitization markets *should* be protected.

PROPERLY UTILIZED, SECURITIZATION IS EFFICIENT

Securitization effectively allocates risk with capital.[17] It enables companies to access capital markets directly, in most cases at lower cost than the cost of issuing direct debt, such as bonds or commercial paper.[18] It avoids middleman inefficiencies.[19] It also helps to transform financial assets, such as loans, into cash for new extensions of credit (indeed, the breakdown of securitization markets led to the recent credit crunch).[20]

These positives might be outweighed, however, by securitization's negatives revealed by the subprime crisis. There are several potential negatives: for example, the originate-to-distribute model of securitization might create moral hazard; securitization can create servicing conflicts; and securitization can foster overreliance on mathematical models.[21]

Regardless of whether securitization's benefits outweigh these negatives, there is no question that securitization is an efficient financing tool if these negatives are effectively addressed. And these negatives can be addressed by refocusing on basic securitization structures and asset types in order to attract investors, emphasizing cash flow securitizations in which there are the traditional 'two-ways out',[22] and avoiding highly complex securitization products like ABS CDO transactions which magnify leverage.[23] This view is shared by leading economists, such as Yale's Professor Gary Gorton who concludes:

> There are no such issues [as occurred in the subprime crisis] with securitization generally, or with the use of off-balance sheet vehicles for the securitization of [other than subprime mortgage loan] asset classes. Other securitizations are not so sensitive to the prices of the underlying assets and so they are not so susceptible to bubbles.[24]

The abuse of securitization may have contributed to the subprime crisis. By regenerating credit, however, securitization can also help get us out of it.[25]

PROTECTING SECURITIZATION MARKETS

I return now to the question of how securitization markets can be protected. These markets are already subject to many prescriptive regulatory protections,[26] and more are likely to be imposed in response to the subprime crisis. I have recently argued, for example, that future financial regulatory reforms should be focused on three categories of market failures – conflicts, complacency and complexity[27] – as well as on a possible fourth category: a type of tragedy of the commons that also can give rise to systemic financial market failures.[28] History, however, has shown that financial markets evolve faster than regulation can adapt.[29] Moreover even market participants themselves cannot always predict how markets may break down.[30]

Prescriptive regulation, even if highly restrictive, therefore cannot always prevent market breakdowns.[31] Markets need a safety net for when prescriptive regulation inevitably fails. Such a safety net can be provided by creating a market liquidity provider of last resort (hereinafter 'market liquidity provider') to help stabilize irrationally panicked financial markets – such as securitization markets in which the price of securities is falling significantly below their intrinsic value – thereby averting a downward price spiral that could trigger a systemic cascade.[32]

Ideal markets would not need a market liquidity provider of last resort. If financial securities are underpriced, investors will step in immediately to buy them. Real markets, however, do not always work this way. In a panicked market, for example, private investors may not act rationally – as the subprime crisis has shown.[33] Individuals at investing firms also may not want to jeopardize their reputations (and jobs) by causing their firms to invest at a time when other investors have abandoned the market.[34] Empirical evidence confirms that individuals engage in this type of 'herd behavior'.[35]

Private investors are also risk averse,[36] and the fact that disclosure has become so complex that investors are uncertain how much securities are worth increases the perception, if not reality, of risk. Private investors also would have greater real risk if – as almost certainly would be the case – the size of their investment is insufficient to ensure market stabilization. They then face the risk that a continuing fall in market prices could systemically impact the real economy (such as by shutting down credit markets, as occurred in the subprime crisis), thereby jeopardizing even the intrinsic value of their purchased securities.[37] Furthermore even if they are confident that the intrinsic value of the purchased securities exceeds the amount of their investment,[38] they may not want to risk having to wait until maturity of the securities to profit.[39]

A market liquidity provider with the financial ability to stabilize markets is needed to correct these market failures.

OPERATIONAL MECHANICS

A market liquidity provider should have the capacity to invest (or, as explained below, to hedge) sufficiently large amounts to stabilize markets and also, if necessary, to wait until final maturity of the securities in which it invests. Such an entity would likely have to be governmental,[40] although it may well be able to obtain at least partial funding from the private sector.[41]

There are at least two ways that a market liquidity provider could act. First, it could choose to purchase market securities, at a price deeply discounted from the original market price and also much lower than the estimated intrinsic value of the securities purchased[42] but still high enough to stabilize market prices above the panicked free-fall level. Say, for example, that the intrinsic value of a type of mortgage-backed securities (or 'MBS') is estimated to be in the range of 80 cents on the dollar. If the market price of those securities had fallen significantly below that number,[43] say to 20 cents on the dollar, the market liquidity provider could purchase these securities at, say, 60 cents on the dollar, thereby stabilizing the market and still making a profit. To induce a holder of the mortgage-backed securities to sell at that price, the market liquidity provider could, for example, agree to pay a higher 'deferred purchase price' if the securities turn out to be worth more than expected.[44] This is just one (simplified) example of the flexible pricing approaches used in structured financing transactions to buy financial assets of uncertain value which could be adapted to a market liquidity provider's purchases.[45]

Alternatively a market liquidity provider could attempt to stabilize the market by entering into derivatives contracts to strip out risks that the market has the greatest difficulty hedging – in effect, the market's irrationality element – thereby stimulating private investment. By hedging – and not actually purchasing securities directly – the market liquidity provider would appear to be taking less investment risk, and thus its function may be seen as more politically acceptable.[46] The Obama Administration in the United States presently appears to be considering this latter type of public-private partnership approach in its revised financial bailout plan.[47]

It is essential, of course, that the market liquidity provider's price-setting and hedging be insulated from inevitable investor lobbying pressure to pay more than the securities are worth. Strict integrity not only would ensure fairness and give taxpayers a chance to profit but also would instill securitization markets with confidence in valuing these types of securities.[48]

COSTS AND BENEFITS

These types of targeted market investments should generate relatively minimal costs, and certainly lower costs than those of a governmental lender of last resort to financial institutions – the traditional role of the US Federal Reserve Bank and other central banks.[49] By providing a lifeline to financial institutions, a lender of last resort can foster 'moral hazard' by encouraging these entities – especially those that believe they are 'too big to fail' – to be fiscally reckless.[50] These loans will also not be repaid if the institution eventually fails.

In contrast a market liquidity provider, especially if it acts at the outset of a market panic,[51] can profitably invest in securities at a deep discount from the original market price and still provide a 'floor' to how low the market will drop.[52] Buying at a deep discount will mitigate investor moral hazard and also make it likely that the market liquidity provider will be repaid.[53]

Furthermore by focusing on markets, a market liquidity provider can minimize the too-big-to-fail dilemma of a lender of last resort to institutions. This is because, by stabilizing financial markets, the market liquidity provider will minimize the likelihood that institutions invested in those markets will ultimately fail, thereby reducing the times when a lender of last resort would be needed. If in the subprime crisis, for example, the securitization markets had not broken down, institutions like Bear Stearns, AIG and Citigroup would not have needed to be bailed out.[54] In economic terms, therefore, any safety-net subsidies created by a marker liquidity provider of last resort will be much smaller than those created by a lender of last resort.[55]

FUNDING ILLIQUIDITY

A market liquidity provider also could be used to address temporary problems of funding illiquidity. This might occur, for example, when a market for short-term investments becomes illiquid, threatening to undermine long-term investments that are funded by the short-term investments – such as investments in long-term financial assets, like bonds, funded by short-term asset-backed commercial paper issued by a securitization conduit.[56] In that case, to minimize moral hazard, the market liquidity provider should limit its financing to situations where market participants have reasonably used short-term funding to invest in long-term assets and the subsequent short-term market illiquidity is unexpected.[57]

APPLICATION TO THE SUBPRIME CRISIS

A market liquidity provider could have at least mitigated the severity of the subprime crisis. If such an institution had existed at the outset of the crisis, it could have stepped in at that time to strategically purchase (or hedge) sufficient quantities of mortgage-backed securities to stabilize securitization markets, thereby deflecting the credit meltdown that ultimately impacted the real economy.[58]

Early in the crisis, for example, the US Treasury Department purchased mortgage-backed securities issued by Fannie Mae and Freddie Mac.[59] As a result of these purchases, the 'national average 30-year fixed mortgage rate [fell] a full percentage point, to just over 5 per cent, setting off a huge refinancing boom'.[60] These purchases did not, however, address the much larger – and more fundamental – problem of mortgage-backed securities that are not already effectively government-guaranteed.

The original Troubled Assets Relief Program, or 'TARP', under the Emergency Economic Stabilization Act of 2008 also contemplated government purchases of mortgage-backed securities, at least partly for the purpose of stabilizing market prices.[61] The intent was for a governmental entity to purchase mortgage-backed securities from banks and other financial institutions at a price above the collapsed 'market' price but, hopefully, discounted from what the securities are intrinsically worth. This would effectively recapitalize these institutions with more transparently valuable assets (cash).[62]

The TARP plan, however, ran into immediate political hurdles based on misunderstanding the distinction between market price and intrinsic value. Because the purchase price paid by the government would have to be above 'market' to avoid even further counterparty write-offs, there was a populist perception that the government would be unjustifiably bailing out Wall Street.[63] Partly for these reasons, and partly because economists misjudged (in my opinion) the accounting and legal feasibility of purchasing securities directly,[64] TARP money was ultimately used mostly to purchase priority equity interests in troubled financial institutions. Those purchases did little, however, to stabilize market prices of the securities or to revitalize securitization markets.[65]

If the TARP funds had in fact been used to purchase MBS, as originally contemplated, market prices might have stabilized.[66] If the government were now to attempt to use any remaining TARP funds to purchase MBS, however, it may be a case of 'too little, too late'. By ignoring the breakdown of securitization markets for so long, the government may already have gone beyond a tipping point in the ability of market purchases alone to correct the problem. This is because the systemic impact of the credit crunch is shrinking the real economy and individuals are losing their jobs, making it more likely that obligors on assets backing even prime securities will default.[67] Stabilization is much easier to achieve at the outset of a market panic, before the panic becomes a self-fulfilling prophecy, cutting off credit and cratering the real economy.

This is not to say that even delayed market purchases of securities won't have some salutary effects. Recently, for example, the Obama White House announced that 'the Treasury Department will continue to purchase Fannie Mae and Freddie Mac mortgage-backed securities to promote stability and liquidity in the marketplace'.[68] Similarly the Term Asset-Backed Securities Loan Facility, or TALF, also contemplates investing government funds in certain consumer-asset-backed securities to reduce consumer financing costs, although its results are not yet known.

PRACTICAL CONCERNS

The market-liquidity-provider concept raises several practical concerns. One such concern is whether holders of securities in panicked markets would be willing to sell their securities to a market liquidity provider if, as this chapter contemplates, the price offered is much lower than the intrinsic value of the securities but still much higher than prices in the collapsing market.[69] Some holders, for example, may refuse to sell their securities if they have to mark down value on their financial statements.[70] Some holders may even oppose creation of a market liquidity provider because, even if a given holder does not sell, mark-to-market accounting may require it to mark its securities down to market prices set by the market liquidity provider in its other purchases.[71] These concerns could be addressed, however, by applying (as this chapter contemplates) to those purchases of securities the same flexible pricing approaches used in structured financing transactions to purchase financial assets of uncertain value.[72]

Failed governmental efforts to try to control their currency exchange rates might raise another concern: whether a market liquidity provider, even if governmental, would have sufficient spending power to stabilize irrationally panicked securitization markets.[73] Only Hong Kong was able to control its currency exchange rate, and that was because its reserves, which implicitly included all of China's reserves, were large enough to be credible. There are important distinctions, though, between controlling a currency exchange rate and stabilizing irrationally panicked securitization markets. Controlling a currency exchange rate depends on all of the macroeconomic factors to which the country in question is subject whereas stabilizing panicked securitization markets depends mostly on factors specific to the securities in question. Also because the market liquidity provider should consider acting only when a panicked market is so irrational that the market value of its securities is significantly below their intrinsic value,[74] the market liquidity provider should be able to stem the information asymmetry leading to this valuation differential by explaining the irrationality and, by buying (or hedging) at an above-market price, putting its money where its mouth is. It effectively would be providing to investors in that market the same type of real credibility and comfort that a country's large reserves provide to currency investors.[75]

A third practical concern is whether purchases by a governmental market liquidity provider could have inflationary effects or expose taxpayers to too much risk.[76] If, for example, a market liquidity provider obtains funds to purchase securities directly or indirectly from the Federal Reserve (or a foreign central bank), the government in effect might be printing money to make the purchases – which could be viewed as a form of 'quantitative easing'.[77] That in turn could spark inflation.[78] Similarly if the securities so purchased turn out to be poor investments, the government, and thus taxpayers, would suffer any consequences.

These concerns turn on the quality of the purchases made by the market liquidity provider. If its purchases are fairly priced – a goal I argue is feasible even if the securities purchased have significant valuation uncertainty[79] – the market liquidity provider, and thus taxpayers, will not lose money on the purchases. In that case the purchases should not have significant inflationary effects because the market liquidity provider ultimately will be able to repay the central bank.[80] The government, in other words, will merely have made a favorable investment.[81]

Yet another practical concern is how effective a market liquidity provider would be in a market for securities that are not actively traded. Even without active trading, however, the market liquidity provider should at least set the floor-price standard.[82] Furthermore even non-actively-traded securities are increasingly traded in virtual markets, such as the ABX.HE indices, which mimic active trading.[83]

Finally there may be concern whether the very existence of a market liquidity provider could inadvertently make falling markets even less stable. For example, parties anticipating market-liquidity-provider stabilization of a falling market might sometimes wait to invest in market securities, even if they believe the securities are undervalued, until they see the price offered by the market liquidity provider. Theoretically this should not occur, but the signal sent by a market liquidity provider might be so strong as to not only set a floor but also a ceiling on the market price. The extent to which this might occur cannot be predicted without empirical data.

INTERNATIONAL DIMENSIONS

This chapter so far has discussed the concept of a national market liquidity provider. Financial markets, however, increasingly cross national borders and are becoming interdependent.[84] That, in turn, has increased the global market's exposure to systemic risk.[85] There may well be a role for an international market liquidity provider of last resort (hereinafter, 'international market liquidity provider').

Because this chapter's analysis of a national market liquidity provider is not necessarily tied to the United States or to any other country, the views already expressed in this chapter should be generically applicable. In an international context, however, three issues emerge: is a single regulatory approach to market liquidity desirable?; if so, is it feasible?; and who should act as the international market liquidity provider?

Whether a single regulatory approach to market liquidity is desirable has political ramifications beyond the scope of this chapter. I observe, however, that such an approach may be easier to adopt and administer in a global economy than country-specific regulation. It also may lessen the potential for a regulatory race to the bottom.[86] Assuming it is desirable, is it feasible?

Given the diversity of approaches to financial regulation and supervision among nations, some commentators believe that any single regulatory model would be impractical.[87] The optimal regulatory model, they argue, must be customized for each country in accord with the structure and size of the country's financial system, its specific regulatory and supervisory objectives and its unique historical evolution and political traditions.[88]

These differences do not, however, appear to undermine the concept of an international market liquidity provider. There is nothing inherently country-specific about stabilizing financial market prices. Furthermore political scientists and economists have observed that international cooperation is the natural and most effective response of states that share an interest in averting a common crisis that affects them individually – despite the many historical, cultural and legal differences that distinguish nations.[89] Basel II, for example – whatever its faults – effectively illustrates that a single regulatory scheme for financial risk can be applied, at least in the banking context, across diverse national financial systems.[90] Approximately a hundred countries have signaled they will implement Basel II by 2010.[91]

A single regulatory approach to market liquidity thus appears feasible. Who, then, could act as the international market liquidity provider? There are at least two obvious choices. One is the International Monetary Fund (IMF), which sometimes already takes on this role, albeit with controversy, in extending liquidity to troubled sovereign states. Another choice would be one or more national central banks, such as the US Federal Reserve Bank or the European Central Bank.

Compare, for example, how the IMF and the Federal Reserve might function in an international-market-liquidity-provider capacity. An international market liquidity provider should ideally be able to advance funds in a widely-used international currency, and the Federal Reserve is a source of US dollars.[92] The IMF, in contrast, has no power to create currency. The Federal Reserve also may have an advantage in that it is arguably less bureaucratic than the IMF and thus capable of making quicker decisions.[93] Thus the Federal Reserve (and, by analogy, the European Central Bank) appears to have a better institutional capacity than the IMF to act as an international market liquidity provider.

On the other hand any national central bank (including the Federal Reserve or European Central Bank) acting as an international market liquidity provider would face possible conflicts of interest between its national and international responsibilities. The IMF, in contrast, is a truly international organization. Furthermore, through its access to member-state capital, the IMF can theoretically spread the burden of responding to international systemic risk.[94] The IMF cannot, however, create currency. It would not need that power if it has access to a potentially unlimited amounts of currency,[95] but such access would require reform of the IMF's relationship with its member-states.[96]

There, therefore, is no clear choice who should act, as among existing institutions, as the international market liquidity provider.

CONCLUSIONS

With the rise of disintermediation, financial markets have significantly replaced banks as sources of credit. Financial markets, however, can break down for unexpected reasons. Prescriptive regulation cannot always deter these breakdowns.

Financial markets need a safety net for when prescriptive regulation inevitably fails. Existing governmental safety nets, in the US and abroad, are insufficient because they are structured to protect banks and other financial institutions, not financial markets per se.

This chapter proposes that a market liquidity provider of last resort could function as a safety net, stabilizing irrationally panicked financial markets to avert a systemic downward price spiral. This function should generate relatively minimal costs, and certainly lower costs than generated by existing safety nets which focus on governmental central banks as lenders of last resort to banks and financial institutions. Existing safety nets can foster moral hazard and give rise to significant taxpayer losses when institutions are deemed too big to fail.

I do not propose that existing safety nets be discarded. This chapter's conception of a market liquidity provider of last resort would supplement, not replace, a lender of last resort. The combination, however, would be synergistic: by stabilizing financial markets, a market liquidity provider not only would preserve credit but also would minimize the likelihood that institutions invested in those markets will ultimately fail – thereby reducing the times when a lender of last resort would be needed.

Finally I want to emphasize that this chapter's market-liquidity-provider concept does not contemplate indiscriminate purchases of illiquid securities. Such purchases not only would foster moral hazard for parties that sell or invest in those securities, it also would waste taxpayer money on poor investments. This chapter only contemplates the market liquidity provider acting when market prices collapse substantially below the intrinsic value of the securities, as in a panic.[97] In contrast if prices in the collapsing market accurately reflect intrinsic value, the market should be left to fail. If that failure triggers a panic that happens to cause a more intrinsically sound financial market to collapse or to cause an otherwise-sound financial institution to fail, the market liquidity provider could then decide to protect that sound market, and any applicable lender of last resort could then decide to protect that institution.[98]

NOTES

1. Copyright © 2009 by Steven L. Schwarcz. Portions of this chapter that derive in part from the author's articles, 'Systemic Risk', 97 *Geo. L.J.* 193, 229 (2008), 'Protecting Financial Markets: Lessons from the Subprime Mortgage Meltdown, 93 *Minn. L. Rev.* 373 (December 2008), and 'Regulating Complexity in Financial Markets', 87 *Wash. U. L. Rev.* 211 (2009/2010), available at http://ssrn.com/abstract_id=1240863, are used with permission. Portions of this chapter also derive in part from the author's keynote speech, 'The Case for a Market Liquidity Provider of Last Resort', at the NYU Law School symposium, 'Modernizing the Financial Regulatory Structure', held 20 February 2009 under the auspices of the NYU Journal of Law and Business.
2. Stanley A. Star Professor of Law & Business, Duke University School of Law; Founding/Co-Academic Director, Duke Global Capital Markets Center. E-mail: schwarcz@law.duke.edu. The author thanks Ed Kane, for valuable comments and Nikhil S. Palekar and Arman Tasheneff for helpful research assistance.
3. Joseph E. Stiglitz and Bruce Greenwald (2003), 142; (1994) 727.
4. Eric Dash & Vikas Bajaj (2008) (explaining that, because 'credit is not flowing . . ., [c] rucial parts of the financial system have stopped functioning').
5. Cf. Jack & Suzy Welch (2009), at 78 (stating that 'Healthy banks are to economies as healthy hearts are to people: They keep them alive with the 'lifeblood' of credit.').
6. Steven L. Schwarcz (1994).
7. Technically these debt securities are non-recourse debt securities; they are payable primarily from the financial assets backing them.

8. Steven L.Schwarcz (2008b), at 200. Investors in securitization markets may include banks, but they are then acting as ultimate investors, not intermediaries.
9. Mortimer B. Zuckerman (2009), at 80 (observing that securitization 'once accounted for 70 per cent of our credit while conventional bank lending has dropped to 30 per cent. Unless financial firms can securitize debt and, in turn, rely on investors willing to buy [securities representing] the bundled loans, credit will remain extremely tight.')
10. Ibid.
11. The following account is based on Steven L. Schwarcz (2009c).
12. Simon Gervais and Steven L. Schwarcz, 'Valuation of Risky Cash Flows' (discussing how to calculate the intrinsic value of risky cash flows). The expected value of the underlying cash flows could be estimated, as was done in an English High Court of Justice case involving the Orion Funding SIV in which I served as an expert witness, by examining the mortgage loans backing the securities and ascertaining which were subprime, which were prime, and which were delinquent or in default.
13. Cf. International Monetary Fund (2008) (indicating that the market prices of at least some mortgage-backed securities may be significantly below the expected present values of their future cash flows).
14. Steven L. Schwarcz (2009c).
15. The mission of the European Central Bank (ECB), for example, is to stabilize the price of the European currency. In 'exceptional circumstances', however, the ECB may indemnify national central banks for 'specific losses arising from monetary policy operations' taken for the benefit of the central banking system. Protocol on the Statute of the European System of Central Banks and of the European Central Bank Art. 32.4. Jul. 29, 1992, O.J.C. 191. At the national level in France, the Bank of France has an even narrower mission because it is 'probihited from authorizing overdrafts or granting any other type of credit to the Treasury or to any other public body or undertaking', which places an absolute restriction on central bank lending to virtually any entity. Code Monétaire et Financier (C. Monétaire et Fin.), Chap. 1, Art. L141–2 (Fr.). *See also* Duncan Alford, *The Lamfalussy Process and EU Bank Regulation: Another Step on the Road to Pan-European Regulation?*, 25 *Ann. Rev. Banking & Fin. L.* 389, 392 (2006) ('[n]ational governments or related agencies, such as central banks, typically have lender-of-last-resort responsibility for banks operating within their borders'); Steve H. Hanke, *Currency Boards*, 579 Annals 87, 90, table 2 (2002) (observing that a typical central bank functions, among other things, as a lender of last resort).
16. *Supra* notes 13–14 and accompanying text.
17. Steven L. Schwarcz (2009a) (symposium issue on The Subprime Crisis: Going Forward). *Supra* notes 8–9 and accompanying text.
18. Ibid.
19. Ibid.
20. Ibid.
21. Ibid.
22. Subprime mortgage securitizations had only one way out: home appreciation.
23. Steven L. Schwarcz (2009a).
24. Gary B. Gorton (2008), at 67. Ibid. at 75 (concluding that '[s]ecuritization is an efficient, incentive-compatible, response to bankruptcy costs and capital requirements'); Ethan Penner (2008), at A15 (observing that 'securitization will continue to play an important role – if adapted appropriately').
25. Zuckerman (2009), *supra* note 9.
26. By prescriptive regulation, I mean regulation that restricts behavior.
27. Steven L. Schwarcz (2008a). Running throughout these causes is a fourth cause, cupidity; but because greed is so ingrained in human nature and so intertwined with the other causes, it adds little insight to view it separately.
28. Because the benefits of exploiting finite capital resources accrue to individual market participants whereas the costs of exploitation, which affect the real economy, are distributed among an even wider class of persons, market participants have insufficient

incentive to internalize their externalities. Therefore, even in a simple financial system with no conflicts and hyper-diligent market participants (that is, a financial system with none of the causes of failure indicated *supra* note 27 and accompanying text), systemic risk is theoretically possible, Steven L. Schwarcz (2009c) For a general analysis of systemic risk see Steven L. Schwarcz (2008b).

29. Henry T.C. Hu (1993) at 1499 (explaining why regulators cannot keep up with development of complex financial products).
30. *Regulating Complexity in Financial Markets, supra* note 1.
31. Moreover highly restrictive regulation would create its own inefficiencies. Gerard Caprio, Jr., Ash Demirguc-Kunt and Edward J. Kane (2008), 5 (observing that 'a tightly regulated financial system hampers growth').
32. Cf. Michael D. Bordo, Bruce Misrach and Anna Schwartz (1995) 19 (observing that financial panic will not usually become contagious when a lender of last resort provides adequate liquidity); *Regulating Complexity in Financial Markets, supra* note 30 (discussing how decoupling systems through modularity helps to reduce the chance that a failure in one part of a complex system will trigger a failure in another part); Steven L. Schwarcz (2008b), at 204 (explaining the chain of systemic collapse).
33. Cf. Ben Levisohn (2009), 'How to attack panic', *Bus. Wk.*, 63 (noting that on February 23, 2009 investors pushed the Dow Jones industrial average down 250.89 points to a 12 year low, only to see it gain 236.16 points the next day).
34. Tyler Cowen (2008), at BU 5 (asking why, in the context of the subprime mortgage crisis, 'asset prices don't simply fall enough so that someone buys them and trading picks up again'; and answering: 'why seek "fire sale" prices when you might lose your job for doing so?').
35. *Cf.* Paul M. Healy and Krishna Palepu (2002) (observing that fund manager who estimates a stock is overvalued but does not act on this analysis 'and simply follows the crowd' will not be rewarded for foreseeing the problems, 'but neither will he be blamed for a poor investment decision when the stock ultimately crashes, since his peers made the same mistake'); Stephen M. Bainbridge (2000), 1038 (discussing how herd behavior may have a reputational payoff even if the chosen course of action fails, and arguing that where 'the action was consistent with approved conventional wisdom, the hit to the manager's reputation from an adverse outcome is reduced').
36. Jonathan Berk and Peter DeMarzo (2007).
37. If the real economy is impacted, quality and creditworthiness of the financial assets underlying the purchased securities may be reduced, as when a mortgagor loses her job.
38. *Supra* note 12 and accompanying text (discussing intrinsic value).
39. This risk is exacerbated if the market value of undervalued securities is still falling because investors then would not even break even on near-term resale of the securities.
40. As a governmental entity, a market liquidity provider would bear at least superficial similarity to the US Resolution Trust Corporation (RTC), created in 1989 to clean up the savings and loan (S&L) mess by buying troubled loans. The RTC, however, 'is not a perfect parallel for today's needs' for several reasons, including that it was created to clean up the mess years after it occurred, not necessarily (as this chapter also contemplates for a market liquidity provider) to minimize occurrence of the mess. 'Beyond Crisis Management: Bold Ideas for Solving America's Financial Mess', *Economist*, 18 September 2008. Nonetheless the RTC is a helpful model insofar as it represents a credible and reasonably efficient model of a governmental entity purchasing troubled financial assets. Sudhir Nanda, James E. Owers, & Ronald C. Rogers (1997), 290 (concluding that mispricing of its purchases were not typical but occurred only in limited cases).
41. Steven L. Schwarcz (2008b), at 226–27 (examining how to privatize the role of a market liquidity provider). Cf. *infra* notes 45–48 and accompanying text (proposing that a governmental market liquidity provider could stimulate private investment by entering into derivatives contracts to strip out risks that the market has the greatest difficulty hedging).
42. *Supra* notes 12–13 and accompanying text (discussing intrinsic value).

43. Because markets normally can fluctuate widely, a market liquidity provider should be careful to act only when the market price of securities is falling significantly below their intrinsic value.
44. In the subprime crisis, some types of MBS securities had become so complex that investors were uncertain how much they were worth. Steven L. Schwarcz (2009b) (symposium issue on the subprime mortgage meltdown).
45. These flexible pricing approaches to buying financial assets of uncertain value include using special-purpose entities. Steven L. Schwarcz (2002), § 4:10 (3d ed. 2002 & supplements) (discussing pricing approaches) and ibid. at § 7:3 (discussing the accounting standards governing these pricing approaches, including Financial Accounting Standard (FAS) No. 140). Purchases also could be coupled with taking equity or contingent equity, such as warrants.
46. Cf. Floyd Norris (2009), at A1 (observing that having the government purchase the distressed MBS securities directly would be a 'politically perilous course').
47. Ibid. (reporting that the revised bailout plan would likely depend in part on private investors, such as hedge funds, private-equity funds and perhaps insurance companies, buying distressed MBS, with the US Government guaranteeing a floor value to the securities purchased).
48. Cf. *infra* note 61 (arguing that one rationale for buying MBS under TARP was to establish objective valuations of those securities). Cf. American Securitization Forum, Securities Industry and Financial Markets Association, Australian Securitisation Forum, & European Securitisation Forum, *Restoring Confidence in the Securitization Markets: A Global Initiative* 7 (3 December 2008) (hereinafter '*Restoring Confidence*') (recommending expanding and improving independent, third-party, sources of valuation for specified types of asset-backed securities).
49. The U.S. Federal Reserve Bank certainly acts as a lender of last resort. *See supra* note 16 and accompanying text. *See also* Edmund L. Andrews, 'Fed Assumes the Role of Lender of Last Resort', *International Herald Tribune*, Mar. 12, 2008. The Bank of England, for example, has explicitly acknowledged its role as a lender of last resort in preventing the collapse of Northern Rock, News Release, Bank of England, *Liquidity Support Facility for Northern Rock plc* (Sept. 14, 2007), *available at* http://www.bankofengland.co.uk/publications/news/2007/090.htm ('In its role as lender of last resort, the Bank of England stands ready to make available facilities in comparable circumstances, where institutions face short-term liquidity difficulties.').
50. See, e.g., Eric Dash, 'Saving Citi May Create More Fear', *New York Times*, Nov. 25, 2008, at B1 (reporting that although the efforts to stabilize Citigroup may have been necessary, its rescue may have sent the wrong signal to other firms by encouraging additional risk-taking); Carol J. Loomis, 'Revealed: 15 AIG Bailout Counterparties', Fortune, Mar. 7, 2009 (arguing that the Fed's decision to bail out AIG's counterparties by paying full value for contracts although the short-term values had dropped significantly reduced counterparties' incentives to carefully assess risks in the future); David Wessel, 'Has Fed Risked Creating Moral Hazard?', *Wall Street Journal*, Sept. 20, 2007, at A2 (some consider recent bailouts as socialism for financial industry professionals, capitalism for everyone else); Rajeev Dehejia and Adriana Lleras-Muney, 'Financial development and pathways of growth: state branching and deposit insurance laws in the United States, 1900–1940', 50 *J. Law & Econ.* 239, 243 (2007) (moral hazard problem exists for all lenders of last resort).
51. The timing of purchases will be critical. The market liquidity provider should try to act at the outset of a market panic, before market prices collapse too far. Cf. *infra* notes 66–67 and accompanying text (observing that we may already be past a tipping point in the ability of market purchases alone to remedy the problem). On the other hand the market liquidity provider should be careful not to act when price fluctuations are normal. *Supra* note 43.
52. *Supra* note 43 and accompanying text. The market liquidity provider, and therefore taxpayers, would profit by buying securities at a much lower price than their intrinsic value.

53. Steven L. Schwarcz (2008b), at 229. Investor moral hazard can be further limited if the market liquidity provider adopts a policy of constructive ambiguity, not stating ex ante whether or not it will attempt to stabilize any given market panic and not indicating in advance the purchase price it would offer if it were to attempt to do so. Ibid. at 226–27. Investor moral hazard cannot be eliminated, however, because certain markets may be so important that investors can predict their stabilization with a high degree of certainty.
54. Steven L. Schwarcz (2009c). *Supra* note 13 and accompanying text (explaining that the collapse in market prices meant that banks and other financial institutions holding mortgage-backed securities had to write down their value, causing these institutions to appear more financially risky, in turn triggering concern over counterparty risk and causing the lack of confidence in banks).
55. Cf. Caprio, Demirguc-Kunt and Kane (2008) (arguing that the goal of financial regulation and supervision is 'to manage the [regulatory] safety net so that private risk-taking is neither taxed nor subsidized'); ibid. at 6 (arguing that ideally regulated parties should not have opportunities to 'shift the deep downside of their risk exposures onto the [regulatory] safety net').
56. *Regulating Complexity in Financial Markets, supra* note 1 (referencing 'Policy Statement on Financial Market Developments: The President's Working Group on Financial Markets'), 14 *Law & Bus. Rev. Am.* 447, 455–56 (2008) (suggesting that some 30 per cent contraction of the ABCP market in the US in 2007 was a factor contributing to the financial crisis).
57. *Regulating Complexity in Financial Markets, supra* note 1.
58. *Supra* notes 11–14 and accompanying text. Testimony of Steven L. Schwarcz before the Committee on Financial Services of the US House of Representatives, on 'Systemic Risk: Examining Regulators's Ability to Respond to Threats to the Financial System', 2 October 2007, available at http://www.house.gov/apps/list/hearing/financialsvcs_dem/ht1002072.shtml (explaining how a market liquidity provider of last resort would work). 'Protecting Against Economic Shocks', *Baltimore Sun*, 17 September 2007; 'Fed Must Also Guard Financial Markets', *[Newark] Star-Ledger*, 17 September 2007; 'Markets, Systemic Risk, and the Subprime Mortgage Meltdown', *Huffington Post* (posted 18 March 2008); 'Systemic Risk Meets Subprime Mortgages', *Commentary*, Forbes.com (posted 1 May 2008). *Supra* note 54 and accompanying text.
59. *How Three Economists View a Financial Rescue Plan* (2008), at C4 (describing this as 'the first serious attempt by government to cure the underlying financial disease and not merely its symptoms').
60. Dash and Bajaj (2008).
61. Cf. Alan S. Blinder (2008), at BU 4 (arguing that the TARP's rationales for buying MBS included establishing objective valuations and restarting the markets for these securities, thereby revitalizing mortgage finance).
62. *See* Edmund L. Andrews & Mark Landler, 'U.S. May Take Ownership Stake in Banks', *New York Times*, Oct. 9, 2008, at A1 (explaining that under the Treasury Department's plan, the government's recapitalization plan would 'inject cash directly into banks that request it').
63. Mortimer B. Zuckerman (2008), at 79 (arguing that buying the MBS at above-market prices 'provides a huge, unjustified bailout of Wall Street' by 'rescuing the financial industry from the consequences of its own misjudgments, profligacy, and greed').
64. Nobel prize-winning economist Paul Krugman, for example, has expressed skepticism about the government's ability to price supposedly undervalued securities when the financial markets cannot do so. Paul Krugman, 'A $700 Billion Slap in the Face', *New York Times*, Sept. 24, 2008. Under the US accounting standards, the present value (also called 'fair value') of a troubled asset is determined on the assumption that the asset will be held for a period of time and sold at some future date, so that such value includes future earnings and the asset is expected to generate, less the cost of owning, holding, developing and operating the asset. Financial Accounting Standards Board, FAS 157.
65. Blinder (2008) (arguing that using TARP funds to buy equity in banks, rather than

MBS, 'wasted a precious resource', and likening such misuse to 'another disaster' like the Iraq war and the response to Hurricane Katrina).

66. Cf. *supra* note 61 and accompanying text (observing that MBS purchases under TARP were intended primarily for minimizing counterparty risk and only secondarily for stabilizing market prices).
67. Cf. Dash and Bajaj (2008) (observing that '[i]n a struggling economy, even a seemingly solid loan can turn bad quickly').
68. Excerpt from White House announcement of the Homeowner Affordability and Stability Plan (19 February 2009).
69. *Supra* notes 42–43 and accompanying text.
70. *See, e.g.*, Eric Dash and Gretchen Morgenson, 'Banks Plan to Help May Itself Need Help', *New York Times*, Oct. 19, 2007 (reporting that Japanese banks 'refused to sell or write off troubled loans' during the 1990s, and there is concern that banks with troubled assets would take the same approach in the current crisis, 'refusing to liquidate assets at market levels'); Peter Boone and Simon Johnson, 'To Save the Banks We Must Stand Up to the Bankers', *Baseline Scenario*, Jan. 27, 2009, http://baselinescenario.com/2009/01/27/to-save-the-banks-we-must-stand-up-to-the-bankers/ (arguing that 'banks refusing to sell assets at market value' will be a significant impediment to an effective, large-scale recapitalization of banks); Joshua Zumbrun, 'Geithner's Bank Plan: Winners and Losers', *Forbes*, Mar. 23, 2009 (reporting that 'Currently, markets for these troubled assets are not working because investors are offering to buy for a price lower than that at which the banks are willing to sell').
71. Testimony of Sean W. McCarthy, President and COO, Financial Security Assurance on behalf of the Ass'n of Fin. Guaranty Insurers, *Hearing of the House Committee on Financial Services, Municipal Bond Turmoil: Impact on Cities, Towns, and States*, Federal News Service, March 12, 2008 (investment bankers in the past rejected the idea of the market liquidity provider asserting that investment banks can remarket the assets needing liquidity).
72. *Supra* notes 44–45 and accompanying text.
73. In a more limited context, the U.S. Government has successfully acted as a market liquidity provider during the subprime crisis. Shortly after Lehman Brothers failed, the commercial paper market collapsed. In response, the Federal Reserve created the Commercial Paper Funding Facility ('CPFF') to act as a lender of last resort for that market, with the goal of addressing temporary liquidity distortions by purchasing commercial paper from highly rated issues that could not otherwise sell their paper. *See* Tobias Adrian, Karin Kimbrough and Dina Marchioni, 'The Federal Reserve's Commercial paper Funding Facility', FRBNY Econ. Policy Rev. (forthcoming). These authors conclude that '[t]he CPFF indeed had a stabilizing effect on the commercial paper market', Id. at 11.
74. *Supra* notes 32 and 43 and accompanying text.
75. Any analogy of the market-liquidity-provider concept to The Bank of Japan's failed attempt to support the Tokyo Stock Exchange's Nikkei index would also be inappropriate. The Nikkei is an index of shares of 225 companies selected to be representative of the Tokyo Stock Exchange as a whole and thus the price of those shares turns on a multitude of macroeconomic factors, including Japan's financial condition.
76. Another practical concern, outside this chapter's scope, is that a market liquidity provider might become ineffective due to political pressures on what assets to buy and how to manage those assets. Cf. Luc Laeven and Fabian Valencia (2008), at 14 (finding based on empirical evidence that the effectiveness of government-run asset-management firms, in the US and elsewhere 'has been quite mixed: better where the assets to be disposed have been primarily real estate, less good where loans to large politically-connected ruins dominated').
77. The term 'quantitative easing' is ill defined, but it generally refers to any central bank policy that tries to affect financial markets through approaches other than directly controlling interest rates. Because a form of quantitative easing was first used,

unsuccessfully by the Bank of Japan in 2001 to fight deflation (Mark M. Spiegel (2006), the term sometimes has a negative connotation.
78. Edmund L. Andrews and Jackie Calmes (2008), (reporting that other than controlling the federal funds rate, the Fed's tools – including those contemplated under TALF – would all 'involve borrowing . . . by the Fed, which amounts to printing money in vast new quantities', which could be 'extremely inflationary').
79. *Supra* notes 44–45 and accompanying text.
80. Inflation occurs when the money supply increases compared to the real gross domestic product. Financing market liquidity purchases by printing new money may temporarily increase the money supply. However, subsequent repayment will lower the money supply.
81. Even if the market liquidity provider occasionally makes poor investments, some inflationary effects or loss of taxpayer money are small prices to pay for avoiding larger consequences to the real economy. Steven L. Schwarcz (2008b). Cf. ibid at 238 (examining applying a precautionary principle to the cost-benefit balancing).
82. *Supra* note 52 and accompanying text.
83. A potential investor could decide to invest in securities represented by one of the indices, such as ABS CDO securities and other asset- and mortgage-backed securities, without actually purchasing the underlying securities; the indices themselves simulate the risk and reward of trading in these securities.
84. Jayati Ghosh (2005), ('[F]inancial liberalization creates exposure to the following kinds of risk: a propensity to financial crises, both external and internal; a deflationary impact on real economic activity and reduced access to funds for small-scale producers, both urban and rural. This in turn has major social effects in terms of loss of employment and more volatile material conditions for most citizens.'); Gerard Caprio, Patrick Honohan and Joseph E. Stiglitz (2001), 15–17 (observing that the liberalized financial markets 'laid bare the previous inefficiencies and failures in credit allocation' and undermined efforts to valuate the true value of bank capital and the true risk of bank portfolios).
85. Rahul Dhumale, John Eatwell & Kern Alexander (2006), 14.
86. Cf. Elene Spanakos (2000), 241–42, 244 (2000) (arguing that without international standards there will be a 'race to the bottom' in regulatory schemes).
87. David T. Llewellyn (2006), *Institutional Structure of Financial Regulation and Supervision: The Basic Rules,* p. 7, Paper presented at a World Bank Seminar 6 and 7 June 2006 (arguing that '[i]t is an illusion to believe there is a single, superior model of institutional structure that is applicable to all countries'); James A. Hanson, Patrick Honohan, & Giovanni Majnoni (2003), 273–74.
88. Llewewllyn (2006).
89. James D. Fearon (1998), at 271 ('Whether the goal is to control arms racing, reduce the risk of preemptive war, limit global environmental damage, stabilize exchange rates, or reduce protectionism in trade, state leaders . . . coordinate state policies and the actions of the relevant state bureaucracies . . . to gain various benefits of cooperating.'); Richard J. Herring and Robert E. Litan (1994), 120–123 (suggesting systemic risk is analogous to epidemiological risk, in that both can be effectively resolved by international collaboration when 'countries agree on how to act . . . [and their] cooperation advance[s] to the point of establishing an international agency and jointly financing international action to control and attempt to eradicate' the contagion); Edward J. Kane (1992), 257–58 (analogizing the global financial system to the interconnected subsystems of the human body and implying that just as the central immune system is the most efficient way to regulate the health of the body's many subsystems, so is a universal regulatory approach the most efficient means of regulating systemic financial risk).
90. Bank for International Settlements (2007); Ioannis S. Akkizidis and Vivianne Bouchereau (2006), 99–105.
91. Karen Krebsbach (2007), at 22 ('Already more than 100 countries have stated intentions to implement the Basel Capital Accord, known as Basel II.'); Memorandum from the Cent. Bank of Bahr., Basel II Update (First Quarter, 2007) ('Over 100 countries are committed to the implementation of Basel II, with implementation dates ranging from

2005 to 2010.'). The chairman of Basel II concedes, however, that implementing the accord will be extremely difficult. Peter Norman (2005). Some also argue that Basel II may actually prove counterproductive. Dhumale, Eatwell and Alexander (2006), at 263 (arguing that because the majority of developed nations will adopt some variation of Basel II, the G10 countries are likely to exert at least moderate pressure on developing nations to permit foreign banks to operate in their markets under Basel II, which in turn could have a disproportionate impact on the composition of credit risk in those jurisdictions and place foreign banks at a distinct advantage over local banks).

92. Robert Keleher (1999), (arguing that the Federal Reserve Bank 'has international reserve or money-creating powers and, accordingly, can act to satisfy increased demands for liquidity [and also] can act to create liquidity quickly via open market operations rather than through the slower, more cumbersome discount window mechanism', though tying this argument in part to the US dollar being the dominant reserve currency).
93. Ibid at 7 (the IMF 'cannot create reserves or international money, cannot act quickly enough to serve as an international LOLR, and does not operate in a transparent manner. Further, IMF lending currently (indirectly) serves to bail out insolvent institutions, something wholly inappropriate for an international LOLR.').
94. Tobias Knedlik (2006) (describing the IMF's substantial access to capital from more than 20 member states).
95. Ibid at 8 ('In the case of a global crisis . . . almost unlimited reserves would be necessary').
96. Ibid at 26 (discussing how the IMF could obtain 'quantitatively unlimited' access to member-state funds).
97. *Supra* note 32 and accompanying text.
98. In order to be able to differentiate between these circumstances – as well as to differentiate normal market fluctuations – a market liquidity provider would monitor and analyze securities markets on an ongoing basis. Its staff therefore should have the requisite expertise and experience to do so.

REFERENCES

Akkizidis, Ioannis S. and Vivianne Bouchereau (2006), *Guide to Optimal Operational Risk and Basel II*, Boca Raton: Auerbach Publications.

American Securitization Forum, Securities Industry and Financial Markets Association, Australian Securitisation Forum, & European Securitisation Forum (2008), *Restoring Confidence in the Securitization Markets: A Global Initiative*.

Andrews, Edmund L. and Jackie Calmes (2008), 'Fed Cuts Key Rate to a Record Low', *New York Times*, 17 December.

Bainbridge, Stephen M. (2000), 'Mandatory Disclosure: A Behavioral Analysis', 68 *University of Cincinnati Law Review* 1023.

Bank for International Settlements (2007), 'Basel II and Financial Institution Resiliency', 27 June, available at http://www.bis.org/review/ro80304a.pdf.

Berk, Jonathan and Peter DeMarzo (2007), *Corporate Finance*, New York: Pearson Addison Wesley.

'Beyond Crisis Management: Bold Ideas for Solving America's Financial Mess', *Economist*, 18 September 2008.

Blinder, Alan S. (2008), *Missing the Target With $700 Billion, New York Times*, 21 December.

Bordo, Michael D., Bruce Misrach and Anna Schwartz (1995), 'Real Versus Pseudo-International Systemic Risk: Some Lessons From History', NBER Working Paper Series (No. 5371).

Caprio, Gerard, Ash Demirguc-Kunt and Edward J. Kane (2008), 'The 2007 Meltdown in Structured Securitization: Searching for Lessons Not Scapegoats', www.ssrn/abstract_id=1293169.

Caprio, Gerard, Patrick Honohan and Joseph E. Stiglitz (2001), *Financial Liberalization: How Far, How Fast?*, Cambridge: Cambridge University Press.

Cent. Bank of Bahr (2007), *Basel II Update* http://www.cbb.gov.bh/cmsrule/media/pdf/policydevelopment/Consultations/Basel_II_Update_Q1_2007.pdf.

Cowen, Tyler (2008), 'It's Hard to Thaw a Frozen Market', *New York Times*, 23 March.

Dash, Eric and Vikas Bajaj (2008), 'In 2009, Economy Will Depend on Unlocking Credit, *New York Times*, 31 December.

Dhumale, Rahul, John Eatwell and Kern Alexander (2006), *Global Governance of Financial Systems: The International Regulation of Systemic Risk*, New York: Oxford University Press.

Excerpt from White House announcement of the Homeowner Affordability and Stability Plan, 19 February 2009.

Fearon, James D. (1998), 'Bargaining, Enforcement, and International Cooperation', 52 *International Organization*, Spring 1998.

Fed Must Also Guard Financial Markets, [Newark] Star-Ledger, 17 September 2007.

Gervais, Simon and Steven L. Schwarcz, 'Valuation of Risky Cash Flows' (working paper on file with author).

Ghosh, Jayati (2005), 'The Economic and Social Effects of Financial Liberalization: A Primer for Developing countries, United Nations Department of Economic and Social Affairs, Working Paper No. 4 http://www.un.org/esa/desa/papers/2005/wp4_2005.pdf.

Gorton, Gary B. (2008), 'The Panic of 2007', NBER Working Paper 14358.

Hanson, James A., Patrick Honohan and Giovanni Majnoni (2003), *Globalization and National Financial Systems*, New York: Oxford University Press.

Healy, Paul M. and Krishna Palepu (2002), *Governance and Intermediation Problems in Capital Markets: Evidence from the Fall of Enron*, forthcoming in *J. Econ. Persp*, www.ssrn.com.

Herring, Richard J. and Robert E. Litan (1995), *Financial Regulation in the Global Economy*, Washington: The Brootings Institution.

How Three Economists View a Financial Rescue Plan (2008), *New York Times*, 22 September.

Hu, Henry T.C. (1993), 'Misunderstood Derivatives: The Causes of Informational Failure and the Promise of Regulatory Incrementalism', 102 *Yale Law Journal* 1457.

International Monetary Fund (2008), *Containing Systemic Risks and Restoring Financial Soundness*, Global Fin. Stability Rep (April).

Kane, Edward J. (1992), 'Government Officials as a Source of Systemic Risk in International Financial Markets', in Franklin R. Edwards and Hugh T. Patrick (eds), *Regulating International Financial Markets: Issues and Policies*, Boston: Kluwer.

Keleher, Robert, Joint Economic Committee (1999), 'An International Lender of Last Resort, the IMF, and the Federal Reserve' (Comm. Print).

Knedlik, Tobias (2006), 'Implementing an International Lender of Last Resort', Halle Institute for Economic Research, IWH-Discussion Paper No. 20.

Krebsbach, Karen (2007), 'International-Rule Adoption May Harm Emerging Economies', *US Banker*, April.

Laeven, Luc and Fabian Valencia (2008), 'Systemic Banking Crises: A New Database', IMF Working Paper WP\08\224 (November 2008).
Llewellyn, David T. (2006), 'Institutional Structure of Financial Regulation and Supervision: The Basic Rules', Paper presented at a World Bank Seminar June 2006 info.worldbank.org/etools/library/latestversion.asp?232743.
Nanda, Sudhir, James E. Owers and Ronald C. Rogers (1997), 'An Analysis of Resolution Trust Corporation Transactions: Auction Market Process and Pricing', 25 *Journal Real Estate Economics* 271.
Norman, Peter (2005), 'Basel II Chairman Says Rules Will Be Hard to Implement', *Financial Times*, 11 April.
Norris, Floyd (2009), 'US Bank Bailout to Rely in Part on Private Money', *New York Times*, 9 February.
Penner, Ethan (2008), 'The Future of Securitization', *Wall Street Journal*, 10 July.
'Protecting Against Economic Shocks', *Baltimore Sun*, 17 September 2007.
Schwarcz, Steven L. (1994), 'The Alchemy of Asset Securitization', 1 *Stanford Journal Law Business & Finance* 133.
Schwarcz, Steven L. (2002), *Structured Finance, A Guide to the Principles of Asset Securitization*, Practising Law Institute.
Schwarcz, Steven L. (2008a), 'Protecting Financial Markets: Lessons from the Subprime Mortgage Meltdown', 93 *Minnesota Law Review* 373.
Schwarcz, Steven L. (2008b), 'Systemic Risk', 97 *Georgetown Law Journal* 193.
Schwarcz, Steven L. (2009a), 'The Future of Securitization', 41 *Connecticut Law Review* 1313.
Schwarcz, Steven L. (2009b), 'Disclosure's Failure in the Subprime Mortgage Crisis', 2008 *Utah Law Review* 1109, http://papers.ssrn.com/sol3/papers.cfm?abstract_id=1113034.
Schwarcz, Steven L. (2009c), 'Understanding the "Subprime" Mortgage Crisis', 60 *S. C. L. Rev* 549, http://ssrn/abstract_id=1288687.
Schwarcz ,Steven L. (2009d), 'The Case for a Market Liquidity Provider of Last Resort', keynote speech, NYU Law School symposium, 'Modernizing the Financial Regulatory Structure', held 20 February 2009.
Spanakos, Elene (2000), 'Note: Harmonization of International Adequacy Rules for Securities Firms: An Argument to Implement the Value At Risk Approach by Adopting Basle's Internal Model Methodology', 26 *Brooklyn Journal of International Law* 221.
Spiegel, Mark M. (2006), 'Did Quantitative Easing by the Bank of Japan "Work"?', *FRBSF Econ. Letter No. 2006–28*, 20 October.
Stiglitz, Joseph E. and Bruce Greenwald (1994), 'Meir Kohn, Financial Institutions and Markets. Systemic Risk, and the Subprime Mortgage Meltdown', *Huffington Post*, 18 March 2008.
Stiglitz, Joseph E. and Bruce Greenwald (2003), *Towards a New Paradigm in Monetary Economics*, Cambridge: Cambridge University Press.
'Systemic Risk Meets Subprime Mortgages', *Commentary*, Forbes.com, 1 May 2008.
Welch, Jack and Suzy (2009), 'For a Fast-Acting Stimulus Plan . . .', *Business Week*, 16 February.
Zuckerman, Mortimer B. (2009), 'No Time to Lose', *US News & World Report* (March).
Zuckerman, Mortimer B. (2008), 'We Deserve a Better Bailout', *US News & World Report*, 20 October.

5. Overdependence on credit ratings was a primary cause of the crisis

Frank Partnoy*

INTRODUCTION

A primary cause of the recent credit market turmoil was overdependence on credit ratings and credit rating agencies. Without such overdependence, the complex financial instruments, particularly collateralized debt obligations (CDOs) and structured investment vehicles (SIVs), which were at the center of the crisis, could not, and would not, have been created or sold. Long-term sustainable policy measures should take into account both regulatory and behavioral overdependence on ratings.

In the first part of the chapter, I describe how over time credit rating agencies[1] ceased to play the role of information intermediaries. By the time market participants recently began to securitize large amounts of subprime mortgages, rating agencies were available, not to provide information about the risk associated with the securitized instruments, but to facilitate the use of 'regulatory licenses'[2] by enabling structurers to create and maintain tranches of these instruments with unjustifiably high credit ratings. This role went well beyond the standard reputational model of the role of rating agencies.

In the second part of the chapter, I suggest how future policy might minimize overdependence on credit ratings by removing regulatory licenses and by implementing 'shock therapy' mechanisms to wean investors off ratings mnemonics. I also analyze how regulators and market participants can learn from the flaws in rating agency models to avoid repeating similar mistakes. In particular, I focus on the misapplication of historical data with respect to estimates of expected default probability, recovery and correlation. Finally, I assess how market measures of these estimates, based on actual prices of traded assets, might substitute for credit ratings for both regulatory and behavioral purposes.

SOME BACKGROUND AND THEORY: REPUTATION VS. REGULATORY LICENSES

Historically, information intermediaries have arisen because of information asymmetry between buyers and sellers, particularly in markets where sellers have superior information but cannot costlessly convey this information to buyers.[3] If buyers are economically rational, prices in a market with information asymmetry will reflect the average quality of a product, and sellers with superior products will bear the cost of the information asymmetry. Consequently, sellers in such a market will have an incentive to disclose the superior nature of their product so that they can receive the highest price. In financial markets, to the extent sellers cannot credibly make such disclosures, there are incentives for information intermediaries to play this role.

Information-gathering firms that certify asset quality typically must satisfy three criteria before their certification will be credible to outside investors. First, the certifying agent must have reputational capital at stake in the certification activity. In other words, the certifying agent credibly must be able to pledge that it will suffer a loss, related either to litigation or declining reputation, if its certification is systematically biased or false. Second, this expected loss must exceed the expected gain from false certification. Third, the agent's services must be costly and the cost must be related to the informational asymmetry between buyer and seller.

In the early debt markets, credit rating agencies evolved to play an informational intermediary role, from the nineteenth-century mercantile credit rating agencies through John Moody's application to bonds.[4] Moody's insight was that he could profit by selling to the public a synthesis of complex bond data into a single letter rating.

For the most part, credit rating agencies fit this reputational investor-pay model until the mid-1970s, when, not coincidentally, the Securities and Exchange Commission (SEC) began relying substantively on credit rating agencies for regulatory purposes and the agencies shifted to an issuer-pay model.[5] As the regulatory dependence on ratings increased, rating agencies became more profitable and also began providing ratings of transactions designed to achieve particular ratings. During the late 1980s and early 1990s, bankers and issuers created a range of highly-rated asset-backed transactions and collateralized bond obligations, as well as derivative product companies, financial guarantor transactions and AAA-rated arbitrage vehicles. The first SIVs and asset-backed CDOs were created during this period.

As the credit rating agency model shifted from investor-pay to issuer-pay, the conditions necessary for the existence of a well-functioning information intermediary faltered. The rating agencies faced little or no risk of loss from inaccurate ratings, while the potential gains from inaccurate ratings increased. Ratings substantially lagged the revelation of public information about rated issuers and instruments, and rating agencies repeatedly were forced to revise ratings substantially downward. As rating agencies began rating substantially greater numbers of issuers and instruments, the resources expended per rating necessarily declined, and the cost of providing a rating became disconnected from the information gap between investors and issuers. Finally, the rating agencies' businesses became progressively more profitable, even as the informational value of their ratings declined.

During the 1990s, overdependence on credit ratings led many market participants to create highly-rated fixed income instruments that carried attractive yields relative to comparable assets, but that also carried new risks typically not associated with highly-rated bonds. The bond market crisis in 1994–95 was driven by structured notes and other derivatives transactions, including mortgage-backed transactions, which were designed to achieve high ratings, even though they carried other embedded risks. More recently, overdependence on credit ratings played a significant role in the collapse of Enron.[6]

With respect to mortgages, 'first-level' securitizations were a response to the investment grade 'cliff' noted by W. Braddock Hickman,[7] and later Michael Milken, who saw that portfolios of sub-investment grade rated bonds outperformed more highly-rated bonds on a risk-adjusted basis. Market participants adapted this insight to mortgages of various types, which could be pooled into new highly-rated fixed income instruments. Surprisingly, this 'cliff' persisted over time, in both corporate bond and mortgage markets; the large yield discontinuity between investment grade and below-investment grade ratings did not disappear even after large amounts of securities were issued. To the contrary, in the early 2000s, rating agency models, and assumptions about historical default, recovery and correlation, suggested that extant mortgage-backed securities could be repackaged and resold in ways that would outperform, not only the mortgage-backed securities themselves, but other comparably rated securities.

THE GROWTH OF 'SECOND-LEVEL' MORTGAGE SECURITIZATION

As the credit derivatives market was experiencing record growth, fixed income structurers and investors, with the assistance of credit rating agencies, searched for assets that could be securitized to create highly-rated fixed income instruments with attractive yields relative to comparable investments. For the first time, banks began seriously considering 'second-level' securitizations of 'first-level' mortgage-backed securities (which were securitizations of mortgages).

The fundamental economic rationale for 'second-level' securitizations is not obvious. After all, the underlying mortgage assets already have been securitized. Indeed, the mortgage-backed securities market was already a deep market, driven by high demand from both originators and investors. Mortgage-backed securities were issued in a competitive environment in large numbers, and already were rated by the rating agencies. 'First-level' securitization transactions were a response to gaps and inefficiencies in the underlying market for individual assets. To the extent mortgages were being allocated or bundled inefficiently, or in ways not desired by investors, one might have expected that continuous 'first-level' securitization would evolve to ameliorate these inefficiencies. Put another way, if there had been a more efficient way of pooling mortgages, or a pocket of unsatisfied demand for particular pool portfolios or structures, investors likely would have demanded it, and then banks would have created and supplied it.

Yet the proliferation of 'second-level' mortgage-backed CDOs and SIVs suggested that billions of dollars of 'first-level' mortgage-backed securities appeared to be mispriced. Market participants could pool those securities into new special purpose entities with tranched capital structures, and sell the slices of those structures for more than the value of the underlying mortgage-backed securities. These transactions, too, persisted over time, so much so that the appetite for 'second-level' mortgage securitizations drove financial intermediaries both to originate new and increasingly risky mortgages, and to create synthetic exposure to mortgages, which then could be resecuritized through tranched special purpose entities, again at higher prices than the underlying mortgage-backed securities were trading in the market.

To obtain ratings for 'second-level' mortgage securitizations, both the structurers and the rating agencies used models based on earlier corporate bond-backed transactions, which provided a methodology for labeling the risks associated with mortgage securities-backed transactions. Bankers increasingly sought to combine the underlying securities and to stratify capital structures in ways that would create new investment grade-rated securities. In particular, CDOs and SIVs were designed to create large tranches of AAA-rated assets backed by lower-rated mortgage-backed securities.

Even after a mortgage-backed security had been re-securitized through cash-flow based CDOs, market participants suggested that there was no reason why investors couldn't take on exposure to a particular mortgage-backed security more than once. Arrangers created synthetic exposure based on side bets derived from the value of the underlying mortgage-backed securities so that investors could obtain exposure to the performance of a pool of mortgages without having an investment vehicle or special purpose entity actually buy the mortgage-backed securities. Synthetic CDOs and SIVs obtained exposure through derivatives transactions, most commonly credit default swaps.

CREDIT RATINGS AS DRIVERS OF 'SECOND-LEVEL' SECURITIZATIONS

The linchpin of a CDO or a SIV backed in whole or part by synthetic assets was the credit rating. Investors typically did not examine the underlying assets of a synthetic CDO or SIV in any detail or at all. One might criticize them for not doing so, except that the underlying assets frequently were not even specified when the deal was sold. Instead, investors relied on parameters set by the arrangers, bankers and rating agencies to constrain the assets that could be purchased originally, and held over time.

If the credit rating agencies, and their clients, had used reasonable and accurate models and assumptions, then in principle these transactions might not have been problematic. However, these parties faced financial incentives to use unreasonable and inaccurate assumptions and models to complete deals and thereby earn greater fees. These incentives were especially strong given the expected absence of any reputational consequence, particularly for individuals involved in transactions, who essentially could sell long-term options obligating their firms while pocketing shorter-term bonuses for themselves. The way to obtain sufficiently attractive ratings to pay the high transaction costs and fees for the various arranging parties, and still generate attractive yields for purchasers, was to use models and assumptions that did not reflect the actual risk of the underlying mortgages, including risks that already were impounded in the price of those securities in the market for mortgage-backed securities.[8]

The simplest way to generate unwarranted high ratings was to use outdated and inapplicable historical assumptions with respect to the underlying mortgage-backed securities. The inputs to the relevant models were straightforward: expected default rate, recovery rate upon default, and, for portfolios of assets, the correlation of expected defaults. The rating agencies created models, with the assistance of bankers and arrangers, that generated tranche credit ratings for 'second-level' deals based on these inputs. Those models, in turn, typically depended on assumptions with respect to the expected statistical distribution that returns on the underlying collateral would follow.

Given these assumptions and models, arrangers were then free to find collateral that would generate the most attractive tranche yields, subject to ratings-based constraints. The restrictions on collateral typically were based on credit ratings; in other words, the 'second-level' securitization methodology depended on previous 'first-level' securitization ratings. As the prices of mortgage-backed securities rose, along with housing prices, it was difficult to generate 'second-level' deals with highly-rated tranches without using increasingly unreasonable assumptions. As collateral became more expensive and ratings of that collateral lagged increasing market prices, accurate and timely ratings would have appeared lower than would have been warranted. This lag provided a rationale for increasingly aggressive assumptions with respect to 'second-level' deals.

Paradoxically, when housing prices began to fall, but ratings on 'first-level' securitizations did not, the historical ratings methodology made 'second-level' securitizations increasingly attractive. If one could buy AAA-rated mortgage-backed securities that had fallen in price, but still use the same historical default, recovery and correlation assumptions associated with AAA ratings in the relevant model, one could create a highly-rated, high-yielding set of 'second-level' transactions. As long as mortgage-backed securities ratings lagged market prices, as those prices declined, CDOs and SIVs backed by that collateral would appear increasingly attractive.

Rating agency assumptions and models did not accurately capture the risk associated with 'second-level' securitizations.[9] Default rate assumptions were derived from historical information, including default data about other asset categories as well as asset price correlations, rather than default correlations. Moreover, assumptions for 'second-level' deals were based on ratings of mortgage-backed securities, even when both the rating agencies and other participants in the resecuritization transactions were aware that both the credit quality of the underlying mortgages had declined and that the expected default correlations associated with those mortgages had increased. Nevertheless, the simulations the agencies ran to calculate tranche ratings were based on stale and inaccurate assumptions.

Rating agency correlation assumptions were particularly important.[10] Inaccurate correlation assumptions based on incorrect statistical models enabled parties to structure deals with high ratings on senior tranches, given that the expected correlation of defaults of mortgage-backed securities was higher than the estimates used for the models.[11] The rating agencies have struggled to understand the importance of correlation assumptions for CDOs and SIVs, even as those assumptions supported a sharply increasing number of 'second-level' securitizations. Moody's conducted an in-depth study of corporate bond correlation, which led to a new Monte Carlo simulation-based market tool in 2004 for measuring the credit risk of synthetic transactions; it revised its methodology for structured finance asset correlations a year later.[12] The inputs for Standard & Poor's (S&P) simply remained constant for years.[13] By 2006 and 2007 at the latest, it was apparent that the relevant mortgage asset correlations underlying CDOs and SIVs were significantly higher than the rating agencies had assumed. By February 2008, Moody's had downgraded at least one tranche of 94.2 per cent of subprime residential mortgage-backed deals it had rated in 2006.[14]

In sum, the proliferation of 'second-level' securitization transactions is consistent with substantial overdependence on credit ratings. If ratings had been accurate, or put another way, if investors had relied on ratings only to the extent they were accurate, then there would have been little incentive for 'second-level' securitizations. But because investors were willing to buy CDO and SIV tranches simply because of their high ratings and high yields, either because of regulatory reliance on ratings or because the mnemonic device of ratings came to play an overly-important private role, CDO and SIV tranches had higher-than-justified ratings, even though they held collateral that already had been securitized. Without overreliance on ratings, investors more likely would have looked through the complexity of CDO and SIV transactions to the underlying mortgage-backed securities, and prices more accurately would have reflected market estimates of default probability, recovery and correlation.

REGULATORY VS. BEHAVIORAL OVERDEPENDENCE

To what extent was overdependence on ratings driven by regulation? I previously have argued that rating agencies increasingly sell 'regulatory licenses' rather than information, and that ratings are not 'opinions', but instead are keys that unlock the financial markets for regulated entities.[15] Regulators recently have endorsed this explanation, and the SEC has proposed rules to eliminate certain aspects of regulatory dependence on ratings.[16]

In addition, it is apparent that, even putting aside regulatory influences, at least some market participants independently over rely on ratings. At its core, this overreliance likely derives from decades of regulatory dependence on ratings, but it has become a more widespread, behavioral phenomenon. Ratings are part of financial culture. Even after the massive dislocation associated with the recent crisis, and the abysmal performance of the rating agencies, market participants have continued to rely on letter ratings. One conclusion is that even if all explicit references to ratings were removed from regulation, some residual implicit overreliance would remain.

An interesting perspective on this behavioral point arises from the fact that the major banks selling 'second-level' securitizations also misperceived the risks associated with the highest-rated tranches. Indeed, it appears that bank officers were so confident about the high ratings of super-senior CDO tranches that they concluded that such tranches posed virtually no risk. One reason, if not the primary reason, why they misperceived such risks was overreliance on credit rating agency assumptions and models. Some of this overreliance derived from bank regulations that depend on credit ratings; the rest was cultural.

Most strikingly, sanguine assessments of super-senior risk, and assumptions that senior tranches protected by AAA-rated junior tranches could not default, appeared to be so obviously correct that banks' exposure to these tranches apparently remained hidden from senior managers, investors and regulators. No bank publicly disclosed risks associated with super-senior tranches before the crisis began. Bank directors and officers claimed, perhaps falsely, that they were unaware of risks associated with these tranches. Moreover, many regulators apparently were unaware of the exposure as well. The Bank of England, in its Financial Stability Report, noted that banks were net buyers of credit protection in 2006; that estimate apparently did not reflect the large amounts of notional credit protection sold by banks in super-senior transactions.[17] These estimates are set forth in Figure 5.1 below.

Much of the blame for overdependence on ratings can be placed on regulation, and I set forth below some measures designed to eliminate this overdependence. But market participants also independently overrelied on ratings. High ratings replaced independent judgment, particularly when 'second-level' transactions created the illusion of thick bands of highly-rated protective tranches. The collapse of senior securities of both CDOs and SIVs illustrates that 'second-level' securitizations require an analysis of something more than just tranche ratings. Because these instruments are so much more complex than the underlying 'first-level' securitizations, they generate a greater need for investigation, and paradoxically are more amenable to overreliance on ratings.

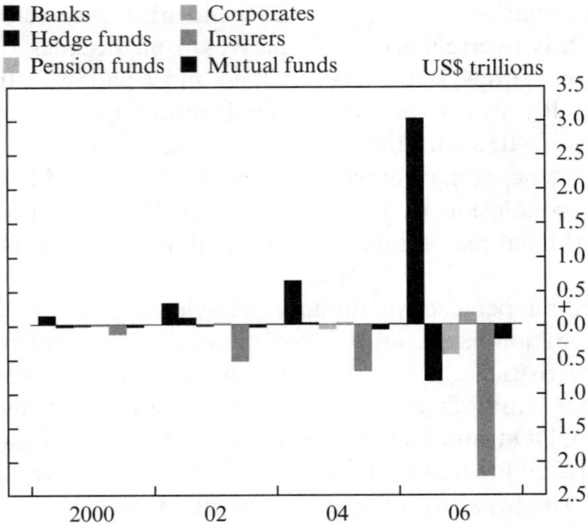

Note: Amount netted across long and short positions.

Sources: BBA and Bank Calculations.

Figure 5.1 Outstanding global amounts of credit protection bought by institutions

SOME POLICY PRESCRIPTIONS

If the story about overreliance on credit ratings is even partially correct, what is to be done? There are two categories of policy responses, some of which already have been proposed. First, regulators should eliminate explicit reliance on credit ratings. To the extent regulators are concerned that such an approach would leave a substantive void, there are many substitutes for ratings, including market measures of risk, as described below. Second, regulators should implement some form of 'shock therapy' to jar market participants from overreliance on ratings. The use of mnemonics is highly path dependent, and unless there are strong reasons for participants to switch, they will not.

With respect to the first point, the SEC already has proposed removing references to Nationally Recognized Statistical Rating Organizations (NRSROs) in its own rules. For example, Rule 2a-7 of the Investment Company Act limits a money market fund's portfolio investments to securities that have received credit ratings from NRSROs in one of the two highest short-term rating categories.[18] The SEC recommended replacing this NRSRO 'regulatory license' with a requirement that money market fund boards of directors determine 'that each portfolio instrument presents minimal credit risks'.[19] Likewise, other SEC proposals would replace several other rules that depend explicitly on NRSRO ratings.

Notwithstanding the intense lobbying effort against these proposals, the SEC should implement them as final. Moreover, other regulatory bodies should similarly excise references to credit ratings. In the United States, the most efficient mechanism for doing this would be for Congress formally to remove references from statutes, and then to hold hearings to encourage various agencies to remove any additional remaining references in both formal rules and informal policies.

Perhaps the most important regulatory references to ratings are in international banking regulations, particularly under the Basel II agreement of the Basel Committee on Banking Supervision. Basel II explicitly allows banking regulators to permit banks to use credit ratings from approved rating agencies in calculating their net capital reserve requirements. International regulators should remove this provision, and in place of letter ratings substitute market-based measures, such as credit spreads or credit default swap prices and/or discretionary estimates of default probability, expected recovery and correlation. The Bank for International Settlements has long been a leader in publicizing problems associated with the use of ratings in structured finance.[20] It now should explicitly disclaim the use of ratings in regulation generally.

Ratings and rating agencies also have been subsidized by other forms of regulation, and those subsidies should be removed as well. NRSROs are specifically exempt under US securities law from Section 11 liability and Regulation FD; they should not be. Nor should rating agencies be exempt from liability for statutory and common law private claims based on any freedom of speech or journalistic privilege rationales. Historically, the rating agencies have interposed First Amendment objections in civil litigation, with some success.[21] As new cases based on 'second-level' securitizations arise, judges should distinguish those prior cases, and make it clear that rating agencies are subject to civil liability and are not protected by any First Amendment privilege. Legislators also should consider clarifying the viability of private rights of action against rating agencies.

The rating agencies' position that ratings are merely 'opinions', and therefore are entitled to the same protection as other 'speakers', is specious in the context of complex securitization transactions. Ratings of 'second-level' securitizations are not protected speech, and rating agencies are doing much more than merely speaking. They have a high level of initial and ongoing involvement in these deals, at early and later stages, and receive significantly higher fees for them. Rating agencies determine the capital cushions that are required for particular tranches; they provide capital matrix parameters that govern the operation of special purpose entity issuers; they are involved in the operation of the issuers on an ongoing basis; they instruct the asset manager regarding the kinds of assets the issuers can acquire, both initially and over time; and the deal documentation for these transactions typically includes descriptions of the simulation models the rating agencies use to determine the relative proportions of an entity's capital structure, as well as the necessary over-collateralization ratios and triggers, both initially and over time. Moreover, unlike corporate bond transactions, CDOs and SIVs require a much more in-depth analysis by the rating agencies, including the use of their mathematical models and assumptions. For these reasons, judges should reject the claim that ratings of 'second-level' securitizations are merely 'opinions'.

With respect to the second point regarding 'shock therapy', regulators should encourage investors not to apply the same ratings and analysis to corporate bonds versus structured finance assets.[22] Ratings of these instruments are categorically different, and it was and is a mistake for anyone to use the same mnemonic for each category. A highly-rated CDO does not pose the same risks as other highly-rated securities, including the collateral underlying the CDO. To the extent regulators and investors continue to rely on ratings, which they should not, at minimum their rating-based rules should distinguish between the symbology of corporate bonds and structured finance instruments, if not other categories as well. Ideally, regulators and investors should find independent means of assessing the risks of different investments within different categories. Forcing investors to split ratings among categories should lead private actors to reassess their approach to risk.

Disclosure with respect to credit derivatives and credit rating-based transactions also must improve. Current disclosure of notional amounts and value-at-risk (VAR) does not enable investors to assess the risks associated with default, expected recovery and correlation of fixed income exposure. One reason for the recent collapse of major financial institutions such as Bear Stearns, Lehman, Fannie Mae, Freddie Mac and AIG was the lack of transparency with respect to 'second-level' securitizations. When no one has enough information to evaluate the risk of portfolios held by financial institutions, the valuation of their issued securities becomes at best a guess. At minimum, bank regulators should require that financial institutions disclose to examiners not only VAR-related measures, but also more robust worst-case analyses and stress tests based on a wide range of assumptions about expected default, recovery and correlation. Requiring such disclosures also would encourage market participants to rely on these measures directly, instead of letter ratings. It also would encourage dissemination of risk disclosure to bank officers and directors.

As regulators and investors seek substitutes for credit ratings, they should consider looking to market measures and prices. Notwithstanding recent market volatility and dislocations, market prices provided a far more accurate assessment of risk than credit ratings. Such prices and related market measures are available from true information intermediaries, which now play a modern version of the role John Moody originally envisioned in the early twentieth century: providing valuable information about credit risk. Most prominently, Markit Group Limited provides credit default swap pricing and other data that investors could use to assess the risk of their portfolios over time. It would vastly improve policy and market efficiency if regulators and investors relied on this kind of data instead of credit ratings.

An example based on data from Markit is set forth in Figure 5.2 below. The chart depicts the daily 5-year Bear Stearns senior credit default swap

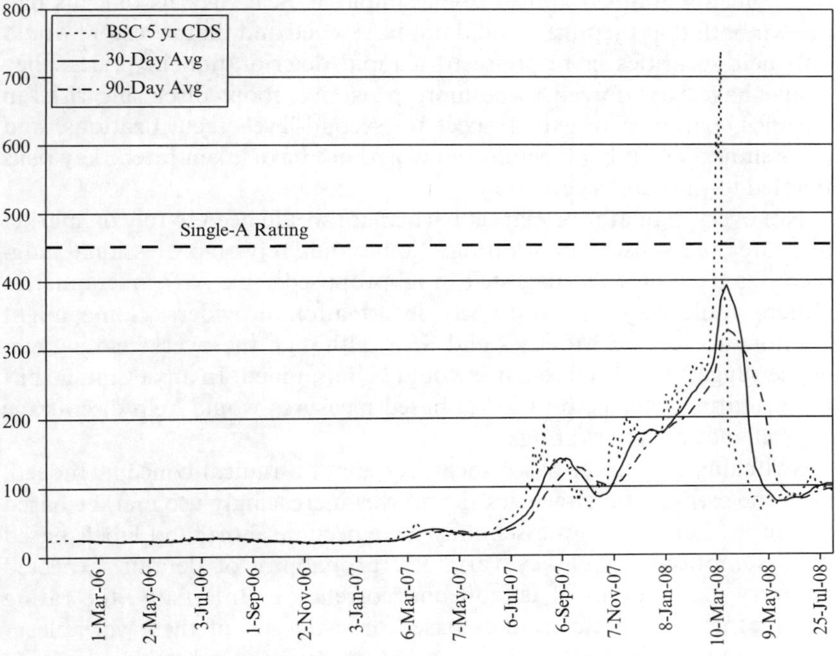

Source: Markit.

Figure 5.2 Bear Stearns 5-Year CDS market spreads (bp)

closing spreads, along with a 30- and 90-day rolling average of these spreads. Note that the credit ratings applicable to Bear Stearns's senior debt were constant at single-A throughout this period.

To the extent regulators or institutions are concerned about the volatility of market based measures, it would be straightforward to reference a rolling average like one of those depicted above. Reliance on market measures instead of credit ratings likely would have led institutions with exposure to Bear Stearns securities to assess their exposure more closely during the period leading up to that firm's collapse. Instead of regulating and making investment decisions based on a Bear Stearns credit rating that remained unjustifiably high and unchanged during that bank's crisis and collapse, regulators and institutions instead could have looked to a rolling average of market measures. Credit default swap spreads provided an early warning to market participants regarding Bear Stearns.

Moreover, the use of market measures would have beneficial ex ante effects, particularly if regulators also adopt the heightened disclosure requirements outlined above. For example, if Bear Stearns officials had known both that their firm would not be rescued and that investors would sell their securities in response to a rapid deterioration in prices, they would have been forced to be more proactive about disclosing risks in advance, particularly with respect to 'second-level' securitizations, and perhaps as a result bank employees would not have taken on the key risks that led to the bank's collapse.

Not every regulator or market participant would need to rely on market measures as a substitute for ratings. Some could rely on professional judgment, as the SEC has suggested in its proposed Rule 2a-7 amendments. Others could rely on third-party information providers. Some might continue to rely on Moody's and S&P, although the overwhelming evidence suggest that such reliance would be misguided. In any event, a shift to permitting reliance on market-based measures would help discourage overreliance on letter ratings.

Switching to market-based measures is not a radical concept. Indeed, even the credit rating agencies themselves increasingly use market-based measures. Letter ratings essentially have become shorthand labels based on assumptions about key variables: probability of default, expected recovery in the event of default and correlation. Internally, the rating agencies generate letter ratings based on estimates of these variables.[23] At minimum, regulators and market participants should switch to relying on actual estimates of these variables instead of letter ratings that amalgamate the variables in an opaque, outdated and incomprehensible fashion.

CONCLUSION

Causation is a complex concept. It has both 'but for' and 'proximate' elements. As a matter of 'but for' causation, there is a strong argument that credit ratings and credit rating agencies caused the crisis. 'Second-level' mortgage-backed securitizations, particularly CDOs and SIVs, explicitly depended on rating agency letter ratings. Without those ratings, the transactions could not, and would not, have happened. Without the ability to obtain high ratings for CDO and SIV tranches, there would have been little appetite for overpriced lower-rated mortgage collateral. Without that appetite, there would have been little pressure leading to the proliferation of subprime mortgages, because those mortgages could not have been offloaded through 'second-level' securitizations. Without the proliferation of low quality mortgages, there would not have been a dramatic housing market rise and fall, with the attendant ripple effects.

It is more difficult to say whether credit ratings were a 'proximate' cause of the crisis, but there are strong arguments here as well. Overreliance on ratings led banks to hold super-senior exposure they otherwise would have assessed more carefully. Overreliance on ratings led regulators to misperceive the extent to which speculation on subprime mortgages had spread, or to where. Overreliance on ratings led institutional investors to take on hidden correlation bets, which their directors, officers and shareholders did not understand.

Overreliance on ratings was a central component of the credit crisis. In responding to the crisis, and in planning and implementing reforms, regulators should not focus exclusively on proposals related to lending abuses, bank rescues, credit expansion and macroeconomic or cyclical factors. They should not miss the crucial role of credit ratings.

NOTES

* George E. Barrett Professor of Law and Director of the Center on Corporate and Securities Law, University of San Diego.

1. By credit rating agencies, I am referring to Nationally Recognized Statistical Rating Organizations (NRSROs), as that term was defined during the early 2000s, and in particular to the two major NRSROs, Moody's Investor Service and Standard & Poor's Rating Services.
2. By regulatory license, I mean the property rights associated with the ability of a private entity, rather than a regulator, to determine the substantive effect of legal rules. Partnoy (1999), p. 622.
3. Partnoy (1999), pp. 633–36.
4. Partnoy (1999), pp. 637–38.
5. More precisely, the regulatory dependence on credit ratings began in 1973, when the SEC proposed amending broker-dealer 'haircut' requirements, which set forth the

percentage of a financial asset's market value a broker-dealer was required to deduct for the purpose of calculating its net capital requirement. Rule 15c3–1, promulgated two years later, required a different 'haircut' based on the credit ratings assigned by NRSROs. See 17 C.F.R. 240.15c3–1. Since the mid-1970s, statutes and regulations increasingly have come to depend explicitly on NRSRO ratings. See Partnoy (1999), pp. 690–703.

6. The following assessment from Senator Joseph Lieberman, whose Senate committee held the first hearings on Enron, was typical: 'The credit-rating agencies were dismally lax in their coverage of Enron. They didn't ask probing questions and generally accepted at face value whatever Enron's officials chose to tell them. And while they claim to rely primarily on public filings with the SEC, analysts from Standard and Poor's not only did not read Enron's proxy statement, they didn't even know what information it might contain.' Senate Committee on Governmental Affairs 2002.
7. Hickman (1958).
8. Mason and Rosner (2007).
9. The SEC investigation of the credit rating agencies found that they struggled to adapt to the complexity of mortgage-backed structured finance deals. Securities and Exchange Commission (2008c), p. 12 ('One analyst expressed concern that her firm's model did not capture "half" of the deal's risk, but that "it could be structured by cows and we would rate it".'). The SEC also found that '[r]ating agencies made "out of model" adjustments and did not document the rationale for the adjustment.' Ibid., p. 14.
10. Hull and White (2006); van Deventer (2008), p. 7 ('Management has often discovered that the working-level staff has been depending heavily on models, like the copula approach, that were known or should have been known to be wrong.').
11. Moody's Investors Service (2006), p. 10.
12. Moody's Investors Service (2005a), pp. 5–6; Moody's Investors Service (2005b),
13. Partnoy (2006).
14. Moody's Investors Service (2008), p. 3.
15. Partnoy (1999).
16. Securities and Exchange Commission (2008b).
17. Bank of England (2008), Chart 2.17. The Bank for International Settlements had been warning about overreliance on ratings since early 2005. Bank for International Settlements (2005).
18. Investment Company Act, Rule 2a-7(a)(10), (21).
19. Securities and Exchange Commission (2008b), p. 40125.
20. Bank for International Settlements (2005).
21. Partnoy (2006).
22. The SEC has proposed such a split. Securities and Exchange Commission (2008a).
23. With respect to mortgage-backed securities, prepayment risk also is a relevant variable. Prepayment risk was an important factor during the 1994–95 interest rate crisis, but did not play a major role during the recent subprime crisis.

REFERENCES

Bank of England (2008), 'Financial Stability Report', http://www.bankofengland.co.uk/publications/fsr/2008/fsrfull0804.pdf, April.

Bank for International Settlements, Committee on the Global Financial System (2005), 'The Role of Ratings in Structured Finance: Issues and Implications', http://www.bis.org/publ/cgfs23.pdf, January.

Hickman, W. Braddock (1958), *Corporate Bond Quality and Investor Experience: A Study by the National Bureau of Economic Research, New York*, Princeton: Princeton University Press.

Hull, John C. and A. White (2006), 'Valuing Credit Derivatives Using an Implied Copula Approach', *Journal of Derivatives*, **14**(2), 8–28.

Investment Company Act, Rule 2a-7(a)(10), (21).

Mason, Joseph R. and J. Rosner (2007), 'Where Did the Risk Go? How Misapplied Bond Ratings Cause Mortgage Backed Securities and Collateralized Debt Obligation Market Disruptions', SSRN Working Paper: http://ssrn.com/abstract=1027475, 3 May.

Moody's Investors Service (2005a), 'Collateralised Debt Obligations: A Moody's Primer', March.

Moody's Investors Service (2005b), 'Moody's Revisits its Assumptions Regarding Structured Finance Default (and Asset) Correlations for CDOs', June.

Moody's Investors Service (2006), 'Moody's Modeling Approach to Rating Structured Finance Cash Flow CDO Transactions', September.

Moody's Investors Service (2008), 'A Short Guide to Subprime', March.

Partnoy, Frank (1999), 'The Siskel and Ebert of Financial Markets?: Two Thumbs Down for the Credit Rating Agencies', *Washington University Law Quarterly*, **77**, 619–712.

Partnoy, Frank (2006), 'How and Why Credit Rating Agencies Are Not Like Other Gatekeepers', in Fuchita, Yasuyuki and R. E. Litan (eds), *Financial Gatekeepers: Can They Protect Investors?*, Washington: Brookings Institution Press, pp. 59–102.

Securities and Exchange Commission (2008a), 'Proposed Rules for Nationally Recognized Statistical Rating Organizations', http://www.sec.gov/rules/proposed/2008/34–57967.pdf, 16 June.

Securities and Exchange Commission (2008b), 'References to Ratings of Nationally Recognized Statistical Rating Organizations', *Federal Register*, **73**(134), 40124–40142

Securities and Exchange Commission (2008c), 'Summary Report of Issues Identified in the Commission Staff's Examinations of Select Credit Rating Agencies', http://www.sec.gov/news/studies/2008/craexamination070808.pdf, July.

Senate Committee on Governmental Affairs (2002), press release, 'Financial Oversight of Enron: The SEC and Private-Sector Watchdogs', October 8.

van Deventer, Donald R. (2008), 'Fair-Value Accounting, CDOs and the Credit Crisis of 2007–2008: Complexity and Model Risk in the Collateralized Debt Obligation Market Are Severe', *Bank Accounting & Finance*, **21**(6), 3–8.

6. Federal preemption, regulatory failure and the race to the bottom in US mortgage lending standards

Patricia A. McCoy*

INTRODUCTION

In the debate over the Great Recession of 2008–2009, much attention has been paid to whether consumer financial protection should continue to be dispersed among state and federal regulators or transferred to a single federal agency dedicated solely to consumer protection, as the Obama Administration has proposed. In this chapter, I argue that the Administration's proposal is essential for three reasons. First, during the housing bubble, our system of fragmented regulation drove lenders to shop for the easiest legal regime. Second, the ability of lenders to switch charters put pressure on banking regulators – both state and federal – to relax credit standards. Finally, banking regulators have routinely sacrificed consumer protection for the short-term profitability of banks. Creating one, dedicated consumer credit regulator charged with consumer protection would establish uniform standards and enforcement for all lenders and help prevent another death spiral in lending.[1]

The reasons for the breakdown of the home mortgage market and the private-label market for mortgage-backed securities are well known by now. In this chapter, I focus on lax lending standards for residential mortgages, which were a leading cause of today's credit crisis and recession. Our broken system of mortgage finance and the private actors in that system – ranging from mortgage brokers, lenders, and appraisers to the rating agencies and securitizers – bear direct responsibility for this breakdown in standards.

The story does not stop there. In 2006, depository institutions and their affiliates, which were regulated by federal banking regulators, originated about 54 per cent of all higher-priced home loans. In 2007, that percentage shot up to 79.6 per cent (Avery et al. (2008), p. A124). In some states, mortgages originated by state banks and thrifts and independent nonbank lenders were regulated under state anti-predatory lending laws. In other states, however, mortgages were not subject to meaningful regulation. Consequently, the credit crisis resulted from regulatory failure as well as broken private risk management. That regulatory failure was not confined to states, moreover, but pervaded federal banking regulation as well.

Neither of these phenomena – the collapse in lending criteria nor the regulatory failure that allowed it – was an accident. Rather, they occurred because mortgage originators and regulators became locked in a race to the bottom to relax loan underwriting and risk management. The fragmented US system of financial services regulation exacerbated this race to the bottom by allowing lenders to shop for the easiest regulators and laws.

During the housing bubble, consumers could not police originators because too many loan products had hidden risks. Those risks were ticking time bombs. Lenders did not take reasonable precautions against default because they were able to shift the credit risk to investors through securitization. Similarly, regulators failed to clamp down on hazardous loans in a myopic attempt to boost the short-term profitability of banks and thrifts.

I begin by examining why reckless lenders were able to take market share away from good lenders and good products. Next, I describe our fragmented financial regulatory system and how it encouraged lenders to shop for lenient regulators. Then I document regulatory failure by federal banking regulators. Finally, I end with an evaluation of the Obama Administration's proposal for a separate Consumer Financial Protection Agency.

WHY RECKLESS LENDERS WERE ABLE TO CROWD OUT THE GOOD

During the housing boom, the residential mortgage market was relatively unconcentrated, with thousands of mortgage originators. Normally, we would expect an unconcentrated market to provide vibrant competition benefiting consumers. On the contrary, however, highly risky loan products containing hidden risks – such as hybrid adjustable-rate mortgages (ARMs), interest-only ARMs, and option payment ARMs – gained market share at the expense of safer products such as standard fixed-rate mortgages and FHA-guaranteed loans.[2]

These nontraditional mortgages and subprime loans inflicted incalculable harm on borrowers, their neighbors, and ultimately the global economy. As of 30 June 2009, almost one-seventh of US residential mortgages (13.16 per cent) were at least one month past due or in foreclosure. This was the highest rate 'ever recorded' since statistics started being kept in 1972 (Mortgage Bankers Association (2009)). By year-end 2008, every sixth borrower owed more than his or her home was worth (Corkery (2008)). The proliferation of toxic loans was the direct result of the ability to confuse borrowers and to shop for the laxest regulatory regime.[3]

The Growth in Dangerous Mortgage Products

During the housing boom, hybrid subprime ARMs, interest-only mortgages, and option payment ARMs captured a growing part of the market. We can see this from the growth in nonprime mortgages.[4] Between 2003 and 2005, nonprime loans tripled from 11 per cent of all home loans to 33 per cent (Federal Deposit Insurance Corporation (2006)).

If we unpack these numbers, it turns out that hybrid ARMs, interest-only mortgages, and option payment ARMs accounted for a growing share of nonprime loans over this period. Option payment ARMs and interest-only mortgages went from 3 per cent of all nonprime originations in 2002 to well over 50 per cent by 2005 (see Figure 6.1). Low- and no-documentation loans increased from 25 per cent to slightly over 40

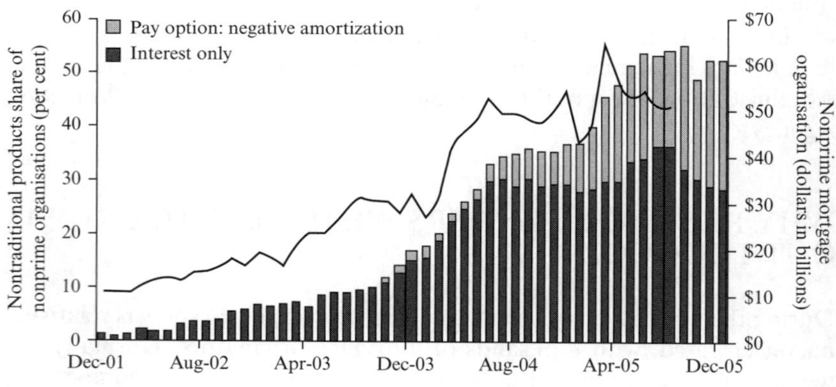

Notes: Nonprime mortgage originations data are securitized originations of Alt-A and subprime product. Data on nonprime mortgage originations are not fully available after August 2005 and are not displayed.

Sources: Loan Performance Corporation (Alt-A and B&C mortgage securities database). FDIC Outlook, *Breaking New Ground in U.S. Mortgage Lending* (Summer 2006), available at www.fdic.gov/bank/analytical/regional/ro20062q/na/2006_summer04.html.

Figure 6.1 Growth in nontraditional mortgages, 2002–2005

per cent of subprime loans over the same period. By 2004 and continuing through 2006, about three-fourths of the loans in subprime securitizations consisted of hybrid ARMs (Federal Deposit Insurance Corporation (2006); McCoy et al. (2009)).

As the product mix of nonprime loans became riskier and riskier, two default indicators for nonprime loans increased substantially. Loan-to-value ratios went up and so did the percentage of loans with combined loan-to-value ratios exceeding 80 per cent. This occurred even though the credit scores of borrowers with those loans remained relatively unchanged between 2002 and 2006. At the same time, the spreads of rates over the bank cost of capital tightened. To make matters worse, originators layered risk upon risk, with borrowers who were the most at risk obtaining low equity, no-amortization, reduced documentation loans (see Figure 6.2).

Many of these risky mortgage instruments were made in areas where housing was least affordable, such as California, Florida and Arizona,

ARMS

	Orig Yr	CLTV	CLTV>80	Seconds	Full Doc	IO%	DTI	FICO<700	Investor	WAC	SpdtoWAC
Prime	2002	66.4	4.1	1.9	56.0	46	31.0	20.7	0.7	5.5	–
	2003	68.2	10.1	10.9	48.6	53	31.8	21.8	1.6	4.6	–
	2004	73.5	20.7	23.1	51.2	71	33.5	22.0	2.1	4.5	–
	2005	74.1	21.7	26.8	47.3	81	33.6	18.9	1.9	5.4	–
	2006	75.3	26.2	35.3	33.6	91	37.2	19.5	2.3	6.2	–
Alt A	2002	74.3	20.8	2.7	29.3	26	35.4	46.4	9.9	6.3	0.8
	2003	78.0	33.3	23.4	28.1	56	35.3	44.7	12.9	5.6	1.0
	2004	82.6	46.9	39.1	32.6	75	36.2	44.3	15.3	5.5	1.0
	2005	83.5	49.6	46.9	28.3	83	37.0	40.5	16.5	6.0	0.6
	2006	85.0	55.4	55.4	19.0	87	38.3	44.2	13.5	6.8	0.6
Subprime	2002	81.2	46.8	3.7	66.9	1	40.0	93.4	4.7	8.5	3.0
	2003	83.5	55.6	9.9	63.5	5	40.2	91.6	4.9	7.5	2.9
	2004	85.3	61.1	19.1	59.9	20	40.6	90.6	5.3	7.1	2.6
	2005	86.6	64.4	28.1	55.9	32	41.2	89.7	5.4	7.3	1.9
	2006	86.7	64.0	31.0	54.6	20	42.1	91.8	5.7	8.2	2.0

Spreads declined

% Full Doc declined

Not much change in FICO or DTI

Legend:
CLTV: Combined loan-to value ratio
Full Doc: Full documentation loans
IO: Interest-only loans
DTI: Average debt-to-income ratios
FICO: Fair Isaac Company credit score
WAC: Weighted average coupon (measuring spread)

Source: Loan Performance data as of November 2006, UBS, April 16 2007, Thomas Zummerman 'How Did We Get Here and What Lies Ahead'.

Figure 6.2 *Underwriting criteria for adjustable-rate mortgages, 2002–2006*

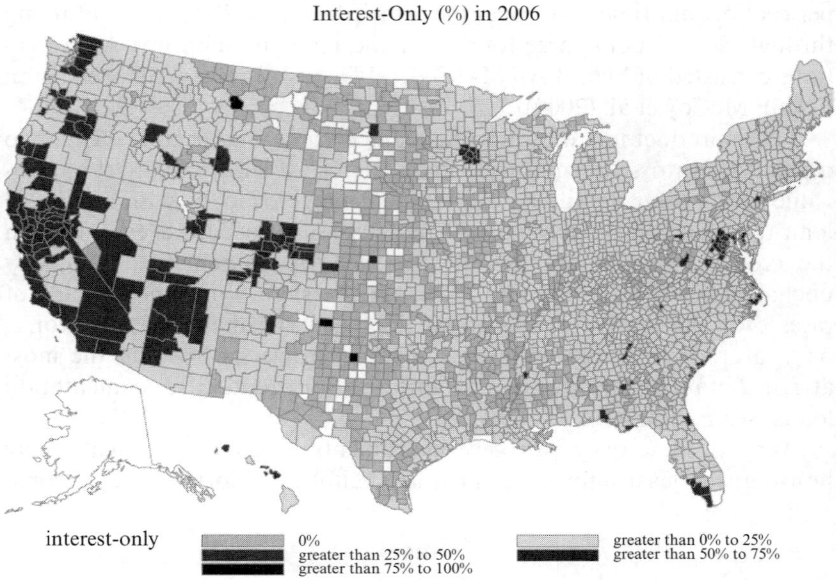

Source: Anthony Pennington-Cross, *Mortgage Product Substitution and State Predatory Lending Laws*, Presentation at the 2008 mid-year meeting of the American Real Estate and Urban Economics Association, Washington, D.C., May 27, 2008.

Figure 6.3 Geographic distribution of interest-only loans, 2006

leading to concentrated areas of unsustainable housing values (see Figures 6.3 and 6.4). This concentration of risky loans put the entire local markets at risk, due to the sudden and extreme withdrawal of credit in the aftermath of the bursting of the real estate bubble (Wachter et al. (2008)).

The combination of easing credit standards and a growing economy resulted in a sharp increase in homeownership rates through 2004. As the credit quality of loans steadily grew worse over 2005 through 2007,[5] however, the volume of unsustainable loans grew and homeownership rates dropped (Abraham et al. (2008)) (see Table 6.1).

The explosion of nontraditional mortgage lending was timed to maintain securitization deal flows after traditional refinancings weakened in 2003. The major take-off in these products occurred in 2002, which coincided with the winding down of the huge increase in demand for mortgage securities through the refinance process. Coming out of the recession of 2001, interest rates fell and there was a massive securitization boom for mortgage refinancing that was fueled by low interest rates. In response to

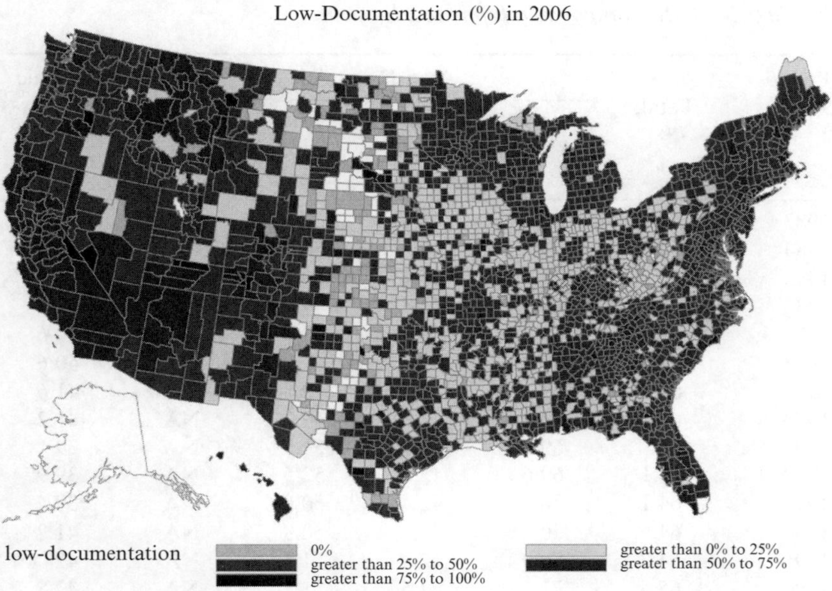

Source: Anthony Pennington-Cross, *Mortgage Product Substitution and State Predatory Lending Laws*, Presentation at the 2008 mid-year meeting of the American Real Estate and Urban Economics Association, Washington, D.C., May 27, 2008.

Figure 6.4 Geographic distribution of low-documentation loans, 2006

the refinancing boom, the private-label securitization industry grew significantly in capacity and profits.

But in 2003, rising interest rates ended the potential for refinancing of prime mortgages at ever lower interest rates, leading to an increased need for another source of mortgages to maintain and grow the rate of securitization and the fees it generated. The 'solution' adopted by mortgage originators and securitizers was to expand the mortgage market by increasing the offering of nontraditional mortgages, especially interest-only loans and option payment ARMs that allowed negative amortization (see Figure 6.1). This expansion of credit swept a larger portion of the population into the potential homeowner pool, driving up housing demand and prices, and consumer indebtedness. Consumer indebtedness grew so fast that, between 1975 and 2007, total household debt soared from around 43 per cent to nearly 100 per cent of gross domestic product (Board of Governors of the Federal Reserve System, Bureau of Economic Analysis).

Table 6.1 U.S. homeownership rates, by year

Period	U.S. Total, %	Non-Hispanic, %				Hispanic %
		White Alone	Black Alone	Other race alone	Two or more races	
1983	64.9	69.1	45.6	53.3	NA	41.2
1984	64.5	69	46	50.9	NA	40.1
1985	64.3	69	44.4	50.7	NA	41.1
1986	63.8	68.4	44.8	49.7	NA	40.6
1987	64	68.7	45.8	48.7	NA	40.6
1988	64	69.1	42.9	49.7	NA	40.6
1989	64	69.3	42.1	50.6	NA	41.6
1990	64.1	69.4	42.6	49.2	NA	41.2
1991	64	69.5	42.7	51.3	NA	39
1992	64.1	69.6	42.6	52.5	NA	39.9
1993	64.1	70.2	42	50.6	NA	39.4
1994	64	70	42.5	50.8	NA	41.2
1995	64.7	70.9	42.9	51.5	NA	42
1996	65.4	71.7	44.5	51.5	NA	42.8
1997	65.7	72	45.4	53.3	NA	43.3
1998	66.3	72.6	46.1	53.7	NA	44.7
1999	66.8	73.2	46.7	54.1	NA	45.5
2000	67.4	73.8	47.6	53.9	NA	46.3
2001	67.8	74.3	48.4	54.7	NA	47.3
2002	67.9	74.7	48.2	55	NA	47
2003	68.3	75.4	48.8	56.7	58	46.7
2004	69	76	49.7	59.6	60.4	48.1
2005	68.9	75.8	48.8	60.4	59.8	49.5
2006	68.8	75.8	48.4	61.1	59.9	49.7
2007	68.1	75.2	47.8	60.3	59	49.7

Source: U.S. Census Bureau.

The growth in nonprime mortgages was accomplished through market expansion of nontraditional mortgages and by qualifying more borrowing through easing of traditional lending terms. For example, while subprime mortgages were initially made as 'hard money' loans with low loan-to-value ratios, by the height of their growth, combined loan-to-value ratios exceeded those in the far safer prime market (see Figure 6.3). While the demand for riskier mortgages grew fueled by the need for product to securitize, the potential risk due to deteriorating lending standards also grew.

Consumer Confusion

If borrowers had been able to distinguish safe loans from highly risky loans, risky loans would not have crowded out the market. But numerous borrowers were not able to do so, for three reasons. First, hybrid subprime ARMs, interest-only mortgages, and option payment ARMs were baffling in their complexity. Second, it was impossible to obtain binding price quotes early enough to permit meaningful comparison shopping in the nonprime market. Finally, borrowers usually did not know that mortgage brokers got higher compensation for steering them into risky loans.

Hidden risks

The arcane nature of hybrid ARMs, interest-only loans, and option payment ARMs often made informed consumer choice impossible. These products were highly complex instruments that presented an assortment of hidden risks to borrowers. Chief among those risks was payment shock – in other words, the risk that monthly payments would rise dramatically upon rate reset. These products presented greater potential payment shock than conventional ARMs, which had lower reset rates and manageable lifetime caps. Indeed, with these exotic ARMs, the only way interest rates could go *was* up. Many late vintage subprime hybrid ARMs had initial rate resets of three percentage points, resulting in increased monthly payments of 50 per cent to 100 per cent or more (Bair (2008)).

For a borrower to grasp the potential payment shock on a hybrid, interest-only, or option payment ARM, he or she would need to understand all the moving parts of the mortgage, including the index, rate spread, initial rate cap, and lifetime rate cap. On top of that, the borrower would need to predict future interest rate movements and translate expected rate changes into changes in monthly payments. Interest-only ARMs and option payment ARMs had the added complication of potential deferred or negative amortization, which could cause the principal payments to grow. Finally, these loans were more likely to carry large prepayment penalties. To understand the effect of such a prepayment penalty, the borrower would have to use a formula to compute the penalty's size and then assess the likelihood of moving or refinancing during the penalty period (Federal Reserve System (2008a), p. 1674; Federal Reserve System (2008b), pp. 44524–25). Truth-in-Lending Act disclosures did not require easy-to-understand disclosures about any of these risks (McCoy (2007)).

Inability to do meaningful comparison shopping

The lack of binding rate quotes also hindered informed comparison-shopping in the nonprime market. Nonprime loans had many rates, not one, which varied according to the borrower's risk, the originator's compensation, the documentation level of the loan, and the naïveté of the borrower. Between their complicated price structure and the wide variety of products, subprime loans were not standardized. Furthermore, it was impossible to obtain a binding price quote in the subprime market before submitting a loan application and paying a non-refundable fee. Rate locks were also a rarity in the subprime market. In too many cases, subprime lenders waited until the closing to unveil the true product and price for the loan, a practice that the Truth in Lending Act rules countenanced. These rules, promulgated by the Federal Reserve Board, helped foster rampant 'bait-and-switch' schemes in the subprime market (Federal Reserve System (2008a), p. 1675; McCoy (2007)).

As a result, deceptive advertising became the stock-in-trade of the nonprime market. Nonprime lenders and brokers did not advertise their prices to permit meaningful comparison-shopping. To the contrary, lenders treated their rate sheets – which listed their price points and pricing criteria – as proprietary secrets that were not to be disclosed to the mass consumer market. Subprime advertisements generally focused on fast approval and low initial monthly payments or interest rates, not on accurate prices.

While the Federal Reserve exhorted people to comparison-shop for nonprime loans (Board of Governors of the Federal Reserve System (2009)), in reality, comparison-shopping was futile. Nonprime lenders did not post prices, did not provide consumers with firm price quotes, and did not offer lock-in commitments as a general rule. Anyone who attempted to comparison-shop often had to pay multiple application fees for the privilege and, even then, might not learn the actual price until the closing if the lender engaged in a bait-and-switch.

As early as 1998, the Federal Reserve Board and the Department of Housing and Urban Development were aware that nonprime mortgage lenders did not provide Truth in Lending Act disclosures early enough in the application process to allow meaningful comparison shopping. That year, the two agencies issued a report diagnosing the problem. In the report, HUD recommended changes to the Truth in Lending Act to require mortgage originators to provide binding price quotes before taking loan applications. The Federal Reserve Board dissented from the proposal, however, and it was never adopted (Board of Governors of the Federal Reserve System and Department of Housing and Urban Development (1998), pp. 28–29, 39–42). To this day, the Board has still not revamped Truth in Lending disclosures for closed-end mortgages.

Perverse fee incentives
Finally, many consumers were not aware that the compensation structure rewarded mortgage brokers for riskier loan products and higher interest rates. Mortgage brokers only got paid if they closed a loan. Furthermore, they were paid solely through upfront fees at closing, meaning that if a loan defaulted, the losses would fall on the lender or investors, not the broker. In the most pernicious practice, lenders paid brokers thousands of dollars per loan in fees known as yield spread premiums (or YSPs) in exchange for loans saddling borrowers with steep prepayment penalties and higher interest rates than the borrowers qualified for, based on their incomes and credit scores.

In sum, these three features – the ability to hide risk, thwart meaningful comparison-shopping, and reward steering – allowed lenders to entice unsuspecting borrowers into needlessly hazardous loans.

The Crowd-out Effect

The ability to bury risky product features in fine print allowed irresponsible lenders to out-compete safe lenders. Low initial monthly payments were the most visible feature of hybrid ARMs, interest-only loans, and option payment ARMs. During the housing boom, lenders commonly touted these products based on low initial monthly payments while obscuring the back-end risks of those loans (Haviv and Kaiser (2007); Reckard (2007)).

The ability to hide risks made it easy to out-compete lenders who offered fixed-rate, fully amortizing loans. Other things being equal, the initial monthly payments on exotic ARMs were lower than on fixed-rate, amortizing loans. Furthermore, some nonprime lenders qualified borrowers solely at the low initial rate alone until the Federal Reserve Board finally banned that practice in July 2008.[6]

Of course, many sophisticated customers recognized the dangers of these loans. That did not deter lenders from offering hazardous nontraditional ARMs, however. Instead, the 'one-size-fits-one' nature of nonprime loans permitted lenders to discriminate by selling safer products to discerning customers and more lucrative, dangerous products to naïve customers. Sadly, the consumers who were least well equipped in terms of experience and education to grasp arcane loan terms ended up with the most dangerous loans (Lax et al. (2004), pp. 552–54).

In the meantime, lenders who offered safe products – such as fixed-rate prime loans – lost market share to lenders who peddled exotic ARMs with low starting payments. As conventional lenders came to realize that it didn't pay to compete by offering good products, those lenders expanded into the nonprime market as well.

THE REGULATORY STORY: RACE TO THE BOTTOM

Federal banking regulators added fuel to the fire by allowing reckless loans to flourish. It is a basic tenet of banking law that banks should not extend credit without satisfactory evidence of their borrowers' ability to repay. Federal banking regulators[7] had ample authority to enforce this tenet through safety and soundness supervision and vigorous consumer protection. Nevertheless, they refused to exercise their substantial powers of rule-making, formal enforcement, and sanctions to crack down on the proliferation of poorly underwritten loans until it was too late. Their abdication allowed irresponsible loans to multiply. Furthermore, their green light to banks to invest in investment-grade subprime mortgage-backed securities and CDOs left the nation's largest banks heavily burdened with toxic assets. These problems were a direct result of the country's fragmented system of financial regulation, which caused regulators to compete for turf.

The Fragmented US System of Mortgage Regulation

In the United States, the home mortgage lending industry operates under a fragmented regulatory structure which varies according to entity (McCoy and Renuart (2008)). Banks and thrift institutions are regulated under federal banking laws and a subset of those institutions – namely, national banks, federal savings associations, and their subsidiaries – are exempt from state anti-predatory lending and credit laws by virtue of federal preemption. In contrast, mortgage brokers and independent non-depository mortgage lenders escape federal banking regulation but have to comply with all state laws in effect. Only state-chartered banks and thrifts in some states (a dwindling group) are subject to both sets of laws.

Under this dual system of regulation, depository institutions are subject to a variety of federal examinations, including fair lending, Community Reinvestment Act, and safety and soundness examinations, but independent nondepository lenders are not. Similarly, banks and thrifts must comply with other provisions of the Community Reinvestment Act, including reporting requirements and merger review. Federally insured depository institutions must also meet minimum risk-based capital requirements and reserve requirements, unlike their independent non-depository counterparts.

Some federal laws applied to all mortgage originators. Otherwise, lenders could change their charter and form to shop for the friendliest regulatory scheme.

Applicable Law

Despite these differences in regulatory regimes, the Federal Reserve Board did have the power to prohibit reckless mortgages across the entire mortgage industry. The Board had this power by virtue of its authority to administer a federal anti-predatory lending law known as 'HOEPA'.

Federal Law

Following deregulation of home mortgages in the early 1980s, disclosure became the most important type of federal mortgage regulation. The federal Truth in Lending Act (TILA), passed in 1968 (15 U.S.C. §§ 1601–1693r), mandates uniform disclosures regarding cost for home loans. Its companion law, the federal Real Estate Settlement Procedures Act of 1974 or RESPA (12 U.S.C. §§ 2601–2617), requires similar standardized disclosures for settlement costs. Congress charged the Federal Reserve with administering TILA and the Department of Housing and Urban Development with administering RESPA.

In 1994, Congress augmented TILA and RESPA by enacting the Home Ownership and Equity Protection Act (HOEPA) (15 U.S.C. §§ 1601, 1602(aa), 1639(a)–(b)). HOEPA was an early federal anti-predatory lending law and prohibits specific abuses in the subprime mortgage market. HOEPA applies to all residential mortgage lenders and mortgage brokers, regardless of the type of entity.

HOEPA has two key provisions. The first is HOEPA's high-cost loan provision, which regulates the high-cost refinance market (15 U.S.C. § 1602(aa)(1)–(4); 12 C.F.R. § 226.32(a)(1), (b)(1)). This provision seeks to eliminate abuses consisting of 'equity stripping'. It is hobbled, however, by its extremely limited reach – covering only the most exorbitant subprime mortgages – and its inapplicability to home purchase loans, reverse mortgages, and open-end home equity lines of credit (15 U.S.C. § 1602(i), (w), (bb); 12 C.F.R. § 226.32(a)(2); Gramlich (2007b), p. 28). Lenders learned to evade the high-cost loan provisions rather easily by slightly lowering the interest rates and fees on subprime loans below HOEPA's thresholds and by expanding into subprime purchase loans.

HOEPA also has a second major provision, which gives the Federal Reserve Board the authority (1) to prohibit unfair or deceptive practices in connection with mortgage loans and (2) to bar practices that are abusive or against the interest of the borrower in connection with the refinancing of mortgage loans (15 U.S.C. § 1639(*l*)(2)). This provision is potentially broader than the high-cost loan provision because it allows regulation of both the mortgage lending and refinancing markets, without regard to interest rates or fees. However, the second provision is not self-activating. Instead, it depended on action by the Federal Reserve Board to implement the provision, a step which the Board did not take until July 2008.

State Law

Before 2008, only the high-cost loan provision of HOEPA was in effect as a practical matter. That provision had a serious Achilles heel, consisting of its narrow coverage. Even though the Federal Reserve Board lowered the high-cost triggers of HOEPA effective in 2002, the provision still only applied to 1 per cent of all subprime home loans (Gramlich (2007b), p. 28).

After 1994, it increasingly became evident that HOEPA was incapable of halting subprime abuses. By the late 1990s, some cities and states were already contending with rising foreclosures and some jurisdictions were contemplating regulating subprime loans on their own. Many states already had older statutes on the books regulating prepayment penalties and occasionally balloon clauses. These laws were relatively narrow, however, and did not address other types of new abuses that were surfacing in subprime loans.

Consequently, in 1999, North Carolina became the first state to enact a comprehensive anti-predatory lending law (N.C. GEN STAT. § 24–1.1E (2000)). Soon, other states followed suit and passed anti-predatory lending laws of their own. These newer state laws implemented HOEPA's basic design but frequently expanded coverage or imposed stricter regulation on subprime loans. By year-end 2005, 29 states and the District of Columbia had enacted one of these mini-HOEPA laws. Some states also passed stricter disclosure laws or laws regulating mortgage brokers. By the end of 2005, only six states – Arizona, Delaware, Montana, North Dakota, Oregon, and South Dakota – lacked laws regulating prepayment penalties, balloon clauses, or mandatory arbitration clauses, all of which were associated with exploitative subprime loans (Bostic et al. (2008)).

Critics, including some federal banking regulators, have blamed the states for igniting the credit crisis through lax regulation. Certainly, there were states in which mortgage lending was largely unregulated, and there were other states where mortgage regulation was weak. Mortgage brokers were loosely regulated in too many states. Similarly, the states never agreed on an effective, uniform system of mortgage regulation.

Nevertheless, this criticism of the states disregards the hard-fought efforts by a growing number of states – which eventually grew to include the majority of states – to regulate abusive subprime loans within their borders. During this period, state attorneys general and state banking commissioners spearheaded some of the most important enforcement actions against deceptive mortgage lenders.[8]

The Ability to Shop for Hospitable Laws and Regulators

State-chartered banks and thrifts and their subsidiaries had to comply with the state anti-predatory lending laws. So did independent nonbank lenders and mortgage brokers. For the better part of the housing boom, however, national banks, federal savings associations, and their mortgage lending subsidiaries did not have to comply with those state laws due to federal preemption rulings by their federal regulators. This became a problem because federal regulators did not replace the preempted state laws with strong federal underwriting rules.

Federal Preemption

The states that enacted anti-predatory lending laws did not legislate in a vacuum. In 1996, the federal regulator for thrift institutions – the Office of Thrift Supervision or OTS – promulgated a sweeping preemption rule declaring that henceforth federal savings associations and their operating subsidiaries did not have to observe state lending laws (12 C.F.R. §§ 559.3(h), 560.2). Initially, this rule had little practical effect because the subprime market was small and any state anti-predatory lending provisions on the books back then were fairly narrow (Bostic et al. (2008); Office of Thrift Supervision (2000), pp. 17814–16).

Following adoption of the OTS preemption rule, federal thrift institutions and their subsidiaries were relieved from having to comply with state consumer protection laws. That was not true, however, for national banks, state banks, state thrifts, and independent nonbank mortgage lenders and brokers.

The stakes rose considerably starting in 1999, when North Carolina passed the first comprehensive state anti-predatory lending law. As state mini-HOEPA laws proliferated, national banks lobbied their regulator – a federal agency known as the Office of the Comptroller of the Currency or OCC – to clothe them with the same federal preemption as federal savings associations. They succeeded and, in 2004, the OCC issued its own preemption rule banning the states from enforcing their laws impinging on real estate lending by national banks and their operating subsidiaries[9] (12 C.F.R. §§ 7.4000, 7.4007–7.4009, 34.4). In a companion 'visitorial powers' rule, the OCC denied permission to the states to enforce their own laws that were *not* federally preempted – state lending discrimination laws are one example – against national banks and their subsidiaries. After a protracted court battle, the controversy ended up in the US Supreme Court, which upheld the OCC preemption rule[10] (*Watters v. Wachovia Bank, N.A.*, 550 U.S. 1 (2007); Wilmarth (2004)).

OTS and the OCC had institutional motives to grant federal preemption to the institutions that they regulated. Both agencies depend almost exclusively on fees from their regulated entities for their operating budgets. Both were also eager to persuade state-chartered depository institutions to convert to a federal charter. In addition, the OCC was aware that if national banks wanted federal preemption badly enough, they might defect to the thrift charter to get it. Thus, the OCC had reason to placate national banks to keep them in its fold. Similarly, the OTS was concerned about the steady decline in thrift institutions. Federal preemption provided an inducement to thrift institutions to retain the federal savings association charter.

The Ability to Shop for the Most Permissive Laws

By 2004, as a result of federal preemption, state anti-predatory lending laws applied to state-chartered depository institutions and independent nonbank lenders, but not to national banks, federal savings associations, or their mortgage lending subsidiaries. The only anti-predatory lending provisions that national banks and federally chartered thrifts had to obey were HOEPA and agency pronouncements of 'guidance' on subprime and nontraditional mortgage loans[11] (Board of Governors of the Federal Reserve System et al. (1999); Office of the Comptroller of the Currency (2000); Office of the Comptroller of the Currency et al. (2001); Office of the Comptroller of the Currency (2003a); Office of the Comptroller of the Currency (2003b); Office of the Comptroller of the Currency (2005); Department of the Treasury et al. (2006); Department of the Treasury et al. (2007)). Of these, HOEPA had extremely narrow scope. Meanwhile, agency guidances lacked the binding effect of rules and their content was not as strict as the stronger state laws.

This dual regulatory system allowed mortgage lenders to play regulators off one another by threatening to change charters. Mortgage lenders are free to operate with or without depository institution charters. Similarly, depository institutions can choose between a state and federal charter and between a thrift charter and a commercial bank charter. Each of these choices allows a lender to switch regulators.

A lender could escape a strict state law by switching to a federal bank or thrift charter or by shifting its operations to a less regulated state.

Similarly, a lender could escape a strict regulator by converting its charter to one with a more accommodating regulator.

Countrywide, the nation's largest mortgage lender and a major subprime presence, took advantage of this system to change its regulator. One of its subsidiaries, Countrywide Home Loans, was supervised by the Federal Reserve. This subsidiary switched and became an OTS-regulated entity as of March 2007. That same month, Countrywide Bank, N.A., ditched its national bank charter, under OCC supervision, and switched to a federal thrift charter, under OTS supervision. Reportedly, OTS promised Countrywide's executives to be a 'less antagonistic' regulator if Countrywide switched charters to OTS. Six months later, the regional deputy director of the OTS West Region, where Countrywide was headquartered, was promoted to division director. Some observers considered it a reward (Appelbaum and Nakashima (2008); Schmitt (2008)).

The result was a system in which lenders could shop for the loosest laws and enforcement. This shopping process put pressure on regulators at all levels – state and local – to lower their standards or relax enforcement. What ensued was a regulatory race to the bottom.

REGULATORY FAILURE

Federal preemption would not have been such a problem if federal banking regulators had replaced state laws with tough rules and enforcement of their own. Those regulators had ample power to stop the deterioration in mortgage underwriting standards that mushroomed into a full-blown crisis. However, they refused to intervene in disastrous lending practices until it was too late. As a result, federally regulated lenders – as well as all lenders operating in states with weak regulation – were given *carte blanche* to loosen their lending standards free from meaningful regulatory intervention.

The Federal Reserve Board

The Federal Reserve Board had the statutory power, starting in 1994, to curb lax lending not only for depository institutions, but for all lenders across-the-board. It declined to exercise that power in any meaningful respect, however, until after the nonprime mortgage market collapsed.

In the mortgage lending area, the Fed's supervisory process has three major parts, with breakdowns apparent in two out of the three. The only part that appeared to work well was the Fed's role as the primary federal regulator for state-chartered banks that are members of the Federal Reserve System.[12]

As the second part of its supervisory duties, the Fed regulates nonbank mortgage lenders owned by bank holding companies but not owned directly or indirectly by banks or thrifts. During the housing boom, some of the largest subprime and Alt-A lenders were regulated by the Fed, including the top- and third-ranked subprime lenders in 2006, HSBC Finance and Countrywide Financial Corporation. The Fed also regulated Wells Fargo Financial, Inc. The Fed's supervisory record with regard to these lenders was mixed. On one notable occasion, in 2004, the Fed levied a $70 million civil money penalty against CitiFinancial Credit Company and its parent holding company, Citigroup Inc., for subprime lending abuses (Board of Governors of the Federal Reserve System (2004)). Apart from that order, the Fed did not take public enforcement action against the nonbank lenders that it regulated. That may be because the Federal Reserve did not routinely examine the nonbank mortgage lending subsidiaries under its supervision, which the late Federal Reserve Board Governor Edward Gramlich revealed shortly before his death in 2007. Only then did the Fed kick off a 'pilot project' to do routine examinations of the nonbank lenders under its jurisdiction for loose underwriting and compliance with federal consumer protection laws (Gramlich (2007a), pp. 8–9; Kroszner (2007)).

Finally, the Board is responsible for administering most federal consumer credit protection laws, including HOEPA. When former Governor Edward Gramlich served on the Fed, he urged then-Chairman Alan Greenspan to exercise the Fed's power to address unfair and deceptive loans under HOEPA. Greenspan refused, preferring instead to rely on non-binding statements and guidances[13] (US House of Representatives (2008), pp. 35, 37–38). This reliance on statements and guidances had two disadvantages: one, major lenders routinely dismissed the guidances as mere 'suggestions' and, two, guidances did not apply to independent nonbank mortgage lenders.

The Federal Reserve did not relent until July 2008, when, under Chairman Ben Bernanke's leadership, it finally promulgated binding HOEPA regulations banning specific types of unsound and abusive mortgage loans. Even then, the regulations were mostly limited to higher-priced mortgages, which the Board defined as mortgages with interest rates that exceed the average prime offer rate for comparable transactions by 1.5 percentage points or more for first-lien loans or by 3.5 percentage points or more for second-lien loans. Although shoddy nontraditional mortgages below those rate triggers had also contributed to the credit crisis, the Federal Reserve's new HOEPA rules left those loans – plus prime loans – mostly untouched[14] (Federal Reserve System (2008b), p. 44536). The rules, while badly needed, were too little and too late.

In the home mortgage area, the Board similarly abdicated its responsibility to keep Truth-in-Lending Act disclosures abreast of market developments. The last time the Board did a major overhaul of the TILA rules for closed-end mortgages was in *1981*. These TILA disclosures worked tolerably well under the old market conditions featuring fixed-rate mortgages. In the 1990s, however, the market changed with the introduction of risk-based pricing. By that time, the Fed's sorely outdated Truth-in-Lending Act disclosures were not equipped to produce accurate, timely disclosures for subprime loans and exotic adjustable-rate mortgages.[15] Nevertheless, the Fed dragged its feet on issuing new rules. It did not get around to issuing a narrow new rule under TILA on bait-and-switch tactics and payment shock disclosures until 30 July 2008, and when it did, Congress immediately passed legislation declaring the rule insufficient[16] (compare Federal Reserve System (2008b) with Mortgage Disclosure Improvement Act of 2008 (MDIA)). As for comprehensive reform, the Board did not even initiate a full review of its TILA rules for closed-end mortgages until 2007. It finally proposed revisions to those rules in August 2009[17] (Federal Reserve System (2009)).

On 23 October 2008, in testimony before the US House of Representatives Oversight Committee, former Chairman Greenspan admitted that 'those of us who have looked to the self-interest of lending institutions to protect shareholder's equity (myself especially) are in a state of shocked disbelief'. House Oversight Committee Chairman Henry Waxman asked Greenspan whether 'your ideology pushed you to make decisions that you wish you had not made?' Greenspan replied (US House of Representatives (2008), pp. 36–37):

> Mr. GREENSPAN. . . . [Y]es, I found a flaw, I don't know how significant or permanent it is, but I have been very distressed by that fact. . . .
> Chairman WAXMAN. You found a flaw?
> Mr. GREENSPAN. I found a flaw in the model that defines how the world works, so to speak.
> Chairman WAXMAN. In other words, you found that your view of the world, your ideology, was not right, it was not working.
> Mr. GREENSPAN. Precisely. That's precisely the reason I was shocked, because I had been going for 40 years or more with very considerable evidence that it was working exceptionally well.

(Greenspan (2008)).

Regulatory Lapses by the OTS and the OCC

Federal preemption might not have devolved into a crisis of systemic proportions if the OTS and the OCC had replaced state regulation for their regulated entities with a comprehensive set of binding rules prohibiting lax underwriting of home mortgages. But they did not. In lieu of binding rules, federal banking regulators, including the OTS and the OCC, issued a series of 'soft law' advisory letters and guidelines against predatory or unfair mortgage lending practices by insured depository institutions. Federal regulators disavowed binding rules during the run-up to the subprime crisis on grounds that the guidelines were more flexible and that the agencies enforced those guidelines through bank examinations and informal enforcement actions (Office of the Comptroller of the Currency (2004)). Informal enforcement actions were usually limited to negotiated, voluntary agreements between regulators and the entities that they supervised, which made it easy for management to drag out negotiations in order to soften any restrictions and gain more time for compliance. Furthermore, examinations and informal enforcement are highly confidential, making it easy for a lax regulator to hide its tracks.

The Office of Thrift Supervision

Although OTS was the first agency to adopt federal preemption, it managed to fly under the radar during the subprime boom, overshadowed by its larger sister agency, the OCC. After 2003, while commentators were busy berating the OCC preemption rule, OTS allowed the largest federal savings associations to embark on an aggressive campaign of expansion through option payment ARMs, subprime loans, and low-documentation and no-documentation loans.

Autopsies of failed depository institutions in 2007 and 2008 show that five of the seven biggest failures were OTS-regulated thrifts. Two other enormous thrifts during that period – Wachovia Mortgage, FSB and Countrywide Bank, FSB – were forced to agree to hasty takeovers by large bank holding companies to avoid failing. By 31 December 2008, thrifts totaling $355 billion in assets had failed in the previous 16 months on OTS' watch.

The reasons for the collapse of these thrifts evince fundamental regulatory lapses by OTS. Almost all of the thrifts that failed in 2007 and 2008 – and all of the larger ones – succumbed to massive levels of imprudent home loans. IndyMac Bank, FSB, which became the first major thrift institution to fail during the current crisis, in July 2008, manufactured its demise by becoming the nation's top originator of low- and no-documentation loans. These loans, which became known as 'liar's loans', infected both the subprime market and loans to borrowers with higher credit scores. By 2006 and 2007, over half of IndyMac's home purchase loans were subprime loans and IndyMac Bank approved up to half of those loans based on low or no documentation.

Washington Mutual Bank, popularly known as 'WaMu', was the nation's largest thrift institution in 2008, with over $300 billion in assets. WaMu became the biggest US depository institution in history to fail on 25 September 2008, in the wake of the Lehman Brothers bankruptcy. WaMu was so large that OTS examiners were stationed there permanently onsite. Nevertheless, from 2004 through 2006, despite the daily presence of the resident OTS inspectors, risky option ARMs, second mortgages, and subprime loans constituted over half of WaMu's real estate loans annually. By 30 June 2008, over one-fourth of the subprime loans that WaMu originated in 2006 and 2007 were at least 30 days past due. Eventually, it came to light that WaMu's management had pressured its loan underwriters relentlessly to approve more and more exceptions to WaMu's underwriting standards in order to increase its fee revenue from loans (Goodman and Morgenson (2008)).

Downey Savings & Loan became the third largest depository institution to fail in 2008. Like WaMu, Downey had loaded up on option ARMs and subprime loans. By the time OTS finally had to put Downey into receivership, over half of Downey's total assets consisted of option ARMs and non-performing loans accounted for over 15 per cent of the thrift's total assets.

In short, the three largest depository institution failures in 2007 and 2008 resulted from high concentrations of poorly underwritten loans, including low- and no-documentation ARMs (in the case of IndyMac) and option ARMs (in the case of WaMu and Downey) that were often only underwritten to the introductory rate instead of the fully indexed rate. During the housing bubble, OTS issued no binding rules to halt the proliferation by its largest regulated thrifts of option ARMs, subprime loans, and low- and no-documentation mortgages. Instead, OTS relied on oversight through guidances. IndyMac, WaMu, and Downey treated the guidances as optional, however, as evidenced by the fact that all three made substantial numbers of hazardous loans in late 2006 and in 2007 in direct disregard of an interagency guidance on nontraditional mortgages issued in the fall of 2006 and subscribed to by OTS that prescribed underwriting ARMs to the fully indexed rate (Department of the Treasury et al. (2006)).

The fact that all three institutions continued to make loans in violation of the guidance suggests that OTS examinations failed to result in enforcement of the guidance. Similarly, OTS fact sheets on the failures of all three institutions show that the agency consistently declined to institute timely formal enforcement proceedings against those thrifts in order to stop the lending practices that resulted in their demise. In sum, OTS supervision of residential mortgage risks was confined to 'light touch' regulation in the form of examinations, non-binding guidances, and occasional informal agreements that did not work.

The Office of the Comptroller of the Currency

The OCC has asserted that national banks made only 10 per cent of subprime loans in 2006. (Dugan (2008)). But this assertion fails to mention that national banks moved aggressively into Alt-A low-documentation and no-documentation loans during the housing boom. This mattered a lot, because the biggest national banks are now considered 'too big to fail' and pose systemic risk on a scale unmatched by independent nonbank lenders. We might not be calling Citibank and Bank of America 'zombie banks' today had the OCC stopped them from expanding into toxic mortgages, bonds, and structured investment vehicles.

Like OTS, 'light touch' regulation was apparent at the OCC. Unlike OTS, the OCC did promulgate one rule, in 2004, prohibiting mortgages to borrowers who could not afford to repay. However, the rule was vague in design and execution, allowing lax lending to proliferate at national banks and their mortgage lending subsidiaries through 2007.

Despite the 2004 rule, through 2007, large national banks continued to make large quantities of poorly underwritten subprime loans and low- and no-documentation loans. In 2006, for example, fully 62.6 per cent of the first-lien home purchase mortgages made by National City Bank, N.A., and its subsidiary, First Franklin Mortgage, were higher-priced subprime loans. Starting in the third quarter of 2007, National City Corporation reported five straight quarters of net losses, largely due to those subprime loans. Just as with WaMu, the Lehman Brothers bankruptcy ignited a silent run by depositors and pushed National City Bank to the brink of collapse. Only a shotgun marriage with PNC Financial Services Group in October 2008 saved the bank from FDIC receivership.

The five largest US banks in 2005 were all national banks and too big to fail. They made heavy inroads into low- and no-documentation loans. The top-ranked Bank of America, N.A., had a thriving stated-income and no-documentation loan program which it only halted in August 2007, when the market for private-label mortgage-backed securities dried up. Bank of America securitized most of those loans, which may be why the OCC tolerated such lax underwriting practices.

Similarly, in 2006, the OCC overrode public protests about a 'substantial volume' of no-documentation loans by JP Morgan Chase Bank, N.A., the second largest bank in 2005, on grounds that the bank had adequate 'checks and balances' in place to manage those loans.

Citibank, N.A., was the third largest US bank in 2005. In September 2007, the OCC approved Citibank's purchase of the disreputable subprime lender Argent Mortgage, even though subprime securitizations had slowed to a trickle. Citibank thereupon announced to the press that its new subsidiary – christened 'Citi Residential Lending' – would specialize in nonprime loans, including reduced documentation loans. But not long after, in early May 2008 after Bear Stearns had narrowly dodged failure, Citibank was forced to admit defeat and dismantle Citi Residential's lending operations.

The fourth largest US bank in 2005, Wachovia Bank, N.A., originated low- and no-documentation loans through its two mortgage subsidiaries. Wachovia Bank originated such large quantities of risky Alt-A loans that by the first half of 2007, Wachovia Bank was the twelfth largest Alt-A lender in the country. These loans performed so poorly that between 31 December 2006 and 30 September 2008, the bank's ratio of net write-offs on its closed-end home loans to its total outstanding loans jumped 2400 per cent. Concomitantly, the bank's parent company, Wachovia Corporation, reported its first quarterly loss in years due to rising defaults on option ARMs made by Wachovia Mortgage, FSB, and its Golden West predecessor. Public concern over Wachovia's loan losses triggered a silent run on Wachovia Bank in late September 2008, following Lehman Brothers' failure. To avoid receivership, the FDIC brokered a hasty sale of Wachovia to Wells Fargo after Wells Fargo outbid Citigroup for the privilege.

Wells Fargo Bank, N.A., was in better financial shape than Wachovia, but it too made large quantities of subprime and reduced documentation loans. In 2006, over 23 per cent of the bank's first-lien refinance mortgages were high-cost subprime loans. Wells Fargo Bank also securitized substantial numbers of low- and no-documentation mortgages in its Alt-A pools. In 2007, a Wells Fargo prospectus for one of those pools stated that Wells Fargo had relaxed its underwriting standards in mid-2005 and did not verify whether the mortgage brokers who had originated the weakest loans in that loan pool complied with its underwriting standards before closing. Not long after, as of 25 July 2008, 22.77 per cent of the loans in that loan pool were past due or in default.

As the Wells Fargo story suggests, the OCC depended on voluntary risk management by national banks, not regulation of loan terms and practices, to contain the risk of improvident loans. A speech by the then-Acting Comptroller, Julie Williams, confirmed as much. In 2005, Comptroller Williams, in a speech to risk managers at banks, coached them on how to 'manage' the risks of no-documentation loans through debt collection, higher reserves, and prompt loss recognition. Securitization was another risk management device favored by the OCC.

Three years later, in 2008, the Treasury Department's Inspector General issued a report that was critical of the OCC's supervision of risky loans (Office of Inspector General (2008)). Among other things, the Inspector General criticized the OCC for not instituting formal enforcement actions while lending problems were still manageable in size. In his written response to the Inspector General, the Comptroller, John Dugan, conceded that 'there were shortcomings in our execution of our supervisory process' and ordered OCC examiners to start initiating formal enforcement actions on a timely basis (ibid).

The OCC's record of supervision and enforcement during the subprime boom reveals many of the same problems that culminated in regulatory failure by OTS. Like OTS, the OCC usually shunned formal enforcement actions in favor of examinations and informal enforcement. Neither of these supervisory tools obtained compliance with the OCC's 2004 rule prohibiting loans to borrowers who could not repay. Although the OCC supplemented that rule later on with more detailed guidances, some of the largest national banks and their subsidiaries apparently decided that they could ignore the guidances, judging from their lax lending in late 2006 and in 2007. The OCC's emphasis on managing credit risk through securitization, reserves, and loss recognition, instead of through product regulation, likely encouraged that *laissez faire* attitude by national banks.

Judging by the Results: Loan Performance by Charter

OCC and OTS regulators have argued that their agencies offer 'comprehensive' supervision resulting in lower default rates on residential mortgages. The evidence shows otherwise.

Data from the Federal Deposit Insurance Corporation show that among depository institutions, federal thrift institutions had the worst default rate for one-to-four family residential mortgages from 2006 through 2008 (see Figure 6.5).

The second-worst performance record among depository institution lenders went to national banks. State thrifts had better default rates than either type of federally chartered institution in 2007 and 2008. State banks consistently had the lowest default rates of all.

Among these charter types, the only ones that enjoy federal preemption are national banks regulated by the OCC and federal thrift institutions regulated by the OTS. State banks and state thrift institutions do not. Thus it appears, at least among depository institutions, that federal preemption was associated with *higher* default rates, not lower rates, during 2006 through 2008, when credit standards hit bottom and the mortgage market imploded.

These data do not address whether independent nonbank lenders have

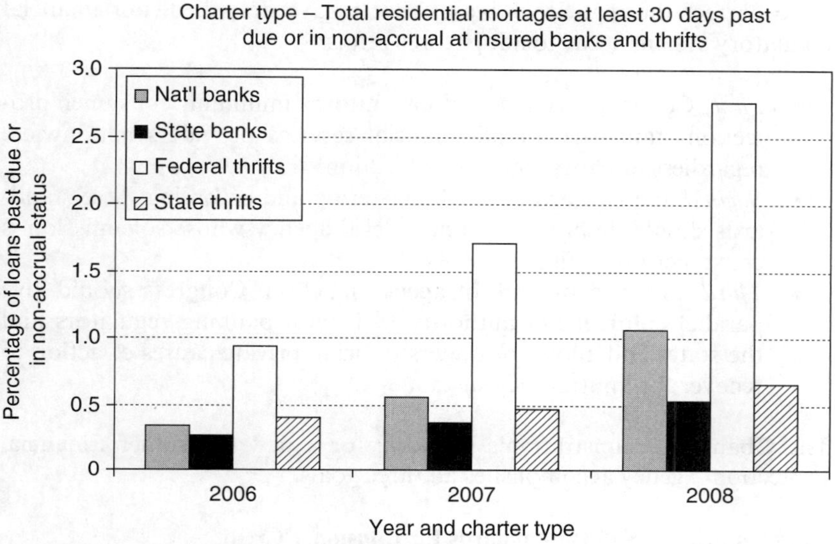

Source: FDIC statistics on depository institutions.

Figure 6.5 Total performance of residential mortgages by depository institution lenders

even higher default rates in some states. That in fact may be the case. Nevertheless, the data undercut the assertion that federal preemption reduces default rates among mortgages by depository institution lenders. To the contrary, the lowest default rates were at state banks and thrifts, which are subject both to state and federal regulation and do not enjoy preemption.

WHAT TO DO

Dual regulation and the resulting crazy quilt of laws encouraged lenders to shop for the lightest rules. In turn, this pressured regulators to weaken their standards and to relax enforcement of safety and soundness and consumer protection laws.

Casting underwriting standards to the wind in a seemingly obscure corner of the consumer credit market ended up triggering a global recession. This crisis shows that the United States ignores consumer protection at its peril. If it was not clear before, we now know that systemic stability and consumer protection are inextricably linked.

To correct the regulatory lapses that I have described, our financial regulatory system needs to adopt three reforms:

- *First*, Congress needs to adopt uniform minimum consumer protection standards for all financial services providers nationwide, regardless of entity, charter or location.
- *Second*, the authority for administering and enforcing these standards should be housed in one federal agency whose sole mission is consumer protection.
- *Third*, to avoid the risk of agency inaction, Congress should give parallel enforcement authority to federal banking regulators and the states and allow consumers to bring private causes of action to recover for injuries they sustain.

The Obama Administration's proposal for a new Consumer Financial Protection Agency accomplishes all three goals.

Uniform Federal Safety Standards for Consumer Credit

The downward spiral in underwriting standards drove home the need for uniform consumer protection standards that apply to all financial services providers. Adopting a uniform federal floor would prevent lenders, brokers and other financial providers from seeking safe haven in legal regimes that do little to protect consumers.

The Obama Administration's proposed Consumer Financial Protection Agency Act of 2009 ('the Act') would solve this problem by creating one set of uniform federal laws that apply to all financial services providers across the country, regardless of entity, charter, or geographic location (Department of the Treasury (2009)). To prevent regulators from competing to relax the interpretation of those laws, furthermore, the Act consolidates the authority to administer those laws in one agency. That agency is the new Consumer Financial Protection Agency ('Agency').

The Act would give the Agency jurisdiction over the following types of consumer financial protection laws and apply almost all of these laws to all financial services providers:

- *Unfair practices*: First, in Section 1031 of the Administration's bill, the Agency would have authority to define and prevent unfair or deceptive acts and practices in consumer financial services. While federal banking regulators have this power, they resisted using it until far too late, after the mortgage market melted down. Section 1031 also represents an improvement over the high-cost loan provisions in HOEPA, which proved too narrow and rigid and failed to address new abuses as they appeared in the mortgage market.

- *Deceptive marketing*: Second, Section 1033 of the bill would authorize the Agency to write rules banning unfair sales practices in consumer financial services. The bill delegates this responsibility to the Agency, due in part to evidence that the Federal Reserve Board was slow to crack down on deceptive marketing practices during the housing bubble. A related provision, Section 1037, would allow the Agency to prescribe the duties of front-line personnel such as loan officers or brokers who deal directly with consumers when selling consumer financial products and to assure that their compensation methods do not undermine those duties.
- *Transparency and disclosure*: Third, Section 1032 would empower the Agency to adopt rules mandating better consumer disclosures. This and other sections of the bill direct the Agency to re-design disclosures based not on speculation, but on empirical tests using real consumers and pilot disclosure forms. The bill would transfer this responsibility to the Agency, in view of the Federal Reserve Board's protracted delay in revamping disclosures. The Agency would also be responsible for producing a badly needed combined TILA-RESPA mortgage disclosure form.
- *Safer loans*: Fourth, in the provision on standard consumer financial products found in Section 1036, the bill would allow the Agency to gently 'nudge' consumers toward safer financial products, such as fixed-rate mortgages, with easy-to-understand terms. Consumers would be offered a relatively safe, plain-vanilla product first. This would make it easier for consumers to comparison shop and help them avoid 'snow jobs' by standardizing the terms of safer products and bringing those products front and center to consumers' attention. At the same time, consumers would remain free to choose different products with other features subject to warnings or other safeguards.
- *Existing consumer financial protection laws*: Finally, the bill would transfer the authority to administer other existing federal consumer financial protection laws to the Agency. These laws would include the Truth in Lending Act, HOEPA, the Real Estate Settlement and Procedures Act, the Fair Credit Reporting Act, the Fair Debt Collection Practices Act, the Equal Credit Opportunity Act, the Fair Credit Billing Act, and the Home Mortgage Disclosure Act.[18]

A Dedicated Federal Agency Whose Sole Mission is Consumer Protection

Federal regulators cannot serve two masters

The housing bubble and hazardous mortgages by federally regulated depository institutions show that we cannot expect consumer protection to be paramount to federal banking regulators. Recent history has shown that the safety and soundness mandate of federal banking regulators regularly eclipses concern for consumer protection. For this reason, the consumer protection function needs to be removed from federal banking regulators and housed in its own agency whose sole mission is consumer protection.

The bank regulatory agencies' own mission statements make it clear that consumer protection is a low priority. For example, the Federal Reserve Board divides its duties into four general areas (Federal Reserve System (2005), p. 1):

- conducting the nation's monetary policy by influencing the monetary and credit conditions in the economy in pursuit of maximum employment, stable prices, and moderate long-term interest rates
- supervising and regulating banking institutions to ensure the safety and soundness of the nation's banking and financial system and to protect the credit rights of consumers
- maintaining the stability of the financial system and containing systemic risk that may arise in financial markets
- providing financial services to depository institutions, the US government, and foreign official institutions, including playing a major role in operating the nation's payments system.

In the Fed's description, monetary policy comes first, followed by banking supervision. Consumer protection does not even merit its own separate bullet point.

Similarly, safety and soundness regulation is the paramount mission of the OCC and OTS. The OCC describes its mission as having four objectives, the last of which is consumer protection (Office of the Comptroller of the Currency, 'About the OCC'):

- To ensure the safety and soundness of the national banking system.
- To foster competition by allowing banks to offer new products and services.
- To improve the efficiency and effectiveness of OCC supervision, including reducing regulatory burden.
- To ensure fair and equal access to financial services for all Americans.

Like the OCC, OTS describes safety and soundness as its principal job (Office of Thrift Supervision, 'Mission and Goals'):

> To supervise savings associations and their holding companies in order to maintain their safety and soundness and compliance with consumer laws, and to encourage a competitive industry that meets America's financial services needs.

In theory, safety and soundness should serve consumer protection. In practice, it has not, as recent experience shows. During the housing boom, federal banking regulators too often mistook short-term profitability, including profits from excessive fees on consumers,[19] with safety and soundness. In their effort to protect the short-term profitability of banks and thrifts, federal regulators often dismissed consumer protection as conflicting with that mission. When agencies derive most of their operating budgets from assessments on the entities they regulate – as do the OCC and OTS – the pressure to sacrifice consumer protection for profit maximization by those entities can be overwhelming.[20]

I served on the Federal Reserve Board's Consumer Advisory Council from 2002 through 2004 and saw firsthand how resistant federal banking regulators were to instituting basic consumer protections during the run-up to the current crisis. Repeatedly over that period, I and other members of that Council warned the Federal Reserve's staff and governors about rising foreclosures and other dangers associated with reckless subprime loans. We urged the Board to exercise its powers under HOEPA to strengthen protections for subprime and nontraditional mortgages, but to no avail. During my tenure on the Council, the late Governor Gramlich told me during a break at one of the Council's public meetings that there was not enough support on the Board to expand HOEPA's protections. These experiences confirmed my belief that banking regulators often dismiss the consumer protection piece of their mission.

Some critics argue that removing consumer protection responsibilities from federal banking regulators and housing them in their own dedicated agency would undercut the safety and soundness of banks. As the current crisis shows, however, entrusting consumer protection to the federal banking agencies is no guarantee of bank safety and soundness. Indeed, having a separate federal watchdog for consumer credit would help place healthy, countercyclical constraints on the tendency of federal banking regulators to sacrifice long-term safety for short-term profits at the top of the credit cycle. It would also encourage forward-looking regulation as new problems arise, instead of laggard, backward-looking regulation of the type recently issued by the Federal Reserve.

Congress could institute mechanisms to avoid agency conflicts or to resolve them if they occur. Such mechanisms could include formal or informal consultation with federal banking regulators or judicial dispute resolution.

A separate federal consumer credit agency offers other strong advantages

In 1995, in the landmark *Twin Peaks* report, Dr. Michael Taylor advised the British Government to separate safety and soundness of the financial system from consumer financial protection and to house them in two distinct agencies (Taylor (1995)). Although Britain rejected that advice and consolidated those functions in the Financial Services Authority, created in 2000, the *Twin Peaks* concept has taken on new life in the US. A wide range of experts across the political spectrum, from the Treasury Department under former Secretary Paulson to the Congressional Oversight Panel, have recommended housing consumer credit protection in its own separate agency[21] (Department of the Treasury (2008), pp. 170–74; Congressional Oversight Panel (2009), pp. 30–37).

A separate federal agency dedicated to consumer protection for all consumer credit offers several distinct advantages. First, it would rescue consumer financial protection from its current orphan state and make consumers the Agency's top priority. Second, it would consolidate industry-wide enforcement in the Agency, meaning that all financial services providers would be subject to the same level of enforcement.

This latter point is necessary to thwart shopping for the easiest regulator. Under the current regime, consumer compliance examinations and enforcement are divided among federal banking regulators and sometimes other agencies, even though the Federal Reserve Board writes the rules for most federal consumer credit laws. Other federal consumer financial protection laws – such as Section 5 of the Federal Trade Commission Act and the Community Reinvestment Act – are individually implemented by the four federal banking regulators with respect to their regulated entities. Each agency can make its own choice about the extent to which it enforces or does not enforce the law. Ending this fragmentation would discourage lenders from switching charters in search of wink-and-nod enforcement.

Finally, transferring consumer credit laws to one agency whose sole mission is consumer protection would provide regulators with a complete overview of the entire consumer credit market, its structure, and emerging issues. Right now, consumer credit regulation suffers from a silo mentality because it is parceled out among so many agencies. Consolidating it in one agency would overcome this mentality. In addition, consolidation would concentrate expertise for consumer financial products in one agency. The provisions of the Act authorizing a research division and periodic reporting requirements are essential to developing and deploying this expertise.

Avoiding Agency Inaction in the Future

Consolidating oversight in one federal agency poses a final concern about agency capture and inaction. The FTC, for example, had a vigorous enforcement record on mortgage abuses during the Clinton Administration but a lackluster record during the George W. Bush Administration, at least until 2008. During that same period, OCC and OTS preemption raised industry capture concerns. These problems are not unique to those agencies. Administrations and agency chairs come and go, which means that over its lifetime, every agency will have periods of drift and inaction. Not every agency head has the wisdom and decisiveness of a Ben Bernanke or Sheila Bair.

The drafters of the Act thought long and hard about this issue and carefully designed the bill to counteract possible agency inaction. The Act takes a two-pronged approach. First, it makes federal consumer financial protection standards a floor, not a ceiling. Second, it vests back-up enforcement authority in fellow federal regulators and in the states.

A minimum federal floor

To address the concern that at some point in the future, the Agency, with respect to its rule-making authority, might drag its feet on needed reforms, the Act specifies that federal consumer financial protection standards will operate as a floor. As such, the federal standards will preempt state laws that are weaker. However, states would remain free to enact stricter consumer protections so long as those protections are consistent with the federal statute. The Agency would retain the power to determine whether a state law was consistent (Section 1041).

A minimum federal floor, rather than a ceiling, is critical for three reasons. First, that approach provides an important safeguard against the possibility that the Agency might adopt unduly weak rules or fail to update the rules. Second, states are closer to local conditions and often more responsive to emerging problems at home. A federal floor would preserve the states' ability to protect their citizens. Finally, giving latitude to the states to adopt stricter standards would preserve the states' important role as laboratories of experimentation. Enabling individual states to test other approaches would help prevent federal rules from becoming ossified. This dual federal-state approach, in fact, may have resulted in lower default rates on mortgages at state banks and thrifts (Figure 6.1).

Bankers have voiced fears that a patchwork of state laws would make compliance too costly and complex. Those fears are vastly overstated. In fact, in the past, when Congress has enacted federal consumer legislation as a floor, only a handful of states passed stronger statutes of their own.[22]

Bankers have managed to adjust to those few variations. In all other states, the federal standard prevails standing alone.

Back-up enforcement power

In financial services regulation, we have starkly different models of enforcement, depending on the regulatory scheme. For national banks and federal savings associations, especially after 2004, the OCC and OTS invoked their visitorial powers to argue that they had sole enforcement power for any consumer protection abuses by their regulated entities. Then they resisted vigorous enforcement action against abusive mortgages, while continuing to assert that no other agency had authority to act in their stead.

In contrast, when the Securities and Exchange Commission succumbed to lax enforcement in the late 1990s and 2000s, state attorneys general retained the power to prosecute securities fraud on their own. That power resulted in landmark actions by the attorneys general of New York, Massachusetts, and Connecticut, among other states, and lit a fire under the SEC to initiate actions of its own. Similarly, in insurance regulation, the decentralization of enforcement among the 50 states meant that when there were serious market conduct problems, some states were likely to take enforcement even if others were not. The Act incorporates these lessons by giving back-up enforcement authority to other federal regulators and the states to provide a strong antidote to any inaction by the Agency.

Vis-à-vis other federal regulators, to avoid traffic jams, the Act gives primary enforcement to the Agency. Other federal regulators, however, can recommend enforcement to the Agency. Furthermore, if the Agency fails to initiate enforcement within 120 days of a recommendation, then the federal regulator that made the recommendation may take enforcement action of its own.[23]

Vis-à-vis the states, the Act gives state attorneys general the power to enforce the Act upon notice to the Agency. The Agency can intervene as of right if it chooses.

These provisions, taken together, would give consumers a needed voice and put an end to the regulatory arbitrage that fueled the credit crisis.

CONCLUSION

During the housing bubble of recent years, our system of financial regulation proved not only fragmented, but fractured. A kaleidoscope of consumer protection regimes, varying by charter, allowed lenders to shop for the friendliest legal regimes. Financial regulators, meanwhile, competed to attract new institutions to their charters by relaxing enforcement of the laws. The denouement was the Great Recession of 2008–2009, which ravaged businesses, depleted the retirement savings of tens of millions of households, and sent unemployment rates soaring over 10 per cent.

This is a matter of national shame. We can no longer afford to dismiss consumer protection as something trivial to the health of the financial system. The Obama Administration's proposal for a new Consumer Financial Protection Agency goes a long way toward ensuring effective consumer financial protection by creating a single federal regulator dedicated to consumer protection and establishing a single set of national consumer protection rules, regardless of charter. The time has come to adopt the Administration's proposal.

NOTES

* George J. and Helen M. England Professor of Law and Director of the Insurance Law Center, University of Connecticut School of Law. My thanks to Lawrence Mitchell and Arthur E. Wilmarth, Jr., both of whom encouraged me to write this work. I also owe an intellectual debt of gratitude to Elizabeth Warren and Oren Bar-Gill for eloquently propounding the behavioral rationales for a Consumer Financial Protection Agency.

1. Although I examine this issue through the lens of mortgage regulation, my discussion is equally relevant to other forms of consumer credit, such as credit cards and payday lending.
2. A hybrid ARM offers a two- or three-year fixed introductory rate followed by a floating rate at the end of the introductory period with substantial increases in the rate and payment (so-called '2–28' and '3–27' mortgages) (Federal Reserve System (2008a)). An interest-only mortgage allows borrowers to defer principal payments for an initial period. An option payment ARM combines a floating rate feature with a variety of payment options, including the option to pay no principal and less than the interest due every month, for an initial period. Choosing that option results in negative amortization (Department of the Treasury et al. (2006)).
3. The discussion in this section was drawn, in part, from McCoy et al. (2009) and Bar-Gill and Warren (2008).
4. I use the term 'nonprime' to refer to subprime loans plus other nontraditional mortgages. Subprime mortgages carry higher interest rates and fees and are designed for borrowers with impaired credit. Nontraditional mortgages encompass a variety of risky mortgage products, including option payment ARMs, interest-only mortgages, and reduced documentation loans. Originally, these nontraditional products were offered primarily in the 'Alt-A' market to people with near-prime credit scores but intermittent or undocumented income sources. Eventually, interest-only ARMs and reduced documentation loans penetrated the subprime market as well.
5. Subprime mortgages originated in 2005, 2006 and 2007 had successively worse default experiences than vintages in prior years (Freddie Mac (2008)).
6. In fall 2006, federal regulators issued an interagency guidance advising option ARM lenders to qualify borrowers solely at the fully indexed rate. Nevertheless, Washington Mutual (WaMu) apparently continued to qualify applicants for option ARMs at the low, introductory rate alone until mid-2007. According to WAMU's securities filings, it was not until 30 July 2007 that WaMu finally updated its 'Bulk Seller Guide' to require

its correspondents to underwrite option ARMs and other ARMs at the fully indexed rate.

7. The four federal banking regulators include the Federal Reserve System, which serves as the central bank and supervises state member banks; the Office of the Comptroller of the Currency, which oversees national banks; the Federal Deposit Insurance Corporation, which operates the Deposit Insurance Fund and regulates state nonmember banks; and the Office of Thrift Supervision, which supervises savings associations.
8. For instance, in 2002, state authorities in 44 states struck a settlement with Household Finance Corp. for $484 million in consumer restitution and changes in its lending practices following enforcement actions to redress alleged abusive subprime loans (Iowa Attorney General (2002)). In 2006, 49 states and the District of Columbia reached a $325 million settlement with Ameriquest Mortgage Company over alleged predatory lending practices (Iowa Attorney General (2006)).
9. National City Corporation, the parent of National City Bank, N.A., and a major subprime lender, spearheaded the campaign for OCC preemption ('Predatory lending laws neutered', (2003)).
10. The Supreme Court recently overturned the OCC visitorial powers rule. *Cuomo v. Clearing House Ass'n, L.L.C.*, 557 U.S. ___, 129 S. Ct. 987 (2009). The OCC and the OTS left some areas of state law untouched, namely, state criminal law and state law regulating contracts, torts, homestead rights, debt collection, property, taxation, and zoning. Both agencies, though, reserved the right to declare that any state laws in those areas are preempted in the future (McCoy and Renuart (2008)).
11. Of course, these lenders, like all lenders, are subject to prosecution in cases of fraud. Lenders are also subject to the Federal Trade Commission Act, which prohibits unfair and deceptive acts and practices (UDAPs). However, federal banking regulators were slow to propose rules to define and punish UDAP violations by banking companies in the mortgage lending area.
12. In general, these are community banks on the small side. In the following discussion on regulatory failure by the Federal Reserve Board, the OTS, and the OCC, the data regarding failed and near-failed banks and thrifts come from federal bank regulatory and SEC statistics, disclosures, press releases, and orders; rating agency reports; press releases and other web materials by the companies mentioned; statistics compiled by the *American Banker*; and financial press reports.
13. Greenspan told the House Oversight Committee in 2008:

    > Well, let's take the issue of unfair and deceptive practices, which is a fundamental concept to the whole predatory lending issue.
    >
    > The staff of the Federal Reserve . . . say[] how do they determine as a regulatory group what is unfair and deceptive? And the problem that they were concluding . . . was the issue of maybe 10 percent or so are self-evidently unfair and deceptive, but the vast majority would require a jury trial or other means to deal with it . . .

    (US House of Representatives (2008), p. 89.)
14. The Board set those triggers with the intention of covering the subprime market, but not the prime market (Federal Reserve System (2008b), pp. 44536–37).
15. As early as 1998, the Federal Reserve Board and the Department of Housing and Urban Development were aware that Truth in Lending Act disclosures did not come early enough in the nonprime market to allow meaningful comparison shopping. That year, the two agencies issued a report diagnosing the problem. In the report, HUD recommended changes to the Truth in Lending Act to require mortgage originators to provide binding price quotes before taking loan applications. The Federal Reserve Board dissented from the proposal, however, and it was never adopted (Board of Governors of the Federal Reserve System and Department of Housing and Urban Development (1998), pp. 28–29, 39–42).
16. In the MDIA, Congress issued a rebuke to the Federal Reserve by mandating stronger payment shock disclosures and notice of any interest rate hikes before the loan closing.

Congress further amended these provisions of the MDIA in the Emergency Economic Stabilization Act of 2008.

17. The Board also seriously delayed revamping TILA disclosures for credit cards, but did issue a comprehensive new final rule on credit card disclosures in January 2009 (Federal Reserve System (2009)).
18. The Agency would also receive responsibility for administering the Consumer Leasing Act, the Electronic Funds Transfer Act, the Truth in Savings Act, the Alternative Mortgage Transaction Parity Act, the S.A.F.E. Mortgage Licensing Act, the Community Reinvestment Act, the privacy provisions in title V of the Gramm-Leach-Bliley Act, and provisions of the Federal Deposit Insurance Act dealing with deposit insurance disclosures (Sections 1002(16), 1011(a)).
19. Examples include regulators' slow response to curtailing large prepayment penalties and their continued indecision on costly overdraft protection.
20. For instance, the OCC derives 95% of its budget from assessments on national banks. The 20 largest national banks contribute almost 60% of those assessments (Bar-Gill and Warren (2008); Wilmarth (2007)).
21. The Committee on Capital Markets Regulation recommended an independent consumer protection agency as another alternative (Committee on Capital Markets Regulation (2009), p. 5). While the Government Accountability Office has not taken a position, it advised that '[c]onsumer protection should be viewed from the perspective of the consumer rather than through the various and sometimes divergent perspectives of the multitude of federal regulators that currently have responsibilities in this area' (General Accountability Office (2009), at 18). See also Schooner (2005), pp. 77–78, 82 ('while there are benefits to combining prudential regulation and consumer protection, serious doubt remains as to whether it is the best arrangement'; '[t]he most sensible approach to correcting the structural defect in the current regime would be to eliminate entirely the federal banking regulators' role in consumer protection').
22. For example, in the Depository Institutions Deregulation and Monetary Control Act of 1980, Congress allowed states to opt out of federal deregulation of usury caps on first-lien residential mortgages. Fourteen states originally opted out, although some of those later repealed their usury caps. Similarly, only six states exercised their right to opt out of federal preemption under the Alternative Mortgage Transaction Parity Act (Renuart and Keest (2005), §§ 3.9.4.1, 3.10.1, 3.10.2).
23. Nothing in the Act affects the enforcement authority of the Department of Justice, the SEC, or the Commodity Futures Trading Commission.

BIBLIOGRAPHY

Abraham, Jesse M., Andrey Pavlov and Susan Wachter (2008) 'Explaining the United States' Uniquely Bad Housing Market', *Wharton Real Estate Review*, **12**, 24.

Appelbaum, Binyamin and Ellen Nakashima (2008) 'Regulator Played Advocate Over Enforcer', *Washington Post*, 23 November.

Avery, R., K. Brevoort and G. Canner (2008) 'The 2007 HMDA Data', *Federal Reserve Bulletin*, A107, www.federalreserve.gov/pubs/bulletin/2008/pdf/hmda07final.pdf.

Bair, Sheila C. (2008) 'Statement of Sheila C. Bair, Chairman, Federal Deposit Insurance Corporation, on Strengthening the Economy: Foreclosure Prevention and Neighborhood Preservation, before the Committee on Banking, Housing and Urban Affairs, US Senate', www.fdic.gov/news/news/speeches/chairman/spjan3108.html, 31 January.

Bar-Gill, Oren and Elizabeth Warren (2008) 'Making Credit Safer', *University of Pennsylvania Law Review* 157, 1.
Board of Governors of the Federal Reserve System (2004) 'Citigroup Inc. New York, New York and Citifinancial Credit Company Baltimore, Maryland: Order to Cease and Desist and Order of Assessment of a Civil Money Penalty Issued Upon Consent', 27 May.
Board of Governors of the Federal Reserve System (2009) 'Looking for the Best Mortgage', www.federalreserve.gov/pubs/mortgage/mortb_1.htm.
Board of Governors of the Federal Reserve System and Department of Housing and Urban Development (1998) 'Joint Report to the Congress, Concerning Reform to the Truth in Lending Act and the Real Estate Settlement Procedures Act', www.federalreserve.gov/boarddocs/rptcongress/tila.pdf.
Board of Governors of the Federal Reserve System et al. (1999) 'Interagency Guidance on Subprime Lending', 1 March.
Bostic, Raphael, Kathleen C. Engel, Patricia A. McCoy, Anthony Pennington-Cross and Susan Wachter (2008) 'State and Local Anti-Predatory Lending Laws: The Effect of Legal Enforcement Mechanisms', *Journal of Economics and Business* **60**, 47–66, full working paper version at papers.ssrn.com/sol3/papers.cfm?abstract_id=1005423.
Committee on Capital Markets Regulation (2009) 'Recommendations for Reorganizing the U.S. Financial Regulatory Structure', 14 January, www.capmktsreg.org.
Congressional Oversight Panel (2009) 'Special Report on Regulatory Reform', January, cop.senate.gov/documents/cop-012909-report-regulatoryreform.pdf.
Corkery, Michael (2008) 'Mortgage "Cram-Downs" Loom as Foreclosures Mount', *Wall Street Journal*, 31 December.
Department of the Treasury (2008) 'Blueprint for a Modernized Financial Regulatory Structure', March, www.treasury.gov.
Department of the Treasury (2009) 'Title X-Consumer Financial Protection Agency Act of 2009', http://www.financialstability.gov/docs/CFPA-Act.pdf.
Department of the Treasury et al. (2006) 'Interagency Guidance on Nontraditional Mortgage Product Risks: Final guidance', *Federal Register* 71: p. 58609, 4 October.
Department of the Treasury et al. (2007) 'Statement on Subprime Mortgage Lending; Final guidance', *Federal Register* 72: 37569.
Dugan, John C. (2008) 'Testimony by John C. Dugan, Comptroller, before the Senate Committee on Banking, Housing, and Urban Affairs', 4 March.
Emergency Economic Stabilization Act of 2008, Pub. L. No. 110–343 (3 October 2008).
Federal Deposit Insurance Corporation (2006) 'Breaking New Ground in U.S. Mortgage Lending, FDIC Outlook', www.fdic.gov/bank/analytical/regional/ro20062q/na/2006_summer04.html, Summer.
Federal Reserve System (2005) 'Purposes & Functions', 9th ed.
Federal Reserve System (2008a) 'Truth in Lending, Part II: Proposed rule; request for public comment', *Federal Register* 73: p. 1672, 9 January.
Federal Reserve System (2008b) 'Truth in Lending, Part III: Final rule, official staff commentary', *Federal Register* 73: p. 44522, 30 July.
Federal Reserve System (2009a) 'Truth in Lending: Final rule', *Federal Register*, 74: 5244, 29 January.

Federal Reserve System (2009b) 'Truth in Lending, Part II: Proposed rule; request for public comment', *Federal Register* 74: p. 43232, 26 August.

Freddie Mac (2008) 'Freddie Mac Update', www.freddiemac.com/investors/pdf-files/investor-presentation.pdf, p. 19, December.

General Accountability Office (2009) 'Financial Regulation: A Framework for Crafting and Assessing Proposals to Modernize the Outdated U.S. Financial Regulatory System', Report No. GAO-09–349T, 4 February, www.gao.gov.

Goodman, Peter S. and Gretchen Morgenson (2008) 'Saying Yes, WaMu Built Empire on Shaky Loans', *New York Times*, 28 December.

Gramlich, Edward M. (2007a) 'Boom and Busts, The Case of Subprime Mortgages', Speech given 31 August, 2007, Jackson Hole, Wyo., at symposium titled 'Housing, Housing Finance & Monetary Policy', sponsored by the Federal Reserve Bank of Kansas City, www.kansascityfed.org/publicat/sympos/2007/pdf/2007.09.04.gramlich.pdf.

Gramlich, Edward M. (2007b) *Subprime Mortgages: America's Latest Boom and Bust*, Washington, D.C.: Urban Institute Press.

Greenspan, Alan (2008) 'Testimony of Dr. Alan Greenspan before the House of Representatives Committee of Government Oversight and Reform, 23 October, 2008', www.oversight.house.gov/documents/20081023100438.pdf.

Haviv, Julie and Emily Kaiser (2007) 'Web lenders woo subprime borrowers despite crisis', *Reuters*, 22 April.

Iowa Attorney General (2002) 'States Settle With Household Finance: Up to $484 Million for Consumers', 11 October, www.iowa.gov/government/ag/latest_news/releases/oct_2002/Household_Chicago.html.

Iowa Attorney General (2006) 'Ameriquest Will Pay $325 Million and Reform its Lending Practices', 23 January, www.state.ia.us/government/ag/latest_news/releases/jan_2006/Ameriquest_Iowa.html.

Kroszner, Randall S. (2007) 'Speech by Governor Randall S. Kroszner At the National Bankers Association 80th Annual convention, Durham, North Carolina', 11 October.

Lax, Howard, Michael Manti, Paul Raca and Peter Zorn (2004) 'Subprime Lending: An Investigation of Economic Efficiency', *Housing Policy Debate* **15**, 533.

McCoy, Patricia A. (2007) 'Rethinking Disclosure in a World of Risk-Based Pricing', *Harvard Journal on Legislation* **44**, 123.

McCoy, Patricia A., Andrey D. Pavlov and Susan M. Wachter (2009) 'Systemic Risk through Securitization: The Result of Deregulation and Regulatory Failure', *Connecticut Law Review* **41**, 1327.

McCoy, Patricia A. and Elizabeth Renuart (2008) 'The Legal Infrastructure of Subprime and Nontraditional Mortgage Lending', in Nicolas P. Retsinas and Eric S. Belsky (eds), *Borrowing to Live: Consumer and Mortgage Credit Revisited*, Boston and Washington, D.C.: Joint Center for Housing Studies of Harvard University and Brookings Institution Press, p. 110.

Mortgage Bankers Association (2009) 'Delinquencies Continue to Climb, Foreclosure Flat in Latest MBA National Delinquency Survey', http://www.mbaa.org/NewsandMedia/PressCenter/70050.htm, 20 August.

Mortgage Disclosure Improvement Act of 2008, Pub. L. No. 110–289, tit. V, § 2502(a)(6), 122 Stat. 2855–2856 (30 July 2008).

Office of Inspector General, Department of the Treasury (2008) 'Safety and Soundness: Material Loss Review of ANB Financial, National Association', Report No. OIG-09–013, 25 November.

Office of the Comptroller of the Currency, 'About the OCC', viewed 28 February 2009, www.occ.treas.gov/aboutocc.htm.
Office of the Comptroller of the Currency (2000) 'Abusive Lending Practices', Advisory Letter 2000–7, 25 July.
Office of the Comptroller of the Currency (2003a) 'Avoiding Predatory and Abusive Lending Practices in Brokered and Purchased Loans', Advisory Letter 2003–3, 21 February.
Office of the Comptroller of the Currency (2003b) 'Guidelines for National Banks to Guard Against Predatory and Abusive Lending Practices', Advisory Letter 2003–2, 21 February.
Office of the Comptroller of the Currency (2004) 'Bank Activities and Operations; Real Estate Lending and Appraisals; Final rule', *Federal Register*, **69**, 1904.
Office of the Comptroller of the Currency (2005) 'OCC Guidelines Establishing Standards for Residential Mortgage Lending Practices', *Federal Register*, **70**, 6329.
Office of the Comptroller of the Currency et al. (2001) 'Expanded Guidance for Subprime Lending Programs', 31 January.
Office of Thrift Supervision, 'Mission and Goals', viewed 28 February 2009, www.ots.treas.gov/?p=MissionGoal.
Office of Thrift Supervision (2000) 'Responsible Alternative Mortgage Lending: Advance notice of proposed rulemaking', *Federal Register* 65: 17811.
'Predatory lending laws neutered' (2003) *Atlanta Journal-Constitution*, 6 August.
Reckard, E. Scott (2007) 'Refinance pitches in sub-prime tone', *Los Angeles Times*, 29 October.
Renuart, Elizabeth and Kathleen E. Keest (2005) *The Cost of Credit: Regulation, Preemption, and Industry Abuses*, Boston: National Consumer Law Center, 3d ed. and annual supplement.
Schmitt, Richard B. (2008) 'Regulator takes heat over IndyMac', *Los Angeles Times*, 6 October.
Schooner, Heidi Mandanis (2005) 'Consuming Debt: Structuring the Federal Response to Abuses in Consumer Credit', *Loyola Consumer Law Review*, **18**, 43.
Taylor, Michael (1995) '*Twin Peaks*': *A Regulatory Structure for the New Century*, London, UK: Centre for the Study of Financial Innovation.
US House of Representatives, Committee on Oversight and Government Reform (2008) 'The Financial Crisis and the Role of Federal Regulators, Preliminary Transcript,' 23 October, oversight.house.gov/documents/20081024163819.pdf.
Wachter, Susan M., Andrey D. Pavlov and Zoltan Pozsar (2008) 'Subprime Lending and Real Estate Markets', in Stefania Perruci (ed), *Mortgage and Real Estate Finance*, London, UK: Risk Books.
Wilmarth, Arthur E. (2004) 'The OCC's Preemption Rules Exceed the Agency's Authority and Present a Serious Threat to the Dual Banking System', *Annual Review of Banking and Finance Law* 23: 225.
Wilmarth, Arthur E. (2007) 'Testimony of Arthur E. Wilmarth, Jr., Hearing before the Subcommittee on Financial Institutions and Consumer Credit of the House Committee on Financial Services', 26 April.

7. Lessons from 2008 US bank failures

William C. Handorf*

Although bank crises commonly occur every 10 to 15 years in some region of the world, the underlying asset classes and countries responsible for such crises shift. The current global banking catastrophe has largely arisen out of unsafe residential real estate lending in the United States and toxic collateralized debt obligations backed by very high-risk classes embedded within mortgage-backed securities. Governmental leaders in many countries have taken unprecedented steps to minimize further disruptions to their financial markets and economies by increasing deposit insurance levels, guaranteeing short-term and long-term debt previously issued by financial institutions, and investing in preferred stock of selected banks whose survival is deemed important. Bank failure is not a new phenomenon and it is not costless.

Countries from all continents have previously incurred significant fiscal costs to bail out unsuccessful banks and recapitalize or nationalize salvageable institutions. If banks are unable to intermediate funds from surplus savings sectors to worthwhile deficit borrowing sectors, economic problems escalate within a country because consumers and businesses are unable to finance the production or consumption of durable goods, working capital or plant and equipment. The consequences of a failing banking system can also be severe when banks finance a sizable portion of governmental debt. A credit freeze precipitates dire economic problems for the remaining fragile financial institutions. This chapter briefly reviews bank risk within the context of the ever-increasing number of bank failures within the US and identifies preliminary lessons for a more thorough study that clearly will be required by Congress, given the massive federal expenditures incurred by the Department of Treasury and the Federal Reserve.

BANK FAILURE

The majority of empirical studies show that depository institutions fail because of the following financial, economic and managerial factors.

Recent experience has differed little from the pattern suggested by history.

- **Financial factors** – Invariably, banks fail because of inadequate capital. Capital ratios decline due to excessive loan losses on high-risk loans. The loans often are not supported by adequate levels of reserves or were not priced appropriately for risk. Capital problems increase if a bank has a concentrated portfolio by type of loan or location of borrowers; that is, the bank does not possess a well diversified portfolio. Other banks incur losses due to investments in high-yielding securities that later default. Banks that pursue a strategy of rapid growth typically originate high-yielding loans and invest in high-yielding securities because management has chosen to fund growth by relying on high-cost liabilities. A business strategy that produces a rapid expansion of liabilities and assets also frequently outstrips capital, incurs high-cost debt and compromises the effectiveness of internal controls designed to control risk and avoid fraud. Once a bank's financial problems are well known by regulators, credit rating agencies and financial markets, liquidity issues arise as the press publishes adverse articles about the bank's low capital and earnings problems.
- **Economic environment** – The financial factors correlating with bank failure are compounded when the economic environment amplifies risk. Commercial loan losses surge during and after an economic recession as business borrowers are unable to generate adequate cash flow to pay interest and repay principal. Consumer loan losses soar as unemployment rates increase and households are unable to service car loans, credit card balances and home loans due to a loss of income. In some cases, regional and community banks suffer asset quality problems if their region of the country experiences a 'boom to bust' scenario. The current US banking crisis has precipitated a nationwide recession. The economic downturn will deepen losses for banks.
- **Managerial malaise** – Ultimately, banks fail because management and the board of directors are unable or unwilling to identify, measure, monitor and control risks in order to ensure a safe and sound institution. Either the bank's business plan is flawed or the bank is unable to remain committed to a viable business model. Fraud perpetrated by management and/or customers produces intensified losses. Failing banks are tempted to gamble for resurrection and therefore place too little emphasis on risk management. Some banks nearing liquidation shrink assets to improve capital-to-

asset ratios. The strategy invariably fails because fixed non-interest expenses must be allocated over a smaller asset base and the bank continues to post losses and dissipate its remaining capital.

The risks enumerated above correlate strongly with traditional regulatory oversight, which focuses on capital, asset quality, management, earnings, liquidity and sensitivity to market risk. Banks fail because capital ratios are eroded by either very quick growth, an inability to control non-interest expenses or losses caused by excessive loan charge-offs compounded by fraud and/or a recession. Capital is of special importance to the assessment of risk by regulatory authorities and credit analysts. Lower capital, erratic profits and increased risks – whether derived from concentrations of high-risk assets, poor strategic and risk management practices resulting from inadequate corporate governance, strained liquidity or too much sensitivity to interest rates or foreign exchange prices – precipitate financial institution problems.

After experiencing several years of very low or even no bank failures, the Federal Deposit Insurance Corporation (FDIC) has been appointed as a receiver or a conservator for 25 failed banks in 2008, and a much higher number of bank failures is projected for 2009. Some of the failures have been small, such as the US $19 million Hume Bank in Missouri. Other failures have been large, such as the US $300 billion Washington Mutual (Wamu). Still other banks, such as National City of Cleveland, Ohio and Wachovia of Charlotte, North Carolina, have been forced by regulators to merge with other stronger depository institutions in order to avoid failure. The FDIC must raise insurance premiums to rebuild their depleted deposit insurance fund. Higher premiums exert more adverse pressure on already low bank profits.

THE RECENT PREDICAMENT

The spreading of the recent financial crisis from the United States to Europe and Latin America shows the risks of excessive leverage and disproportionate reliance on short-term debt. Investors expect firms to earn a

$$\text{Return on Equity} = \text{Leverage Multiplier} \times \text{Return on Assets}$$

$$[\text{Net Income/ Equity}] = [\text{Total Assets/Equity}] \times [\text{Net Income/Total Assets}]$$

return on equity that exceeds their targeted investment return. Return on equity for a bank equals their leverage or equity multiplier multiplied by return on assets.

Managers can increase return on equity either by operating more profitably or by increasing leverage. Higher leverage indicates that banks are financed by more debt and less equity. Equity provides the key source of funding designed to absorb unexpected losses while the allowance for loan losses provides the cushion for expected loan charge-offs. Financial managers can increase return on assets by funding assets with lower-cost, short-term debt rather than long-term debt. Short-term debt typically costs less than long-term debt given the existence of a liquidity premium for long-term securities. Short-term debt must be repaid quickly or rolled over at maturity. Short-term debt increases liquidity risk because cash is difficult to obtain during a financial crisis. The combination of too much leverage and too much reliance on short-term debt at too many financial institutions greatly has increased the severity of the present crisis. Leverage and maturity of debt are important indicators of risk; excessive risk-taking was the foundation of the calamity.

Historically, US banks have failed or encountered operating losses due to asset quality problems arising out of a variety of asset classes, including loans to developing countries, the petroleum sector, the agriculture sector and, more recently, the commercial real estate sector. Residential home loans (and acquisition, development and construction loans for home building) are the primary culprits behind the current wave of bank failures.

The double-digit annual increases in home prices in the US between 2001 and 2005 encouraged speculators and investors to buy more homes and condominiums than were required for immediate occupancy. This incremental demand by speculators and investors pushed up home prices to unsustainable levels. Families that could not qualify for prime, fixed-rate mortgages financed their purchases of high-priced homes by entering into high-risk, non-traditional first mortgages whose interest rates subsequently reset to higher levels and (in many cases) whose principal balances increased with the passage of time. Higher loan payments caused a higher probability of default and larger loan balances precipitated larger losses given default. Many of the same families also borrowed second mortgages to finance their initial down payments and therefore had little, if any, equity in their homes.

Governmental housing policies encouraged home ownership and prodded government-sponsored housing enterprises (that is, Fannie Mae and Freddie Mac) to purchase or guarantee high-risk subprime and Atl-A mortgages. The US central bank kept interest rates too low (for example, at 1 per cent) for too long after the mild recession of 2001. The Federal Reserve's accommodative monetary policy encouraged mortgagors to borrow funds on an adjustable-rate basis and facilitated quick, low-cost growth in the banking sector.

Lax, fraudulent or non-existent underwriting of loans contributed to subsequent loan losses, but mortgage brokers and lenders were unconcerned as long as Wall Street continued to purchase and package the loans in order to create highly-rated mortgage-backed securities and toxic collateralized debt obligations. As delinquencies and foreclosures on mortgage loans soared and housing prices slumped, selected hedge funds began to report sizable losses on mortgage-backed securities. Excessive leverage and over-reliance on short-term debt minimized the ability of all affected institutions to absorb risk and contributed to the deepening of the financial disaster. Nonbank mortgage lenders, investment banks and commercial banks began to fail in 2007 and the failure rates accelerated in 2008. The tempo of failure is unlikely to abate until 2011. Who contributed to the problems and what lessons can be learned to avoid similar crises in the future?

EXPENSIVE LESSONS LEARNED

Although there will be many academic and governmental studies that examine the causes of the current banking crisis in the United States, there is now sufficient evidence to preliminarily identify many of the wrongdoers who contributed to the financial chaos.

- **Central Bank** – The Federal Reserve kept interest rates too low for too long after the mild recession of 2001. Low interest rates encouraged investors and speculators to purchase real estate in California, Arizona, Nevada and Florida funded by adjustable-rate loans. The central bank also failed to recognize that easy access to high-risk mortgage loans, second mortgages and home equity loans allowed investors and families to push up home prices to unsustainable levels. When monthly payments on the non-traditional loans subsequently reset to sharply higher levels, defaults soared.
- **Bank managers and Boards of Directors** – Despite the rapid recent increase in bank failures, 99 per cent of the remaining banks remain safe and sound. Managers of the failing or problem banks did not pursue a viable business plan and did not implement risk management systems that enabled their institutions to identify, measure, monitor and control risk. Bank managers were seduced by seeming

high profits from high-yielding loans and securities and high-fee income from originating subprime and Alt-A loans. Directors simply did not question how much risk they were taking to achieve high returns. For example, Citibank's yield on real estate loans increased from 6 per cent in 2005 to 18 per cent by 2006 when other large banks were reporting yields of 7 per cent on similar loans. Clearly, the global bank was taking on too much risk by originating high-risk loans to high-risk mortgagors or by purchasing high-risk securities.

- **Bank Regulators** – Every federal and/or state regulator waited far too long to criticize interest-only mortgage loans and payment-option loans that allowed unpaid interest to be capitalized and added to loan principal. The regulators ultimately promulgated guidelines that stressed appropriate underwriting, but most of the problem loans that are currently in delinquency or foreclosure status had already been originated. Savings and loans (for example, Downey, IndyMac and Wamu) were especially vulnerable to housing industry problems because of their focus on high-yielding residential lending and lack of diversified loan portfolios.
- **Unregulated loan brokers and nonbank lenders** – Despite the shortcomings of regulators, many loan brokers and nonbank lenders who originated high-risk mortgages to subprime borrowers (that is, borrowers with low credit scores) and Alt-A borrowers (that is, borrowers who did not provide documentation of their income or assets), were not subject to any meaningful supervision. When losses occurred on highly-rated mortgage-backed securities in the summer of 2007, investment banks stopped buying loans from brokers and cut off wholesale lines of credit, thereby causing the hundreds of mortgage brokers and nonbank lenders to fail.
- **Wall Street** – Investment banks share much blame for the crisis. Indeed, selected Wall Street firms encouraged mortgage brokers and nonbank lenders to provide a continuing flow of high-risk mortgages that could be pooled and securitized to create high-yielding, investment-grade securities. Credit rating agencies failed miserably to identify and isolate risks within collateralized debt obligations (CDOs), and many tranches of CDOs rated 'Aaa/AAA' either defaulted or were downgraded to non-investment grade status within only one year of origination. The CDOs were often backed by lower, medium-grade classes from mortgage-backed securities and when foreclosure rates increased and losses given default jumped as home prices declined, losses surged.
- **Public Policy and Government Sponsored Enterprises** – The Bush Administration and the Department of Housing and Urban

Development (HUD) encouraged home ownership and hoped to see 70 per cent of Americans own a home. HUD encouraged Fannie Mae and Freddie Mac to guarantee or purchase subprime and Alt-A mortgages to provide additional funding for families with tarnished credit ratings. As default rates surged on securities backed by subprime and Alt-A mortgages, Fannie Mae and Freddie Mac suffered huge losses that caused their regulator to place the two mortgage enterprises into conservatorship. The 12 Federal Home Loan banks offer low-cost secured loans to member institutions. To date, the Federal Home Loan Bank System has not incurred credit losses on the advances extended to banks because banks must post collateral from performing loans and high-grade securities that comfortably exceed loan balances. Although failing banks have borrowed funds from a regional Federal Home Loan Bank to support growth, access to the credit invariable mitigates temporary liquidity problems as bank regulators and management determine how best to resolve financial problems and seek mergers with qualified institutions.

The lessons learned are not new to any seasoned bank regulator. Rapid growth and high returns should prompt close bank scrutiny.

SUMMARY

Public policy must heed the costly mistakes endured from the Panic of 2008. First, bank inspectors should demand that each bank implement a full risk management system commensurate with the size and complexity of the institution's business plan. The business plan must clearly articulate the mission, goals, milestones and objectives of the bank and include detailed marketing, financial, organizational and risk management plans. Second, bank inspectors must carefully examine any assets with high yields and any banks growing quickly. Third, bank inspectors must ensure that every loan originated and security purchased is evaluated according to current repayment schedules and prospective resets. Fourth, bank inspectors may take comfort in credit rating agency letter grades and accounting firm audit opinions but recognize they too make mistakes; the consequence of errors can be and have been enormous.

To summarize, if an asset class or a bank is performing unusually well, bank regulators and the central bank must question how the results are being achieved and what contingencies might cause serious harm to the institution or the market. Although prudential regulation, including the imposition of stricter capital and liquidity requirements to curb speculative excesses, may reduce the growth of gross domestic product, the costs of lower growth will prove small relative to the subsequent fiscal and societal burdens incurred to resolve a systemic financial crisis. The US and other countries are now sustaining substantial fiscal costs to resolve market, managerial and regulatory mistakes. Consumers and small firms bear much of the adverse consequences even though the majority had no role in creating the underlying problems. Banks restrict credit after a crisis to increase capital ratios. Bankers underwrite loans more conservatively, and the lack of access to credit deepens the recession and lengthens the period of recovery. Early intervention by regulatory supervisors and the central bank could have prevented some of the later costs incurred by the government and its citizens.

Unfortunately, history suggests problems similar to those discussed in this conference will resurface in approximately 15 years. Although the asset categories that trigger future crises will likely be comparable (in terms of risk) to the risky loans and securities that produced the Panic of 2008, future bankers and regulators will remember little from the current crisis. The academic literature refers to this phenomenon of collective amnesia as the 'error learning model'. As time passes, management and regulators will conclude that their risk management systems and risk models have improved sufficiently to permit the origination of high-risk and high-yielding loans and securities without undue financial concern. When the next credit boom leads to the next crisis, the resulting pain caused by large losses and widespread bank failures will guide the financial services industry for another 15 years until the experience (that is, error learning) dissipates and the cycle is renewed.

NOTE

* William C. Handorf, Ph.D., is a professor of finance with the School of Business at the George Washington University located in Washington, DC. In addition, he currently serves as a director with the Federal Home Loan Bank of Atlanta, and previously served as a director with the Federal Reserve Bank of Richmond, where he chaired the Baltimore Branch board of directors. Professor Handorf has over 40 years of experience as a banker, bank regulator, bank consultant and accountant, bank director and academic publishing banking, finance and real estate articles.

8. Defaults and returns in the high-yield bond market: the year 2008 in review and outlook[1]

Edward I. Altman* and Brenda J. Karlin**

The year 2008 proved to be a difficult one for investors in high yield, with more than $50 billion in defaults, the largest dollar amount in six years, and the continuing turmoil in credit markets. Returns versus 10-year Treasuries were at their lowest historical levels, new financings ground to a halt, spreads increased to record levels, and an unprecedented 82 per cent of high-yield bonds outstanding were classified as distressed by year-end.

The default rate rose to 4.60 per cent; while only 67bp above average, this was the highest rate since 2003, and significantly larger than the 0.51 per cent default rate of 2007. The fourth-quarter 2008 default rate was 2.84 per cent, the highest quarterly default rate since the third quarter of 2002.

Default losses on high-yield bonds came in at 2.83 per cent, based on a weighted average recovery rate of 42.5 per cent just after default, slightly below the historical average of 45.1 per cent. The average recovery rate was elevated by the record level of distressed exchanges in 2008. The weighted average recovery on bankruptcy and payment defaults was considerably lower at 27.1 per cent, compared to 52.2 per cent for distressed exchanges. These levels are significantly lower than a year ago, when the recovery rate was at its highest level since 1987.

Returns on high-yield bonds reached historically low levels, ending the year at 25.91 per cent. The excess return versus 10-year US Treasuries was a 46.21 per cent, more than double the previous record low of 20.13 per cent in 2000. Yield-to-maturity spreads versus 10-year US Treasuries increased to 17.31 per cent by year-end 2008, slightly lower than the high it reached in December, but 1164bp greater than year-end 2007.

The distressed ratio of bonds yielding more than 1000bp above the risk-free rate increased precipitously to 82.0 per cent, as of the end of 2008, from 40.2 per cent three months earlier and just 10.4 per cent at year-end 2007. This metric reached its high in November 2008, with 85 per cent of

US high-yield bonds considered distressed. The previous high of 58 per cent was registered in 1991. By month-end January 2009, the volatile distressed ratio dropped to 69.4 per cent.

Estimates of the face value size of the distressed and defaulted debt markets increased significantly to $3.59 trillion, as of 31 December 2008, up significantly from $867 billion one year earlier. This increase is largely attributable to the meteoric rise in the distressed ratio. The market value estimate also increased to approximately $2.20 trillion, up from $1.32 trillion as of the end of the third quarter of 2008, and $708 billion at the end of 2007.

Based on our mortality rate methodology of new issuance in the last ten years, stratified by original bond rating, the Altman forecast for the high-yield bond market's default rate in 2008 was 4.64 per cent, compared to an actual default rate of 4.60 per cent. Based on five different methodologies, the 2009 forecasts ranged from 7.98 per cent (mortality method) to 18.32 per cent (spread method), with the consensus average rate of 13.63 per cent. Through the first quarter of 2009, the default rate was already 3.7 per cent and the weighted average recovery rate approximately 24 per cent.

DEFAULTS, DEFAULT RATES, AND RECOVERIES

Although the high-yield bond default rate in 2008 was only 67bp higher than the historical average, this past year was anything but average in the credit markets. The default rate reversed a two-year downward trend in 2008, rising to 4.60 per cent from an extremely low 0.51 per cent one year earlier. The 2008 rate is based on a market size of $1.091 trillion, up by $15 billion from a year ago. In all, $50.2 billion of defaults, the largest dollar amount since 2002, were recorded in 2008 (Table 8.1).

In the fourth quarter of 2008, the default rate was 2.84 per cent, the largest quarterly default rate since the third quarter of 2002 (Figure 8.1). The most sizeable defaults during the year were GMAC, defaulting on more than $14 billion of outstanding bonds, and Residential Capital (ResCap), which defaulted twice on almost $10 billion. TOUSA, Quebecor, Washington Mutual, Harrah's, Trump Entertainment, and Tribune Co. each defaulted on outstanding bonds totaling more than $1 billion. In all, 63 issuers constituting 154 issues defaulted in 2008, considerably greater than the 19 issuers and 35 issues which defaulted in 2007. The average dollar amount per defaulting issuer in 2008 was $796 million, compared to $288 million in 2007, and $329 million in 2006.

Note also that the default rate in the first quarter of 2009 spiked up to 3.69 per cent even higher than the fourth quarter of 2008 (Table 8.1).

Table 8.1 Historical default rates – straight bonds only excluding defaulted issues from par value outstanding, 1971–2009(Q1) (dollars in millions)

Year	Par value outstanding ($)[a]	Par value defaults ($)	Default rates (%)
2009(Q1)	1 083 600	40 003	3.692
2008	1 091 000	50 169	4.598
2007	1 075 400	5473	0.509
2006	993 600	7559	0.761
2005	1 073 000	36 209	3.375
2004	933 00	11 657	1.249
2003	825 000	38 451	4.661
2002	757 000	96 858	12.795
2001	649 000	63 609	9.801
2000	597 200	30 295	5.073
1999	567 400	23 532	4.147
1998	465 500	7464	1.603
1997	335 400	4200	1.252
1996	271 000	3336	1.231
1995	240 000	4551	1.896
1994	235 000	3418	1.454
1993	206 907	2287	1.105
1992	163 000	5545	3.402
1991	183 600	18 862	10.273
1990	181 000	18 354	10.140
1989	189 258	8110	4.285
1988	148 187	3944	2.662
1987	129 557	7486	5.778
1986	90 243	3156	3.497
1985	58 088	992	1.708
1984	40 939	344	0.840
1983	27 492	301	1.095
1982	18 109	577	3.186
1981	17 115	27	0.158
1980	14 935	224	1.500
1979	10 356	20	0.193
1978	8946	119	1.330
1977	8157	381	4.671
1976	7735	30	0.388
1975	7471	204	2.731
1974	10 894	123	1.129
1973	7824	49	0.626
1972	6928	193	2.786
1971	6602	82	1.242

Table 8.1 (continued)

		%	Standard Deviation (%)
Arithmetic average default rate	1971 to 2008	3.135	3.030
	1978 to 2008	3.405	3.226
	1985 to 2008	4.052	3.365
Weighted average default rate[b]	1971 to 2008	3.932	
	1978 to 2008	3.942	
	1985 to 2008	3.975	
Median annual default rate	1971 to 2008	1.802	

Notes:
[a] As of midyear.
[b] Weighted by par value of amount outstanding for each year.

Source: NYU Salomon Center.

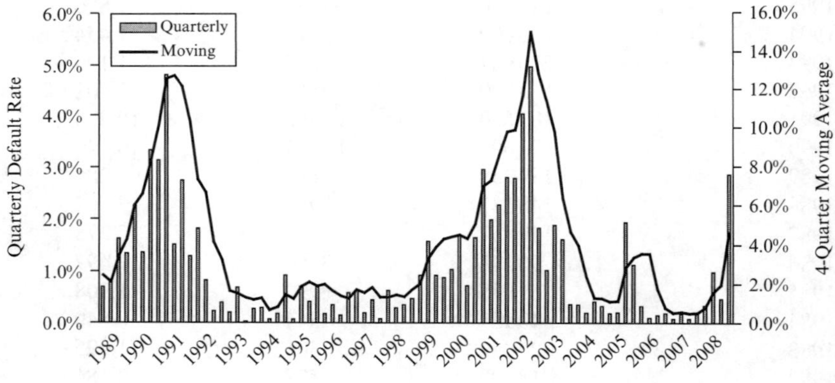

Source: NYU Salomon Center.

Figure 8.1 Quarterly default rate and four-quarter moving average 1989–2008

Pointedly missing from the list of the largest issuers to default is Lehman Brothers Holdings, Inc. Since Lehman's bonds were rated investment-grade prior to bankruptcy and default, they are not included in the default rate. Furthermore, only $1.6 billion of the $5.7 billion in Washington Mutual bond defaults have been included in the default rate

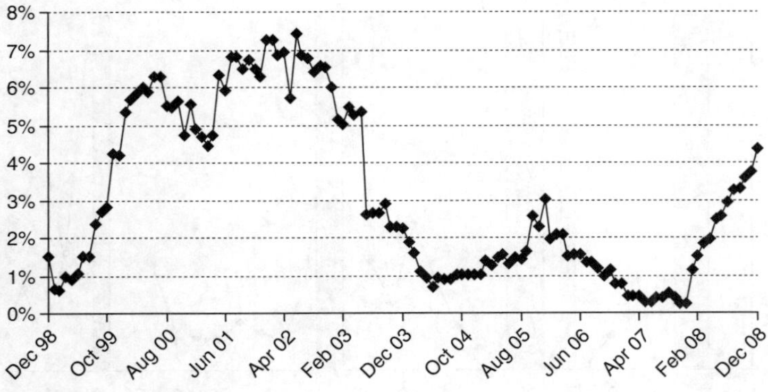

Source: Standard & Poor's LCD.

Figure 8.2 *S&P Leveraged loan index 12-month moving average default rate 1998–2008*

calculation. This amount represents three bonds that Moody's downgraded to noninvestment-grade in March 2008.

In our default statistics, we include only those bonds from distressed exchanges that were actually tendered. For example, in the initial Residential Capital exchange, which occurred in June, we determined that \$5.67 billion of bonds were exchanged out of the \$12.8 billion outstanding. About 59 per cent of GMAC's outstanding bonds were tendered, and less than 40 per cent of the remaining ResCap bonds were actually exchanged. In 2008, thirteen distressed exchanges comprised \$29.7 billion of defaults (59.3 per cent of the total). We will discuss distressed exchanges in greater detail later in this chapter.

In 2008, S&P and Moody's issuer-denominated default rates were 4.02 per cent and 4.43 per cent, respectively. Moody's 6.56 per cent dollar-denominated default rate was greater than its issuer-denominated rate.

The issuer-based default rate for the last 12 months in the US leveraged loan market was 4.35 per cent (Figure 8.2), and 3.75 per cent based on issuance, according to S&P's LCD compilations. This is in contrast to the miniscule rates of 0.24 per cent and 0.26 per cent, respectively, at the end of 2007. Forty-one leveraged loan issuers defaulted in 2008, compared to only two for the entirety of 2007. According to our comparison between high-yield bond defaults and leveraged loan defaults, only 11 firms had both bonds and leveraged loans default in 2008. In the first quarter of 2009, the last 12-month leveraged loan default rate spiked up to 8.02 per cent (dollar denominated) and 4.79 per cent (issuer denominated).

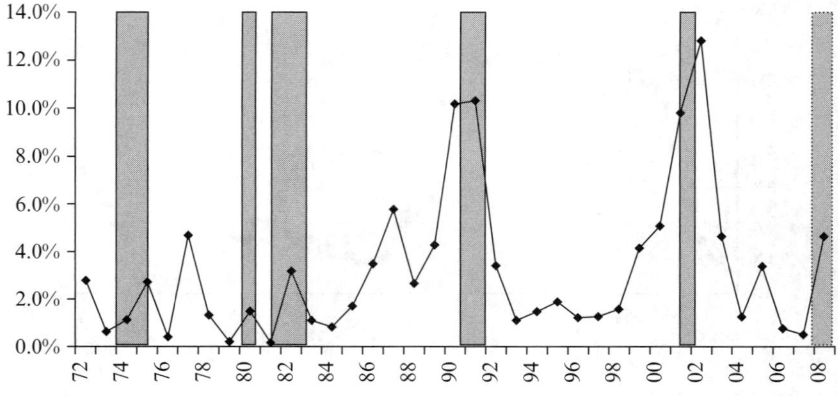

Notes: Periods of Recession: 11/73–3/75, 1/80–7/80, 7/81–11/82, 7/90–3/91, 4/01–12/01, 12/07– Present.

Sources: Table 8.1 of this chapter and National Bureau of Economic Research.

Figure 8.3 Historical default rates and recession periods in the US high-yield bond market, 1972–2008

We recently learned that the US economy went into a recession in December 2007, so 2008 is now included as a recession year. Whereas the default rate began increasing two years, or so, before the start of the two prior recessions, this time the increase in default rates coincided with the beginning (Figure 8.3). In all five prior recessions since 1972, it is clear that default rates peaked near the end, or soon after the end of the recession. With the current recession likely to continue through the entirety of 2009 (or beyond), it is quite likely that the high-yield default rate will continue to rise in 2009, and possibly into 2010.

Bankruptcies

The amount of total liabilities for Chapter 11 bankruptcies in 2008 was \$107.8 billion, based on 145 filings and excluding Lehman Brothers Holdings, Inc. Although approximately 150 per cent larger than the 2007 total of \$72.65 billion, the 2007 total liabilities figure was based on only 38 filings. The 2007 amount was somewhat high due to New Century's filing for bankruptcy with more than \$20 billion in liabilities. Incorporating Lehman Brothers into the 2008 number increases the total liabilities to \$720.8 billion. Tribune Co. was the largest bankruptcy filing in 2008, excluding Lehman Brothers, with \$13.0 billion in liabilities.

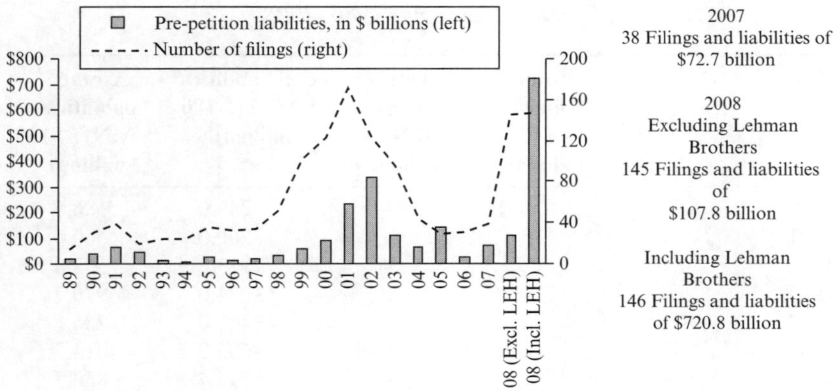

Notes: [a]Minimum $100 million in liabilities.

Source: Table 8.1 of this chapter and NYU Salomon Center bankrupcty filings Database.

Figure 8.4 Liabilities[a] of public companies filing for Chapter 11 protection, 1989–2008

The total amount of 2008 bankruptcy liabilities (including Lehman) was more than twice the previous record amount in 2002. Of the 146 filings, 51 were highly leveraged restructurings, primarily LBOs, sponsored by private equity firms.[2]

The number of billion-dollar bankruptcies in 2008 increased significantly from eight in 2007 to 23, the same number as in 2000, but lower than 2001 and 2002, with 39 and 41, respectively. The majority of the larger bankruptcies were in the financial services, communications, and construction/real estate sectors.

According to New Generation Research, the number of public companies filings was 136 (Table 8.2). The average of total liabilities for all 146 bankruptcy filings in 2008 was $4.9 billion including Lehman Brothers, and $743.4 million excluding Lehman.

In Figure 8.5 we compare the date of default with the Chapter 11 filing date for firms that defaulted on bonds and also went bankrupt going back to 1981. Based on 817 observations from the NYU Salomon Center Master Default and Bankruptcy Databases, both events occurred on the same date in 402 instances (49 per cent). In the remaining 51 per cent of the cases, the lag between the default date and bankruptcy date varied considerably, with decreasing levels as the two dates became further separated from each other. Of course, some defaulting issuers never formally filed

Table 8.2 Historical bankruptcy filings 1980–2008

Year	Total filings[a]	Total filings[b] (>$100 million)	Total filings (≥$1 billion)	Total liabilities[b] ($ MN) (>100 million)	Average liabilities[b] ($ MN) (>100 million)
1980	62	4	0	746.0	186.5
1981	74	6	1	3960.0	660.0
1982	84	12	3	7113.0	592.8
1983	89	14	3	13674.0	976.7
1984	121	12	0	3440.0	286.7
1985	149	14	2	8605.2	614.7
1986	149	11	3	9335.4	850.5
1987	112	12	1	25421.0	2118.4
1988	122	14	2	6905.0	493.2
1989	135	22	10	33538.9	1524.5
1990	115	35	10	41115.1	1174.7
1991	123	51	11	81157.9	1591.3
1992	91	37	14	64224.1	1735.8
1993	86	37	4	17701.1	478.4
1994	70	24	1	8396.0	349.8
1995	85	32	7	27153.0	848.5
1996	86	32	0	11687.0	365.2
1997	83	36	5	18865.9	524.1
1998	122	56	6	32038.3	572.1
1999	145	109	19	70957.1	651.0
2000	179	136	23	98895.8	727.2
2001	263	170	39	22993.1	1352.5
2002	220	135	41	336611.7	2493.4
2003	172	102	26	115171.8	1129.1
2004	92	44	11	39549.7	898.9
2005	86	34	10	141525.2	4162.5
2006	66	32	5	23917.3	747.4
2007	78	38	8	72642.7	1911.7
2008	136	146	23	720805.1	4937.0
Total	**3395**	**1407**	**288**	**2265104.3**	**1609.9**

Notes:
[a] Represents Chapter 7 and 11 public company filings.
[b] Filings with total liabilities greater than $100 million.

Sources: New generation research and NYU Salomon Center.

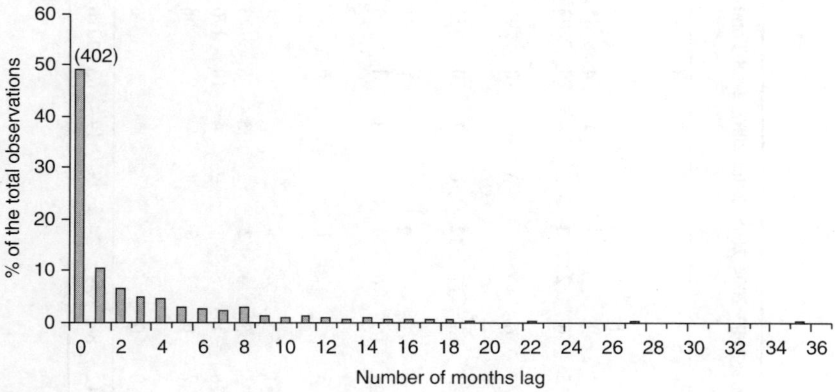

Notes: [a]Based on 817 observations.

Source: NYU Salomon Center.

Figure 8.5 Time differential between default and bankruptcy filing[a] (1981–2008)

for bankruptcy as their problems were settled out of court or the default came as a result of an exchange.

Industry Defaults

Table 8.3 lists the number of high-yield bond defaults by industry. Of the total 63 defaulting issuers in 2008, leisure and entertainment, general manufacturers, and media and communications were industries in which ten firms defaulted. Eight issuers defaulted in the auto/motor carrier sector, six in real estate and construction, and five in both financial services and retailing. The remaining nine defaulting issuers were spread over various industries.

Age of Defaults

Table 8.4 shows the age distribution of defaults in 2008 and for the period 1991–2008. It appears normal that the number of defaults is low in the first year after issuance. What typically follows is an increase in default rates in years two through four. Indeed, 2008 essentially mirrors the cumulative default proportions over 1991–2008, in terms of marginally increasing default frequencies in years one through three, slightly lower rates in years four and five versus three, followed by decreasing frequencies thereafter.

Table 8.3 Corporate bond defaults by industry (number of companies)

Industry	1970–1989	1990	1991	1992	1993	1994	1995	1996	1997	1998	1999	2000	2001	2002	2003	2004	2005	2006	2007	2008	Total
Auto/Motor carrier	6	3					1				1			1			**4**	3		**8**	27
Conglomerates	5	1	3	3								1			1	1					15
Energy	35		4	2	3		1			1	13	1		8	9		**1**		**1**	**4**	83
Financial services	21	7	14	3	2	1	2	1	2	6	1	6	4	5	6	2	**3**	2		**5**	93
Leisure/ Entertainment	9	8	2	4	3	4	3	1	5	5	8	9	6	5	6			3		**10**	91
General manufacturing	26	5	8	8	7	3	8	6	7	6	16	23	43	22	13	17	**12**	6	**7**	**10**	253
Health care	4	2	1	1	1		2			2	8	6	3	4	3		**2**		**1**	**1**	41
Miscellaneous Industries	16	4	4	3	1	1	1		3	3	16	34	38	25	16	6	**1**	4	**3**	**4**	183
Real estate/ Construction	14	7	5	1			2	1	2	1	4	6	4	3		2	**1**			**6**	59
REIT	12			1										1							14
Retailing	10	6	15	6	4	5	6	3	6	6	12	7	12	5	5	3	**2**	2	**3**	**5**	123
Communications	17	3	4	1	1	3	2	2	1	6	11	8	39	26	21	6	**3**	2	**4**	**10**	170
Transportation (non auto)	9	1	2			2			2	1	8	5	7	7	6	2	**5**	1			58
Utilities	2			1				1	1			1		0	0						6
Total	**186**	**47**	**62**	**34**	**22**	**19**	**28**	**15**	**29**	**37**	**98**	**107**	**156**	**112**	**86**	**39**	**34**	**23**	**19**	**63**	**1216**

Source: NYU Salomon Center.

Table 8.4 Distribution of years to default from original issuance date (by year of default), 1991–2008

Years to default	1991		1992		1993/1994		1995		1996		1997		1998		1999		2000	
	No. of issues	% of total	No. of issues	% of total	No. of issues	% of total	No. of issues	% of total	No. of issues	% of total	No. of issues	% of total	No. of issues	% of total	No. of issues	No. of issues	No. of issues	No. of issues
1	0	0	0	0	3	8	32	26	2	8	5	20	2	6	32	26	19	10
2	18	13	0	0	6	16	37	30	3	13	4	16	5	15	37	30	51	28
3	26	19	7	13	5	14	15	12	3	13	4	16	10	30	15	12	56	31
4	29	21	10	19	2	5	14	11	8	33	9	36	3	9	14	11	14	8
5	35	26	8	15	4	11	7	6	1	4	3	12	10	30	7	6	13	7
6	10	7	12	22	8	22	8	6	5	21	0	0	2	6	8	6	5	3
7	4	3	5	9	7	19	10	8	0	0	0	0	1	3	10	8	12	7
8	10	7	4	7	0	0	2	2	0	0	0	0	0	0	2	2	4	2
9	3	2	0	0	0	0	0	0	0	0	0	0	0	0	0	0	3	2
10	2	1	8	15	2	5	0	0	2	8	0	0	0	0	0	0	6	3
Total	**137**	**100**	**54**	**100**	**37**	**100**	**125**	**100**	**24**	**100**	**25**	**100**	**33**	**100**	**125**	**100**	**125**	**100**

Table 8.4 (continued)

Years to default	2001		2002		2003		2004		2005		2006		2007		2008		1991–2008	
	No. of issues	**% of total**	**No. of issues**	**% of total**	**No. of issues**	**% of total**	**No. of issues**	**% of total**	**No. of issues**	**% of total**	**No. of issues**	**% of total**	**No. of issues**	**% of total**	**No. of issues**	**% of total**	**No. of issues**	**% of total**
1	40	12	29	8	18	9	8	10	16	9	2	4	1	3	9	6	187	9
2	69	21	51	15	30	15	7	9	13	7	4	8	1	3	18	12	326	16
3	87	26	61	18	26	13	8	10	9	6	6	12	6	17	34	22	370	18
4	65	19	56	16	23	11	6	8	22	12	5	10	9	26	30	19	308	15
5	27	8	45	13	40	20	10	13	14	8	4	8	3	9	20	13	245	12
6	14	4	21	6	20	10	16	21	17	9	9	17	4	11	10	6	163	8
7	21	6	8	2	25	12	9	12	13	7	6	12	2	6	9	6	134	7
8	5	1	7	2	3	1	6	8	11	6	7	13	5	14	6	4	72	4
9	4	1	12	3	5	2	1	1	5	3	6	12	1	3	7	5	51	3
10	3	1	54	16	13	6	6	8	64	34	3	6	3	9	11	7	178	9
Total	**335**	**100**	**344**	**100**	**203**	**100**	**77**	**100**	**184**	**100**	**52**	**100**	**35**	**100**	**154**	**100**	**2034**	**100**

Source: NYU Salomon Center.

Many bonds that were ten years or older that defaulted in 2008 were originally investment-grade issues. Again, as in 2007, a small proportion (6 per cent) defaulted during the first year after issuance. The historical average is 9 per cent.

Fallen Angel Defaults

Eight issuers (GMAC, Residential Capital, Tribune Co., Washington Mutual, Quebecor, Harrah's, Clear Channel, and Fremont General) were responsible for 48 issues that were investment grade at some time prior to default. This results in a fallen-angel issuer default rate of 3.07 per cent, comparable to the historical average of 3.71 per cent (Table 8.5). The fallen-angel default rate for 1985–2008 is slightly below the historical average annual rate for original issue defaults in the high-yield bond market. This differential, however, is not statistically significant due to a relatively high standard deviation of around 241bp per year between the two rates. Table 8.6 shows the fallen angel proportion of defaults from 1977 to the present. In 2008, 31 per cent of defaulted issues were originally rated investment grade, somewhat above the historical average of 26 per cent.

Default Losses and Recoveries

The weighted-average recovery rate (based on market prices just after defaults) on high-yield bond defaults in 2008 dipped below the historic average of 45.1 per cent to end the year at 42.5 per cent. This is in contrast to the recovery rate of 66.6 per cent in 2007, and is the lowest rate since 2002. The default loss rate in 2008, including the loss of 0.189 per cent (18.9bp) from lost coupons, was approximately 283.2bp (Table 8.7). If we remove fallen angel defaults (48 issues) the loss would have been 341.8bp. Over the 31-year period from 1978 to 2008, the arithmetic average annual loss rate on high-yield bond defaults is 2.29 per cent, 2.67 per cent on a weighted-average basis (Table 8.8).

In 2009 through the first quarter, as noted earlier, the default rate was 3.69 per cent, and, the recovery rate dropped to just 25.4 per cent. This relatively low recovery rate would have been substantially even lower had we not observed a very large bankruptcy at Charter Communications whose recovery was quite high, near the end of the quarter.

Table 8.9 lists the average recovery rate by seniority for 1978–2008. In 2008, 18 of the defaulting issues were senior secured, with an average recovery rate of 30.52 per cent, compared to a historical average of 59.0% (59.1 per cent median). This is lower than the third-quarter recovery of

Table 8.5 Fallen angels versus original issue and all high-yield default rates[a] (in per cent)

Year	Fallen angel average 12-mo. default rate	Original issue speculative grade default rates	All speculative grade bond default rates	Altman dollar weighted annual default rates
2008	3.07	NA	4.02	4.60
2007	0.86	1.00	0.97	0.51
2006	1.40	1.23	1.26	0.76
2005	2.74	3.70	2.48	3.37
2004	0.83	2.65	2.23	1.25
2003	5.88	5.46	5.53	4.66
2002	6.59	8.55	8.32	12.79
2001	8.46	10.14	10.99	9.81
2000	7.01	7.10	7.03	5.07
1999	4.01	5.10	4.62	4.15
1998	3.31	2.75	2.23	1.60
1997	2.04	2.10	1.71	1.25
1996	1.38	2.00	1.71	1.23
1995	0.25	3.90	3.07	1.90
1994	0.00	2.31	1.70	1.45
1993	1.72	1.99	1.79	1.10
1992	4.50	5.48	5.45	3.40
1991	7.53	10.86	11.66	10.27
1990	5.77	8.30	8.20	10.14
1989	3.74	4.93	5.33	4.29
1988	4.25	3.39	3.95	2.66
1987	4.36	2.92	2.41	5.78
1986	2.46	6.29	4.78	3.50
1985	6.77	4.06	3.24	1.71
Arithmetic average	3.71	4.62	4.36	4.05
standard deviation	2.41	2.74	2.94	3.37

Note: [a] All S&P issuer based except for Altman rates.

Sources: NYU Salomon Center and S&P.

59.24 per cent, primarily due to Tribune Co. senior secured defaults of over $1 billion with a recovery rate of merely 6–7 per cent. Seventy-nine of the issues were senior unsecured with an average recovery rate of 49.6 per cent, compared to a historical average of 37.9 per cent (45.9 per cent

Table 8.6 Defaults by original ratings (investment grade versus non-investment grade), by year

Year	Total no. defaulted issues[a]	Originally rated investment grade (%)
2008	154	31
2007	35	11
2006	52	13
2005	184	49
2004	79	19
2003	203	33
2002	322	39
2001	258	14
2000	142	16
1999	87	13
1998	39	31
1997	20	0
1996	24	13
1995	29	10
1994	16	0
1993	24	0
1992	59	25
1991	163	27
1990	117	16
1989	66	18
1988	64	42
1987	31	39
1986	55	15
1985	26	4
1984	14	21
1983	7	43
1982	20	55
1981	1	0
1980	4	25
1979	1	0
1978	1	100
1977	2	100
Total	**2299**	**26%**

Note: [a] Where we could find an original rating from either S&P or Moody's.

Sources: Moody's, NYU Salomon Center, and S&P.

Table 8.7 2008 Default loss rate

	Unadjusted for fallen angels (%)	Only fallen angels (%)	All except fallen angels (%)	Price adjusted for fallen angels (%)
Background data				
Average default rate	4.598	3.065	8.693	5.964
Average price at default[a]	42.520	48.913	35.056	41.776
Average price at downgrade[a]	82.519	52.52		
Average recovery	42.520	59.275	35.056	46.801
Average loss of principal	57.480	40.725	64.944	53.199
Average coupon payment	8.231	7.116	9.281	8.231
Default loss computation				
Default rate	4.598	3.065	8.693	5.964
X loss of principal	57.480	40.725	64.944	53.199
Default loss of principal	2.643	1.248	5.646	3.173
Default rate	4.598	3.065	8.693	5.964
X loss of 1/2 coupon	4.115	3.558	4.640	4.115
default loss of coupon	0.189	0.109	0.403	0.245
Default loss of principal and coupon	**2.832**	**1.357**	**6.049**	**3.418**

Note: [a] If default date price is not available, end-of-month price is used. Average Default Rate of 'Only fallen angels' is based on number of issuers.

Sources: NYU Salomon Center and various dealer quotes.

median). This rate was bolstered by the large number of issues within this seniority that defaulted, due to a distressed exchange, wherein recovery rates are typically higher.

There were 23 issues that were senior subordinated with an average recovery of 30.3 per cent, compared to a historical average of 31.0 per cent (32.8 per cent median). Four were subordinated with an average recovery

Table 8.8 Default rates and losses,[a] 1978–2009(Q1)(dollars in millions)

Year	Par value outstanding[a] ($)	Par value of default ($)	Default rate (%)	Weighted price after default ($)	Weighted coupon (%)	Default loss (%)[b]
2009(3/31)	1 083 600	40 003	3.69	25.4	9.23	2.91
2008	1 091 000	50 169	4.60	42.5	8.23	2.83b
2007	1 075 400	5473	0.51	66.6	9.64	0.19b
2006	993 600	7559	0.76	65.3	9.33	0.30b
2005	1 073 000	36 209	3.37	61.1	8.61	1.46b
2004	933 100	11 657	1.25	57.7	10.30	0.59b
2003	825 000	38 451	4.66	45.5	9.55	2.76b
2002	757 000	96 858	12.79	25.3	9.37	10.15b
2001	649 000	63 609	9.80	25.5	9.18	7.76
2000	597 200	30 295	5.07	26.4	8.54	3.95
1999	567 400	23 532	4.15	27.9	10.55	3.21
1998	465 500	7464	1.60	35.9	9.46	1.10
1997	335 400	4200	1.25	54.2	11.87	0.65
1996	271 000	3336	1.23	51.9	8.92	0.65
1995	240 000	4551	1.90	40.6	11.83	1.24
1994	235 000	3418	1.45	39.4	10.25	0.96
1993	206 907	2287	1.11	56.6	12.98	0.56
1992	163 000	5545	3.40	50.1	12.32	1.91
1991	183 600	18 862	10.27	36.0	11.59	7.16
1990	181 000	18 354	10.14	23.4	12.94	8.42
1989	189 258	8110	4.29	38.3	13.40	2.93
1988	148 187	3944	2.66	43.6	11.91	1.66
1987	129 557	7486	5.78	75.9	12.07	1.74
1986	90 243	3156	3.50	34.5	10.61	2.48
1985	58 088	992	1.71	45.9	13.69	1.04
1984	40 939	344	0.84	48.6	12.23	0.48
1983	27 492	301	1.09	55.7	10.11	0.54
1982	18 109	577	3.19	38.6	9.61	2.11
1981	17 115	27	0.16	72.0	15.75	0.15
1980	14 935	224	1.50	21.1	8.43	1.25
1979	10 356	20	0.19	31.0	10.63	0.14
1978	8946	119	1.33	60.0	8.38	0.59
Arithmetic average 1978–2008			**3.40**	**45.07**	**10.72**	**2.29**
Weighted average 1978–2008			**3.94**			**2.67**

Notes:

[a] Excludes defaulted issues.

[b] Default loss rate adjusted for fallen angels is 9.3% in 2002, 1.82% in 2003, 0.59% in 2004, 1.56% in 2005, 0.039% in 2006, 0.20% in 2007 and 3.42% in 2008.

Sources: NYU Salomon Center and Figures 1 and 12.

Table 8.9 Weighted average recovery rates on defaulted debt by seniority per $100 face amount, 1978–2008

Default year	Senior secured			Senior unsecured			Senior subordinated			Subordinated			Discount and zero coupon			All seniorities	
	No.	%	$	No.	%	$	No.	%	$	No.	%	$	No.	%	$	No.	$
2008	18	**14**	30.52	79	**63**	49.56	23	**18**	30.25	4	**3**	21.09	1	**1**	2.71	125	42.52
2007	10	**35**	87.24	10	**36**	47.70	6	**21**	63.98	2	**7**	46.53	0	**0**	0.00	28	66.65
2006	9	**18**	90.60	26	**52**	60.90	8	**16**	50.24	1	**2**	60.33	6	**12**	78.31	50	65.32
2005	67	**54**	76.50	44	**36**	45.88	7	**6**	32.67	0	**0**	0.00	5	**4**	74.21	123	62.96
2004	27	**39**	63.67	33	**48**	56.77	2	**3**	37.44	0	**0**	0.00	7	**10**	43.06	69	57.72
2003	57	**28**	53.51	108	**53**	45.40	29	**14**	35.98	1	**0**	38.00	8	**4**	32.27	203	45.78
2002	37	**11**	52.81	254	**75**	21.82	21	**6**	32.79	0	**0**	0.00	28	**8**	26.47	340	26.25
2001	9	**3**	40.95	187	**67**	28.84	48	**17**	18.37	0	**0**	0.00	37	**13**	15.05	281	25.62
2000	13	**8**	39.58	47	**29**	25.40	61	**37**	25.96	26	**16**	26.62	17	**10**	23.61	164	26.74
1999	14	**11**	26.90	60	**47**	42.54	40	**31**	23.56	2	**2**	13.88	11	**9**	17.30	127	32.20
1998	6	**18**	70.38	21	**62**	39.57	6	**18**	17.54	0	**0**	0.00	1	**3**	17.00	34	40.46
1997	4	**16**	74.90	12	**48**	70.94	6	**24**	31.89	1	**4**	60.00	2	**8**	19.00	25	57.61
1996	4	**17**	59.08	4	**17**	50.11	9	**38**	48.99	4	**17**	44.23	3	**13**	11.99	24	45.44
1995	5	**15**	44.64	9	**27**	50.50	17	**52**	39.01	1	**3**	20.00	1	**3**	17.50	33	41.77
1994	5	**23**	48.66	8	**36**	51.14	5	**23**	19.81	3	**14**	37.04	1	**5**	5.00	22	39.44
1993	2	**6**	55.75	7	**22**	33.38	10	**31**	51.50	9	**28**	28.38	4	**13**	31.75	32	38.83
1992	15	**22**	59.85	8	**12**	35.61	17	**25**	58.20	22	**33**	49.13	5	**7**	19.82	67	50.03
1991	4	**3**	44.12	69	**44**	55.84	37	**24**	31.91	38	**24**	24.30	9	**6**	27.89	157	40.67
1990	12	**10**	32.18	31	**27**	29.02	38	**33**	25.01	24	**21**	18.83	11	**9**	15.63	116	24.66
1989	9	**12**	82.69	16	**21**	53.70	21	**28**	19.60	30	**39**	23.95				76	35.97

1988	13	**21**	67.96	19	**31**	41.99	10	**16**	30.70	20	**32**	35.27				62	43.45
1987	4	**13**	90.68	17	**55**	72.02	6	**19**	56.24	4	**13**	35.25				31	66.63
1986	8	**14**	48.32	11	**20**	37.72	7	**13**	35.20	30	**54**	33.39				56	36.60
1985	2	**7**	74.25	3	**11**	34.81	7	**26**	36.18	15	**56**	41.45				27	41.78
1984	4	**29**	53.42	1	**7**	50.50	2	**14**	65.88	7	**50**	44.68				14	50.62
1983	1	**13**	71.00	3	**38**	67.72				4	**50**	41.79				8	55.17
1982				16	**80**	39.31				4	**20**	32.91				20	38.03
1981	1	**100**	72.00													1	72.00
1980				2	**50**	26.71				2	**50**	16.63				4	21.67
1979										1	**100**	31.00				1	31.00
1978				1	**100**	60.00										1	60.00
Total/ Average[a]	**360**	**16%**	**$58.96**	**1106**	**48%**	**$37.85**	**443**	**19%**	**$31.03**	**255**	**11%**	**$31.14**	**157**	**7%**	**$25.83**	**2321**	**$37.81**
Standard dev[a]			**$18.30**			**$13.49**			**$14.23**			**$17.52**			**$20.84**		**$14.04**
Median			**$59.08**			**$45.88**			**$32.79**			**$31.00**			**$19.00**		**$41.78**

Note: [a] Standard deviations are calculated based on the yearly averages.

Sources: NYU Salomon Center from various dealer quotes.

of 21.1 per cent, compared to a historical average of 31.1 per cent (31.0 per cent median). One was issued as a discount note with a recovery of 2.7 per cent compared to a historical average of 25.8 per cent (19.0 per cent median). Twenty-nine issues could not be priced. The historic 31-year median for all high-yield bond defaults stayed constant at 41.8 per cent, while the arithmetic average rose slightly to 37.8 per cent. These latter statistics are based on a sample of over 2300 defaults.

Distressed Exchanges

Distressed Exchanges (DE), a classical restructuring tool, reemerged in 2008. Typically, this tactic is an attempt by an ailing firm to avoid bankruptcy by proposing a fundamental change in the contractual relationship between a debtor and its various creditor classes and is 'voluntarily' agreed upon by a sufficient percentage of relevant creditor claims.

While the most common and dramatic DEs involve a substitution of lower priority equity securities for debt claims, DEs can result from a reduction in the effective interest rate on the debt, a subordination of claims, an extension of time to repay the debt, or a package of new securities that has a total value less than the face value of the original debt claim. An added, critical component is that the original claim sells at a distressed price – usually below 90 cents on the dollar – at the time of the DE announcement.

The first instances of DEs in the modern high-yield bond era were the so-called '3(a)9 exchange', championed by Drexel Burnham Lambert in the 1980s. These exchanges were particularly attractive to distressed firms because they did not require SEC review and could be accomplished quickly, usually in less than a month. A second critical element was that the exchange was tax-free, even if the new securities had a combined value of less than the original claim.

This tax-free exemption changed in the early 1990s, when the reduction in debt was considered a taxable event. This revised tax ruling is still in effect, regardless if the company is distressed. Hence, there is little incentive for a solvent firm to exchange its debt for equity and reduce its leverage when the consequences would be a meaningful increase in taxes. As such, these exchanges will usually only take place when a firm is desperately trying to avoid an even more costly bankruptcy and usually where it has sufficient tax-loss credits to offset the taxable exchange.

While a few earlier studies, for example, Gilson, John and Lang (1990),[3] showed that out-of-court restructurings were considerably less costly than bankruptcies to the debtor firm, in many cases the DE was followed by a bankruptcy anyway. Our own analysis, shows that of 57 DEs completed prior to 2008, at least 26 (46%) were followed by a bankruptcy filing, and several others resulted in a change of ownership of the debtor.[4]

Implications of DEs

DEs have important implications to credit markets. First, nearly all instances of DEs are now categorized as a 'default' in the calculations of default rates – including our own calculations. However, some debate still exists as to whether the entire debt issue involved in a DE should be counted as a default or just the amount that is actually tendered in the exchange. Another debatable issue is which date should be considered as the default date – when the DE is announced or when it is completed. This is particularly relevant for the computation of the recovery rate on the default event.

Our policy is to count a DE that has been accepted by the requisite proportion of claimants at the time the announcement of the tender offer took place, unless there were changes in the terms of the exchange, or other material events took place, as in the case of GMAC (discussed below). In addition, we only count the amount of claims that are tendered, not the total outstanding amount of the debt issue.

DE Defaults in the CDS Market

The corporate market has not experienced any distressed exchanges that triggered CDS in recent years, although it has been observed in the sovereign market. Outside of a prepackaged Chapter 11, apparently US corporations are unlikely to affect an exchange that would qualify as a default under ISDA guidelines. There is an ongoing discussion for a proposal to eliminate a 'modified exchange' as a default trigger in CDS contracts to avoid confusion and costly lawsuits. Therefore, in practice, only traditional defaults including a failure to pay interest or a bankruptcy has qualified as of late.

Reasons for tighter spreads in CDS (versus cash bonds) are liquidity and funding differences, but it is difficult to isolate each factor. Despite improved specifications, we may find debate from time to time as to what constitutes a CDS default event, especially with respect to DEs, unless new regulations are put in place.

Distressed Exchanges in 2008

To say that we observed a resurgence in DEs in 2008 is an understatement. Indeed, the 13 DE issuers in 2008 was nearly double the number of any year since 1984. The amount of DEs ($29.7 billion) was more than three times the total amount of the years 1984–2007 combined. Firms appear to be scrambling to avoid bankruptcy like never before. In addition, since DIP loans and equity infusions are constrained due to the credit crisis, the usual benefits of bankruptcy have been lessened, and the prospect of liquidation in bankruptcy has heightened.

Creditors, on the other hand, are less likely to resist a DE tender because the likely recovery after a DE is greater than in bankruptcy reorganization and certainly greater than in bankruptcy liquidation. Of course, initial DE proposals can be challenged by creditors in the hope that the debtor will sweeten the offer. We have seen several instances of this in 2008, the most publicized being the recently completed GMAC exchange. If the DE goes through, those investors not tendering will continue to have a claim of full-face value should a bankruptcy subsequently occur, but they may become subordinated to those that do tender.

The saga of the GMAC/Residential Capital (second instance of the latter) exchange has been exceptional for several reasons. First, it has involved the US Government in a material way and is, by far, the largest DE in history. The initial DE offer was a complicated package of cash, new debt, and preferred stock advertised as needing a tender of 75 per cent of the outstanding debt amounts of both GMAC and Residential Capital (ResCap) – a subsidiary of GMAC. The 75 per cent was the amount supposedly necessary for the Federal Reserve to grant GMAC status as a bank holding company, thereby giving it access to the Fed's discount window and low-cost debt borrowings.

When it became obvious that the 75 per cent would not be achieved, the US Government trumped that requirement by investing $5 billion directly in GMAC preferred stock and loaning an additional $1 billion to General Motors in order for the company to purchase additional preferred securities. Hence, the 75 per cent exchange was not necessary, and GMAC accepted the 59 per cent of GMAC bonds tendered as well as the 39 per cent tendered to ResCap.

The irony of the GMAC DE is that all creditors, those that tendered and those that did not, were pleased with the exchange since the prices on all existing bonds spiked significantly due to the enormous equity 'bailout' infusion of the government and since a GMAC bankruptcy was averted. Upfront prices on the CDS of the remaining GMAC bonds dropped dramatically, from about 44 points as of the day before the firm won Federal Reserve approval to become a bank holding company to about 10.5 points in early January 2009. Much of the drop occurred after the announced equity infusion. Bond prices also increased by about 30 points after that announcement.

DEs in 2008 accounted for about 21 per cent of the defaulted issuers (13 of 63), but as much as 59 per cent of the defaulted dollar amount. These statistics attest to the significance of the DE phenomenon in 2008. From 1984 through 2008, however, DEs accounted for only about 7.4 per cent of all defaulting issuers and 8.5 per cent of all defaulted dollar amounts (Table 8.10).

Recovery Rates on Distressed Exchanges

Since DEs are not as dramatic a reflection of a firm's distressed status as a bankruptcy or nonpayment of cash interest on debt, one might expect the recovery rate on DE defaults to be higher than other, more serious, distressed situations. Indeed, the data support this intuition. Table 8.1 shows the arithmetic average recovery rate on all DE defaults was 50.8 per cent for 1984–2008, compared to 41.1 per cent for all defaults, and 37.6 per cent for all non-DE defaults (Table 8.11). In 2008, DEs recovered 52.2 per cent while non-DE defaults recovered only 27.1 per cent.

In Table 8.11, we calculate a difference in means test between the arithmetic average recovery rate on the 70 DE issuers (135 issues) during 1984–2008 (46.5 per cent)[5] and the average recovery rate on all non-DE defaults (37.5 per cent) of the same period. We found that given the above, the DE recovery rate is significantly higher ($t = 4.34$) at the 1 per cent confidence level. It is not surprising that bondholders will choose, in many instances, to accept a recovery with certainty from a DE, rather than take the chance of holding out for an uncertain – and likely lower – recovery in bankruptcy. Our results do not include data for situations where a DE offer is rejected.

It is safe to assume that most of these scenarios could possibly be associated with a subsequent bankruptcy petition. Investors still must decide, given the completion of a DE, whether to hold on to the new set of securities from the exchange or sell as quickly as possible. More than likely, if a bankruptcy takes place subsequent to a DE, the default recovery after bankruptcy will be considerably lower than if the investor had sold immediately after the DE. What we do not know is the likely positive average return in those situations where a bankruptcy is permanently avoided after the DE.

Forecast Recovery Versus Actual

The 2008 weighted-average recovery rate of 42.5 per cent was in line with our linear regression default/recovery rate forecasting model prediction (Figure 8.6).[6] We expect recovery rates to continue to decrease in 2009, as default rates rise.

Table 8.10 High-yield bond distressed exchange (D/E) default and recovery statistics, 1984–2008

Year	D/E defaults ($)	Total defaults ($)	D/E defaults (%) to total $	D/E defaults (No. of issuers)	Total defaults (No. of issuers)	D/E defaults (%) to total no. of issuers	D/E recovery rate[a]	All default recovery rate[a]	Difference between D/E & all default recovery rate
2008	29735.11	50168.95	59.3	13	63	20.6	52.21	42.50	9.71
2007	146.83	5473.00	2.7	1	19	5.3	85.17	66.65	18.52
2006	0.00	7559.00	0.0	0	0	0	NA	NA	NA
2005	0.00	36209.00	0.0	0	0	0	NA	NA	NA
2004	537.88	11657.00	4.6	5	39	12.8	58.05	57.72	0.33
2003	1034.94	38451.00	2.7	7	86	8.1	78.52	45.58	32.94
2002	764.80	96858.00	0.8	3	112	2.7	61.22	25.30	35.92
2001	1267.60	63609.00	2.0	5	156	3.2	33.12	25.62	7.50
2000	50.00	30295.00	0.2	1	107	0.9	77.00	26.74	50.26
1999	2118.40	23532.00	9.0	6	98	6.1	65.39	27.90	37.49
1998	461.10	7464.00	6.2	2	37	5.4	17.34	40.46	(23.12)
1997	0.00	4200.00	0.0	0	0	0.0	NA	NA	NA
1996	0.00	3336.00	0.0	0	0	0.0	NA	NA	NA
1995	0.00	4551.00	0.0	0	0	0.0	NA	NA	NA
1994	0.00	3418.00	0.0	0	0	0.0	NA	NA	NA
1993	0.00	2287.00	0.0	0	0	0.0	NA	NA	NA
1992	0.00	5545.00	0.0	0	0	0.0	NA	NA	NA

1991	76.00	18 862.00	0.4	1	62	1.6	31.30	40.67	(9.37)
1990	1044.00	18 354.00	5.7	7	47	14.9	43.15	24.66	18.49
1989	548.90	8110.00	6.8	7	26	26.9	44.53	35.97	8.56
1988	390.30	3944.00	9.9	3	24	12.5	28.40	43.45	(15.05)
1987	33.60	7486.00	0.4	2	15	13.3	40.70	66.63	(25.93)
1986	114.80	3156.00	3.6	4	23	17.4	47.68	36.60	11.08
1985	323.30	992.00	32.6	2	19	10.5	55.04	41.78	13.26
1984	100.10	344.00	29.1	1	12	8.3	44.12	50.62	(6.50)
Totals/ Averages	$38 747.65	$455 860.95	8.5%	70	945	7.4%	50.76[b]	41.11[b]	9.65

Notes:

[a] Weighted-average recovery rates for each year.

[b] Arithmetic average of the weighted-average annual recovery rates; only those years with DEs counted. The arithmetic average of each individual DE (70) for the entire sample period was 46.52% and the average for the non-DE defaults (875 observations) was 37.55%.

Source: NYU Salomon Center.

Table 8.11 Difference in means test between recovery rates: all nondistressed exchange defaults versus distressed exchanges (D/E), 1984–2008

	All defaults excluding D/E (issues)	Distressed exchange (issues)
Sample size	2072	135
Mean recovery rate	37.49	46.52
Standard deviation	25.78	23.25
Variance	664.61	540.35
t-test[a]	4.34108	

Note: [a] $t = \dfrac{\overline{X}_T - \overline{X}_C}{\sqrt{\dfrac{var_T}{n_T} + \dfrac{var_C}{n_C}}}$

Source: NYU Salomon Center.

Mortality Rates and Losses

Updated mortality statistics are reported in Table 8.12. This default measurement includes the impact of bond aging by adjusting the base population over time for such disappearances as defaults, calls, and other noncredit-related events. Results are calculated based on the rating at birth and the volume of issuance. Similar statistics for cumulative default rates can be found from rating agency compilations, only the base is usually the number of issuers. These agency-calculated cumulative default rates are based on the number of issuers in a certain rating category at the beginning of the same year, regardless of the rating received when they were issued. Hence, they are not affected by aging, and the statistics are more appropriate for seasoned portfolios.

Since the 2008 default rate was relatively consistent with 1971–2007, the updated mortality rate statistics are similar to one year earlier. For example, the one- and five-year B-rated category had cumulative mortality rates of 2.77 per cent and 27.6 per cent in 2008 compared to 2.78 per cent and 27.56 per cent in 2007. We utilize our mortality rate statistics in one of our default forecasts at the end of this report.

Mortality losses in Table 8.13 indicate a parallel story to the mortality rate statistics. Most losses are quite similar to – or lower than – the end of 2007, due to the lower recoveries in 2008.

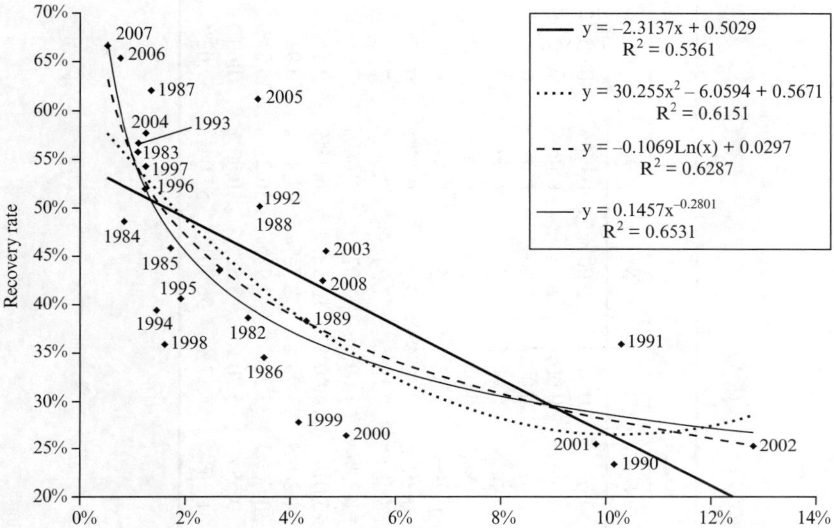

Note: Regression equations are based on data from 1982–2003, with later years data points inserted to show the model's effectiveness.

Sources: 'The Link Between Default and Recovery Rates: Theory, Empirical Results and Implications', Altman, Brady, Resti, and Sironi, *Journal of Business*, November 2005, and NYU Salomon Center.

Figure 8.6 Recovery rate/default rate association, dollar weighted average recovery rates to dollar weighted average default rates, 1982–2008

Returns and Spreads

Table 8.14 shows the return on high-yield bonds for 2008 was −25.91 per cent, the lowest annual return since 1978. The excess return (loss) versus 10-year US Treasury bonds was −46.21 per cent, as the reality of an ongoing recession and the specter of increasing defaults and declining recoveries continued to lead investors to relatively risk-free investments. The absolute return had previously plunged even further to −33.67 per cent in December.

The spread between the yield-to-maturity on high-yield bonds versus 10-year Treasuries increased by 693bp from 1038bp at the end of the third quarter to a year-end total of 1731bp, the highest year-end spread in the history of the Citi High-Yield Market Index. To illustrate the rise in yield

Table 8.12 Mortality rates by original rating – all rated corporate bonds[a] (1971–2008)

		Years after issuance									
		1	**2**	**3**	**4**	**5**	**6**	**7**	**8**	**9**	**10**
AAA	Marginal	0.00%	0.00%	0.00%	0.00%	0.03%	0.02%	0.01%	0.00%	0.00%	0.00%
	cumulative	0.00%	0.00%	0.00%	0.00%	0.03%	0.05%	0.06%	0.06%	0.06%	0.06%
AA	Marginal	0.00%	0.00%	0.28%	0.13%	0.02%	0.01%	0.00%	0.00%	0.03%	0.01%
	cumulative	0.00%	0.00%	0.28%	0.41%	0.43%	0.44%	0.44%	0.44%	0.47%	0.48%
A	Marginal	0.01%	0.06%	0.02%	0.07%	0.05%	0.08%	0.04%	0.25%	0.10%	0.03%
	cumulative	0.01%	0.07%	0.09%	0.16%	0.21%	0.29%	0.33%	0.58%	0.68%	0.71%
BBB	Marginal	0.38%	3.07%	1.43%	1.20%	0.70%	0.28%	0.32%	0.17%	0.13%	0.37%
	cumulative	0.38%	3.44%	4.82%	5.96%	6.62%	6.88%	7.18%	7.34%	7.46%	7.80%
BB	Marginal	1.12%	2.41%	4.32%	2.20%	2.46%	1.23%	1.60%	1.07%	1.68%	3.38%
	cumulative	1.12%	3.50%	7.67%	9.70%	11.92%	13.01%	14.40%	15.32%	16.74%	19.55%
B	Marginal	2.77%	6.72%	7.26%	8.42%	5.96%	4.28%	3.90%	2.35%	1.97%	0.93%
	cumulative	2.77%	9.30%	15.89%	22.97%	27.56%	30.66%	33.37%	34.93%	36.21%	36.81%
CCC	Marginal	7.86%	15.30%	18.66%	11.66%	4.08%	9.55%	5.70%	5.62%	0.80%	4.60%
	cumulative	7.86%	21.96%	36.52%	43.92%	46.21%	51.35%	54.12%	56.70%	57.04%	59.02%

Note: [a] Rated by S&P at issuance based on 2137 issues.

Sources: S&P and NYU Salomon Center.

Table 8.13 *Mortality losses by original rating – all rated corporate bonds*[a] *(1971–2008)*

		Years after issuance									
		1	**2**	**3**	**4**	**5**	**6**	**7**	**8**	**9**	**10**
AAA	Marginal	0.00%	0.00%	0.00%	0.00%	0.01%	0.01%	0.01%	0.00%	0.00%	0.00%
	cumulative	0.00%	0.00%	0.00%	0.00%	0.01%	0.02%	0.03%	0.03%	0.03%	0.03%
AA	Marginal	0.00%	0.00%	0.04%	0.04%	0.02%	0.01%	0.00%	0.00%	0.02%	0.00%
	cumulative	0.00%	0.00%	0.04%	0.08%	0.10%	0.10%	0.10%	0.10%	0.12%	0.12%
A	Marginal	0.00%	0.03%	0.01%	0.06%	0.03%	0.03%	0.02%	0.06%	0.07%	0.00%
	cumulative	0.00%	0.03%	0.04%	0.10%	0.13%	0.16%	0.17%	0.23%	0.30%	0.30%
BBB	Marginal	0.30%	2.06%	1.22%	0.48%	0.45%	0.19%	0.13%	0.10%	0.08%	0.21%
	cumulative	0.30%	2.35%	3.55%	4.01%	4.44%	4.62%	4.74%	4.84%	4.91%	5.12%
BB	Marginal	0.65%	1.39%	2.55%	1.28%	1.47%	0.65%	0.88%	0.46%	0.87%	1.21%
	cumulative	0.65%	2.04%	4.53%	5.76%	7.14%	7.74%	8.56%	8.98%	9.77%	10.86%
B	Marginal	1.85%	4.70%	4.92%	5.62%	3.93%	2.35%	2.50%	1.32%	1.02%	0.67%
	cumulative	1.85%	6.46%	11.07%	16.06%	19.36%	21.26%	23.23%	24.24%	25.01%	25.51%
CCC	Marginal	5.18%	10.86%	13.25%	8.50%	2.86%	7.16%	4.27%	4.33%	0.48%	2.94%
	cumulative	5.18%	15.48%	26.68%	32.91%	34.83%	39.49%	42.08%	44.59%	44.85%	46.47%

Note: [a] Rated by S&P at issuance based on 1930 issues.

Sources: S&P and NYU Salomon Center.

Table 8.14 Annual returns, yields, and spreads on 10-year treasury and high-yield bonds,[a] 1978–2008

Year	Return (%)			Yield to maturity (%)		
	High yield	Treasury	Excess returns	High yield	Treasury	Spread
2008	(25.91)	20.30	(46.21)	19.53	2.22	17.31
2007	1.83	9.77	(7.95)	9.69	4.03	5.66
2006	11.85	1.37	10.47	7.82	4.70	3.11
2005	2.08	2.04	0.04	8.44	4.39	4.05
2004	10.79	4.87	5.92	7.35	4.21	3.14
2003	30.62	1.25	29.37	8.00	4.26	3.74
2002	(1.53)	14.66	(16.19)	12.38	3.82	8.56
2001	5.44	4.01	1.43	12.31	5.04	7.27
2000	(5.68)	14.45	(20.13)	14.56	5.12	9.44
1999	1.73	(8.41)	10.14	11.41	6.44	4.97
1998	4.04	12.77	(8.73)	10.04	4.65	5.39
1997	14.27	11.16	3.11	9.20	5.75	3.45
1996	11.24	0.04	11.20	9.58	6.42	3.16
1995	22.40	23.58	(1.18)	9.76	5.58	4.18
1994	(2.55)	(8.29)	5.74	11.50	7.83	3.67
1993	18.33	12.08	6.25	9.08	5.80	3.28
1992	18.29	6.50	11.79	10.44	6.69	3.75
1991	43.23	17.18	26.05	12.56	6.70	5.86
1990	(8.46)	6.88	(15.34)	18.57	8.07	10.50
1989	1.98	16.72	(14.74)	15.17	7.93	7.24
1988	15.25	6.34	8.91	13.70	9.15	4.55
1987	4.57	(2.67)	7.24	13.89	8.83	5.06
1986	16.50	24.08	(7.58)	12.67	7.21	5.46
1985	26.08	31.54	(5.46)	13.50	8.99	4.51
1984	8.50	14.82	(6.32)	14.97	11.87	3.10
1983	21.80	2.23	19.57	15.74	10.70	5.04
1982	32.45	42.08	(9.63)	17.84	13.86	3.98
1981	7.56	0.48	7.08	15.97	12.08	3.89
1980	(1.00)	(2.96)	1.96	13.46	10.23	3.23
1979	3.69	(0.86)	4.55	12.07	9.13	2.94
1978	7.57	(1.11)	8.68	10.92	8.11	2.81
Arithmetic annual average						
1978–2008	9.58	8.93	0.65	12.33	7.09	5.24
Standard deviation	13.54	11.44	14.61	3.19	2.76	2.97
Compound annual average						
1978–2008	8.76	8.38	0.38			

Note: [a] Year-end yields.

Sources: E. Altman 'Revisiting the High-Yield Bond Market', Financial Management, Vol. 21, Summer 1992, NYU Salomon Center, and Citi.

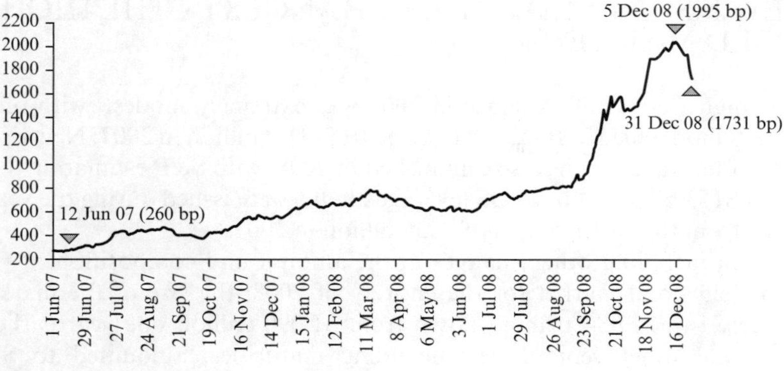

Source: Citi.

Figure 8.7 YTM spread between high-yield bonds and 10-year treasury notes, 1 Jun 07–31 Dec 08

required by high-yield bond investors, Figure 8.7 shows the spread trend from its all-time low of 260bp in June 2007, to the peak spread of 1995bp in December, then its decline for the remaining three weeks of 2008. The option-adjusted spread topped 2000bp in this period.

Due to the exceptionally poor absolute and relative returns in 2008, the arithmetic and geometric average annual return spread versus 10-year US Treasuries for 1978–2008 dropped to just 0.65 per cent and 0.38 per cent, respectively, compared to 2.21 per cent and 2.28 per cent one year earlier. One might conclude that the high-yield asset class is no longer attractive, as a result of these low historical excess returns. However, one should be reminded that a low cumulative historic relative return is not unprecedented, and could also be considered an excellent opportunity for future returns.

The cumulative arithmetic excess return spread dropped to 0.01 per cent for 1978–1990, then came roaring back to a positive 26.05 per cent in 1991. Again, from 1978–2000, the average annual excess return fell to 1.65 per cent and even lower (0.93 per cent) for 1978–2002, before rebounding by 29.37 per cent in 2003, and reaching a cumulative average annual peak of 2.38 per cent by 2006. So, the key question today is: Will the high-yield bond market rebound in 2009 after two years of poor relative returns (as in 1991) or will the drought last for three years, as it did during 2000–02?

NEW ISSUES AND OTHER CHANGES IN THE HIGH-YIELD MARKET

New high-yield bond issuance in 2008 was extremely modest, with only $50.3 billion issued in total – compared to $141.2 billion in 2007. New issuance of leveraged loans also diminished in 2008, with S&P estimating that about $153 billion of new, US leveraged loans were issued during the year, down from the all-time high of $535 billion in 2007.

When including other changes in the amount and composition of the high-yield bond market for the entirety of 2008, the size of the market decreased to $1.084 trillion, down from $1.090 trillion one year earlier. Calls and other repurchases, including maturities, amounted to $39 billion, and along with fallen angels ($38.9 billion), rising stars ($26.6 billion), non-distressed exchanges ($20.3 billion) and defaults and other minor changes, the resultant total market size at year-end, was $1.084 trillion (see Table 8.15).

Credit Quality and Trends in New Issuance

Figure 8.8 shows the proportion of new issue dollars rated B- or lower by S&P for 2008, and annually for 1993–2008. The proportion of this low-quality segment was 15.03%, well below the proportion of 51.25% from a year earlier and the average of 39.22% for 2004–07. This annual percentage is not unusual for times of financial distress and is reminiscent of 2001 and 2002.

Proportion and Size of the Distressed and Defaulted Public and Private Debt Markets

The distressed and defaulted debt proportion of the high-yield plus defaulted debt markets in the United States comprised roughly 85.2 per cent, as of 31 December 2008, up considerably from the 19.8 per cent one year earlier (see Figure 8.9). The cause of this staggering increase is the unprecedented growth of distressed debt (bonds selling at 1000bp, or more, above the risk-free, 10-Year US Treasury rate). This so-called 'distressed ratio' jumped from 10.4 per cent of the high-yield bond market, as of year-end 2007 to 82.0 per cent, eclipsing the previous high of 58 per cent set in 1991. As a result, the distressed segment comprised 67 per cent of the total high-yield plus defaulted debt market ($1.318 trillion) as of year-end, while the defaulted segment increased to 18 per cent, its highest level since 2003.

The defaulted bond amount total is derived by adding the new defaults

Table 8.15 Market changes in 2008 and size of the high-yield bond market (dollars in billions)

Size of market (as of December 2007)	**$1089.9**
New issues	$50.3
Fallen angels	$38.9[a]
Rising stars	$(26.6)[b]
Defaults	$(50.2)
Calls	$(4.2)
Repurchases/Tenders	$(19.1)
Maturities	$(15.7)
Exchanges	$20.3[c]
Size of market (as of December, 2008)	$1083.6

Notes:
[a] First downgrade to non-investment grade from either Moody's or S&P.
[b] Must be investment grade with both Moody's and S&P.
[c] Estimate.

Sources: NYU Salomon Center and Citi.

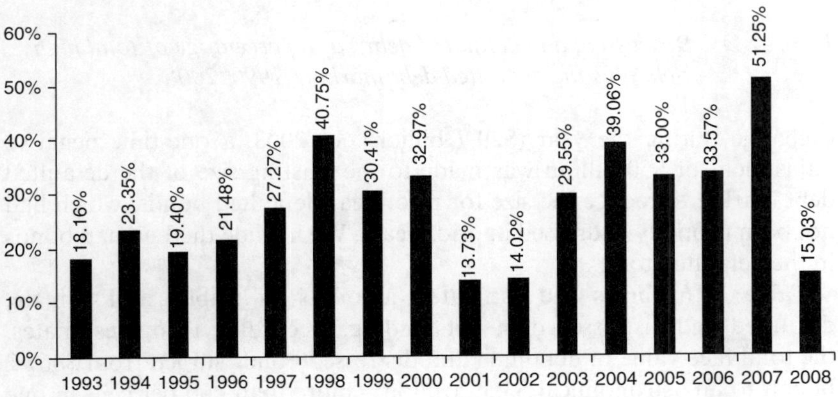

Source: S&P LCD.

Figure 8.8 Percentage of new high-yield issues rated B- or below, 1993–2008 (based on the amount of issuance)

of 2008 ($50.17 billion) to the existing defaulted bonds as of year-end 2007, subtracting those bonds of firms whose reorganization plans were deemed effective and have emerged from Chapter 11 ($16.71 billion and, finally, by deducting the value of bonds which defaulted, as part of a distressed

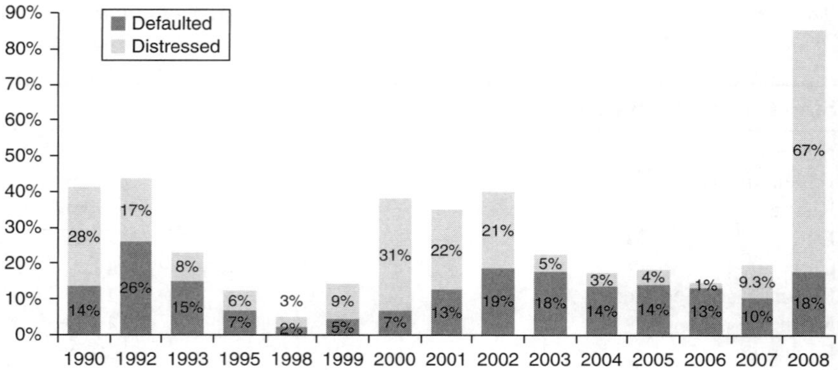

Notes:
[a] Defined as yield-to-maturity spread greater than or equal to 1000bp over comparable Treasuries.
[b] 2008 defaulted debt includes $149.2 billion defaulted bonds by Lehman Brothers and includes a one-time adjustment for prior year defaulted bonds no longer trading.
[c] $1.318 trillion as of December 31, 2008.
[d] Some years not available as no survey results are available.

Source: NYU Salomon Center.

Figure 8.9 Distressed[a] and defaulted debt,[b] as a percentage of total high yield plus the defaulted debt market,[c] 1990–2008[d]

exchange during the year ($29.7 billion). In 2008, a one-time negative adjustment of $50 billion was made to the existing size of the defaulted debt market to reduce the size for prior year defaulted bonds, which had not been properly addressed in prior years. We include the Lehman bonds in the defaulted total.

Table 8.16 shows the estimated amounts of public and private, defaulted and distressed debt outstanding. According to our estimates, the total face value of defaulted and distressed bonds surged from $867.2 billion to an astronomical $3.59 trillion – more than 400 per cent in one year. Distressed debt increased in one year from about $114 billion in 2007 to almost $889 billion, reflecting the significant rise in the distressed ratio. It should be noted that the distressed ratio has been highly volatile of late; witness its decline in the first month of 2009 from 82 per cent to 69 per cent.

We continue to use a private-to-public debt ratio of 2.2 times to estimate the amount of defaulted and distressed private debt (mainly bank loans, mortgages, and trade debt). Applying the 2.2 ratio to our public debt totals, we estimate the face value of private defaulted and distressed debt

Table 8.16 Estimated face and market values of defaulted and distressed debt, 2006–2008 (dollars in billions)

	Face value ($)			**Market value ($)**			
	31 Dec 06	**30 Dec 07**	**31 Dec 08**	**31 Dec 06**	**30 Dec 07**	**31 Dec 08**	**Market/ Face ratio**[d]
Public debt							
Defaulted	156.2	127.3	234.4[a]	101.5	76.4	40.7	0.25
Distressed	17.9	113.6	888.5[b]	13.4	85.2	488.7	0.55
Total public	**174.1**	**240.9**	**1122.9**	**115.0**	**161.6**	**529.4**	
Private debt							
Defaulted	406.1	331.0	515.6[c]	365.5	281.4	299.1[c]	0.60
Distressed	46.6	295.3	1954.8[c]	44.3	265.7	1368.3[c]	0.70
Total private	**452.7**	**626.3**	**2470.4**	**409.7**	**547.1**	**1667.4**	
Total public and private	**626.8**	**867.2**	**3593.2**	**524.7**	**708.7**	**2196.8**	

Notes:

[a] Calculated using: (2007 defaulted population) + (2008 defaults) – (2008 emergences) – (2008 distressed restructurings).

[b] Based on 82.0% of the size of the high-yield market ($1083.6 billion).

[c] Based on a private/public ratio of 2.2; likely inflated in 2008 because not all of Lehman Brothers' liabilities should be subject to the 2.2 ratio.

[d] The market/face value ratio was 0.60 for public defaulted debt, 0.75 for public distressed debt, 0.85 for private defaulted debt and 0.90 for private distressed debt in 2007.

Source: NYU Salomon Center.

is $2.5 trillion. The total face value of public and private, defaulted and distressed debt as of 31 December 2008, is an estimated $3.6 trillion (Table 8.16). This is a staggering increase of about $2.7 trillion from one year earlier, due, in part, to Lehman's defaults, as well as the increase in the distressed ratio. Figure 8.10 shows that the total face value of distressed and defaulted debt is at record amounts, far surpassing the previous high of $942 billion as of year-end 2002.

We have significantly revised downward our market-to-face value ratios of defaulted and distressed debt so as to recognize the fall in prices of outstanding defaulted debt.[7] Applying these market-to-face value ratios to our face value totals results in a total market value estimate of $2.2 trillion (Figure 8.10).

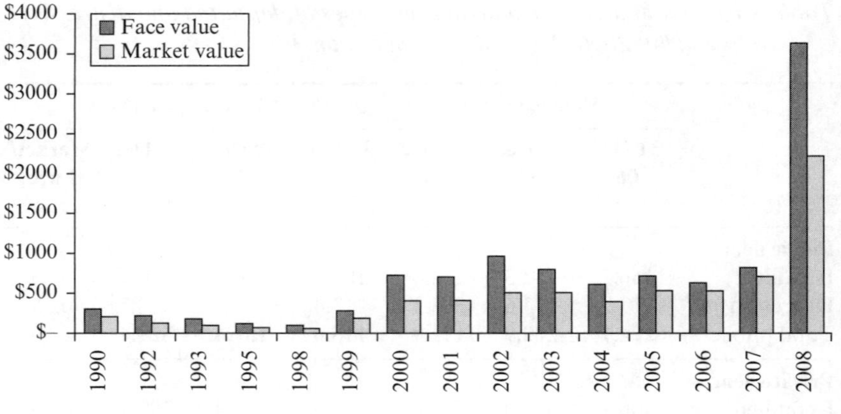

Source: NYU Salomon Center.

Figure 8.10 Size of the defaulted and distressed debt market, 1990–2008 (dollars in billions)

FORECASTING DEFAULT RATES AND RECOVERIES

We are pleased and a bit surprised that our forecast of 4.64 per cent for the 2008 high-yield bond default rate, estimated a year ago,[8] was extremely close to the actual 2008 rate, which came in at 4.60 per cent (Table 8.17). However, we now know that if GMAC had not concluded its distressed exchange in late December, the 2008 rate would have been below 3 per cent.

Using our standard mortality rate forecasting method (see below), our forecasts were higher than the actual rates in 2006 and 2007, when credit markets were abnormally buoyant. We expect our 2009 default rate forecast to be on the low side, using the same mortality rate methodology. After all, the mortality rate incidences of the past have been based on six recession periods (see Figure 8.3) covering only about six-and-a-half years of the 38 in our sample period (1971–2008). A nonrecessionary, macroeconomic climate dominates our statistics, and with a severe recession in place coming into 2009, we expect the mortality rate methodology to underestimate the actual default results. For this reason, we also consider scenario analyses and market-based statistics to provide useful estimates of future results.

Table 8.17 Mortality rate-based forecasts of default and recovery rates in the high-yield bond market, 2007–2009

Year	Default rate	Default amount ($ billion)	Recovery rate
2007 (forecast)	2.50%	$27.5	59.4%
2007 (actual)	0.51%	$5.5	66.6%
2008 (forecast)	4.64%	$53.1	35.8%/39.6%[a]
2008 (actual)	4.60%	$50.2	42.5%
2009(forecast)	7.98%	$86.4	30.0%/31.8%[a]

Note: [a] Based on the log-linear and linear default/recovery rate regressions (see Figure 8.6).

Sources: Mortality Rates (Table 8.12) and NYU Salomon Center.

Mortality Rate-Based Forecast

Utilizing the updated mortality rate statistics in (Table 8.12) and inputting new issuance statistics per rating class over the past ten years, we estimate that the 2009 default will be 7.98 per cent, with a recovery rate of about 30 per cent (Table 8.17). Our forecast includes the expected size of the high-yield bond market for 2009, as well. Since we forecast a substantial amount of defaults in 2009, we do not anticipate the size of the market growing this year.

Scenario-Based Forecasts

Based on recent work, we observed the behavior of default rates during the two most recent recessions, 1991 and 2001. Our forecasts are based on the proportional breakdown of the three major high-yield noninvestment-grade rating categories (Ba, B, and Caa) just before these recessions (Table 8.18) and the subsequent default experience from these categories (Table 8.19).[9] We then applied the breakdown of rating class percentages as of year-end 2008 (Table 8.18) to estimate default rates for 2009, given the 1991 and 2001 recession scenarios.

The resulting default rate forecast for 2009 is 15.4 per cent, given a 1991 default scenario, and 12.3 per cent given a 2001 scenario, which are much higher than our mortality rate estimate and assume that factors such as market conditions, structure, and so on will remain quite similar as in the two prior recessions.

Table 8.18 Rating distributions prior to recessions (per cent of issuers)

	1990	2000	2007	2008[a]
Ba	54	32	29	43
B	44	54	57	35
Caa	2	14	14	22

Note: [a] Year-end based on Moody's, S&P, and Fitch ratings in 2008 (based on dollar amounts); Moody's only in prior years.

Table 8.19 Scenario based forecasts of default in the high-yield bond market, 2009

	Subsequent one-year 1991	Default rate 2001	2009 forecasts[a] 1991/2001 scenarios
Ba	4%	2%	1.7% / 0.9%
B	6%	11%	5.6% / 3.9%
Caa	37%	34%	8.1% / 7.5%
H.Y. default rate	11.0%	10.6%	15.4% / 12.3%

Note: The total is based on the summation of the three rating category contributions.

Sources: M. Fridson: *Distressed Debt Investor* (September 28, 2006, April 17, 2008) and NYU Salomon Center.

Market-Based Methods for Forecasting Defaults

In our third-quarter 2008 report,[10] we introduced two alternative methods for forecasting default rates. The first relies on the market's spread on high-yield bonds compared to 10-year US Treasuries. The second utilizes the proportion of high-yield bonds selling at 1000bp over 10-year US Treasuries. In both cases, we regress the market-based measure in period (t) and the subsequent one-year default rate in period (t+1). Based on the spread on 31 December 2007, this method predicted a 4.62 per cent 2008 default rate, essentially a perfect forecast. As of the end of September 2008, we estimated through this method that the cumulative default rate for the next 12 months, ending September 2009, would be 11.1 per cent.

We have updated our regression analysis for results through 2008 (Figure 8.11) and the resulting equation is essentially unchanged since the actual 2008 default rate fell on the regression line. We have input the most up-to-date spread of 15.51 per cent, as of 30 January 2009; the resulting

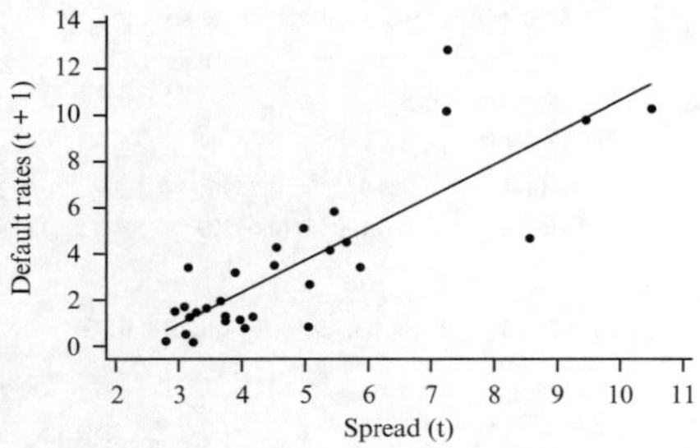

The regression equation is
Default rate = –3.25 + 1.39* Spread

Predictor	Coef	SE Coef	T	P
Constant	–3.2490	0.9072	–3.58	0.001
Spread	1.3904	0.1741	7.99	0.000

S = 1.86079 R-Sq = 69.5% R-Sq(adj) = 68.4%

Compare with prediction based on mortality rate approach (7.98%)

Application

Applying spread (12 Jun 07) of 260 bp, $P_D = -3.25 + 1.39*2.60 = 0.364\%$
Applying spread (31 Dec 08) of 566 bp, $P_D = -3.25 + 1.39*5.66 = 4.617\%$
Applying spread (30 Jan 09) of 1,551 bp, $P_D = -3.25 + 1.39*15.51 = 18.316\%$

Sources: Figures 1 and 30, NYU Salomon Center, and Citi Yield Book.®

Figure 8.11 Market-based forecast: default rate (t+1) versus spreads (t) (1978–2008)

one-year default rate forecast is 18.32 per cent. Again, this rate is far greater than the mortality-rate forecast and even higher than our scenario analysis estimate.

A second market-based method utilizes the distressed ratio, that is, the proportion of the high-yield bond market trading at least 1000bp over Treasuries. The updated regression equation for 2008 is shown in Figure 8.12 Adding the January 30, 2009, distressed ratio of 69.4 per cent – an astonishingly high ratio, but not as high as the 85 per cent figure in mid-December 2008 or 82 per cent as of year-end 2008 – the distressed ratio model reveals an expected 14.16 per cent default rate for year-end 2009.

An important caveat of market-based measures as indicators of future default rates is the potentially large impact on such measures as spreads or the distressed ratio from the liquidity premium demanded by investors. This is especially relevant in the current recession and stressed condition of credit markets. It is difficult to know how much of the spread is due to a flight to quality away from all risky security markets. Since we are mainly concerned with the market's underlying estimates about default and recovery rates, the liquidity premium's impact should be considered and isolated. Anecdotally, estimates of 300–500bp, relating to the market's risk premium due to liquidity conditions, have been suggested recently. If

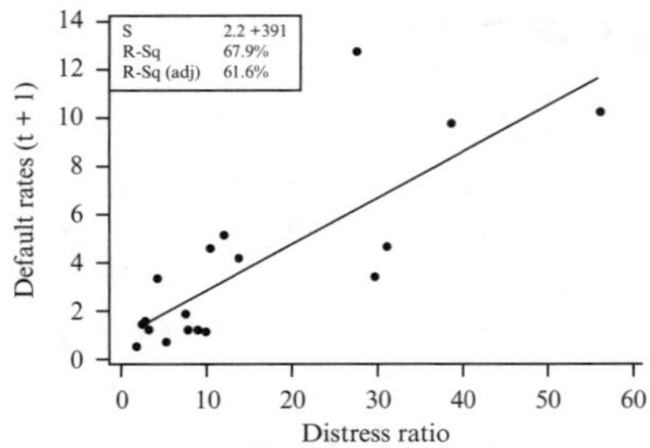

The regression equation is
Default rate = 0.942 + 0.190* Distressed ratio

Predictor	Coef	SE Coef	T	P
Constant	0.9422	0.7596	1.24	0.233
Distressed ratio	0.19045	0.03579	5.32	0.000

S = 2.24391 R-Sq = 63.9% R-Sq(adj) = 61.6%

Compare with prediction based on mortality rate approach (7.98%)

Application

Applying distressed ratio (30 Jun 07) of 1.20%, P_D = 0.935 + 0.193*1.20 = 1.031%
Applying distressed ratio (31 Dec 07) of 10.42%, P_D = 0.810 + 0.193*10.42 = 2.820%
Applying distressed ratio (30 Jan 09) of 69.40%, P_D = 0.942 + 0.190*69.40 = 14.159%

Sources: Merrill Lynch & Co. and NYU Salomon Center, and Figure 1.

Figure 8.12 Market-based forecast: default rate (t+1) versus distressed ratio (t)

the latter, the default rate forecast would be reduced to about 12.0 per cent utilizing the spread forecasting method.

DEFAULT AND RECOVERY CONCLUSIONS

Considering the various forecasting methods, we observe that the forecast range is between 7.98 per cent (mortality rate) and 18.32 per cent (spreads). There is no obvious way to reach a consensus from the different techniques, so we simply took the average of the five to obtain our 13.63 per cent 2009 forecast and a default amount of $147.6 billion (Table 8.20)[11]. Inputting this estimate into our recovery regression (Table 8.6), we estimate that 2009's high-yield bond default recovery rate will be 24.27 per cent, based on our log-linear model, and 18.75 per cent based on our linear model.

As noted earlier, the default and recovery rates in the first quarter of 2009 registered 3.69 per cent and 25.4 per cent respectively, pretty much in line with our forecasts based on the average of the five models.

Table 8.20 2009 default and recovery forecasts: summary of forecast models

Model	**2009 Default rate forecast**	**Default amount (dollars in billions)**	**2009 Recovery rate forecast**[a]
Mortality rate	7.98%	$86.4	30.00%
Scenario (2001)	12.30%	$133.2	25.37%
Scenario (1991)	15.40%	$166.8	22.97%
Spread	18.32%	$198.4	21.11%
Distressed ratio	14.16%	$153.3	23.87%
Average of models	13.63%	$147.6	24.27%

Note: [a] Based on the log-linear regression (Figure 8.6).

Sources: Several prior figures.

NOTES

* Max L. Heine Professor of Finance, NYU Stern School of Business, ealtman@stern.nyu.edu

** Research Associate at the NYU Stern School of Business, bjw215@nyu.edu.

1. An earlier version of this chapter was a working paper at the NYU Salomon Center, Stern School of Business, February 2009.
2. List compiled by E. Griffith, published on www.pehub.com, 5 January 2009.
3. S. Gilson, K. John and L. Lang (1990), 'Troubled Debt Restructurings: An Empirical Study of Private Reorganization of Firms in Default,' *Journal of Financial Economics*, 27:315.
4. Seventeen (30%) were eventually acquired and 11 (19%) were still operating in 2009.
5. The average of the annual weighted average DE recovery rates was 50.8%.
6. 'The Link Between Default and Recovery Rates: Theory, Empirical Results and Implications', Altman, Brady, Resti and Sironi, *Journal of Business*, November 2005.
7. Altman NYU Salomon Center Indexes of portfolios of defaulted bonds and bank loans and estimate for private debt.
8. *Altman 2007 High-Yield Bond Default and Return Report,* J. Fenn, Citi, 6 February 2008.
9. Martin Fridson first reported this scenario approach in his article in the *Distressed Debt Investor*, 28 September 2006.
10. *Altman High-Yield Bond Default and Return Report,* J. Fenn, Citi, 5 November 2008.
11. The actual default rate in 2009 reached a relatively high 10.74% (the second highest annual rate ever), but somewhat below our estimate (and for that matter everyone else's estimate as well). Combined with an enormous input of liquidity into the financial system by the U.S. Federal Reserve System of almost $2 trillion and a great recovery in global stock markets, the financial system averted implosion and recovered impressively. The yield spread (Figure 8.7) dropped to almost normal levels by year-end 2009. The crisis did motivate the Financial Reform Bill (Dodd-Frank Act of 2010) as the nation attempts to avert future financial crises.

9. Regulating the financial markets by examinations

Tamar Frankel

SUMMARY

This chapter proposes changing future government examinations of market intermediaries and focusing on bubbles and crashes as the main dangers to the financial system and the economy. Prior substantive regulation has an undesirable effect on innovations and freedom of the markets. Regulating after a crash (when the 'horse has left the barn') is undesirable and ineffective. Therefore the chapter proposes tighter and closer examinations somewhat different from the current ones: (1) Examine more frequently when market prices rise (not when they have fallen). (2) Examine entities that are too large to fail; those that are highly leveraged; those whose shares-prices rise steadily with little or no fluctuation; and entities that have obtained exemptions from regulation. (3) Examiners should search for violations of the law (and the spirit of the law), but not economic or financial rationalizations. (4) Examiners should be experts, highly paid and incentivized to remain in government employ. Expert information about the markets will hopefully reduce the impact of bubbles and inevitable crashes and the loss of investors trust that decimates the financial system.

INTRODUCTION

It is time to reevaluate the regulation of the financial markets. This reevaluation should include the fundamental regulatory philosophy and its implementation. For the past 60 years two principles guided market regulation. One principle was disclosure by securities issuers to investors. The second principle underlying market regulation was self-regulation by the financial intermediaries, subject to the supervision of the Securities and Exchange Commission (SEC). Added to these two principles were three underlying governing directives. First: Always calculate and balance the benefits of regulation against the cost of regulation to the issuers and intermediaries in the markets: the corporations, the dealers, brokers, advisers and financial planners as well as the insurance salespersons and exchanges. Second: Innovations are the lifeline of the financial system and the banner of American financial leadership. Third: The function of the market regulator – the SEC – is to enforce the law mainly by prosecuting violations. In light of the failure of America's financial system by innovations, competitiveness, disclosure and prosecution, we should reexamine the principles and directives, and consider alternatives.

This chapter proposes a somewhat different approach to market regulation. Under this Proposal the current system may remain in place or be revised slightly, as its basic operation has been in effect for years. Disclosure, self-regulation and enforcement should remain, but the emphasis of market regulation should shift to ongoing examinations; and these examinations should focus on market bubbles and crashes.

To be sure, bubbles are not easily identified. Market prices can be volatile because they reflect the state of the economy, which is what they should do. Markets can be unstable because they can develop bubbles that inevitably result in crashes, which they should not bring about. Besides, the financial markets have changed in the past 30 years. They are far more complex and volatile than they were for many years. They cover the globe, and with the aid of new technology they function worldwide instantaneously. Therefore it is difficult and dangerous to regulate rising prices and attempt to determine whether they might reflect bubbles. And even though crashes can be deadly to the economy, the cost of 'cleaning up' the results of a crash by regulation after the fact may be very high.[1] Besides, it may not be helpful to regulate severe crashes after they have occurred. Wrongful actions that led to bubbles and inevitable crashes are unlikely to be repeated immediately after the crash. Rather other destructive activities might be practiced in the near future.

Some people might view crashes as desirable. After all crashes correct 'bubbly' market prices. However, crashes can be catastrophic when they undermine the public's trust in the market and in the institutions that have established the market practices. Public trust is crucial for the financial system, its institutions and the people who have the power to direct the institutions. Therefore the price of market corrections may be too high as compared to alternative controls that could intervene before devastating 'market corrections' take over. However market regulation poses a dilemma. There are disadvantages to regulating the markets *before* rising prices clearly demonstrate bubbles, and there are disadvantages of regulating the markets *after* destructive crashes.

Under the Proposal in this chapter market regulators should follow a process similar to bank regulation. They should continuously examine financial market intermediaries and even large issuers. Regulators should be most diligent in the 'good times', when market prices rise. They should examine the large corporations and institutions and those whose share prices consistently rise rather than fluctuate. Most importantly regulators should closely examine the institutions and structures that received relief from legal constraints and were allowed to engage in innovative practices. Exemptions from the law must be coupled with close government watchfulness.

However, unlike the bank regulators and the Treasury Department, market regulators should not seek to affect the economic incentives and drivers of rising market prices, even as market prices rise to the bubble stage. Market regulators should aim at detecting violations of existing law, including violations of the spirit of the law, as well as market customs and practices that follow the norms of the law. Government examiners should look for situations which present known problems in new forms. The cost of recruiting and training appropriate and able examiners will be high, yet likely to dwarf the cost of 'cleaning up' after crashes.[2] When examinations uncover violations of the existing law, prosecution should take place. When, in the course of examinations, serious weaknesses in current laws appear, the weaknesses should be reported; suggestions and alternatives should be considered, and then and only then should the laws be amended.

What would be the results of such examinations? There is evidence that rising bubbles are accompanied by rising violations of the law or the spirit of the law. The regulators' continuous examination, their very existence and the interpretation of the data they bring, may help nip in the bud some of these violations before they spread out to contaminate the system; market practices can be influenced and redirected, and at the same time the pressure to soaring bubbles that could lead to disastrous crashes can be controlled or reduced.

Just as the markets have changed in the past 30 years to become more volatile and fast-moving, their regulation should move towards a more flexible complementary system and be readjusted continuously. While regulators are responsible for enforcing the law, they should obtain market data and understand its implication to law and market practices. After all these components create the environment in which the financial system should function and the law that governs it should be effective. Continuous examinations are the least disruptive and most efficient way to help adjust market regulation to the reality of today's financial market.

The outline of this chapter is as follows. The chapter opens with an examination of market bubbles and crashes: What are they, and how they evolve; and the reasons for, and objections to, focusing on bubbles and crashes. The analysis of these extreme market gyrations includes an examination of investors' gullibility, which may lead to or affect the creation of bubbles. That is when investors rely solely on the actions of others and ignore consideration of their own knowledge and judgment.

Part Two poses the question: What should regulators do? It opens with a discussion of what regulators should *not do*: they should not regulate before clear bubbles arise, and should not regulate after the disastrous crashes have clearly appeared. Imposing regulation too early can discourage innovation and results in unintended consequences. Imposing regulation after a crash has occurred is likely to address past wrongs rather than the future ones. This section suggests that there is little need for new laws to address the current problems.

Part Three outlines a Proposal of what market regulators *should do*. They should follow the model of bank and institutional regulation: examinations. This section outlines generally what regulators should examine, who they should examine, the priorities and the limitations on their power.

Part Four focuses on the examiners, their education, compensation, objectives, status and culture of interaction among themselves and with the personnel of the examined entities, their agency and Congress.

This chapter concludes with a short discussion of alternatives to examination, such as the market gatekeepers, internal regulation and self-regulatory bodies, and concludes that they have failed to limit the pressure to, and rise of, bubbles. Therefore a new approach may be more desirable, while these private sector regulators can continue to function to the best of their abilities and within their limitations.

PART ONE: OF BUBBLES AND CRASHES

The Recent Frequent Rise of Bubbles and Inevitable Crashes

During the past 20 years market bubbles have appeared more frequently than during the previous 50 years,[3] and like all bubbles they were inevitably followed by market crashes.[4] After all this is the nature of bubbles. Full of hot air, they usually burst rather than float easily and safely down. The recent crash, combining the enormous bubble of subprime mortgage-backed securities[5] with the failure of the auctions for 'auction rate securities'[6] and the mammoth derivative markets, is shaking not only the financial system and the economy of the United States but the economies of other countries as well.[7] Financial markets have functioned poorly, and some not at all. Information may have been available in the markets. Understanding the information, however, was the province of the very few. Investors relied on each other, the blind leading the blind – a classic bubble.

How can bubbles be identified?

Although the signal of bubbles is rising prices, not all rising prices represent bubbles, and not all bubbles present a danger to the financial system. After all some bubbles, such as the 1990s initial public offerings (IPOs) in technology stocks, involved not only worthless or fraudulent corporate promotions but also enormously successful innovative enterprises, such as Yahoo and Google (although Google arrived publicly later, in 2004). Similarly, even though arguably true bubbles result in crashes,[8] some crashes might have been caused by factors other than bubbles.[9] Besides crashes can be honest and true 'corrections' of market prices. Such corrections do not necessarily result in investors's mistrust in the markets. After a 'blip', markets quickly resume their healthy volatility rather than result in horrendous losses.

Not all bubbles are triggered by predictable or identified actors

Bubbles and crashes can be triggered by events and actors that are hard to predict or single out. For example, bubbles and crashes can be caused by sudden readjustments in the estimation of the amount of equity in the market. Some theorists suggest that bubbles start with 'noise traders', creating 'noise'.[10] That is, their successful trades induce other investors to trail after the traders, sometimes by becoming noise traders themselves, sometimes by following the market trends. And there are always the newspapers and newsletters and various advisers that increase noise.[11] These result in a cascade or as it is sometimes called – a herd phenomenon.

Unintended consequences of regulation can blow air into a price-bubble

Arguably the regulators contributed to the 2007–08 crash. After raising interest rates they lowered the rates drastically, and offered banks 'cheap money'. This policy rewarded banks that have been taking unjustifiable (and perhaps illegal) risks with the depositors' money. The 'run' of investors in the market was rational. It was the government that was gullible at not putting a stop to what the banks were doing. Government regulators believed that the banks needed money to lend but were solvent, but did not check or verify the belief. They were gullible. And those who knew that the banks were insolvent may have been following faith: an unquestioning belief that self-interest will take care of the banks' problems. Thus, in his testimony before Congress, Alan Greenspan, the Chairman of the Federal

Reserve Board during the bubble period, has admitted that 'he had been wrong to think banks' ability to assess risk and their self-interest would protect them from excess'.[12]

Regardless of how bubbles start, they present stock prices that far exceed the true value of the securities to anyone

The excess price is so high as to make it clear at some point that the price represents 'hot air' rather than any substance. Sometimes other factors demonstrate the problem, such as when a significant number of AAA rated securities fail to perform, as in the case of the mortgage-backed securities. At this point investors recreate the story of the child who watched the naked Emperor and declared that the Emperor had no clothes.

Why Should Regulators Focus on Bubbles?

For a number of reasons, bubbles harm the financial system as well as many investors and intermediaries

First, bubbles inevitably end in crashes. This fact does not mean that regulators should always act on the appearance of bubbles. It means, however, that they should pay attention to market bubbles. To be sure markets can indeed correct some bubbles and excesses, without self-destruction,[13] and some bubbles are amenable to cure without much harm to the financial system. Such bubbles are better than others because they produce not only harm but also some good.[14] In all cases, however, crashes shock individuals, corporations and the financial system, and sometimes rattle the economy. Arguably such shocks are less desirable than any good bubbles might produce.

Second, bubbles harm the financial system by helping convert investors' trust into gullibility or by resulting in investors' gullibility. The importance of trust in the financial system and its intermediaries cannot be emphasized enough. The welfare of the financial markets and their liquidity in general depend on investors' trust and on a measure of trust among the financial intermediaries. If the banks do not trust each other, interbank lending shrinks and involves high costs.[15] If investors do not trade, markets dry up.[16]

During bubbles investors trade; in fact they trade furiously. However during these periods investors become gullible rather than trusting. 'Trust' in this chapter means 'a reasonable belief that the other party or parties tell the truth and will abide by their promises'.[17] The definition of trust excludes gullibility and faith. Even though trust, gullibility and faith are based on belief, they differ with respect to the basis for the belief. In trust, belief is reasonable, based on a modicum of verification. Gullibility is a belief that is not reasonable and is not based on any measure of verification. The buyer of the Brooklyn Bridge is not trusting but gullible. And faith rejects legitimacy of verification altogether.

Bubbles are driven by investors' gullibility – unreasonable trust. Investors' trust in prices and behavior rather than their own judgment and knowledge becomes gullibility. Crashes that follow often produce investors' mistrust – extreme and unreasonable as much as gullibility is. In both cases the markets experience a herd phenomenon. Thus trust in the markets can be destroyed by bubbles and their aftermath – crashes.

Market bubbles and crashes offer signals that can help determine the level of investors' trust as compared to the level of their gullibility. In fact gullibility can not only signal bubbles but also be their cause. That is when market prices are far higher than any reasonable price, investors succumb to the market trends they see and not to what they know.[18] Reliance on others and rejection of one's own judgment are the features of gullibility.

Not only the investment decisions of individual investors but also the trades of mutual fund managers are influenced by their peers' actions[19] and there is some indication that herding by mutual funds influences prices.[20] The rise in popularity of investment clubs and of day-trading in the 1990s was probably due in part to a self-feeding effect in which individuals learned from the media or word-of-mouth that many others were day-trading. Several theoretical models of securities market trading[21] and market crashes[22] embody cascade or cascade-like features.[23] Bubbles can be described as 'information cascades'. That is 'when individuals, having observed the actions and possibly payoffs of those ahead of them, take the same action regardless of their own'.[24] Bubbles rise when people follow what others do, in the hope of gain. A crash can be described as when people do the same in the hope of avoiding losses. Investors can be caught in 'being in the market', as reasonable investors were in October 2008.[25]

To be sure it may be reasonable to follow others who are more experienced or for other rational explanations. In addition following others may be rational in saving one's time and attention. And finally following others may be a signal (even though weak) that the market is rising or falling. But when people follow others for no reason except that others do it, the followers turn gullible. Market prices may become less reliable when investors no longer ask, nor care about, *what* they are buying or what they know about what they are buying, and determine their trades solely or mostly on the basis of continuous rise in prices on the assumption that others are buying as well. In a crash, the same trend appears, only in the reverse.[26]

Public policy underlying the regulatory system is aimed at maintaining investors' trust

Many legal rules are based on this objective, imposing limitations and duties to enhance investors' reasonable belief in the truthfulness and reliability of the issuers and the intermediaries of the financial system. The securities acts require issuers to offer much information about their securities and operations. This information is then revised by the staff of the Securities and Exchange Commission.[27] Sophisticated investors receive the information without the revision of the Commission's staff,[28] presumably on the assumption that they can either ask the issuers for explanations and more information or that they understand and can make a judgment about the reliability of the information and the value of the offered securities. Required information, however, supports trust by providing a reasonable belief in the truth of the offered information. Other regulation presumably strengthens belief in the reliability of the issuers' promises. However, the belief is not complete. It leaves space for the investors' judgment and evaluation of whether the securities are suitable for them.

The bone of contention in interpreting the securities acts often centers on the description and evaluation of the investment risk involved in the offered securities. Rarely, if ever, do investors complain about gain. They bring court cases upon investment losses. Being a prediction of the future, the evaluation of the risk depends in part on the information investors receive and its source. If information is too complex and especially if it can easily change with small adjustments in the environment, the value of the information to support verification is greatly reduced. Sales talk and advice of financial intermediaries, tainted with deep conflicting interest, may emphasize positive future probabilities and lower risk. These undermine the reliability of the information.

It makes sense to focus on market bubbles as signaling the level of investor trust because the pattern of market bubbles has repeated itself for many years

We can study again the famous Black Tulip Mania in seventeenth-century Holland,[29] the South Sea Bubble in eighteenth-century England,[30] Law's bank issuance of obligations in eighteenth-century France,[31] America's bubbles and crashes in the 1920s,[32] 1987,[33] and the bubble and crash in the 1990s and beginning of the 2000s.[34] Some bubbles rose higher than others, and some crashes fell lower than others. But they consistently appear in the markets of different countries throughout the centuries, and have been studied.

Past and present bubbles are distinguishable, yet alike

We can learn much from the past bubbles because bubbles and crashes in the securities markets are similar, regardless of time and place.[35] We can distinguish the bubbles of the past from the recent ones based on the different information. In the sixteenth century investors knew that they traded in securities based on black tulips. This knowledge may have precluded a bubble today. But the cascades – the unthinking herd-drive behavior grounded in human nature – seems to have changed little.

The 'tulips' of today are instruments and assets that are not understood. Derivatives, auction-rate notes and some asset-based securities are of this sort. Nonetheless, sophisticated institutions and people traded in them. Perhaps the time will come when everyone would understand the math and technical language for evaluating derivatives; but not today.

Arguably today's investors' ignorance is similar to the investors' ignorance of the past

In the past, many investors did not know how to read, while most of today's investors can read. Today's regulatory system is aimed at making investors financially literate, and helping them to rely on their own investment judgment. Nonetheless the recent bubbles occurred in the markets for securities backed by assets which investors did not understand and did not have the tools to understand. In such cases investors must rely on others not only because in a specialized society everyone must rely on the expertise of others, but also because very few investors could understand the nature of the information that was offered to them. The more highly specialized the information was, the harder it is to evaluate causation and the future, the more reliable and trustworthy the specialists had to be. This does not mean that the specialists can give a clear-cut answer to investors. It may mean that the specialists may have to tell investors that *a risk exists, and they cannot evaluate it*.

For example, sophisticated investors were offered higher interest rate for auction-rated notes. These securities were long-term obligations that became short-term if and when they were bought in short-term auctions. At that time it seemed that auctions would draw traders. But if they did not, the buyers will remain holding long-term notes, while they need cash. Implied or expressed obligations of the market makers could cover this risk. However, information about the ability of the market makers to absorb failed auctions was not disclosed nor examined. In fact market makers held an inventory of these notes. As compared to the investors, the position of these market makers was doubly precarious; their interests seemed identical to the interests of their client note-buyers. Both needed liquidity.[36]

Nonetheless buyers believed the brokers-market makers that they can receive higher interest at the same risk level as 'money in the bank'. Those who did not need the money on short notice could take the risk. But those who were obligated to pay the money short-term took enormous risks. The chance of the market failure was small, but the risk for these particular investors was very large. There came a point when the specialists became omnipotent and trust edged closer to faith – a belief that the specialists were honest and reliable and should not be questioned – or gullibility – trusting the conflicted brokers-market makers. The brokers-market makers possessed inventory that had to be sold. Hence brokers were under pressure to convince new buyers. The buyers had unreasonable trust in the brokers, having forgotten or not fully realizing the brokers' conflicting interest. Buyers became gullible. This is the aspect of the markets to which regulators should attend.

PART TWO: THE REGULATORS' DILEMMAS

Preventing Bubbles

Regulators can attempt to anticipate and regulate possible harmful activities before they actually occur, and thus 'plan' the financial system or the economy. Yet no one is prescient; regulators may make mistakes. Regulation in advance of possible bubbles may preclude innovations and retard the economy.[37] The harms of this approach to investors and the financial system could far outweigh its potential benefits. Arguably bubbles and crashes rise time and again under different names. But not everyone can see through the labels to the substance; even experts might not recognize 'old tricks in new guises'. Hence American law rarely imposes on securities issuers any particular product or design or price. Rather regulation requires the issuers to disclose and describe the offered securities and their features, and leaves the choice to the buyers-investors.[38]

Alternatively regulators can wait until harmful activities are clearly established and launch investigations for violations of the law, and prosecute or settle the charges. Examining the behavior that led to the bubbles, regulators might find and close loopholes in the law that facilitated the rise of bubbles.

Finding out when market liquidity is likely to produce a bubble is not feasible

While liquidity is good, too much liquidity may lead to bubbles. Liquidity is a valuable feature of markets and is good. Liquidity can encourage economic activity. It enables investors to offer their savings to others for productive use, and at the same time recoup their money back if and when they need it. Yet liquidity can induce lenders to lend more, and if the pool of reliable lenders is exhausted, to increased lending to risky borrowers. This increase can demolish the markets, as it has done in the United States in 2008. Thus liquidity, like other good things, may lead to bubbles. In fact every good and beneficial thing can turn bad and destructive, even food and water, fresh air and medicine. All sustain humans and can kill humans. The eternal question is: How to keep and encourage the good while discourage or prevent, the same good from becoming bad. How to sense the heat coming from a potential 'hot zone' which starts the slippery slope towards the bubble?

Finding out when speculating, borrowing and risk-taking are likely to become excessive and bad

Not all speculation is bad. Speculation by investors may depend on the individual's age and activities or on outside preventive power.[39] Innovative adults experience satisfaction in 'pushing the envelope', and are excited in taking the risk of failure and punishment.[40] After all the essence of innovation is breaking out of accepted patterns of thought and action; chafing at restrictions, sometimes passionately, and testing the regulators the way children test authorities.[41] Similarly some borrowing and risk-taking is good, but at some point it can lead to disaster. When regulators refuse to consider leverage in the 'rogue financial system', they allow the good to creep towards the bad side. Precisely when such a change occurs is difficult, and perhaps impossible, to gauge.

Similarly regulators cannot identify the transition from good trustworthy rising market prices to bad 'public exuberance' or gullibility. In 1996 Alan Greenspan expressed this regulatory dilemma: 'How do we know when irrational exuberance [namely bubbles] has unduly escalated asset values, which then become subject to unexpected and prolonged contractions . . .? And how do we factor that assessment into monetary policy?'[42] He was right and wrong at the same time, as he later admitted.[43] The main reason for his mistake, however, was faith and unshaken belief that self-interest of market intermediaries on the one hand, and investors' power on the other hand will guide the market and take care of excesses. Just let them be!

Professor Geoffrey Miller noted the difficulties that a central bank faces when it moves to control potential bubbles, such as the effect of the bank's actions on other countries, international relationships, issues of the bank's authority and potential conflict with other regulatory authorities and political considerations, among others.[44] He concluded:

> that the central bank should not be charged with principal responsibility for policing against price rises in discrete industrial sectors. Other authorities should then carry that responsibility, aware of the general social utility of allowing the price system to operate free of government intervention. If these authorities do intervene, they should use regulatory tools targeted at only the affected sector and not elsewhere.

The central bank should monitor economic developments and 'alert the appropriate authorities'. And only when the bubble threatens the economy should the central bank 'use monetary policy to counteract such a bubble'.[45] While these words were written in 1996 with respect to the bubble in Japan, they could apply with equal force to the bubbles and crashes in the United States.

The passive regulators and move to the 'hot zone' is well illustrated in the United States. For example, the government corporations of Fannie Mae and Freddie Mac were useful but then crossed to the 'hot zone', having grown to manage over $3 trillion, holding an enormous number of failing mortgage loans, and posing a threat to the American economy. On 30 August 2008 the *Wall Street Journal* reported that in the first month of his service as the Secretary of the Treasury, two deputies of Henry Paulson 'flagged Fannie Mae and Freddie Mac as significant risks to the economy. Mr. Paulson didn't share their level of concern.' When he was at Goldman Sacks, these corporations were not on his list. But '[t]wo years later, they're at the top of his list'.[46] In September 2008 Fannie Mae and Freddie Mac were nationalized![47] The government removed their management, acquired their assets, their debts and liabilities.

If not a 'first' in the United States, this step of nationalizing a semi-private business corporation is certainly unusual, in stark conflict with the lore that the markets should and would resolve problems of excesses. The decision to take over these two semi-government corporations, in the environment of a crisis, may be viewed later as a mistake or a brilliant solution, but it is difficult to judge it until its results become clear in the future. The most difficult task of anyone, including investors and regulators, is to predict whether and when financial innovation will tend to turn from good contributions towards bad destruction, and discover this turnabout 'hot zone' sufficiently early on.

In the United States, Regulators Did not Act During the Rise of Bubbles

During the rise of bubbles Congress and the regulators have tended to relax regulatory prohibitions and offer exemptions from legal constraints to innovative financial activities.[48] During this period Congress and the regulators have adopted a light touch in enforcing the existing law.

When bubbles burst and crash, Congress and the regulators have taken a very active and public role, and new laws were passed when fraud was uncovered.[49] There can be many reasons for this trend. While the concern of the public may be identified when a 'run' is on the way,[50] it seems that the bubble heat is harder to detect. Perhaps regulators believed that there is little they can do to cool down the heat of a bubble. Arguably a rising bubble is less preventable, as one researcher averred. According to him empirical data raises doubts about 'the effectiveness of margin regulations, the prime example of this type of antibubble law, in real-world markets'.[51] Whatever the reason, regulators not only did not take steps to cool down a bubble but to some extent released strict regulation and to help it rise. With a crash, however, regulators pursue and investigate frauds, prosecute and enact new rules to clarify vague prohibitions.

In the United States, Regulators Act After the Crash

While regulators relax rules and adopt a 'wait and see' policy during the rise of bubbles, they take steps to tighten regulation and impose new ones. They examine crashes with great care to determine why and how the 'horse got out of the barn'. Figuratively speaking they may even create new locks for the barn door. But next time the horse may leave the barn through another door, while the locked door can become a hazard if a fire starts in the barn. It seems that there is no winning policy for regulators: Advance planning is bad. 'Wait and see' may be bad. And 'after the fact' rules to meet crises may be obsolete and bad. If discovered, destructive activities are not prohibited at the time when they were committed, they cannot be prosecuted. And future destructive activities cannot yet be imagined.

The recent consequences of the 'wait and see' approach have been serious. In 2007 and 2008, when the crash of subprime mortgage-backed securities was percolating in the American financial system and rippling steadily throughout the economy, arguments about what regulators should do have reached new heights. Congress and the regulators not only passed laws and took regulatory action.[52] They became active partners to the financial system. Congress allocated funds to failing institutions;[53] the Federal Reserve Board distributed money and negotiated deals to save whatever is possible from the debacle of financial institutions,[54] as well as to offer relief to millions of homeowners slated for eviction from their homes.[55] Moreover, in an unprecedented step, the government *nationalized* semi-government corporations – Fannie Mae and Freddie Mac.[56] Thus the regulators and the government have been offering a helping hand to blunt market solutions that became too painful or, as an economist would say: too costly.

After a crash United States regulators conduct investigations. The SEC, the regulator of the securities markets, is investigating the crash and violations of the law

The SEC launched a widespread investigation of mutual funds in 2004 after revelations about market timing wrongs,[57] and followed the investigations and the prosecutions with a new batch of rules. The Commission recently launched a far-flung investigation to find out what happened to auction-rate notes, how they were sold and whether the laws were violated.[58] This investigation began after it became clear that auction-rate notes resulted in massive losses (and former gains) when the auction processes failed.[59] The investigation led to compromises and settlements that involved quick compensation to needy investors who believed that they were buying and holding near-cash securities and found themselves holding five-to-thirty-year notes.[60]

More recently, during the 2008 'turmoil' in the financial markets, the SEC announced that the Enforcement Division and its Director would 'expand their ongoing investigations by undertaking a series of additional enforcement measures against market manipulation'. The Division would 'obtain disclosure from significant hedge funds and other institutional traders of their past trading positions in specific securities' and require those institutions 'to secure all of their communication records in anticipation of subpoenas for these records'.[61] The expanded examination would include the 'unusual step'[62] of 'obtaining statements under oath from market participants'.[63]

Failures of particular corporations that reach and shake the public are usually followed by new regulations. The recent Sarbanes-Oxley Act[64] is such an example. There are voices cautioning against adding substantive rules.[65] The Sarbanes-Oxley Act has received a concentrated howl of protests.[66] Regulation has been blamed for the crashes.[67] Regulators have been blamed for self-interest, self-aggrandizement and subtle or not so subtle corruption,[68] and inaptitude and having been captured by the regulated entities.[69] In fact a Commissioner of the Securities and Exchange Commission preached for restricting the Commission's activities.[70] The call is for substituting economists for lawyers at the Commission's staff.[71] For these regulators, law is economics and economic values should become the values of the law. These voices express deep mistrust of, with a whiff of hostility to, government regulation and government regulators and above all – to law.

There are voices calling for more and stricter regulation[72]

These voices raise serious doubts about the efficiency of the informed markets, especially in light of the complexity of the current financial instruments and institutions and the inability to publicize what is truly important to understand in the securities that are offered and the trading that is taking place.[73] In fact a recent study concluded that investors trust their brokers, dealers, financial advisers and financial planners, and do not distinguish between them. Neither do they care to know the difference.[74] They trust rather than protect themselves from these intermediaries. In addition the subprime mortgage-backed securities 'markets' consisted of three or four rating agencies that followed the same pattern and competed among themselves for the favors of customers who press for high ratings.[75] This is not the 'invisible hand' that Adam Smith envisioned.

Thus serious issues relate to the timing of regulation and activist regulators
Before bubbles rise, new regulation can stifle innovation and healthy growth. After the market crashes, it is doubtful whether 'post mortem' new laws are worth the cost. After all it is likely that the next bubbles might rely on different forms of fraud which would make use of different environmental opportunities. Knowledge gleaned from these investigations may not be sufficient to guide against future systemic risks.

Prosecutions, to the extent that they lead to significant punishments, such as long prison terms for high-ranking executives, might have a deterrent effect;[76] but not for long. The regulators change, the executives change and the environment – economic, financial and political – changes to make memories hazy and distant. Deterrence, without a continuing signal of threat, fades. If regulators wait too long, we may and will experience a crash that can crash more than market prices, and injure the financial system. If regulators do not wait long enough they may freeze innovations, which is the United States' economic bloodline.

The Effect of the Changes in the Financial Markets

There are serious questions about the effect of any new regulation of the financial markets. The markets have changed and in-depth knowledge about these changes is missing. In the past 30 years the traditional financial system ceased to be. In the past the financial system was composed of market intermediation, in which brokers, dealers, advisers, financial planners and formal and informal exchanges brought together buyers and sellers of financial assets, and institutional intermediation, composed of intermediaries who issued their own obligations to one party and then turned around and bought the obligations of other parties, thus intermediating among these parties by becoming a party to each of them. These are the commercial and investment banks, savings and loan associations, various savings banks, credit unions and mutual funds.

During the past 30 years there arose new types of intermediation, such as the securitization process. This process starts with traditional institutional intermediaries, such as banks, and proceeds through an intermediate institution (Special Purpose Entity) (similar to a mutual fund), to the market, where the Special Purpose Entity issues securities, and the development of a secondary market in these securities by market intermediaries. Both institutional and market intermediaries have been engaged in creating this hybrid intermediation form. Derivatives markets have flourished. Banks contain investment banks and the latter contain the former, and both manage insurance as well.

The particulars and details of the present market are less known. Yet to a great extent the laws on the books are out of sync with current market structures and practices.[77] The laws that govern market and institutional intermediaries differ. The regulation of banks, insurance companies and mutual funds, for example, is far more intrusive and imposes greater restrictions on the business of these intermediaries than the regulation of market intermediaries. And as the size and diversity of market intermediaries has grown, they no longer pass other issuers' securities from sellers to buyers, but have come to closely resemble institutional intermediaries, such as banks, that issue their own obligations and receive the obligations of others. They pose 'banking dangers' to the financial system, where their obligations and assets no longer match. Yet their regulation did not change.

Regulators are not always aware of market changes as they occur, and learn about these developments later, if not too late. Even when they receive the information, they might not have the personnel to decode the meaning of the changes. Consequently the regulators might establish priorities and reactions without recognizing the importance or even the existence of other activities.

PART THREE: A PROPOSAL: WHAT REGULATORS SHOULD DO: ACTIVISM BY EXAMINATION

Market Regulators Should Conduct Continuous Examinations; They Should Act as the 'Police Officer on the Beat'

The police officer on the beat does not carry a gun. He carries a baton. That officer has the authority to stop suspicious persons or activities and ask questions. That officer moves in the neighborhood and learns the terrain, the inhabitants, their foibles and their strengths. The officer recognizes those who present more danger and those who present less danger.

That officer learns to identify the gang leaders and their followers. And that officer shares the information with her colleagues without making an arrest or firing a shot.[78]

To be sure, this comparison to the regulators of the financial system is not entirely precise. Police officers on the beat rarely work in neighborhoods where residents have more authority, including more money and more armed men, than the officers and their backing do. Controlling the residents of more violent neighborhoods with a baton might be far more difficult, yet not necessarily futile. The very presence of the police may remind the residents of the law and its potential enforcement. Some neighborhoods need fewer police to protect neighbors from each other, and more protection from outsiders. Yet in all cases police are there to protect.

The Ongoing Examinations

Market regulators should follow a process similar to bank regulation

They should continuously examine financial market intermediaries and large issuers. Banking examination can offer a model. In large banks examiners reside more or less continuously for a number of years. The same system can apply to market intermediaries such as the large broker-dealers, large mutual fund advisers-managers and the large pension funds that are self-managed. Some of these institutions are currently subject to examinations, but the visits of the examiners are not sufficiently frequent. Examinations should be continuous, if possible at least once a year. Examinations should be designed for each form of intermediary to fit its functions and the possible danger it poses to the system. This approach is already taken not only in the banking system but also by the Securities and Exchange Commission's examiners of mutual fund managers and advisers.

Examinations and regulation should intensify and become more frequent when market prices rise rather than when markets crash and prices fall

This recommendation suggests a drastic reversal of the current practice. In light of the analysis above the hope for cooling the hot zone of bubbles is during their rise and before they crash, not after they crash. Similarly regulators should be most diligent in 'good times,' when market prices rise. The rises may be due in part to better economic conditions or to violations of the law. Examining and strictly regulating violations during these periods might dampen the investors' ardor leading to excesses and bubbles. While violations of the law can be broadly interpreted, examiners should refrain from intruding on the business judgment of the examined entities. This is the difference between regulation of financial institutions, such as banks, and financial market intermediaries, such as broker dealers. It may well be that if examiners note persistent imprudent activities, they might report them. But the focus of the examinations should be on violations of the law. And there is a high probability that some highly imprudent activities will fall within the prohibitions of the law, especially if such activities threaten the financial system.

Examinations and regulation should focus on entities and institutions that are too large to fail[79]

The obvious reason for these examinations is to help predict and prevent the failure of such enterprises that may affect the financial system as a whole. The examinations should lead to restrictions that may not apply to smaller corporations. Perhaps some regulation should precede these examinations but, in light of the current information, these large institutions have violated current laws; there may be no need for more except to detect and stop them.

To be sure, global institutions are likely to experience more violations. Nonetheless they should be required to establish strict internal supervision, with the help of government guidance. And if institutions are concerned about offering examiners a view of proprietary materials, this concern, as well as similar ones, can be resolved by special protections for such material.[80] No large institution can be allowed to borrow or speculate to the extent of endangering the financial system and requiring the taxpayers that suffer from its management's actions to foot the bill of its rescue. That is the purpose of the examinations.

Examinations should focus on financial entities that are highly leveraged

Such entities, especially if they are sufficiently large, can pose a threat to the financial system. In addition they may offer a dangerous example to competitors and drive to rising leverage beyond the hot zone of bubbles. Here, again, the main purpose is to examine and uncover the level of leverage rather than regulate it. That is because some businesses may have levels of leverage that are higher than others without endangering their existence or the competitive position of their competitors, while others may pose such dangers.

Examinations should focus on entities whose share prices rise without fluctuations[81]

The reason for these examinations is that more often than not performance that is 'too good to be true', is not true. Absence of volatility usually involves fraud and violations of the law. The sooner such frauds are uncovered the better off the investors and the financial system will be. At the same time such performance has led too many investors, including sophisticated investors to trust and invest in these enterprises. That is when the government's examination is crucial.

These institutions should draw attention not because all these institutions are presumed fraudulent, but because they, more than others, could reflect the 'too good to be true' syndrome. One could argue that regulators' attention of this sort would provide a disincentive for the corporations to succeed, or to succeed consistently in the market. That may indeed be the case for some corporate managers. However, incentives to show consistent performance may balance and overcome the incentives to hide success and thereby hide from the regulators' attention. Besides if the corporations' books are subject to examination, then the attempt to hide failures and substitute them for success is more likely to be discovered. That possibility can deter attempts to 'manage' the financial data.

This is also the time when investors' trust may turn into gullibility and when investors could become a herd rather than the aggregate of rational, investigating investors.[82] It is precisely the time when no 'education' of the investors can help; no information and learning can affect investors who see an opportunity to profit quickly and very handsomely – because 'everyone does it' and everyone becomes richer.

Finally examinations must cover corporations and entities that have received exemptions from the law

The reason for this examination-focus is that by definition, freedom from legal constraints may be used well or abused. The legal constraints were imposed because the prohibited activities could bring about undesirable social results. The exemptions can be granted to allow for innovations, and probably subject to some constraints, but not all possible fraudulent uses of the relief. Securitization of mortgages took advantage of the exemption from the Investment Company Act of 1940,[83] because the process could not be practiced under the constraints of the Act. The exemption included prohibitions and conditions, but did not include a prohibition on pyramid structures. The structure was practiced under the umbrella of the exemption and produced much harm.[84]

Examiners should focus only on detecting violations of existing laws

This includes the spirit of the laws, as well as focusing on market customs and practices. They should not attempt to determine whether the market is evolving a bubble or a crash. But they should look for signals that these trends might produce.

What are the Purposes and Boundaries of Examinations?

Examiners should gain information and understanding of the data

Even if the staff of the SEC is powerless to chastise the very large institutions, staff examination can help the SEC gain more information, and understanding, and become vigilant. Examiners should gather data with a view of determining whether the examined organization was: (1) violating specific provisions of the law, (2) violating standards established in law or (3) conducting activities that may lead to violating the standards of the law but that are not prohibited by law.

Little need be said about the discovery of clear blatant violations of specific provisions of the law. Such a discovery protects market actors and the financial markets and the examined enterprises have nothing to complain about. But examinations that focus on the standards of the law and potential legal violations raise the question of whether the examiners could and would avoid involvement in precisely what this Proposal rejects. That is could they include the economic and financial evaluation of the examined entities' activities? The answer is that they should, if they focus on the law, but not necessarily on merely the forms or narrow interpretation of the law. Their purpose is fact finding and not regulation. They should report rather than decide what the results of their finding would be.

However, how can examiners focus only on the law when, in their opinion, some of the activities violate standards and principles and policies on which, in their opinion, the law is based, and even more seriously, activities which in the opinion of the examiners – should be prohibited, although they are not presently prohibited? Will these examiners not engage in economic regulation?

The answer to that is functionally the examiners should do nothing but examine. Their findings should be transferred to others, who will make the policy decision. However, expert examiners should be the interpreters of the facts they are reporting. The more expert they are, and the more expertise the data requires for understanding, the greater their discretion is going to be. In such cases the examiners will have to interpret their opinions and explain to the decision-makers the principles, policies and judgments that the examiners have made. If they considered costs and financial issues, they should report these as well. But to the extent possible, the examiners should not attempt to judge the economic, financial and business decisions of the investigated enterprises. The implications of the facts uncovered, however, should be expounded and explained.

Examiners should learn about financial innovations and the developments in the markets

It is not enough for examiners to know the law and to understand the data. It is just as important for examiners to grasp the 'market practices and understandings' and notice their various implications. The United States would have greatly benefited from an expert explanation of Enron Corporation's actions and securitization activities. An evaluation of auction-rate notes would have been helpful as well. And an understanding of the rating agencies' systems, their conflicts and their attitudes would have been desirable. An insight into the structure of securitization that allowed for pyramid structures would have saved the financial system billions of dollars.

Had regulators known about the prevalence of market timing by mutual funds advisers, they would have acted before the practice became so widespread. Had regulators been aware of the army of mortgage brokers that grew by leaps and bounds during a very short period, and had they been on notice of the precise type of borrowers that the mortgage brokers were targeting, and had regulators understood the terms of the mortgages, they might have been alert to the rating agencies's AAA rating. They could have just asked the rating agencies how such terms could bring about these high ratings. They might have found out that the buyers did not read nor examine the terms of the loans. Perhaps the examiners might have even uncovered the identity of the borrowers. They might have discovered the fact that neither borrowers nor investors have read or examined the terms of the loans. Had regulators understood how the rating agencies performed their functions, America might not have suffered a crisis in 2008. Had they perceived the magnitude, impact and risks of derivatives, they might have reconsidered the overall exemptions that covered the $600 trillion of these derivatives.[85]

Justifications for the Proposal

In addition to the disadvantages of regulating financial markets before bubbles reach the crash stage or after market crashes, strong *continuous examinations* offer a number of advantages.

First, examinations are not a new regulatory device

They are not new for the regulators, or for the institutions and persons subject to the regulation. After all corporations, and especially financial intermediaries, such as banks, broker-dealers and advisers of mutual funds are used to examinations. Examinations would be far less bewildering to the public and to the regulators. The proposed change might involve the details and frequency of the examinations but not the very introduction of the examination process. In addition a move to more continuous examinations should hardly change the applicable laws. Further the examiners' expertise would supplant the missing expertise of the investors. It leaves intact, but without full reliance, the private sector gatekeepers that have also not been very successful.

Examinations can be flexible

If a corporation or a financial institution has passed examinations with few difficulties, its examinations should become shorter even if they will not become less frequent. A similar approach was adopted by the SEC. Institutions that passed examinations with fewer problems might be visited less frequently than those that had problems to be corrected. Accountants have adopted the system by which, if they encounter more than the usual problems, they begin to examine more of the materials before them, and as more problems are uncovered, more materials are examined.[86] The same approach could be taken by the regulators-examiners.

Examinations can deter violations of the law

To be sure, deterrence can be achieved by harsh and jarring lessons, such as lifelong prison sentences that executives have received. That can scare others in similar positions. However, examinations on an ongoing basis can be a more effective deterrent because although they are low-key rather than jarring, they are continuous reminders of the watchful eyes of the law. Habits are hard to establish, but also hard to change.[87] If good habits are inculcated, then, even in a changing environment and changing personnel, institutional habits can survive.

Thus examinations can be compared to the annual doctor's checkup or dentist visits. They are usually preventive. If problems appear, they can be fixed before they become far more serious. And they are expected, accepted and recognized for what they are – preventive measures. Examiners might research this issue and bring it to the attention of the substance-regulators, who can act before transactions fail.

Both examiners and examined can benefit from interacting with each other

These parties can develop limited cooperative relationships rather than corroding hostile ones, without necessarily losing sight of the main objective of the examinations. Most importantly if the public is aware of the examinations, as the public is currently aware of the examinations of banks by the Federal Deposit Insurance Corporation, the public's trust in the markets may deepen. This trust strengthens the financial system and benefits the actors in the system.

By moving from prosecution after the fact to ongoing examinations the financial system is likely to experience less destructive bubbles and crashes

Bubbles and crashes are indeed likely to continue, regardless of rules and regulations. However, a move from after-crash prosecution to ongoing long-term examinations, with sensitivity to violations of the law that are likely to accompany bubbles, may minimize the devastating impact of crashes. A wide-open door can be left to innovations, as examiners spot those innovations that lead to undermining the law and trust in the financial system. Following the innovations might help regulators later halt their impact in time. Moreover, for the regulators, examinations, although consistent and long-term, are likely to be less costly than court litigation, especially against well-endowed defendants who are using well-staffed law firms.

Most importantly changing the focus from prosecution to examination can take place piecemeal, by stages, starting from the most leveraged and larger institutions. These institutions might have the innovative personnel, and pose the greatest danger to the system. This is where examiners can learn. But if examiners find that the danger lies elsewhere, they might move to that part of the financial system, for example, the incubators of derivatives, or the brokers or real estate appraisers, or insurance companies' banking specialties.

Currently a more significant portion of the SEC's resources is devoted to enforcement by prosecution, including investigation of particular offenses

The Commission's Office of Compliance is far smaller. As compared to the banking regulators, the SEC examination force is even smaller. This allocation of resources should change. Most of the Commission's funds should be allocated to examinations, and to investigations leading to prosecution. For example, the Securities and Exchange Commission examines broker-dealers.[88] Yet these examinations did not uncover the highly leveraged and risky position of mammoth broker-dealers such as Merrill Lynch[89] and Bear Stearns,[90] both of which were sold in a fire sale with different degrees of help from the Federal Reserve Board.[91]

The examiners should acquire full information

Yet not all information should become public. Whether and to what extent they could make their conclusions public must be left for the difficult 'devilish details'.

Disadvantages and Criticisms

This proposal involves costs and dangers of regulators' capture

Examiners who command high expertise should be well compensated. Currently the difference between the pay of SEC examiners and the equivalent in the private sector is significant.[92] Expert examiners cannot be wooed to government employment if their current standard of living is significantly lowered. They must be paid salaries which may be higher than the current government pay scales. The sources of such experts are academia and the private sector. It may be possible to draw from both sectors a sufficient number of experts who might spend their time and contribute their knowledge for a specified period.

In addition expert examiners may move to the private sector and deal with the entities that they examined in a revolving door. That would open an earlier door to examiners' capture by the 'examinees'. The issues of the revolving door and the capture of regulators by regulated entities are not new. They have been dealt with, more or less successfully throughout the years. Examiners might be assigned to particular entities for a number of years and then moved to others. After leaving the government, examiners might be barred from consulting with the same type of entity, not only with the examined entities, for a number of years. And the more recognition, prestige, compensation and the less frenzy and pressure the examiners experience the more likely they are to choose examiners as their career.

This proposal raises the everlasting issue of trust in the financial markets and the cry for freedom from regulation

Private sector management has limited trust in Congress or in the regulators. As previously mentioned, regulators are among those blamed for the 2008 financial and economic crisis. In the United States such mistrust is a good feature. Powerful institutions force other powerful institutions to be more accountable. Conflicts among powerful constituencies in society increase freedom more than if these constituencies become friendly. Therefore one could expect a strong and lasting protest from the private sector leaders. In fact the Chamber of Commerce has already raised the battle cry and announced its intention to fight, presumably for its conservative members. Similarly a large union has been holding Boeing Corporation and demanding long-term job security.[93] Sometimes, as is the case recently, mistrust is mutual. James Grant suggests that America is 'losing confidence in Washington with the administration losing faith in capitalism'.[94] In such an atmosphere ongoing examinations and suggestions for improvements, rather than prosecutions and investigations, may offer the better approach. Each party can flex its muscles to show and yet cooperate.

Is this proposal too ambitious?

Arguably it is. It embraces too many different situations, subject to different laws, which may require different regulator reactions. These cannot offer an overview of the financial system from above. Therefore such examinations are less useful.

There are a number of answers to this criticism. First, the Proposal in this chapter is limited to the financial markets and their intermediaries such as the brokers, dealers, financial planners, money managers of mutual funds, pension funds and other pooled investments. It does not cover financial institutions such as banks, insurance companies and savings and loan associations. Second, even though the financial markets and their intermediaries are regulated by many laws, the underlying policy of the markets' regulation is grounded in disclosure. Thus, until recently, regulators of market intermediation dealt with issues concerning what and how information should be disseminated to the markets, and the nature of the violations of disclosure and non-disclosure rules. Market regulation has also relied on private sector gatekeepers: the lawyers, accountants and various types of advisers and salespersons, as well as compliance officers and boards of directors. And yet, none, alone and together, has managed to stem the avalanche of violations of the law. In fact some of the gatekeepers sought to provide and were rewarded for pointing to loopholes into which actors could wriggle through to presumed legality.

The recent market crash awakened the country to the realization that the large market intermediaries resemble banks and other institutional intermediaries. Market intermediaries are no longer individuals or small groups of individuals but huge institutions whose failure can devastate the system and perhaps the economy. In addition information concerning many financial assets is far too complex for disclosure in the usual way. This information requires expert readers to decipher, understand and evaluate. In a recent book *Panic* Michael Lewis accuses Robert Merton, Myron Scholes and the innovative Black-Scholes model as being one of the causes for modern crashes.[95] However, there were many other complicated instruments that could not be grasped and evaluated. And while these innovations purported to assure investors by seemingly reducing market risk, in fact, they did not. Further because the entire financial system has been moving from institutions to markets, market failures can harm the system and economy as much, if not more, than the failure of the banking system and its progenies.

Thus even though the laws that govern various forms of market trading differ, the issues and problems that financial markets raise are very few and surprisingly similar. Solving these problems or reducing their impact is crucial to the revival and maintenance of the financial system. These problems involve less rules or standards. They involve far more people's nature, their trust, society's culture and containment of private power by accountability and supervision.

Why not consider an alternative to government examination, such as self-regulation by market intermediaries?

Examination can be divided into internal self-regulation of individual institutions by compliance officers or outsourced compliance private sector entities. Self-regulation can also be performed by membership organizations, such as FINRA, the stock exchanges and the bar associations, or associations such as members of the medical profession.

To be sure these institutions impose some responsibility on their members, but not perhaps as rigorously as is needed. These self-regulatory organizations are beset by conflicts within their members. They serve the interests of the trade or profession and not only or perhaps not mostly the interests of the public and the financial system. Their strict self-regulation might come after a crash, but is unlikely to become vigilant with a bubble.[96] The recent bubble has demonstrated the inadequacy of private self-regulating organizations.

What about disclosure as an alternative to enhanced examinations?

This Proposal does not suggest eliminating disclosure from the regulatory arsenal. Perhaps it should be enhanced, even as the number of prosecutions may be reduced. Unfortunately disclosure alone is ineffective in many cases of bubbles, such as when the relevant information is highly technical and requires not only specialized knowledge but also specialized tools before it can be deciphered. To understand the disclosed material requires professional knowledge, similar to law and medicine. Disclosure to market participants should remain at a level accessible to a model of unsophisticated investors in our day and age.

In addition not all relevant information can be disclosed without injury to the examined institutions and corporations. Some information is proprietary and calls for protection as business secrets. Such information, however, could be sheltered in the hands of government examiners under the current law.[97] And if this law is insufficient to protect the examined institutions, it is not difficult to add appropriate protections to the current law.

The Policy Concern

Market regulators might intrude on the private sector leading to a planned economy

We clearly do not choose a planned economy. However regardless of our choice, when market intermediaries in the financial system do not exercise self-controls and so bring about a destructive bubble the government should interfere before the financial system enters the hot zone.

This Proposal is limited to examinations, proposing a change in the focus of regulating financial market intermediaries. The Proposal draws on the regulation of institutional financial intermediaries such as banks, but not completely. It leaves far more space for the markets and limits substantive regulation. The Proposal is based on the principle that market regulators should not and would not impose their views on the economic and financial decisions of market actors.

However, neither should regulators remain passive and silent during rising bubbles. They should not wait for crashes to indicate more specifically where the problems lie. Investigations of past facts do not necessary teach what will trigger future bubbles and crashes that are bound to rise, and the frauds that may accompany them or bring them about. By watchful following of the market actors, regulators might learn when to interfere in a dangerous trend and how to lightly affect its direction.

This Proposal shifts the regulatory emphasis to examination from mere disclosure on the one hand and active prosecution on the other hand. The Proposal shifts to government examiners some of the burden that is currently imposed without much success on the investors. To be sure investors do affect the markets. They also create the bubbles and the crashes. And these are the markets' main problems today.

CONCLUSION

Law without enforcement is a dead letter; enforcement without information is an empty word. Investors do not enforce the law, regardless of the information they receive. They rarely avoid the intermediaries' fraud or inducements. Investors' reaction to information may destroy the financial system by bubbles and crashes. To prevent such destruction law must be enforced continuously, and that can be achieved only by ongoing government information-gathering. Examination can be used on a trial basis without drastic changes in our current regulatory system.

Thorough examinations by experts as a strong pattern of regulatory behavior might reduce the threats to the financial system at (ultimately) a lower cost to taxpayers, to the economy, and to our way of life. The very existence of vigilant examinations can serve to lower the risk of serious violations of the law. Most importantly the existence of expert examinations can help create a more reliable culture on Wall Street and greater support to the public's trust in the financial system.

NOTES

1. The International Monetary Fund put the costs for aggregate write downs based on global holdings of US-originated and securitized mortgage, consumer, and corporate debt at $1.4 trillion in October 2008. International Monetary Fund (2008). The International Labour Organization estimates that the financial crisis will increase an unemployment by 20 million people. Press Release, International Labour Fund, ILO Noted that Global Financial Crisis Increased Unemployment by 20 Million (20 October 2008) (on file with author). In 1989 this author worried about high market volatility and wrote *'What Can Be Done About Stock Market Volatility?'* Frankel (1988).
2. John P. Mello Jr. (2004), at E2 (summarizing book discussing 'the culture that led to the creation and the bursting of the stock market bubble at the turn of the millennium').
3. Dennis Atkins (2008), at 54, LEXIS, News Library, Curnws File (noting that there have been five 'systemic cris[e]s in financial markets during the past 20 years').
4. Paul De Grauwe and Marianna Grimaldi (2004), http://www.aup.fr/pdf/wpseries/AUP_wp07-DeGrauwe.pdf.
5. Greg Farrell (2008), at 3B. For a short description of the bubble and crash see Tamar Frankel (2008).
6. *Breakdown of Auction Rate Securities Markets: Testimony Concerning the SEC's Recent Actions with Respect to Auction Rate Securities: Hearing Before the H. Comm. on Financial Servs.* (2008) (statement of Linda Chatman Thomsen, Director, Division of Enforcement , US Sec. & Exch. Comm'n).
7. *Wall Street to Main Street: Is the Credit Crisis Over and What Can the Federal Government Do to Prevent Unnecessary Systemic Risks in the Future?: Hearing Before the Joint Economic Comm.* (2008) (statement of Rep. Hinchey) ('Our economic circumstances are negatively impacting other countries in a very dire way. . ..').
8. Ibid at 27 (stating that boom leads to 'financial distress,' a decline in prices, a 'specific signal that precipitates the crisis,' and a 'decline in investor optimism' which 'may lead to panic').
9. Frank Partnoy (2000), 757–60 (2000) (stating 'moral hazard' argument that 'markets crash due to distortions caused by financial guarantees'); ibid at 760–62 (stating 'information asymmetry' argument that 'markets crash because of the information gap between investors and issuers').
10. Erik F. Gerding (2006), (citing Robert J. Shiller (2000), 135–68; Andrei Shleifer (2000), 112–74 (2000)). 'Noise traders' are defined as investors 'who make irrational investment decisions on the basis of herding behavior and behavioral biases who became full-time traders for their own accounts'. Ibid.
11. Andrei Shleifer & Lawrence H. Summers (1990), at 19, 23 (defining 'noise traders' as investors who respond to 'pseudo-signals' such as 'advice of brokers or financial gurus'); ibid at 25 (arguing that if noise traders are successful other investors might imitate them); ibid at 28–29 (arguing that 'trend chasers' 'follow positive feedback strategies' and some join with the noise traders); ibid at 29–30 (arguing that positive feedback traders played a role in the 1987 bubble and crash).
12. Kara Scannell and Sudeep Reddy (2008), at A1, LEXIS, Busfin Library, Wsj File.
13. Hideaki Sakawa (2006) (stating that under efficient market hypothesis, in a market with rational arbitrageurs, they sell stock when its market price exceeds its fundamental price, causing price to fall).
14. Jason Potts (2004), 15, 18 ('Bubbles are good because they promote variety and experimentation in an economic system.'); ibid at 18–19 (arguing that this is so because bubbles increase access to finance and reduce the cost of failure, providing incentive for structural change).
15. Marc Lifsher and Evan Halper (2008), pt. A, at 12, LEXIS, News Library, Curnws File ('Interest rates on loans between banks rose, telegraphing that banks were reluctant to lend to one another.').
16. To be sure market lenders should distinguish between lack of liquidity and insolvency.

Lenders will rationally make loans backed by illiquid assets. Lenders do not lend to insolvent institutions by 'throwing good money after bad'. If, for example, banks are in fact insolvent, but the regulators of the financial system perpetuate the myth that the banks are only illiquid, then the solvent banks should be mistrustful.

17. Tamar Frankel (2006), 49 (defining 'trusting others' as 'believing that others tell the truth and will keep their promises').
18. Arguably such reasonable investors may be realistic rather than gullible. Some say: You cannot fight a market. But reasonable persons who succumb also destroy the market. 'That is the markets' tyranny. They eat rational people and gullible people. That is why regulation must be unrelentingly information-based and, as you say, continuous, if we want to have orderly markets'. E-mail by Ann Rutledge (on file with author).
19. Harrison Hong et al. (2005), *cited in* Sushil Bikhchandani et al. (2008).
20. Russ Wermers (1999), 'Mutual Fund Herding and Its Impact on Stock Prices', 54 *J. Fin.* 581 (1999), cited in Bikhchandani (2008), 334.
21. Christopher Avery and Peter Zemsky (1998), 'Multi-Dimensional Uncertainty and Herd Behavior in Financial Markets', 88 *Am. Econ. Rev.* 724 cited in Bikhchandani (2008), 334.
22. In Ho Lee (1998), 'Market Crashes and Informational Avalanches', 65 *Rev. Econ. Stud.* 741 (1998), cited in Bikhchandani (2008), 334.
23. Bikhchandani (2008), 334 (authorities in the text were removed to footnotes); David Hirshleifer and Siew Hong Teoh, 'Herding and Cascading in Capital Markets: A Review and Synthesis', 9 *Eur. Fin. Mgmt.* 25 (2003), cited in Bikhchandani (2008), 334.
24. Sushil Bikhchandani et al. (2008), http://www.dictionaryofeconomics.com/article?id=pde2008_I000103 (abstract).
25. Such investors could remain in the market and forced to lose all they had or withdraw and incur significant losses. Investors who are 'on the sideline' because they disagreed with market prices are not in the market.
26. Tamar Frankel (2005), Many victims of con artists, the 'marks', for example, rarely focus on the business and economic considerations relating to what the con artists offer for sale ('The business of a con artist is marketing investments in stories about a business, not investments in a business.'). Cons use an effective method of diverting investors' attention to extraneous facts, and giving the impression of public demand for the securities they offer. Cons do that by limiting the supply themselves. Ibid at 56 ('Scarcity for investors, both individuals and institutional, is a forceful drawing signal.'); 'Regulators Sound Alarm on Affinity Scams', *Canada NewsWire*, 29 January 2002, LEXIS, News Library, Curnws File (stating that Canadian securities regulators warn against '[i]nvestments that are open to a select few' and investments that 'require an investor to make a quick decision'). Con artists also promote investments in 'a business that is impossible to verify'. Tamar Frankel (2006), 19; Tamar Frankel (2005), 59–60 (unpublished manuscript, on file with author) (discussing 'schemes that are impossible to verify' as the investment is in a remote location or another country or another part of the United States); Lisa Singh (2000), LEXIS, News Library, Arcnws File (noting that purported investment was an abandoned gold mine, to which access was very difficult).
27. Securities Act of 1933, § 5, 15 USC § 77e (2000).
28. Rule 144A, 17 CFR § 230.144A (2008) (exempting from registration qualified resales of securities to qualified institutional buyers).
29. Charles P. Kindleberger (2005), 99–100; Charles Mackay (1932), 1–45, 90–97, cited in Institute for Economic Democracy, *Market Bubbles and Crashes,* http://www.ied.info/articles/an-honest-bank-is-so-simple-you-can-run-it/market-bubbles-and-crashes (last visited 28 September 2008).
30. Charles P. Kindleberger (2005), 110–11; Charles Mackay (1932), 46–88, available at http://www.thesouthseabubble.com/thesouthseabubble.html, cited in Tamar Frankel (1988), 991; *The South Sea Bubble,* http://www.thesouthseabubble.com (last visited 29 September 2008) (modernized version of Mackay text).

31. Charles P. Kindleberger (2005), 110–11.
32. John Kenneth Galbraith (1979), *The Great Crash, 1929*.
33. Senate Report No. 101–300, at 29–38 (1990); ibid at 30–31 (concluding that before the crash 'the securities markets were overvalued . . . and a decline in market values was inevitable').
34. Eugene N. White (2006); ibid. at 6 (noting that stock indices peaked in 1999–2000 and crashed in 2002).
35. Charles P. Kindleberger (2005), 9–12 (noting similarities among manias and among panics); ibid at 10–11 (stating thesis that 'the cycle of manias and panics results from the pro-cyclical changes in the supply of credit').
36. The unanticipated event that triggered the enormous losses in this case was a relatively distant event – the failure of the borrowers under the terms of subprime loans.
37. Edythe S. Miller (1993), 30 (noting belief that 'regulation stifles the innovation required for technological advance by inhibiting profits').
38. Louis Loss and Joel Seligman (1998) (stating that 'the philosophy embodied in the [Securities Act] is one of disclosure').
39. Dr. Kevin Leman (2007), at 3F, LEXIS, News Library, Curnws File ('Kids are always going to push the edge of the envelope to see if you are willing to draw the parameters in their life,'; according to psychologist).
40. Joseph A. Schumpeter (1975), 81–86 (discussing principle of 'Creative Destruction' in which capitalism creates and destroys economic structures).
41. Ibid.
42. Alan Greenspan, Chairman of the Board of the Federal Reserve System, 'The Challenge of Central Banking in a Democratic Society', Remarks Given at the Annual Dinner and Francis Boyer Lecture of the American Enterprise Institute for Public Policy Research, Washington, DC (5 December 1996), quoted in Geoffrey P. Miller (1996), 1053.
43. Kara Scannell and Sudeep Reddy (2008), at A1, LEXIS, Busfin Library, Wsj File.
44. Geoffrey P. Miller (1996).
45. Ibid. at 1057.
46. Deborah Solomon (2008), at A1, A6.
47. Alex Berenson (2008), at C7, LEXIS, News Library, Nyt File (stating that 'Fannie Mae and Freddie Mac . . . were effectively nationalized earlier this month').
48. Rule 3c-7, 17 CFR § 275.3c-7 (2008) (exempting an important part of the securitization process from the Investment Company Act of 1940). Significant exemptions were awarded to Enron Corporation. Enron Corp. (1997), LEXIS, Fedsec Library, Secrel File (application for exemption); Enron Corp., Investment Company Act Release No. 22,560 (13 March 1997), LEXIS, Fedsec Library, Secrel File (exemptive order).
49. Sarbanes-Oxley Act of 2002, Pub. L. No. 107–204, 116 Stat. 745 (codified as amended in scattered sections of 15, 18 USC).
50. Kris James Mitchener (2007).
51. Erik F. Gerding (2007).
52. Housing and Economic Recovery Act of 2008, Pub. L. No. 110–289, 122 Stat. 2654 (to be codified in scattered sections of 11, 12, 15, 31, 37, 38, 42, 44, 47, 50 USC); Mortgage Forgiveness Debt Relief Act of 2007, Pub. L. No. 110–142, 121 Stat. 1803 (to be codified in scattered sections of 26 USC); Truth in Lending, 73 Fed. Reg. 44,522 (30 July 2008) (to be codified in scattered sections of 12 CFR pt. 226) (Federal Reserve rule 'to protect consumers in the mortgage market from unfair, abusive, or deceptive lending and servicing practices'); Statement on Subprime Mortgage Lending, 72 Fed. Reg. 37,569 (10 July 2007) (statement issued by banking agencies 'to clarify how institutions can offer certain adjustable rate mortgage (ARM) products in a safe and sound manner, and in a way that clearly discloses the risks that borrowers may assume').
53. Bob Davis et al. (2008), at A1, LEXIS, Busfin Library, Wsj File (noting Federal Reserve 'decision to lend Bear Stearns temporary funding' and 'take over $30 billion of its least-liquid securities'; actions 'went against decades of Fed efforts to avoid measures that favor a particular company or market').

54. Susanne Craig et al. (2008), at A1, LEXIS, Busfin Library, Wsj File (noting that Secretary of the Treasury 'helped structure a rescue of Bear Stearns . . ., which included an agreement that the Federal Reserve . . . would take on $30 billion in Bear Stearns's assets if J.P. Morgan Chase & Co. would buy [Bear Stearns]'); Steven Syre (2008), at A1, LEXIS, Curnws Library, Bglobe File (stating that 'Federal Reserve promised short-term loans for Freddie Mac and Fannie Mae if necessary').
55. *Monetary Policy: Hearing Before the S. Comm. on Banking, Housing, and Urban Affairs,* 110th Cong. (2008), Fed. News Serv., LEXIS, Legis Library, Fednew File (statement of Ben Bernanke, Chairman, Federal Reserve) (stating that '[t]he Federal Reserve continues to work with financial institutions, public officials, and community groups around the country to help homeowners avoid foreclosures' and '[has] called on mortgage lenders and servicers to pursue prudent loan workouts and [has] supported the development of streamlined, systematic approach to expedite the loan modification process').
56. Fed. Housing Fin. Agency, Statement of FHFA Director James B. Lockhart (7 September 2008), http://www.ofheo.gov/newsroom.aspx?ID=456&q1=0&q2=0; Alex Berenson, *Fearing Worse to Come, Investors Drive Dow to Biggest Loss Since '01*, NY Times, 16 September 2008, at C7, LEXIS, News Library, Nyt File (stating that 'Fannie Mae and Freddie Mac . . . were effectively nationalized earlier this month').
57. Office of Compliance Inspections & Examinations (2004), 9 n.11.
58. *Breakdown of Auction Rate Securities Markets: Testimony Concerning the SEC's Recent Actions with Respect to Auction Rate Securities: Hearing Before the H. Comm. on Financial Servs.,* 110th Cong. (2008) (statement of Linda Chatman Thomsen, Director, Division of Enforcement, US Sec. & Exch. Comm'n), (noting that broker-dealer firms misled customers and violated federal securities laws).
59. Ibid (noting that as result of market failure, customers were unable to sell securities).
60. Ibid ('firms misrepresented . . . that [auction rate securities] were safe, highly liquid investments that were equivalent to cash or money market funds').
61. US Sec. & Exch. Comm'n (2008b).
62. Miriam Miquelon Weismann (2004), 109 (stating that requiring filing of sworn statement under oath in 2002 WorldCom scandal was 'highly unusual step').
63. US Sec. & Exch. Comm'n (2008a); 15 USC § 78u(a)(1) (Supp. V 2005) (authorizing Commission to require filing of statements under oath).
64. Sarbanes-Oxley Act of 2002, Pub. L. No. 107–204, 116 Stat. 745 (codified as amended in scattered sections of 15, 18 USC).
65. Jon Hilsenrath (2008), at A2, LEXIS, Busfin Library, Wsj File (noting arguments that increasing regulation brings risks including regulatory arbitrage, undermining market discipline, and discouraging innovation or risk-taking).
66. Henry Manne (2005), at A10, LEXIS, Busfin Library, Wsj File (arguing that 'strict enforcement of Sarbanes-Oxley . . . is costly beyond any conceivable benefits').
67. *Too Much Regulation Caused Housing Crisis* (2008), LEXIS, News Library, Curnws File (blaming 2008 housing crisis on Community Reinvestment Act and regulations issued in 1995).
68. George Sutton (2002), 974 (arguing that 'failure of the regulatory system contributed to 'banking and deposit insurance crisis of the 1980s and that one bank failure would not have occurred 'without complacent, incompetent or corrupt regulators'); Keith R. Fisher (2004), 1071–72 (describing typical fraud and mismanagement in 'savings and loan debacle,' arguing that '[n]one of this could have been accomplished without the cooperation of unusually inept (and occasionally corrupt) regulators'); ibid at 1072 n.199 (arguing that former Federal Home Loan Bank Board ignored Bank Secrecy Act violations and 'altered examination reports that would have revealed potential currency reporting violations at a thrift in Puerto Rico, whose president was also vice-chair of the Federal Home Loan Bank of New York').
69. Alan O. Sykes (1989), 1168 ('[T]he economic theory of regulation suggests that regulators are often 'captured' by the regulated, in part because regulated entities control the information flow to the regulators, and in part because the regulators often aspire

to lucrative private sector positions in the regulated entities following their exit from public service.') (citing George J. Stigler (1971), 'The Theory of Economic Regulation', 2 *Bell J. Econon.* 3; Richard A. Posner (1974), 'Theories of Economic Regulation', 5 *Bell J. Econ.* 335; Sam Peltzman (1976), 'Toward A More General Theory of Regulation', 19 *J.L. & Econ.* 211.

70. Paul S. Atkins (2007) (stating that the SEC 'should be asking whether [its] rules are coming at such a pace or such a level of complexity and expense that they are discouraging new industry entrants or forcing small firms out of the industry').
71. Ibid (arguing that 'SEC tends to be lawyer-dominated and lawyer-driven' and that it often neglects 'economic justification for and consequences of regulatory actions').
72. Bryce Ward and Ed Whitelaw (2008), at D01, LEXIS, News Library, Curnws File ('The 30-year push to eliminate . . . regulation must end. Markets require clear rules and mechanisms to enforce those rules. Without rules and enforcement, crises occur and people lose trust in markets. Without trust, markets fail and the economy suffers.').
73. William Neikirk (2008), News section, at 1, LEXIS, News Library, Curnws File (noting statement by former Federal Reserve board member that regulation is necessary in view of more complex financial products); Kara Scannell and Aaron Lucchetti (2008), at C2, LEXIS, Busfin Library, Wsj File (noting SEC commissioner statement that new rules for complex structured products will be 'disclosure-based' so that investors will be 'able to understand what they're looking at').
74. Angela A. Hung et al. (2008), 112–13 (concluding that investors 'expressed high levels of satisfaction' with their professionals' services, but are confused about the legal duties of broker-dealers and investment advisers; they also view financial advisors and financial consultants as more similar to investment advisers than to brokers).
75. Staff of Office of Compliance inspections & Examinations, Div. of Trading & Mkts. & Office of Econ. (2008), 23 (2008), (noting inherent conflict of interest in 'issuer pays' model in which issuer of security being rated pays for rating); ibid at 25–26 (noting indications that employees responsible for market share or other business interests indicated their concerns to marketing staff).
76. Pete Carey (2008), LEXIS, News Library, Curnws File (quoting law professor saying that sentence of prison term and fine is a 'sharp deterrent message'). Tamar Frankel (2006), 172–73 (2006) (suggesting that prison sentences may not be effective deterrent for white-collar criminals). For a description and preparation of corporations subject to current SEC examinations see *SEC Examinations: A Primer For Advisers & Mutual Funds*, Compliance Rep., 20 May 2005, LEXIS, News Library, Arcnws File.
77. *Accounting: All's Fair*, Economist, 18 September 2008, at 36; Steve Forbes (2008), at 18; Paul B.W. Miller and Paul R. Bahnson (2008), at 15 (arguing that marking to market makes things worse).
78. Ricardo Duran (1995), at B01, LEXIS, News Library, Arcnws File (noting that police ask questions of suspected gang; gained trust of residents; share information with other law enforcement). 'In 2004, the SEC began requiring advisers to hire their own chief compliance officer and to implement formal compliance policies and procedures. Following this, reports of an eight-page SEC document titled 'Examination Request List' surfaced, describing the SEC's extensive adviser audit program.' Eric Clarke (2006), LEXIS, News Library, Arcnws File.
79. Cornelius Hurley (2008).
80. Cf. 5 USC § 552(b)(4) (2000) (providing exemption from Freedom of Information Act for 'trade secrets and commercial or financial information obtained from a person and privileged or confidential').
81. Robert L. Bartley (2002), LEXIS, Busfin Library, Wsj File (noting that Enron's year-end share prices increased for three of four years affected by accounting restatement and share price increased for part of fourth year before first 'revelations'); Bethany Mclean (2001), at 122, LEXIS, Busfin Library, Fortun File (questioning, before scandal was revealed, why Enron share price was high relative to earnings; suggesting that 'lack of clarity' about company 'raises a red flag'); Tamar Frankel (2006), 170–71.

82. David S. Scharfstein and Jeremy C. Stein (1990); cf. Daniel Kearney (2005), 314 ('Network effects arise whenever a good's value is dependent on the number of other people using that good or a complementary good. A telephone, for instance, is only worth something when someone else owns one, or when you expect someone else to own one – and the more people there are who own one, the more valuable a phone is.'); Michael Klausner (1995), 773 n.50 (stating that potential sources of network externalities include '[i]ncreased use of a produc[t,] . . . wider availability of information regarding a product, market signaling effects of widespread use, and fashion or style').
83. 15 USC § 80a-1–65 (2006); 17 CFR § 270.3c-7 (2008).
84. Fund of funds structures are very restricted under the Investment Company Act of 1940, 15 USC § 80a-12(d)(1) (2006). Rule 3c-7, 17 CFR §270.3c-7 (2008) does not contain this prohibition or a similar prohibition.
85. Barrett Sheridan (2008), LEXIS, News Library, Curnws File (noting that $600 trillion is 'the rough figure cited in many news reports for the total size of the derivatives market').
86. Jonathan Weil (2003), at C1, LEXIS, Busfin Library, Wsj File (stating that many accounting firms only perform 'sample testing of accounts, barring absence of acute problems that should spur further digging').
87. Tamar Frankel (2006).
88. US Sec. & Exch. Comm'n (2007) (Investment Company examinations include pricing procedures, fund expenses, disaster recovery planning, selective disclosure).
89. Carrick Mollenkamp et al. (2008), at A1, LEXIS, Busfin Library, Wsj File (Merrill Lynch is acquired by Bank of America).
90. Robin Sidel et al. (2008), at A1, LEXIS, Busfin Library, Wsj File.
91. Carrick Mollenkamp et al. (2008), at A1, LEXIS, Busfin Library, Wsj File (Merrill Lynch is acquired by Bank of America).
92. US Sec. & Exch. Comm'n. (2002) Salaries of employees in the government sector may be significantly less than those of comparable employees in the private sector. *Salary Survey Report for Job: Branch Manager: Banking*, http://www.payscale.com/research/US/Job=Branch_Manager%2c_Banking/Salary/by_Employer_Type (last updated 4 December 2008).
93. J. Lynn Lunsford (2008), at A1, LEXIS, Busfin Library, Wsj File.
94. James Grant (2008), at W1, LEXIS, Busfin Library, Wsj File.
95. Michael Lewis (2008), 3.
96. Tamar Frankel (1997).
97. Securities Exchange Act of 1934, § 21(a)(1), 15 USC § 78u(a)(1) (2006) (granting SEC discretion to publish information concerning violations).

REFERENCES

15 USC §§ 78, 80 (2000).

17 CFR §§230, 270, 275 (2008).

5 USC § 552 (2000).

'Accounting: All's Fair', *Economist*, 18 September 2008, 2008 WLNR 17853079.

Atkins, Dennis (2008), 'Gloom Across the Globe', *Courier Mail* (Australia) 26 January.

Atkins, Paul S. (2007), *Comm'r, US Sec. & Exch. Comm'n, Remarks Before the National Association for Business Economics*, 13 March, http://www.sec.gov/news/speech/2007/spch031307psa.htm.

Bartley, Robert L. (2002), 'Thinking Things Over: Enron: First, Apply the Law', *Wall Street Journal*, 11 February.

Berenson, Alex (2008), 'Fearing Worse to Come, Investors Drive Dow to Biggest Loss Since '01', *New York Times*, 16 September.

Bikhchandani, Sushil et al. (2008), *Information Cascades,* in Steven N. Durlauf and Lawrence E. Blume (eds), 4 The New Palgrave Dictionary of Economics (2nd edn), 329.

Breakdown of Auction Rate Securities Markets: Testimony Concerning the SEC's Recent Actions with Respect to Auction Rate Securities: Hearing Before the H. Comm. on Financial Servs., 110th Cong. (2008), http://www.sec.gov/news/testimony/2008/ts091808ct.htm.

Carey, Pete (2008), 'Brocade Ex-CEO Reyes Sentenced to 21 Months in Prison', *San Jose Mercury News*, 17 January.

Clarke, Eric (2006), 'Steps for Surviving an SEC Audit', *Investment News*, 6 November.

Craig, Susanne et al. (2008), 'Street Scenes: The Players Remaking Financial World', *Wall Street Journal*, 19 September.

Davis, Bob et al. (2008), 'US Mulls Next Steps in Crisis – Easing Constraints on Loans Is Likely; Markets Still Edgy', *Wall Street Journal*, 18 March.

Duran, Ricardo (1995), 'Policing Effort Cheers Moreno Valley Residents', *Press-Enterprise*, 19 February.

Enron Corporation (1997), *Investment Company Act Release No. 22,515, 22,560*, 14 February.

Farrell, Greg (2008), 'SEC Slams Credit-Rating Agencies Over Standards; Says Firms Dropped Ball on Bonds Backed by Subprime Loans', *USA Today*, 9 July.

Fed. Housing Fin. Agency (2008), *Statement of FHFA Director James B. Lockhart*.

Fisher, Keith R. (2004), 'Regulation of Lawyers Post-Enron', 37 *U. Mich. J.L. Reform* 1017.

Forbes, Steve (2008), 'How Capitalism Will Save Us', *Forbes*, 10 November, 2008 WLNR 20505055.

Frankel, Tamar (1988), 'What Can Be Done About Stock Market Volatility?' 69 *Boston University Law Review* 991.

Frankel, Tamar (1997), 'Should Funds and Investment Advisers Establish A Self-Regulatory Organization?', in Clifford T. Kirsch (ed), *The Financial Services Revolution: Understanding the Changing Roles of Banks, Mutual Funds and Insurance Companies*, New York: McGraw Hill.

Frankel, Tamar (2005), 'Con Artists and Their Victims (A Story of Ponzi Schemes)', unpublished manuscript, on file with author.

Frankel, Tamar (2006), *Trust and Honesty: America's Business Culture at a Crossroad*, New York: Oxford University Press.

Frankel, Tamar (2008), 'The Problems of Securitizing Subprime Loans', 1 *Asian Bus. Law*. 20.

Galbraith, John Kenneth (1979), *The Great Crash, 1929*, Boston: Houghton Mifflin.

Gerding, Erik F. (2006), 'The Next Epidemic: Bubbles and the Growth and Decay of Securities Regulation', 38 *Conn. L. Rev*. 393.

Gerding, Erik F. (2007), 'Laws Against Bubbles: An Experimental-Asset-Market Approach to Analyzing Financial Regulation', 2007 *Wis. L. Rev*. 977.

Grant, James (2008), 'The Confidence Game', *Wall Street Journal*, 18 October.

Grauwe, Paul De and Marianna Grimaldi (2004), 'A Theory of Bubbles and Crashes', American University of Paris, Working Paper No. 7.

Hilsenrath, Jon (2008), 'Markets Police Themselves Poorly, but Regulation Has Its Flaws', *Wall Street Journal*, 21 July.

Hong, Harrison et al. (2005), 'Thy Neighbor's Portfolio: Word-Of-Mouth Effects in the holdings and Trades of MoneyManager', 60 *J. Fin.* 2801.

Housing and Economic Recovery Act of 2008, Pub. L. No. 110–289, 122 Stat. 2654 (to be codified in scattered sections of 11, 12, 15, 31, 37, 38, 42, 44, 47, 50 USC); Mortgage Forgiveness Debt Relief Act of 2007, Pub. L. No. 110–142, 121 Stat. 1803 (to be codified in scattered sections of 26 USC).

Hung, Angela A. et al. (2008), *Investor and Industry Perspectives on Investment Advisers and Broker-Dealers*, LRN-RAND Center for Corporate Ethics, Law, and Governance, http://www.sec.gov/news/press/2008/2008-t_randiabdreport.pdf.

Hurley, Cornelius (2008), 'Commentary: Getting it Right the Next Time on 'Too Big to Fail', *Reuters*, 29 September, http://www.reuters.com/article/reutersComService4/idUSTRE4857XQ20080929.

International Labour Fund (2008), *ILO Noted that Global Financial Crisis Increased Unemployment by 20 Million.*

International Monetary Fund (2008), *Global Financial Stability Report.*

Kearney, Daniel (2005), Note, 'Network Effects and the Emerging Doctrine of Cybertrespass', 23 *Yale L. & Pol'y Rev*. 313.

Kindleberger, Charles P. (2005), *Manias, Panics, and Crashes* (5th edn), New York: Wiley.

Klausner, Michael (1995), 'Corporations, Corporate Law, and Networks of Contracts', 81 *Va. L. Rev*. 757.

Leman, Dr. Kevin (2007), '3-Year-Old Son Too Young for Preschool', *Tuscon Citizen*, 25 December.

Lewis, Michael (2008), 'Introduction: Inside Wall Street's Black Hole', in Lewis (ed) *Panic: The Story of Modern Financial Insanity*, New York: W.W. Norton.

Lifsher, Marc and Evan Halper (2008), 'Financial Crisis: Ripple Effects', *Los Angeles Times*, 4 October.

Loss, Louis and Joel Seligman (1998), *Securities Regulation* (3rd edn), New York: Aspen Publishers.

Lunsford, J. Lynn (2008), 'Boeing Strikers Dig In Heels Even as Economy Turns Sour', *Wall Street Journal*, 23 October.

Mackay, Charles (1932), *Memoirs of Extraordinary Popular Delusions and the Madness of Crowds*.

Manne, Henry (2005), 'Life After Donaldson', *Wall Street Journal*, 6 June.

Mclean, Bethany (2001), 'Is Enron Overpriced?', *Fortune*, 5 March.

Mello Jr., John P. (2004), 'Book Review', *Boston Globe*, 8 February.

Miller, Edythe S. (1993), 'Some Market Structure and Regulatory Implications of the Brave New World of Telecommunications', 27 *J. Econ. Issues* 19.

Miller, Geoffrey P. (1996), 'The Role of a Central Bank in a Bubble Economy', 18 *Cardozo Law Review* 1053.

Miller, Paul B.W. and Paul R. Bahnson (2008), 'The Spirit of Accounting: Don't Blame Mark to Market for the Subprime Bubble', *Accounting Today*, 2 June, 2008 WLNR 10394460.

Mitchener, Kris James (2007), 'Are Prudential Supervision and Regulation Pillars of Financial Stability? Evidence from the Great Depression', 50 *J. Law & Econ.* 273.

Mollenkamp, Carrick et al. (2008), 'Crisis on Wall Street as Lehman Totters,

Merrill Is Sold, AIG Seeks to Raise Cash – Fed Will Expand Its Lending Arsenal in a Bid to Calm Markets', *Wall Street Journal*, 15 September.

Monetary Policy: Hearing Before the S. Comm. on Banking, Housing, and Urban Affairs, 110th Cong. (2008), Fed. News Service.

Neikirk, William (2008), 'Call Grows for Tough Financial Regulation; Candidates, Congress Consider Intervening in Banking Markets', *Chicago Tribune*, 28 March.

Office of Compliance Inspections & Examinations, Div. of Trading & Mkts. & Office of Economics (2008) Analysis, *US Sec. & Exch. Comm'n Summary Report of Issues Identified in the Commission Staff's Examination of Select Credit Rating* Agencies, http://www.sec.gov/news/studies/2008/craexamination070808.pdf.

Office of Compliance Inspections & Examinations (2004), *Sec. & Exch. Comm'n Examinations of Investment Companies and Investment Advisers*, http://www.sec.gov/news/extra/apx-ts031004lar.pdf.

Partnoy, Frank (2000), 'Why Markets Crash and What Law Can Do About It', 61 *U. Pitt. L. Rev*. 741.

Potts, Jason (2004), 'Liberty Bubbles', *Policy* (Australia), Spring 2004, 15 http://www.cis.org.au/policy/spring04/Spring04-3.pdf.

'Regulators Sound Alarm on Affinity Scams', *Canada NewsWire*, 29 January 2002.

Sakawa, Hideaki (2006), 'Market Makers' Price-Correction Behavior Towards Synchronization Risk', Osaka Univ. 21st Century COE Program Discussion Paper No. 96, http://www2.econ.osaka-u.ac.jp/coe/dp/dp_no.96rev.pdf.

Sarbanes-Oxley Act of 2002, Pub. L. No. 107–204, 116 Stat. 745 (codified as amended in scattered sections of 15, 18 USC).

Scannell, Kara and Aaron Lucchetti (2008), 'Credit Crunch: SEC to Seek Rule on Added Disclosure by Bond-Rating Firms – Proposals Unlikely To Quell Criticism that More Be Done', *Wall Street Journal*, 11 June.

Scannell, Kara and Sudeep Reddy (2008), 'Greenspan Admits Errors to Hostile House Panel', *Wall Street Journal*, 24 October.

Scharfstein, David S. and Jeremy C. Stein (1990), 'Herd Behavior and Investment', 80 *Am. Econ. Rev*. 465.

Schumpeter, Joseph A. (1950), *Capitalism, Socialism and Democracy* (3rd edn, 1995), New York: Harper & Row.

Senate Report No. 101–300 (1990).

Sheridan, Barrett (2008), *600,000,000,000,000?,* Newsweek (int'l ed.) 27 October.

Shiller, Robert (2000), *Irrational Exuberance*, Princeton: Princeton University Press.

Shleiter, Andrei (2000), *Inefficient Markets: An introduction to Behavioural Finance*, New York: Oxford University Press.

Shleifer, Andrei and Lawrence H. Summers (1990), 'The Noise Trader Approach to Finance', *J. Econ. Persp*, Spring 1990, 19.

Sidel, Robin et al. (2008), 'J.P. Morgan Buys Bear in Fire Sale, as Fed Widens Credit to Avert Crisis – Ailing Firm Sold for Just $2 a Share in US-Backed Deal', *Wall Street Journal*, 17 March.

Singh, Lisa (2000), 'Fool's Gold', *Dallas Observer*, 16 November.

Solomon, Deborah (2008), 'The Fannie & Freddie Question', *Wall Street Journal*, 30 August.

Statement on Subprime Mortgage Lending, 72 Fed. Reg. 37569 (10 July 2007).

Sutton, George (2002), 'Penn Square Bank – 20 Years Later: A Personal

Recollection of the Causes and Effects of the Banking and Deposit Insurance Crisis of the 1980s', 27 *Okla. City U.L. Rev.* 969.
Sykes, Alan O. (1989), 'Reformulating Tort Reform', 56 *U. Chi. L. Rev.* 1153.
Syre, Steven (2008), 'Washington Throws Long Lifeline Rescue; Aims at Fannie, Freddie, and US Economy', *Boston Globe*, 15 July.
'Too Much Regulation Caused Housing Crisis', *Home News Trib.* (East Brunswick, N.J.), 1 October 2008.
Truth in Lending, 73 Fed. Reg. 44522 (30 July 2008) (to be codified in scattered sections of 12 CFR pt. 226).
US Sec. & Exch. Comm'n. (2002), *Pay Parity Implementation Plan and Report*, 6 March, http://www.sec.gov/news/studies/payparity.htm.
US Sec. & Exch. Comm'n (2007), *Office of Compliance Inspection and Examinations – Highlights*, 5 February, http://www.sec.gov/about/offices/ocie/ocie_highlights.shtml.
US Sec. & Exch. Comm'n (2008a), *SEC Expands Sweeping Investigation of Market Manipulation: Measure Will Require Statements Under Oath by Market Participants* (Release No. 2008–214), 19 September, http://www.sec.gov/news/press/2008/2008-214.htm.
US Sec. & Exch. Comm'n (2008b), *Statements of SEC Chairman Christopher Cox and Enforcement Division Director Linda Thomsen Regarding Immediate Commission Actions to Combat Market Manipulation* (Release No. 2008–209), 17 September, http://www.sec.gov/news/press/2008/2008-209.htm.
Wall Street to Main Street: Is the Credit Crisis Over and What Can the Federal Government Do to Prevent Unnecessary Systemic Risks in the Future?: Hearing Before the Joint Economic Comm., 110th Cong., Fed. News Service, 14 May 2008.
Ward, Bryce and Ed Whitelaw (2008), 'The Economists', *Sunday Oregonian*, 21 September.
Weil, Jonathan (2003), 'Accounting Scheme Was Straightforward but Hard to Detect', *Wall Street Journal*, 30 March.
Weismann, Miriam Miquelon (2004), 'Corporate Transparency or Congressional Window-Dressing? The Case Against Sarbanes-Oxley as a Means to Avoid Another Corporate Debacle: The Failed Attempt to Revive Meaningful Regulatory Oversight', 10 *Stan. J.L. Bus. & Fin.* 98.
White, Eugene N. (2006), 'Bubbles and Busts: The 1990s in the Mirror of the 1920s', Nat'l Bureau of Econ. Research Working Paper No. 12138, http://www.nber.org/papers/W12138.pdf.

10. The sewers of Jefferson County: disclosure, trust and truth in modern finance

Theresa A. Gabaldon

INTRODUCTION

In one sense, the story of Jefferson County's sewer debt is a case study; in another, it is a morality tale. As a case study, it provides an opportunity to examine how the subprime mortgage crisis roiled the waters of municipal finance, contributing to a state of affairs in which governmental issuers of securities having nothing to do with subprime lending found themselves swamped with debt service. As a morality tale, it unhappily cautions against trust at the same time that it reminds us that trust of a sort is an inevitability of the modern age. As a logical matter, this reminder should prompt a rethinking of the disclosure to be made in connection with financings (municipal or otherwise). Perhaps more important, it should demand a great deal more systemic attention to the development of the conditions that nurture the trust that must be mustered to make modern finance continue to work.

The first section of this chapter provides background on what promises to be the most significant failure of municipal finance in history. The next examines the disclosures that were and were not made along this particular road to perdition. There follows an inquiry into the disclosure and other needs of the various players, followed in turn by an analysis of the trust and trustworthiness exhibited by some of these same characters. This analysis suggests that trustworthiness is critical to the functioning of sound financial systems, but concludes that in some instances it is not enough, and must be supplemented by a demand for absolute truth.

BACKGROUND

The Consent Decree

In 1993, the United States government sued Jefferson County, Alabama, for a number of violations of the federal Clean Water Act. The consent decree terminating the litigation in 1996 required the construction of sewer projects and improvements ultimately costing the County in excess of three billion dollars.[1] The initial construction costs were financed primarily by the issuance of long-term fixed-rate debt payable solely out of sewer revenues. These revenues were to be generated by the imposition of fees on the users of the sewer system. Notwithstanding staggering rate increases (eventually totaling 328 per cent), the sewer fees flowing into County coffers did not leave it flush with resources. In fact, it became apparent by the early 2000s that a debt restructuring was necessary. A refinancing program was commenced in late 2002, with JP Morgan Securities, Inc. ('JPMorgan') at the helm as the well-compensated lead underwriter.

The Refinancing

As conceived by JPMorgan, the refinancing plan called for the replacement of fixed rate debt with variable-rate debt coupled with a series of interest rate swaps intended to provide a 'synthetic fixed rate', The idea was that although the County was paying variable rates of interest, the variations were supposed to be offset by the amounts it would receive from transactions in which it paid a fixed rate and received a rate tied to LIBOR.[2] It was anticipated that this LIBOR-pegged rate would fluctuate with essentially the same market conditions driving the variable interest rates on the County's sewer debt. The swaps were provided (obviously, for a fee) by JPMorgan, Bank of America, Lehman Brothers, and Bear Stearns.

Jefferson County's own floating-rate sewer debt was insured by one of four insurers. These four were Financial Guaranty Insurance Company ('FGIC'), XL Capital Assurance Inc. (now known as Syncora Guarantee, Inc.), Financial Security Assurance, Inc., and Ambac Financial Group, Inc. This insurance, for which the County paid approximately 50 million dollars, was intended to reduce the County's cost of borrowing because each insurer then carried a AAA credit rating, which was higher than the County's own A rating.[3] Traditionally, municipal debt insurance providers, including the ones from which the County made its purchases, had pursued no other line of business and were referred to as 'monoline' insurers.

The floating-rate debt issued by the County had two components:

variable rate demand warrants and auction rate warrants. Holders of the variable rate demand warrants were permitted to tender their warrants for repurchase on seven days' notice; payment of the repurchase price was secured by standby purchase agreements provided (for a fee paid by the County) by a consortium of banks assembled by JPMorgan. The standby agreements could be terminated by the banks if the relevant bond insurer's rating were downgraded to below-investment grade, if the insurer failed to pay claims, or if the insurer became insolvent. Moreover, if the banks were required to purchase the warrants at a time when they could not be remarketed, the County would become obligated to retire them over a period of four years, rather than over the warrants' much longer original life of 30 to 40 years.

In the case of the auction rate warrants, the interest rate was reset by a periodic auction process in which holders and buyers would identify the amount of warrants they were willing to (respectively) hold or purchase at a rate they designated. A single interest rate would be set at the level necessary to sell all warrants. If the bidding was inadequate to sell all warrants, the auction would fail, and an interest rate would be determined by a formula in the indenture pursuant to which the warrants were issued. JPMorgan and Bank of America served (for a fee) as the broker-dealers soliciting and accepting orders to hold or purchase the warrants. One of the historic functions of a broker-dealer in this setting was to participate as a purchaser in order to prevent auction failure. Until 2008, no auction of municipal debt securities had failed.

The Problem

Some accounts of the Panic of 2008–2009 start with relaxed monetary policies facilitating the overuse of credit by virtually all economic sectors (Soderquist and Gabaldon (2009), iii–vi).[4] This overuse was most notorious in the housing market, where a bubble in prices was exacerbated by lax (or even predatory) lending practices. These practices often involved qualifying borrowers for loans based on very low initial interest rates that would increase over time. The prevailing theory, however, was that continued increases in housing prices would permit the borrowers to refinance before any rate increase. It was recognized that some of the mortgages thus generated were of questionable value, but thought that the risk of any particular mortgage going into default could be offset by combining it with other mortgages. Interests in pooled mortgages were sold using a process referred to as 'securitization'. This process frequently involved the purchase of insurance in order to improve the credit rating of the interests sold. Most famously, this insurance took the form of credit default swaps (a financial product insuring against third party default). All four of the insurers of Jefferson County's sewer debt became dissatisfied with the profitability of their traditional line of business and chose to branch out into insuring mortgage-backed securities and the execution of credit default swaps.

Eventually, the housing market plateaued and then reversed, while homeowners' payments on variable rate loans increased. Mortgages began going into default in unanticipated numbers and the companies insuring mortgage-backed securities and/or executing credit default swaps were called upon to make good. As they did so, they began to lose money hand over fist, and their own credit ratings began to decline.

Soon after the credit ratings of FGIC, et al., started their slide, the holders and purchasers of Jefferson County's auction-rate debt demanded vastly increased interest rates to compensate for the perceived increase in risk. In addition, in a show of prudence, if not loyalty, the banks participating as broker-dealers in the auction process refused to act as back-up purchasers; without their support, auctions began to fail. The indenture's default formula for setting interest resulted in much higher rates than the County had anticipated.

Not to be outdone in fiscal willies by their auction-rate purchasing brethren, holders of the County's variable-rate demand warrants became worried that the banks providing the standby repurchase agreements would terminate those agreements if the credit-worthiness of the bond insurers sufficiently declined. The holders of the demand warrants therefore unanimously tendered, forcing the banks to purchase the warrants. The interest rate thereafter contractually owed the banks was, again, much higher than the County had expected to pay.

At the same time the interest rates paid by the County were increasing on both its auction-rate and demand warrants, LIBOR sunk to historic lows. This meant that the amounts the County was receiving from its swaps were drastically declining. The fixed rate it was paying, of course, did not decline. The swaps could not, however, be unwound without the payment of termination penalties deemed by the County to be prohibitive. As the result of all these developments, although the County had believed its synthetically fixed interest rate would be slightly in excess of 4 per cent, it found itself shelling out something in excess of 10 per cent.

Perhaps most disastrously, however, the banks' standby repurchases of the County's variable-rate demand warrants triggered the County's obligation to pay off those warrants over an accelerated four-year term. The amounts the County was forced to pay in total debt service vastly exceeded the revenues produced by the sewer system.[5] Although the sewer debt indeed is a 'limited obligation' of the County, and payable only out of sewer revenues,[6] the County's own credit rating was downgraded to 'junk' status and it found itself unable to put together another refinancing. The largest municipal bankruptcy in history became a very real possibility.[7]

And, Oh Yes, the Corruption

Evidently, municipal securities transactions have provided a cesspool of opportunity for private gain at public cost (Retnasaba (2006)). Jefferson County's sewer debt was no exception. As it turns out, even if the variable rate restructuring otherwise had been well-advised, the County was vastly overcharged (by something like $100,000,000, or six times the prevailing rates) by the banks providing the credit swaps (Selway and Braun (2008)). In addition, one former County Commissioner has pled guilty to accepting bribes in connection with the refinancing; another (who is currently the Mayor of Birmingham, Alabama) has been indicted as well as sued civilly by the Securities and Exchange Commission ('SEC' or 'Commission'). The SEC has also sued two other individuals involved in the refinancing and has authorized an enforcement action against JPMorgan (JPMorgan (2009), 157). More investigations are pending.[8] It is piling on, but irresistible, at this point also to note that at least 21 former Jefferson County officials or contractors who worked on sewer improvement projects have been indicted for federal crimes related to those projects (although not necessarily relating to their financing).

Who Were the Victims?

The dust has not settled, but it is fairly clear that the ultimate victims of the Jefferson County sewer debacle were not the third-party purchasers of the debt. In the case of the variable-rate demand warrants, demand was exercised by the holders and satisfied by the standby banks. In the case of the auction-rate warrants, it is true that there were auction failures. This doubtless meant that there was some loss of liquidity for the holders; at the same time, however, they became entitled to a default rate of interest that was substantially in excess of what they might have expected when they purchased their warrants. Moreover, it appears that the (initially faithless) auction broker-dealers (JPMorgan and Bank of America) have been brought to heel, forced, in a settlement with the New York State Attorney General, to purchase the auction warrants.

Several of the banks participating in the original structuring of Jefferson County's refinancing are, then, holding the bag they stitched. It must be noted, however, that as of this writing they are holding it wide open and shaking it insistently to receive the high interest rates triggered by the auction rate failures and standby repurchases, as well as to require that the County pay off the demand warrants over a four-year term. Litigation is (predictably) underway.[9]

The residents of Jefferson County believe themselves to be the true victims in the story, and have taken to the streets in cars bearing bumper stickers with the catchy slogan 'Wipe Out Sewer Debt' (Selway and Braun (2008)). They have some justification. At least one (and probably more) of their elected representatives took bribes for agreeing to what a court in the aforesaid litigation later characterized as 'a risky attempt' to minimize the County's debt burden. Assuming, as is almost certainly the case, that there were elected decision makers who were not accepting bribes in connection with the refinancing transactions,[10] the majority of those decision makers nonetheless were disastrously mistaken about the soundness of what they were doing. The sewer users (many of whom surely are experiencing some of the other aftereffects of the subprime meltdown), are, as of June 2009, paying or protesting sewer use fees that rival or in some cases are greater than their other utilities (ibid.); they also are facing the demands of the bag-holding banks that additional user fees be implemented. Moreover, other routine services ordinarily provided by Jefferson County appear to be on the line.

Frankly, it may be the fact that sewer use is so – um – basic that the dilemma of the residents of Jefferson County seems particularly poignant (unless, of course, you're into toilet humor). Poignancy or bad jokes aside, one is easily tempted to analogize those residents to the shareholders of a corporation, the managers of which have made spectacularly bad decisions. Factoring poignancy back in, however, prompts the realization that corporate shareholders may lose money – or, in the case of Enron, entire retirement nest eggs – without losing the ability to rely on the government to dispose of human waste at affordable cost. There is also an argument to be made that the vaunted ability of shareholders to vote with their feet does not readily extend to the ability of a County resident to pick up and relocate. Looking at the matter a bit differently, however, those inclined to allow practical experience to affect their scrutiny may conclude that the attempted resident vs. shareholder distinctions actually go to show that the questions posed truly are only those of degree.[11] It is hard for people to pick up and move, even though using the toilet has become expensive; it also is hard for many people to come home from a hard day at work and decide to sell investments in mismanaged companies, especially if the mismanagement is hard to detect. Thus, it may be the plight of the residents of Jefferson County that should inform our contemplation of the plight of shareholders of mismanaged companies, rather than the other way around. To the extent that the matter-of-fact response is that people who are too tired to pay attention to their investments should buy mutual funds, the question of trust is joined.

Related to this line of inquiry, moreover, is the question of just what constitutes mismanagement, and whether mismanagement is a betrayal of trust. What can, or should, we be able to expect of either commercial or municipal managers when it comes to relying on the advice of so-called experts and/or jumping on the bandwagons of financial euphoria? These are questions to be considered below, following an examination of the disclosures made by Jefferson County on its path to watery financial ruin.

HOW MUCH DISCLOSURE, AND TO WHOM?

To be sure, there were a number of disclosures made at the time of Jefferson County's debt refinancing. Set out below are (1) a brief discussion of the legal requirements governing those disclosures, (2) a description of the disclosures that actually were made, and (3) an evaluation of whether those disclosures were meaningful.

Disclosure Requirements

It is well established that municipal issuers are subject to the antifraud provisions of the United States federal securities laws (Gabaldon (2009), 748). Thus, when they speak regarding their financial condition they must be candid and avoid half-truths. Prompting municipal disclosure, however, has been problematic for two reasons. First, municipal offerings always have been exempt from registration under the Securities Act of 1993 (15 USC sec. 77c(1)) and the Securities Exchange Act of 1934 (15 USC sec. 78c12(a)(ii)). Second, Congress voted in the 1970s to prohibit the SEC from requiring municipal issuers to otherwise make any pre-issuance filings (15 USC sec. 78o2(d)(1)).

In the wake of a succession of municipal bond scandals, the Commission nonetheless has proven itself to be fairly inventive. Relying on its broad statutory authority to regulate brokers and dealers, it has imposed a rule making it unlawful for any such broker or dealer to participate in an underwriting of municipal securities in excess of $1,000,000 unless it has obtained and reviewed the issuer's official statement. The official statement must '[set] forth information concerning the terms of the proposed issue of securities; [and] information, including financial information or operating data, concerning such [issuer] of municipal securities and those other entities, enterprises, funds, accounts, and other persons material to an evaluation of the Offering . . .' (17 CFR. sec. 240.15c2–12(f)(3)). That is the long and the short of the mandate, however; in stark contrast to the regime imposed on non-municipal issuers there are no long lists of detailed information to be provided nor precise forms to be followed.

There really are only two fairly specific requirements supplementing the more general one described. One is a description of the issuer's agreement with the underwriter subsequently to provide the public with annual financial information and disclosure of certain material events. (As a technical matter, the SEC does not require municipal issuers to make continuing disclosure, but their agreement to do so is a condition of the ability of any broker or dealer to participate in an offering (ibid). Discharge of this contractual obligation frequently has been observed in the breach and a description of any such defalcation by the issuer within the last five years is the second specifically required disclosure (ibid).

The Disclosures of Jefferson County

Lengthy official statements were prepared in connection with Jefferson County's debt restructurings. A brief perusal quickly reveals the following tidbits and/or categories of information: (1) an introductory section with a description of the debt's exempt tax status, summary terms and a number of cautionary statements related to any so-called 'forward-looking' information that was to follow; (2) an amplified description of the terms of the warrants to be issued pursuant to the official statement, including a one-paragraph explanation of the County's planned credit swaps; (3) very brief summaries of information descriptive of the bond insurers, the standby purchase banks, and the auction broker-dealers (in each case obviously provided by the subject of the description and disclaimed by the County); (4) a lengthy section talking about Jefferson County's wondrous new sewage system (complete with a step-by-step account of exactly what happens to effluent); (5) a lengthy section talking about the County itself, including the number of its public school children and the various departments of the University of Alabama at Birmingham's Health Complex; and (6) the required representation that the County had agreed to make continuing disclosure.

Not surprisingly, the offering statements did not mention the overpricing of the County's new credit swaps, nor the now-admitted fact that at least one County Commissioner had accepted bribes from the lead underwriter.[12] Perhaps less expectedly, they also failed to mention that the County had received an expert opinion to the effect that the County was on the verge of becoming unable to pay off its existing debt unless sewer revenues dramatically (and probably unrealistically) increased.[13] Given that there was absolutely no guarantee that the County's interest rate and repayment schedule would improve as a result of the refinancing, this lack of disclosure initially seems disappointing – particularly since hindsight reveals that the County's debt service actually took such a distinct turn for the worse. This disappointment is heightened by the fact that the County had, in the past, attached to its official statements opinions by the same expert to the effect that its sewer revenues would be adequate to service its sewer debt.

There are two obvious responses to this cavil that can be made on behalf of the County. The first is that whether or not the County could have paid off its old bonds was not determinative of the question of whether it could make the payments on its restructured debt. The County expected, thanks to the advice of JPMorgan, that its payments on its new, whiz-bang variable-rate debt at least initially would be lower than the amounts payable on the old, fixed-rate debt. Moreover, although a description of the County's various covenants about implementing rate increases probably constituted a forward-looking representation that there would be adequate sewer revenues to satisfy the new holders, that representation was preceded by a specific warning that political or other conditions might prevent the county from generating the requisite amounts. This warning was an obvious attempt to invoke application of the judicially developed 'bespeaks caution' doctrine to establish the County's lack of liability if future events failed to conform to current prediction.[14] Although it is not clear that this protection would extend to the failure to disclose known information (such as the fact that an unfavorable expert opinion had been received), neither is it clear that it would not (since, after all, the expert's opinion itself was forward-looking).[15]

The second obvious response is that purchasers of Jefferson County's debt were not relying on the County's credit; they were relying on the AAA rating of the debt insurers – otherwise, of course, the debt would have carried the County's credit rating rather than that of the insurers. From that perspective, the only material disclosure would consist of a description of the terms of the debt and information about the insurers and, perhaps, about the banks providing the standby purchase agreements; the extended description of the County and its state-of-the art sewers actually included in the official statement arguably was just for the amusement of the reader or was a form of advertising for possible tourism.

As far as disclosure about the insurers was concerned, the information provided effectively consisted of a representation of parentage (that is, which large holding company owned each insurer and was specifically disavowing responsibility for its debt), a sentence-length description of capitalization, some indication that each was a monoline insurance company, and a recital of the top-flight credit ratings boasted by each.

The reader also was told how to go about obtaining each insurer's audited financial statements, if so inclined. Disclosure about the banks providing the standby purchase agreements and auction broker-dealer services was on a par with that relating to the insurers (with, of course, a different description of the relevant line of business).

Whether or not disclosure relating to the insurers was adequate, the argument that purchasers should not really care about the County's ability to pay its debts highlights the ambiguity of the role of municipal debt insurance, making it seem quite arguable, as a matter of theory, that the securities being issued were those of the insurers, not those of the County.[16] This is a characterization worth contemplation with respect to bond markets more generally, with arguable consequences (detailed below) as to the types of disclosure that should be made and the types of regulation that should attach.

No Match

As indicated above, the official statements relating to Jefferson County's debt restructuring contained quite a bit of newsy disclosure about the County. It was, however, relatively quite light on 'information, including financial information or operating data, concerning . . . those other entities, enterprises, funds, accounts, and other persons material to an evaluation of the Offering'. The analytic task thus becomes a comparison of the needs of various parties for protection, the needs of those parties for disclosure as a form of protection, and the suitability of the disclosures actually made.

The needs of the debt-purchasers

The institutions purchasing Jefferson County's restructured sewer debt obviously were seeking a security that was, well, actually secure. They were, in the case of the holders of the variable-rate demand warrants, diligent and, in the case of the holders of the auction-rate warrants, lucky that the New York State Attorney General was on their side. In any event, they generally appear to have moved on to other investments, leaving some of the banks that participated in the restructuring holding the toxic waste.

In retrospect, it seems clear that they got the protection they sought, not in the form of bond insurance, but in the form of commitments from banks that managed to stay solvent long enough to live up to their obligations. Ironically, the purpose of the standby purchase agreements or, for that matter, the broker-dealers' anticipated auction participation, was to provide temporary liquidity, not lasting protection – that, of course, was the purpose of the debt insurance. One way to look at it, then, is that the debt purchasers found themselves falling off an investment cliff in the company of the insurers, but snagged the back of their pants on a twig on the way down.

Another way to look at the situation, though, is that investors who wish for security really should think about both a belt and suspenders. In shopping for these items, they presumably should get enough information to make an informed choice about the various trade-offs between form and function. Although the information provided in Jefferson County's disclosure documents about insurers, standby purchasers, and broker-dealer banks was minimal, it is not at all apparent that more really would have been of help. What prudent investors needed to know, but what could not have been forthcoming at the time, was that at some point in the not very distant future municipal debt insurers were going to start making some very bad judgments about insuring mortgage-backed securities and executing credit default swaps in a big, big way.[17] Thus understood, it seems patent that the most meaningful protection for the would-be purchasers of secure municipal debt is meaningful regulation of insurers.

On the other hand, additional disclosure with respect to the management and prospective business models of those insurers could not be a bad thing. This would extend to ongoing disclosure as well.[18] It is evident that credit ratings have been regarded as the surrogate for these disclosures and now just as evident that, as sometimes assigned, they should not have been.[19] The extent to which markets have relied on this surrogacy is well illustrated by the Jefferson County debacle. A later part of this chapter will address this reliance as a question of whether it was misplaced trust.

The needs of the bag-holding banks

The banks providing standby purchase agreements and the banks participating as auction broker-dealers appear to be the only current holders of Jefferson County's debt. They obviously had a different motivation in involving themselves in the affairs of Jefferson County than did the original purchasers, and received compensation in return for their willingness to assume the risk that their obligation to provide short-term liquidity would become something else. That does not mean, of course, that they did not wish to quantify that risk, and thus they should have had some of the same concerns as the original purchasers about the credit-worthiness of the debt insurers.

The banks, moreover, had only the insurers between themselves and losing their pants if Jefferson County could not pay its sewer debt. This presumably means that they would be somewhat more interested than the original debt purchasers in actually obtaining information about the County's sewer revenues and the likelihood that the income stream would be sufficient to satisfy the sewer debt service. As noted above, a piece of information bearing on that issue was omitted from the official statement. Still, official statements are not prepared for the benefit of participating banks and there is no reason to think that the banks did not privately receive any information they desired, even including the expert opinion about the inadequacy of revenue to service existing debt. Particularly in light of the past use of expert opinions as attachments to Jefferson County official statements, it almost certainly would have occurred to participating banks to inquire into the matter.

The Needs of the Insurers

The insurers needed enough information about Jefferson County and its sewers to know how much to charge for the policies they issued. There is no reason to think they did not receive that information, although if they were misled they would have cause for complaint. It is possible that they relied too heavily on the County's underlying sewer bond rating; if so, it is to their shame. What is more to their shame, of course, is the bad decisions they made about becoming involved with mortgage securitizations. It would seem, then, that what they really needed was protection from themselves, presumably in a form to be provided by insurance regulators.

The needs of the credit rating agencies

Credit rating agencies seem to be doing very nicely, thank you (in fact, financially thriving), notwithstanding their role in the run on municipal standby purchasers and other panic-related events (Evans and Salas (2009)). In popular view, they may need (the way a child 'needs' a good spanking) a firmer commitment to doing their jobs, said commitment to be brought about by regulation or a restructuring of their compensation schemes (Partnoy (2010)). It seems quite likely that a rating agency spokesperson might make the claim that better information should have been forced on the agency by the various rated entities, with the follow-up point that the public really should realize that you can't rate for a risk that isn't yet quite recognized. The response to these contentions appears below in connection with the discussion of credit rating agency trustworthiness.

The needs of the citizens of Jefferson County

An attempt was made earlier in this chapter to analogize the citizens of Jefferson County to the shareholders of a mismanaged company. The analogy may, with some strain, be continued to say they indeed are in a position similar to that of shareholders insofar as they relied on management to take the funds that they provided and apply them on their behalf.

The analogy is complicated by the introduction of user fees; moreover, it breaks down in small ways because of the migration of citizens, the receipt of benefits by some who have not paid for their entitlement, and so on. Its biggest failing doubtless is that the benefits produced by a county or other governmental entity simply are not thought of as corporate profits – it is more a matter of a conceptual zero-sum game in which the capital pooled is supposed to be expended for goods and public services in an amount exactly equaling (over time) the amount of the capital provided. This means, among other things, that whatever financial interest a citizen has, it certainly cannot be regarded as a 'security' for purposes of United States securities law.[20] There is no doubt, however, that if citizens indeed were security holders, they would have been expected to take ongoing interest in any financial disclosures generated by the entity in which they were invested (including those that were or should have been contained in the official statement). As a matter of federal law, they also would have been entitled to receive ongoing disclosure specifically designed to allow them to make informed voting decisions.

The purpose of the analogy, flawed as it is, is to demonstrate that there were some very real parties-in-interest whose possible need or desire for disclosure in connection with Jefferson County's financial dealings were, as a matter of routine, overlooked. As this suggests, the citizens of Jefferson County are hardly unique: whatever protection they and other purported beneficiaries of municipal finance are to have, it evidently is not going to come from self-help enlightened by disclosure.[21]

DISCLOSURE BY WHOM, AND WHY?

At this juncture, it is interesting to pause for a reminder that, as Jefferson County poses for its swan dive, the Securities and Exchange Commission has chosen to become involved. The Commission's involvement presumably manifests the opinion that at least part of what is at issue indeed is some sort of failure of disclosure in connection with the purchase or sale of securities.[22] Even though the SEC's concern may turn out exclusively to focus on bribery and swap pricing, it is worthwhile to inquire briefly into the matter of just who was issuing securities and thus should have been responsible for such public disclosures as were required.

In most of the world, the decision to regulate transactions in financial interests now turns primarily on whether those interests are something in which there is likely to be active public trading. In the United States, securities regulation is somewhat more expansive. Certainly, concern with the likelihood of public trading is discernible in the legislative choice to declare that such instruments as stock, bonds, and debentures are securities,[23] as well as in the decision to exempt from registration requirements (although not from anti-fraud rules) transactions not involving any public offering.[24] There are, however, a number of instruments included in the definition of 'security' that do not, on their face, demand suitability for trading. These include 'evidences of indebtedness' and 'notes'. The Supreme Court has declared that suitability for trading is a factor, but only a factor, to be considered in determining whether something denominated a 'note' is a security.[25]

Although the County's warrants are not denominated 'bonds' they surely are quite close (and, in fact, frequently are referred to as 'bonds' by those having reason to discuss them). Moreover, they would seem to satisfy the judicially devised tests for the 'evidences of indebtedness' and 'notes' parts of the United States definition of a 'security'. In any event, no one seems seriously worried about whether they are or are not covered by at least parts of the federal securities laws. As noted above, securities issued by municipalities are covered by anti-fraud provisions and the SEC forces some amount of municipal public disclosure, albeit through the backdoor of regulating broker-dealer conduct.

As a general matter, public disclosure requirements extend to all material information that is issuer-specific (Soderquist and Gabaldon (2006), 95); the description set out above of the mandatory contents of a municipal official statement seems to be in accord. Disclosure requirements probably do not capture, however, information that relates to non-issuer-specific information that is publicly available. For instance, it has been held that an issuer need not disclose what is going on in gas prices even if those prices have a significant impact on the issuer's results of operation, provided that the correlation itself is disclosed or obvious.[26] As a technical matter, it is said that such information is not material because it adds nothing to the total mix of information that is available to would-be investors. It would be easy for Jefferson County, then, to argue that this analysis extends to a municipal issuer's disclosures about well-known bond insurers or standby banks. If information is publicly available about those insurers or banks, and it is obvious why that information is relevant to the offering, the information is not technically material and should be no part of the issuer's burden to reveal. This analysis would seem to prevail notwithstanding the SEC's requirement that the official statement obtained by underwriters include information about 'those other entities, enterprises, funds, accounts, and other persons material to an evaluation of the Offering' (17 CFR. sec. 240.15c2–12(f)(3)), since public availability evidently cancels materiality in the eyes of at least some courts.

This form of argument, like the actual disclosure in Jefferson County's official statements, obviously is driven by critical assumptions about what information really is publicly available about a well-known debt insurer or bank. Once recognized, however, the issue seems to complement, or perhaps even converge with, the question raised above as to just whose securities the purchasers of Jefferson County's sewer debt were buying. In extending this examination, it should first be recognized that even if it is a point of concession that Jefferson County was offering securities, there is no reason another entity might not have been offering its securities as well.

There seem to be at least three paths to take in identifying additional issuers of securities in the context of Jefferson County's sewer refinancing. The choice between them is not critical, since all three lead in the same direction.

The first route is the path of practicality. The initial purchasers of Jefferson County's restructured debt were purchasing the right to be repaid by the debt insurers. Were this not true, they would not have accepted the rate of interest associated with a AAA rated debt instrument; they would have held out for something higher. Their conduct when the credit rating of the insurers started to slide is further evidence of this thesis; as spelled out above, the demand debt holders immediately demanded payment, and the auction debt holders refused to bid to hold the debt any longer. This is true even though nothing about the County and its then-existing ability to pay its obligations seems to have changed.[27] In other words, the transaction tanked only because of a credit issue that was not the County's. Thus, although the insurers' promises to pay were denominated 'insurance policies', the right to be paid that the purchasers were receiving might just as well have been called an 'evidence of indebtedness' or a 'note' (which, as indicated above, both are securities under United States law). Proper characterization could be critical because 'insurance policies' issued by regulated companies automatically are exempt from registration under the Securities Act of 1933, whereas 'evidences of indebtedness' and 'notes' of these entities are not (15 USC sec. 77c(8)). Because municipal bond insurance, a product not developed until 1971 (AFGI (2009)), may lack similarity to insurance policies known at the time the exemption was adopted, it is not at all clear that the exemption should apply. The Supreme Court has recognized that the extent of the insurance policy exemption is not co-extensive with the types of instruments known in 1933,[28] but has called for an in-depth inquiry into factors that simply have not been adequately examined in the context of municipal bond insurance.

The second path is one of literalism. In addition to the stock, bonds, debentures, notes, evidences of indebtedness and other instruments defined as securities for purposes of the federal securities, is the 'guarantee of . . .

any of the foregoing' (15 USC sec. 77b(a)(1)). This more-or-less proves that an offering of the security of one issuer can be coupled with the offering of the guaranteeing security of another, for guaranteeing one's own securities would be pointless. One reason for including guarantees in the definition of 'security' may well have been to stay out of the thicket of figuring out the precise entity's credit on which a purchaser might be relying. In any event, this analysis should make it obvious that municipal bond insurance policies are securities, even if they do turn out to be exempt from registration.[29]

The third path invokes something like a 'sham transaction' analysis.[30] If someone really were investing only in the securities of Jefferson County, they really should have been accepting the risk that Jefferson County would not be able to pay off the debt those securities represented. The purchasers of the County's restructured debt were not willing to take that risk. What they really wanted to do was to buy someone else's debt, and it seems fair to say that they actually did so.[31] For all intents and purposes, the transaction could have been recast as a loan to the insurers, who turned around and loaned the money to Jefferson County (happily diversifying their risk, of course, by loaning to many others as well). Of course, if that had transpired, not only would the insurers not have issued insurance policies, but the purchasers might not (without the issuance of a revenue ruling or two by the United States Treasury) have been entitled to interest that was exempt from federal income taxation.

After practicality, literalism, and sham transaction theory have had their say, it does seem that municipal debt insurance is, to put it nicely, a bit of hokum that exists because there is a market for tax exempt income that is safer than municipal issuers can make it themselves. Municipal issuers might, of course, pay higher rates to compensate for the risk of investing in their naked securities, but that would result in increased costs to the citizenry. Municipalities might, on the other hand, borrow from lenders who are able to diversify sufficiently as to value the risk differently than does the average person or institution buying municipal debt today. That is, in effect, what they are doing.

Nonetheless, there are drawbacks to frankly acknowledging the nature of the scheme. One is that the whole municipal tax exemption thing has been in place for quite a long time and the markets for tax-exempt obligations presumably are structured in reliance – over 50 per cent of municipal debt issues are insured (AFGI (2009)). If former insurers were theoretically reconfigured as the only lenders receiving tax exempt interest, there would be quite a few unsettled expectations. Forcing a reconfiguration involving actual lending would also be unsettling. In fact, reconfiguring insurers as private lenders would destroy the only aspect of the current scheme that is not obvious hokum. This is the involvement of insurance regulators. If, in fact, insurers actually were adequately regulated in a merit sense, their involvement as insurers would add value. Unfortunately, it is hard to be inspired by the performance of insurance regulators in permitting monoline municipal insurers to go for a day at the races (that is, move heavily into insuring securitizations and guaranteeing credit default swaps).

Going forward, it probably is the case that purchasers of insured municipal debt will be somewhat more concerned, and thus more curious, about the insurers' *bona fides*. Insurance regulators may step into the breach, proclaiming stricter scrutiny, tougher standards or what-have-you. Credit rating agencies already are taking their lumps, and doubtless will be proclaiming stricter scrutiny, tougher standards and the like. It is possible that more public disclosure of insurers' affairs will be required. One method of bringing about such a change might be for the SEC to fiddle with its current, somewhat toothless, rule calling for disclosure relating to 'other entities' material to the offering. This easily could be adjusted to an outright demand that municipal issuers (or their underwriters) find out, and reveal, more about their insurers than previously the case.

When push comes to shove, however, it is not at all clear just what could be said or, indeed, that any level of municipal disclosure could meaningfully address problems like those posed, and faced, by Jefferson County. What could the County have been expected to say in 2002 or 2003 about what its insurers were going to do in the future? Even if the County had refinanced in 2006, at a time when the relevant municipal debt insurers already were hip deep in securitizations, what might the County have been expected to find out, much less say? In fact, throughout the boom years of the securitization craze there were lots of entities disclosing their involvements in securitizations, credit swaps and so on. To call the descriptions of those involvements opaque would be polite. More important, the risks of securitization failure were not revealed because they simply were not recognized by anyone to whom the markets were willing to listen.

SO TRUST US

Sadly, then, one of the major lessons of securitization as seen through the lens of Jefferson County is just how irrelevant disclosure really can be in the modern age. The complexity of financial models, the pace of change, and, thus, the speed at which the wizards of Wall Street can make mistakes simply preclude meaningful discourse about some dangers. It might as well be understood that, as to some risks, the only disclosure to be had is 'you're going to have to trust us on this one'. It doubtless is too straightforward a suggestion to work, but it might even be best to create clear categories of transactions to be labeled 'trust us' transactions. The primary benefit would then be to call attention to the real question of whether the speaker is worthy of trust.

It has been said that 'a major function of trust is to help reduce the uncertainty and complexity of life in society' (Mitchell (1993), 432). This is well illustrated by the tale of Jefferson County. The citizens of Jefferson County obviously had to trust their elected representatives to do whatever it took to accomplish the complex task of disposing of sewage (indeed, the Official Statements make rocket science look easy by comparison). Just as clearly, the purchasers of the County's debt, as well as the County Commissioners and the standby and auction banks involved in the restructuring, trusted the nice folks at the credit rating agencies to do the complex work of evaluating the debt's insurers. In both instances, it might occur to the reader to wonder whether trust was misplaced.[32]

Trust in Jefferson County

The disappointments

As the music comes to a stop, it is the citizens of Jefferson County who are looking for a place to sit. In one sense, it does not seem disturbing or unfair to have a 'pay as you go' plan – that is, to require the citizens to pay for the fancy new sewage treatment facilities that they currently are enjoying. According to them, however, they just, well, can't afford it. It may be that the original consent decree was unrealistic, from the standpoint of the County's ability to pay for the new facilities, or it may be that population patterns and growth had an adverse effect on that ability. It may be that all the fraud and kickbacks associated with the construction of the facilities drove the cost too high to be borne. All that is water down the drain, or, at any rate, beyond the scope of a chapter relating to financial panic.

What is within the scope of analysis, however, is the fact that if the insurers of Jefferson County's sewer debt had not gambled on securitizations and lost, the County would not be facing a four-year repayment plan for its variable-rate demand warrants, and the interest rates it would be paying would be substantially less, presumably better aligning with the rates the County still is receiving on its overpriced swaps. What, if anything, could the County Commissioners have done to avoid finding themselves and their constituents in their current position?

Certainly, it would be nice if some of them hadn't taken bribes. Certainly, it would be nice if they collectively had figured out the County was paying for its swaps at six times the usual price. They might have even figured out that if someone is selling you a swap, it's because they think they're going to win the bet – and if 'they' are big city banks and 'you' lack similar sophistication, 'they' are probably right. In this sense, of course, finance is much like the extended warranties they sell at Best Buy (and is something Orange County, California, found out some years ago). On the other hand, if you really do need continuous service from a product or are really worried that you cannot afford your existing interest rate, you may very well accept the slicker's terms. There is evidence, in fact, that the Commissioners were trying any way they could to reduce the County's interest rates in the short term, but were aware that the refinancing probably would be 'savings negative' after seven years.[33] 'Savings negativity' does not mean, however, that the Commissioners automatically were consigning the County to bankruptcy; presumably they expected to continue to raise user fees as much as they could, or perhaps to attempt another refinancing when the time came.

The biggest disappointment for the County and its residents, of course, had to do with the insurers of the County's debt. It would have been more than nice – indeed, downright dandy – if someone acting on the County's behalf had discerned that there was a risk that said insurers would go belly-up/credit-rating-down. Labeling the lack of discernment a breach of trust, however, seems a bit harsh; if it involved a failure of any kind, it seems a forgivable one.

Disappointment vs. betrayal

In identifying instances of misplaced trust, it is relevant to note a distinction made by scholars between trust in intention and trust in ability (Mitchell (1993), 434), as well as to distinguish trust from a demand for absolute truth (ibid, 433). As to the former distinction, it has been suggested that if any relationship requiring trust is to succeed, the beneficiaries of trust must be entitled to rely both on the ability of the trusted to navigate the risks of the future and on the intention of the trusted to discharge the terms of the trust to the best of that ability, without interference by the trusted's personal interests.

Because it is only individuals that can form intent, it is arguable that if one of the conditions of trust involves intention, the ranks of the trusted must be limited accordingly to human beings. On the other hand, there are many colloquial uses of the terms 'trust' and 'trustee' with reference to institutions. There also is a story to be told about constructive intent on the part of institutions. In any event, there surely are instances in which an institution's conflicts of interest will be more or less apparent and tend to undercut the confidence of those who act in reliance on that institution. For the moment, then, the idea that an institution may be trusted will not be rejected, notwithstanding Lawrence Mitchell's insight that trust is an affective relationship between human beings 'in which the trusted party's self-love is transformed by human imagination into fellow-feeling' (2001, 609–10). Moreover, the completely convincing point that institutions cannot trust will be left unexplored, with the excuse that references in this chapter to trust exhibited by institutional purchasers or bag-holding banks should be understood as the trust reposed by their human constituents.

The question of ability – individual or institutional – to discharge the duty of the trusted must be seen as one that is subject to situational limits: no one can do more than can be done. Once resigned to this limitation, it really is only a very short step to saying no one can [reasonably be expected to] do more than can [reasonably be expected to] be done. This step is virtually irresistible when (in the reciprocal of Professor Mitchell's quoted point) the trusted is a human being like ourselves. There may, once again, be a case for distinguishing institutions; this case will be addressed below in the context of credit rating agencies. The Jefferson County Commissioners, however, were and are human beings. As such, they seem sentimentally, if not morally, entitled to a standard of reasonableness. Once that entitlement is recognized, of course, it seems uninspiring but necessary to revisit the condition of intent to do one's best, recasting it as the condition of intent to do what is reasonably required. Luckily, this adjustment can be made without abandoning the intent to avoid the influence of self-interest.

Notwithstanding the evident lack of reasonableness in asking for conduct that is more than reasonable, there may have have been a time when trustees of formal trusts effectively were asked for more, and were more-or-less held as insurers of the correctness of their decisions. Expectations have never been that high for either public officials or corporate directors. Public officials acting in a legislative capacity generally are granted immunity for their official acts, and the (reasonable) judgments of corporate directors are protected by the business judgment rule.[34] What this means for purposes of this chapter is that the law does not usually require that trusted decision makers actually be correct about what will happen as the result of a given decision. Another way to describe the same notion is that uncertainty as to future events imposes legally significant situational limits on the ability of decision makers to discern the 'truth' of what will occur upon the taking of certain actions.

In the case of Jefferson County it is quite easy to apply the concepts of trust in intention and trust in ability, as distinct from a demand for truth. The citizens of the County should have been entitled to trust that the County Commissioners would not take bribes, for taking a bribe invokes self-interest in decision making, making intention questionable. The citizens should have been entitled to trust that the County Commissioners would be diligent enough to ask the right questions about swap pricing and other terms, and smart enough to understand the answers they received. Lack of diligence, by definition, destroys the condition of intention, while lack of financial sophistication would go to lack of ability; in both instances, of course, they are questions of fact the answers to which are not yet clear. A fairly straightforward analysis pertains with respect to the County Commissioner's reliance on its insurers' credit ratings: such reliance did not violate the terms of trust if reasonable. An assessment of reasonableness in this regard logically relates to the trustworthiness of the rating agencies, an issue to be addressed below.

Sustaining the conditions of trust

Before turning to the credit ratings that initially supported and ultimately tanked the Jefferson County refinancing, it is instructive to consider the ways in which the legal system attempts to sustain the conditions that permit citizens to trust their elected representatives, using Jefferson County's own issues as a template for analysis. The once-again-easiest issue to deal with is that unfortunate business about bribery.

The American legal system deplores bribery of public officials.[35] There are, after all, actual statutes against making bribes and against receiving them that already have been invoked by the Justice Department against selected Jefferson County Commissioners. Moreover, the SEC views the conduct in question as a type of fraud and is pursuing remedies against recipients and, evidently, payers.

The extent to which anti-bribery sentiment is felt in fact has led to a specific attempt at prophylaxis in municipal finance. Thus, the federal Municipal Securities Rulemaking Board ('MSRB'), the rules of which are approved and enforced by the Securities and Exchange Commission, has adopted two rules intended to prevent corruption on the part of municipal underwriters. MSRB Rule G-37 prohibits accepting a municipal underwriting within two years of making a contribution to a person in position to influence the underwriting's grant;[36] Rule G-38 prohibits the use of consultants to assist in obtaining municipal business.[37] Both rules aim at stamping out not only overt attempts at bribery, but substantial grey areas as well.

By contrast, the fact that the County Commissioners (with some help from people in pin-striped suits) got the County into a credit mess seems to be just one of those things that didn't work out, with no ramifications other than those that may be meted out in the election booth. There simply are few instances in which elected officials suffer legal consequences for non-feasance (that is, lack of diligence) and, thanks to the various varieties of official immunity, we never even pretend to expect our public servants to be right. As noted above, some part of this determination has been based on human sympathy; another part no doubt turns on the notion that if one has to be right or risk liability, few will be interested in serving in an official capacity. For all intents and purposes, then, the legal reaction to official error is a shrug.

Unfortunately, the 'shrug' approach begs the question of whether, and how, systemic support could be given to municipal representatives as they attempt to do their jobs in connection with financing the projects for which they find themselves responsible. In this regard, the SEC and MSRB probably should give some significant, albeit paternalistic, thought to adopting rules forcing municipal underwriters to be very, very helpful indeed in their explanations to municipal officials. For instance, a specific and written disclosure of prevailing rates for the various services and products (such as swaps) might be in order. Going a bit further, regulators might entertain the idea of rules requiring municipal underwriters to go beyond reasonable efforts and 'speak the truth' to municipalities about various risks. Rules requiring 'truth' in the sense of actual correctness are discussed immediately below in the context of credit rating agencies.

In Ratings We Trust

The disappointments

It is fair to say that just about everyone involved is disappointed as heck in the performance of the agencies that rated the credit of Jefferson County and its insurers. Whether this disappointment is entirely fair, given the timing of the restructuring transactions, is not clear; it does seem, however, that the insurers had begun to stick their toes into securitizations. The following analysis will proceed on the assumption that the rating agencies could have obtained the information that the debt insurers either were, or were about to be, very heavily involved in securitizations.

Disappointment vs. betrayal

When contemplating the issue of the trust in credit ratings exhibited by the Jefferson County Commissioners, the County's debt purchasers and the County's standby and auction banks, a trichotomous inquiry into intent, ability and truth still has an appeal. First, it is no novel insight that the current rating agency structure presents a disturbing conflict of interest insofar as it is the entities that are being rated that pay the rating agencies' fees. One would think that this would suggest they are not trustworthy in the intentions sense. Second, it now is evident to all that serious mistakes were made. Perhaps this was a matter of inattention – an intentions issue – or perhaps it was a question of ability; the rating agencies either were or were not able to do a reasonable job. In any event, it is clear that truth was not discovered.

Sustaining the Conditions of Trust

If anything resembling trust in credit ratings is to be justified, there really should be systemic attention to the conditions of trust. In fact, there is much noise about revising credit rating methods (Evans and Salas (2009)) and something eventually may be accomplished. Certainly, restructuring incentives, perhaps with a shift to user-based fees, should be on the table (Manns (2009)). Perhaps something of the order of a private right of action for those injured by reliance on negligent or reckless ratings could be established (Partnoy (2010)). Another possibility might be the subjection of rating agencies to periodic examinations, with stiff penalties to be imposed if lax practices are discovered.

The most obvious suggestions, however, share a common theme. They seem either to address intention directly or to convert the issue of ability into one of intention, focusing on process and asking only whether rating agencies are trying as hard as reasonably could be expected. They do not seem to ask if there really is any institutional ability to do better (much less demand it), although it seems widely assumed that better linkage of credit ratings and later financial viability is possible. The suggestions described above also stop short of holding rating agencies accountable for truth.

If we continue to choose to have a financial system that is a house of cards resting on the card-table of credit ratings, it would seem to go without saying that we really do want credit rating devices that succeed, not devices that try hard but fail. In other words, this is an area where we legitimately should demand truth rather than the trustworthiness asked of human beings. The only real question has to do with just how to articulate and enforce the demand. As a starting thought, though, it does seem that truth-telling might be prompted by establishing a system for rating the rating agencies and weeding out non-performers. One could imagine, for instance, a method of comparing a credit rating agency's ratings with the rated entities' failures over time, and yanking the charter of sub-performing agencies.

Whether or not basing a credit rating agency's right to exist on a comparison of its predictions and actual outcomes has allure, conceiving of credit ratings in terms of 'truth' may strike some as inapt, simply because a credit rating, like finance more generally, relates to things that will happen in the future. A credit rating also may be viewed, however, as a representation that a rated company either does or does not satisfy one of a set of weighted standards well chosen to correlate with financial viability over some period of time. The failure of a rated entity then may be taken as good evidence either that the relevant standards were not met, or that the standards were not well chosen, and thus as evidence – preferably conclusive evidence – that the rating agency's representation as to one or both was untrue.

Although treating an unacceptable outcome as conclusive evidence of misrepresentation has the marked benefit of simplicity, there will be those who complain that the approach sometimes will be incorrect. The conceptualization of rating as current representation rather than prediction could then, if demanded, afford a rating agency the opportunity to demonstrate to a regulator that the evidence is not persuasive, whether owing to a meteor that hurtled from the sky or some other event that genuinely could not be anticipated. Thus, for instance, if at the time the insurers of Jefferson County's restructured sewer debt issued their policies they (counter factually) had not even thought of starting a move into securitizations, the rating agencies might have nothing to answer for at that time. If, however, the ratings were maintained after the move began, a different picture would take shape. A rating agency challenged on this basis doubtless would attempt the argument that *everyone* was wrong about securitizations. The proper – and only superficially hard-hearted – reply would be, 'But it was *your* job to be right'.

Truth vs. Trust

The difference between government and corporate decision makers, who are human beings, and credit rating agencies, which are not, cannot be overlooked. We may well feel sympathy for our human counterparts and recognize the unfairness of requiring them actually to be right. This does not require extension of the same sentiment and/or reasoning to an entity such as a credit rating agency. There is nothing immoral or unfeeling about expecting a device to do its job; if a barometer does not reliably predict a change in the weather it is thrown out and if modeling software fails in its task it is replaced. It may seem immoral or unfeeling, once human beings are factored in as owners, managers and workers, to call for executing entities for being wrong, but the fact of the matter is that entities frequently are executed for being wrong, and probably with not as much cause. That the mechanism is the market, not the law, does not change the result.

Thus, if one (for purposes of argument) characterizes corporations as devices for making money, it is easy to see that a corporation fails in its purpose if money is not made.[38] It similarly is easy to see that market forces effectively demand corporations to discern the 'truth' of such matters as future public desire for particular commodities. The metric in such instances for judging correctness happens to be the well-known bottom line – or the question of whether they are accomplishing their purpose. In this sense, commercial institutions, unlike their human constituents, are widely held to a 'truth', rather than 'reasonableness' standard.

One of the difficulties with credit rating agencies is, of course, that the bottom line on which the market has judged them has not for years had a direct correlation with what it is that third parties have relied on them to do. It has, instead, related to rating agency ability to discern the 'truth' of how much its services will appeal to the issuers who pay for them. Thus, if rating agencies are to maintain their critical role in the financial system, some metric for judging their accuracy other than the bottom line really must be employed. Interestingly, the articulation of this need prompts recognition that what is at stake (the ability to rely on the representation of the rating agencies as accurate) is not at all the same as the 'trust' of which Niklas Luhmann wrote in saying 'Trust is . . . something other than a reasonable assumption on which to decide correctly, and for this reason models for calculating correct decisions miss the point of the question of trust' ((1979), 88).

Distinguishing trust from reliance on truth does not, however, lead to a necessary loss of interest in such matters as whether credit ratings agencies have conflicts of interest, simply because we have become accustomed to addressing that issue in the context of trustworthiness. Conflicts of interest undermine the search for truth as much as for trust. Thus, incentives that come from those who have a vested interest in anything other than strict truth clearly are suspect. Relaxation of internal processes by those who may find the rating enterprise more profitable or life more pleasant if shortcuts are taken are suspect. Addressing incentives, addressed above in terms of intention, can only complement a demand for truth.

CONCLUSION

Finance is inherently about what will happen in the future. That is, of course, no reason to disregard the lessons of the past. This chapter has attempted to plumb a single, but impressive, failure of modern finance in the hopes of extracting its morals. The Jefferson County sewer refinancing obligingly has given up at least seven arguable insights that are capable of ready summary.

Three of the insights that can be abstracted from the experience of Jefferson County relate to disclosure. The first such insight is that disclosure as currently practiced in the context of municipal finance is probably of little use to anyone. The second is that one of the reasons for the shortfall is failure to recognize the true nature of just who is issuing securities, leading to acknowledgment that debt insurers properly are within this group. The third is that, even with revamping and identification of insurers as issuers, disclosure is not likely to provide the protection that many of the participants in modern municipal securities markets arguably need; in some instances, the only possible course of action is resort to trust.

The next two insights pick up where despair with respect to disclosure leaves off, and have to do with trust. One of these is that trust cannot be justified and therefore would be difficult to sustain without significant attention to its conditions. The next calls for recognition that the law has at least some facility in dealing with problems that are presented by the intentions of a trusted actor, but deals awkwardly, at best, with problems presented by a trusted actor's abilities or lack thereof.

The sixth insight has to do with truth. There are instances in which an attempt to buttress the conditions of trust should be augmented with a full-cry demand that an actor 'speak the truth' or suffer significant legal consequences. Although this would appear to circle back to a requirement of full disclosure, the duty of 'truth' is different in kind, as it calls upon an actor to be right and not just forthcoming. Thus, the representations of certain entities critical to the financial system would be required, in the rearview mirror, to be completely correct on what effectively is a strict liability basis.

The seventh, and final, insight has to do with authorial license. It really is not possible, try as one might, to compose a chapter about sewer bond financing without using a particular expression. This piece thus will close with the observation that the law cannot simply pooh-pooh the plight of municipalities and their citizens as it addresses the mess created by the financial maelstrom of 2008. Attention must be paid.

NOTES

1. The term 'billion' is used in the American sense of one thousand million. If not otherwise attributed, factual background in this chapter is drawn from documents provided to the Securities and Exchange Commission on 3 June 2009, as support for the County's request that it be considered a victim of JPMorgan's fraud in connection with an enforcement action announced in May 2009. Copies are on file with the author.
2. 'LIBOR' stands for 'London Interbank Offered Rate'. It is fixed daily by the British Bankers' Association on the basis of a filtered average of the rates paid by the world's most creditworthy banks and is the most widely used benchmark for short-term interest rates.
3. The A rating was carried on the County's sewer debt; its overall rating at the time was AA.

4. Material relating to the general causes of the Panic of 2008 can, of course, be found throughout this volume.
5. The County contended that the ability to increase user fees was constrained by legal principles prohibiting confiscatory charges, as well as that its ability to collect increased fees would be practically constrained by its inability to cut off service.
6. Although the bond insurers still are contractually obligated to pay off the sewer debt in the event the County is unable to do so, the looming insolvency of those insurers renders it unlikely that the debt holders will be paid. In fact, the New York insurance commissioner already has suspended the ability of Syncora Guarantee, Inc. (formerly XL Capital Assurance, Inc.) to pay any claims.
7. The prior record holder was the bankruptcy of Orange County, California (Gellis (1996), 454).
8. Interestingly, the Commissioner sued by the Securities and Exchange Commission appears to be defending on the basis that he allegedly accepted bribes relating to the County's interest swaps and that those swaps are not securities. This overlooks the connection of his charged perfidy to the sale of the County's debt which, as detailed below, clearly was a security.
9. The history of the litigation is described in the recent opinion rendered as *The Bank of New York Mellon et al v. Jefferson County*, Alabama, *et al*, 2009 U.S. Dist. LEXIS 122093.
10. In this regard, it is quite notable that Bettye Fine Collins, currently the President of the Jefferson County Commission, was, as early as 1996, vigorously complaining to the SEC about the pay-to-play and other corrupt practices affecting the County's financings.
11. Feminist legal commentators, among whom the author groups herself, often contend that analysis devoid of experiential reference is meaningless (Rhode (1990), 621).
12. The offering statements may be obtained from the website of the Municipal Securities Rulemaking Board under CUSIP 472682LH4.
13. This lack of disclosure was noted with some disapproval by the court in the litigation referred to in note 7.
14. The 'bespeaks caution' doctrine essentially provides that forward-looking statements accompanied by meaningful cautions are not material and thus not actionable. One of the fairly early cases in which the doctrine was invoked is *In re Donald J. Trump Casino Securities Litigation–Taj Mahal Litigation*, 7 F.3d 357 (3d Cir. 1993). A similar, statutory safe harbor added to the federal securities laws by the Private Securities Litigation Reform Act of 1995 would not apply (Soderquist and Gabaldon (2006), 276).
15. The law seems to have converged on a point of agreement that whether someone indeed holds an opinion is a matter of fact, but to regard a misrepresentation of that opinion as material only if it would mislead as to underlying facts. *Virginia Bankshares, Inc. v. Sandberg*, 501 U.S. 1083 (1991). This has far from settled the many interesting issues that arise about opinions and predictions. Based on the *Bankshares* reasoning, though, one could construct an argument that failing to reveal a (third party) opinion at all only is materially misleading if it misleads about the likelihood of future events. If the reader already has been told that future events may diverge from stated prediction, the omission of the opinion thus might be seen as immaterial.
16. As stated above in the text, the securities of municipal issuers are exempt from registration under the Securities Act of 1933 (15 USC sec. 77c(1)). Insurance policies and contracts issued by corporations subject to the supervision of a state or federal insurance commissioner similarly are exempt (15 USC sec. 77c(8)). The possible applicability of this exemption is discussed in the text below.
17. In fact, it is clear that the insurers already did have some involvement in guaranteeing securitizations.
18. The desirability of ongoing disclosure is particularly obvious in light of the fact that insurance companies usually are privately held subsidiaries. Matters that would be

material in considering the viability of the subsidiary might assume less significance when addressed in the context of the affairs of the larger enterprise.

19. The assertion in the text is a generic one, and is not limited to the ratings assigned to Jefferson County.
20. The definition of 'security' for purposes of federal securities law is a complex subject, but it is fairly clear that financial return is a requisite.
21. It should be noted that even though there is no reason to think that the citizens of Jefferson County were intended readers of the County's disclosures in connection with its sewer debt restructuring, that is not to say that they might not have been incidental users. Information (or what passes for it) has a way of filtering here, there and everywhere; facts from the County's official statement doubtless stalk the internet and may even have informed the preparation of the County's Wikipedia entry (which, as one might expect, now addresses the collapse of the County's debt restructuring).
22. In addition, there may be sustainable claims that the registered broker-dealers failed to comply with more specific rules of conduct.
23. Discussion of the definition of a 'security' in this chapter contemplates both the definition in the Securities Act of 1933 (at 15 USC sec. 77b(a)(2)) and the Securities Exchange Act of 1934 (at 17 USC sec. 78c(a)(10)). The Supreme Court has held that 'security' is to be given uniform across the two Acts, notwithstanding that there are slightly different articulations. *Tcherepnin v. Knight*, 389 U.S. 332, 338–39 (1967).
24. The exemption from registration is stated at 15 USC sec. 77d(2). It has been judicial and administratively amplified (Soderquist and Gabaldon (2006), 179–93).
25. The factor is described by the Court as 'whether it is an instrument in which there is "common trading for speculation or investment"'. The other factors to consider include whether the transaction in question is prompted by investment motives, the expectations of the investing public, and whether there is some factor that reduces the risk of investment, making regulation superfluous. *Reves v. Ernst & Young*, 493 U.S. 56 (1990). Also of interest in this regard is *Marine Bank v. Weaver*, 455 U.S. 551 (1982), which, in interpreting the part of the definition of 'security' referring to 'investment contracts', referred to the importance of finding that an instrument was 'not designed to be traded publicly'. Ibid at 560.
26. The case referred to in the text is *Kapps v. Torch Offshore, Inc.*, 379 F.3d 207 (5th Cir. 2004).
27. One might try to enunciate an alternative explanation in which the debt holders feared what other debt holders might do (tender in the case of demand warrants and refuse to bid in the case of auction warrants) and anticipated the difficult situation the County would find itself in as a result; the explanation given in the text is far more straightforward. A more plausible, but still not preferred, alternative account might involve a simple panic over a possible impending lack of liquidity or concern that no matter how credit-worthy the County might be, prospective future purchasers would be inclined to place irrationally low values on its debt.
28. The case referred to in the text is *SEC v. Variable Annuity Life Insurance Co. of America*, 359 U.S. 65 (1959). It was invoked in in the request of Messrs. Mudge, Rose, Guthrie & Alexander for an assurance from the staff of the SEC that it would not recommend action in connection with the unregistered first offering of insured municipal bonds. The staff tersely indicated that it was acting 'in reliance' on the opinion of the requesting law firm in stating that it would not recommend an enforcement action if the offering proceeded without registration. 'American Municipal Bond Assurance Corporation', 1972 SEC No-Act, Lexis 2655 (16 June 1972).
29. The SEC never has adopted a contrary position. When requested to concur in the view of Messrs. Mudge, Rose, Guthrie & Alexander that the initial issuance of municipal bond insurance did not involve the issuance of a security, the staff did not do so. Ibid. The staff did, as indicated in the prior note, rely on the opinion of requesting counsel with respect to the issue of the need for registration.
30. The 'sham transaction' doctrine probably is best known in tax law, where it also goes

by the name 'step transaction' theory. The basic notion is that parts of transactions that do not have genuine business reasons should be disregarded for purposes of federal income tax (Graber (2000)). The doctrine has applications in other areas as well (Schwartz (2003)), and dovetails nicely with the repeated references in the federal securities context that substance be elevated over form, also known as the test for 'economic reality'. This test was most famously enunciated by the Supreme Court in *United Housing Foundation, Inc., v. Forman*, 421 U.S. 837, 848 (1975).

31. For an interesting empirical study tending to support this characterization, the reader is encouraged to consult Singh and Nanda (2003).
32. This chapter does not address the very interesting question of whether trust that effectively is forced is really trust at all, or merely surrender. Even if the question is one of surrender, the position of the vulnerable can only be improved by attending to the same matters that are regarded as the conditions of trust.
33. The term 'savings negativity' is a deliberate perversion of the actual phrasing using by the court in *The Bank of New York Mellon, et al v. Jefferson County, Alabama, et al*, 2009 U.S. Dist. LEXIS 122093. The court actually said that '[s]avings were projected to be negative for several years thereafter'. Ibid. at n. 10.
34. There has been much (arguably way too much) written on the business judgment rule. In the view of the author, it provides that pure-minded (that is, non-criminal and non-self-interested) directors cannot be held liable for being wrong, provided only that they acted and decided reasonably. For a more nuanced explication and presentation of other renditions, the reader is invited to peruse Gabaldon (1995), 21–26.
35. Of a piece, accepting a bribe would be a good way for a corporate director to lose the protection of the business judgment rule.
36. The formal reference for the rule is Mun. Sec. Rulemaking Bd., Rule 6–37: Political Contributions and Prohibitions on Municipal Securities Business (2005), available at http://www.msrb.org/MSRB1/rules/ruleg37.htm.
37. The formal reference for the rule is Mun. Sec. Rulemaking Bd., Rule 6–38: Solicitation of Municipal Securities Business (2005), available at http://www.msrb.org/MSRB1/rules/ruleg38.htm.
38. There are alternative conceptions of the corporation that the author would prefer. These include the visions advanced by the school of corporate progressives, the team production theorists, and feminists. (For brief descriptions of these visions, the reader may consult Gabaldon (2006), 540–546.)

REFERENCES

Association of Financial Guaranty Insurers ('AFGI'), AFGI Website, http://afgi.org/invest_faq.htm, accessed 28 June 2009.

Cox, C., Chairman, U.S. Sec. & Exch. Comm'n (2007), 'Speech by SEC Chairman: Integrity in the Municipal Market' (18 July 2007), http://www.sec.gov/news/speech/2007/spch071807cc.htm., accessed 15 June 2009.

Evans, D. and C. Salas (2009), 'Flawed Credit Ratings Reap Profits as Regulators Fail Investors', http://www.bloomberg.com/apps/news?pid=20601101&sid=a6NdKd8CfR2A, accessed 30 June 2009.

Gabaldon, T. (2009), 'Financial Federalism and the Short, Happy Life of Municipal Securities Regulation', **34** *J. Corp. Law* 739.

Gabaldon, T. (2006), 'Like a Fish Needs a Bicycle: Public Corporations and their Shareholders', **65** *U. Md. L. Rev.* 538.

Gabaldon, T. (1995), 'Feminism, Fairness and Fiduciary Duty', **5** *Texas J. Women & L.* 1.

Gellis, A.J. (1996), 'Municipal Securities Market: Same Problems–No Solutions', **21** *Del. J. Corp. Law* 427.
Graber, B. (2000), 'Can the Battle be Won? Compaq, the Sham Transaction Doctrine, and a Critique of Proposals to Combat the Corporate Tax Shelter Dragon', **149** *U. Pa. L. Rev.* 355.
JP Morgan Chase & Co. (7 May 2009), *Quarterly Report (Form 10-Q).*
Luhmann, Niklas (1979), *Trust and Power*, Chichester, UK: John Wiley & Sons, Inc.
Manns, J. (2009), 'Rating Risk after the Subprime Mortgage Crisis: A User Fee Approach for Rating Agency Accountability', **87** *N.C.L. Rev.* 1011.
Mitchell, L.E. (2001), 'The Importance of Being Trusted', **81** *B.U.L. Rev.* 591.
Mitchell, L.E. (1993), 'Fairness and Trust in Corporate Law', **43** *Duke L.J.* 425.
Partnoy, Frank (2010) 'Overdependence on Credit Ratings Was a Primary Cause of the Crisis', Chapter 5 in this volume.
Retnasaba, G. (2006), 'Do Campaign Contributions and Lobbying Corrupt? Evidence from Public Finance', **2** *J.L. Econ. & Pol'y* 145.
Rhode, D. (1990), 'Feminist Critical Theories', 42 *Stan. L. Rev.* 617.
Schwartz, J. (2003), 'Elaborating on Sham Transactions as Evidence of Violations of the Anti-Kickback Statute', **13** *Wash. U.J.L & Pol'y* 357.
Selway, W. and M.Z. Braun (2008), 'JPMorgan Swap Deals Spur Probe as Default Stalks Alabama County', http://www.bloomberg.com/app/mews?sid=aF_18gL LNyn)*pid=20601109, accessed 20 June 2009.
Singh, R. and V.K. Nanda (2003), 'Bond Insurance: What is Special about Munis?', http://ssrn.com/abstract=171412 or DOI: 10.2139/ssrn.171412, accessed 27 June 2009.
Soderquist, Larry D. and Theresa A. Gabaldon (2009), *Supplement to Securities Law* (6th edn), New York, NY: Foundation Press.
Soderquist, Larry D. and Theresa A. Gabaldon (2006), *Securities Regulation* (6th edn), New York, NY: Foundation Press.

11. It's time to resuscitate the shareholder derivative action

Edward Labaton and Michael W. Stocker*

INTRODUCTION

Even in the midst of the spectacle of collapsing automobile giants and banks teetering on the brink of insolvency, little has outraged the public as much as abuses of executive compensation. While the credit crisis and plummeting real estate values may have resulted in more wide-scale damage, the trust and confidence of the American public were profoundly shaken when AIG's board approved hundreds of millions of dollars in bonuses to many of the same executives who had run the company into the ground.

AIG management was hardly alone in pocketing king-size bonuses in the midst of the greatest financial disaster of the last 70 years. In 2007, as the bubble economy began its death plunge, Goldman Sachs, Morgan Stanley, Merrill Lynch, Lehman Brothers and Bear Stearns handed out about $36 billion in performance-related bonuses to top executives. Less than two years later, Lehman was bankrupt, Merrill Lynch had been forced into a shotgun marriage with Bank of America, and Bear Stearns was saved from bankruptcy only by its eleventh-hour rescue by JP Morgan Chase, subsidized by American taxpayers.

Most frustrating to the public is that there is apparently so little that can be done to rein in this outrageous waste of corporate assets. Legislators argue that their hands are tied by the contracts companies have entered into with executives. Boards of directors have thus far shown little appetite for restraining management excesses, in part because structural biases tend to lead directors to promote management's interests over those of shareholders.

Policy makers searching for an answer to these abuses may find it in the past – America's long tradition of shareholder derivative lawsuits. After decades spent in desuetude, hobbled by industry lobbying and unfavorable legal decisions, these suits may at long last be making a comeback as a means to impose meaningful reforms for the benefit of shareholders. To ensure that derivative suits regain their key role in ensuring responsible corporate governance, states would be wise to adopt reforms inspired by recent changes in securities class action litigation.

THE REVIVAL OF THE DERIVATIVE LITIGATION

The US tradition of derivative or shareholder litigation has its roots in the English courts, which began recognizing equitable jurisdiction for shareholder suits in the early nineteenth century (Demott (1987), § 1:01). These actions were acknowledged by the United States Supreme Court as early as 1855, by which time industrialization and the dispersal of stock holdings in the US were leaving shareholders increasingly powerless to remedy malfeasance by company managers. The shareholder derivative action took hold as an important lever these minority shareholders could deploy to resolve disputes with company executives (Swanson (1993), pp. 1351–52).

Derivative suits provide at least two possible benefits for shareholders. The suits may result in material rewards to shareholders, such as disgorged profits. Just as important, the existence of the derivative suits may itself have the effect of policing management misconduct (Thompson and Thomas (2004), p. 1774).

Indeed, in the late 1940s the Supreme Court described the derivative action, a 'remedy born of stockholder helplessness', as the 'chief regulator of corporate management' and as having 'afforded no small incentive to avoid at least grosser forms of betrayal of stockholders' interests' (*Cohen v. Beneficial Industrial Loan Corp.*,[1] pp. 547–49). Ten years later, Eugene Rostow echoed this sentiment in observing that shareholder derivative litigation was 'the most important procedure the law has yet developed to police the internal affairs of corporations' (Rostow (1959), p. 48).

Because the derivative plaintiff acts essentially as a self-appointed spokesperson for the interests of the corporation, courts and legislatures created a 'demand requirement' to help ensure that the (potentially expensive) prosecution of a derivative claim is in fact in the best interests of the corporation, and not merely a form of extortion by a shareholder with an axe to grind. All jurisdictions in the United States require that a would-be shareholder derivative plaintiff must first make a demand on the corporation's board of directors before any action can be filed (American Law Institute (1994), § 7.03). As the Sixth Circuit has recently observed, 'the demand requirement serves several purposes: to allow the directors to occupy their normal status as the conductors of the corporation's affairs, to encourage informal resolution of intracorporate disputes, and to guard against misuse of the derivative remedy' (*McCarthy v. Middle Tennessee Electric Membership Corp.*[2], pp. 407–08).

For much of the twentieth century, the demand requirement did not empower corporations to abort a derivative suit brought against their own directors. However, in the 1970s, US corporations, acting under the imprimatur of sympathetic courts, vastly expanded their ability to abort derivative actions. They did this by distorting an innovation originally intended to protect corporate integrity – the special litigation committee.

Special litigation committees were developed by the Enforcement Division of the Securities Exchange Commission as a way to combat the rash of improper foreign and political payments – bribes – by American corporations. In order to ensure that corporate boards had directors willing to take action against management for such misconduct, the SEC used consent decrees to require corporations to add independent directors to their boards and to appoint those independent directors to serve on independent board committees that would file reports with the SEC. The composition of the special litigation committee was subject to the approval of the Commission, ensuring that this oversight function would be independent of management interests.

The Southern District of New York's 1976 decision in *Gall v. Exxon*[3] saw the special litigation committee concept pressed into an unexpected use. In *Gall*, an Exxon shareholder brought a derivative action against directors of the corporation arising from charges that Exxon had used corporate funds to bribe Italian officials to secure political favors and business advantages. The shareholder alleged claims for, among other things, waste, spoliation and misuse of corporate assets, and asked to reconstitute the company's board of directors in order to ensure board independence.

In response, Exxon's Board of Directors established a special litigation committee composed of current directors, and referred to this committee the task of determining whether Exxon should pursue the shareholder's claims. However, there was one critical difference between the special litigation committees created under SEC consent decrees and the one created by Exxon: the 'independent directors' in *Gall* were selected and approved by the defendant corporation alone, without any review by the SEC.

Based on empirical evidence, scholars have repeatedly expressed skepticism about the independence of committee members selected by corporations, such as those selected in *Gall*. When members of special litigation committee are chosen by incumbent directors who are subject to derivative suits, those incumbent directors are understandably likely to appoint members who are sympathetic to their interests. Moreover, because special litigation committees operate at the pleasure of corporate boards, overly scrupulous committees face dissolution if they press too hard for litigation (Cox (1982), p. 962).

In *Gall*, Exxon's special litigation committee quickly determined that it was not in the best interests of Exxon shareholders to pursue the claims against any current or former Exxon officer or director. Surprisingly, the Southern District of New York did not find the manner in which the special litigation committee was selected to be *per se* improper. Instead, the court placed the burden on the plaintiff to show that the committee's decision was not independent. The court also held that a special litigation committee's decision to abort derivative litigation was subject to the same deference generally given to management decisions under the business judgment rule (*Gall*, p. 515).

Other companies, sensing opportunity, quickly followed Exxon's lead and created special litigation committees to make the determination of whether or not a corporation should permit derivative litigation to go forward. This new use of the special litigation committee as a bulwark against derivative lawsuits was further entrenched by the Supreme Court's 1979 decision in *Burks v. Lasker*.[4] In *Burks* the Supreme Court agreed that corporate directors chosen by the corporation itself could terminate pending derivative litigation.

As a result of judicial acceptance of special litigation committees, the success of derivative suits has come to depend upon whether or not the plaintiff can show that the demand requirement should be excused as futile or that demand was improperly denied. The requirements for showing demand futility vary from jurisdiction to jurisdiction, but generally turn on whether the plaintiff can demonstrate the self interest of board members who would vote on the demand (Swanson (1993), pp. 1351–52). This conflict of interest requirement varies widely in its application, with some jurisdictions requiring that plaintiffs demonstrate the voting board member is actually a named defendant (Swanson (1993), p. 1352).

Plaintiffs seeking judicial review of corporate decisions aborting derivative suits shoulder a similarly heavy burden. Under standards adopted by the American Law Institute, judicial review of corporate decisions not to pursue derivative claims involving the duty of care is limited to determining whether the decision violated the easily-met business judgment rule (American Law Institute 1994, § 7.19(a)(1)). For decisions to reject demands to prosecute derivative claims involving the duty of fair dealing or knowing and culpable violations of the law, the standard of review is whether the board or a committee of the board 'reasonably determined' that dismissal is in the best interests of the corporation (American Law Institute (1994), § 7.10(a)(2)). In examining the ALI's approach, Carol

Swanson rightly describes plaintiffs' burden as 'formidable' (Swanson (1993), pp. 1376–77).

A plaintiff shareholder in a duty of care case typically finds it almost impossible to excuse the demand requirement, or to show that the board of directors' denial of a demand violated the business judgment rule. Accordingly, the derivative action has in the past three decades played almost no role in any cases involving excessive compensation or other allegations of breaches of the duty of due care. Indeed, a 2004 study showed that only about 30 suits per year were being brought against public companies incorporated in Delaware (Thompson and Thomas (2004), p. 1749). Moreover, given the great incentive that special litigation committees have to terminate derivative litigation prematurely, much derivative jurisprudence of the last two decades has turned not on the merits of the underlying claims on behalf of corporations, but on whether or not plaintiffs can avoid these committees by arguing that demand is futile.

Public shock and outrage over the recent financial crisis make this a better time than ever to consider unshackling the derivative suit from the fetters of the demand requirement. This can be undertaken, however, with due attention to the concern expressed by corporate interests that lawyers representing small shareholders may exploit derivative litigation to exact extortionate settlements. The need for stronger policing of corporate boards can be balanced against this claimed potential for mischief by looking to the lead plaintiff provisions of the Private Securities Litigation Reform Act of 1995 ('PSLRA').

In enacting the PSLRA, Congress created a rebuttable presumption that the most adequate lead plaintiff in a class action brought under the federal securities laws is the plaintiff with the largest losses (15 U.S.C. § 78u-4). The goal of the PSLRA's lead plaintiff rule 'is to locate a person or entity whose sophistication and interest in the litigation are sufficient to permit that person or entity to function as an active agent for the class' (*In re Cendant Corp. Securities Litigation*,[5] p. 192). The rationale underlying this rule is that a plaintiff with much at stake is more likely to be acting in the best interests of the class, and better able to oversee the litigation. Indeed, as the PSLRA's legislative history reveals, the intent of this provision is 'to empower investors so that they – not their lawyers – exercise primary control over private securities litigation' ('Report on the Private Securities Litigation Reform Act', p. 4).

Frivolous and attorney-driven derivative lawsuits could be limited with analogous provisions. We agree with the suggestion of Professors Thompson and Thomas that the demand requirement be relaxed for derivative plaintiffs who hold at least 1 per cent of a company's shares (Thompson and Thomas (2004), p. 1787). Because the 1 per cent requirement may not impose sufficient protections in companies with a smaller market capitalization, an alternative minimum required investment of $25 million in shares would ensure that only responsible derivative plaintiffs are given access to the courts. An additional safeguard could be provided by a requirement that a derivative plaintiff have held shares in the corporation for at least six months.

With the imposition of these protections, special litigation committees would not be permitted to abort derivative claims. Moreover, courts in appropriate cases should be empowered to look past the business judgment rule and hold directors to a reasonableness standard where there are allegations of an egregious breach of the duty of care.

NEW LIFE FOR THE CORPORATE WASTE DOCTRINE?

If the derivative suit could be revived with such reforms, shareholders may at last be empowered to deal with one of the root causes of our recent financial crisis: corporate compensation packages that are disconnected from any real measure of company performance.

Whether coincidentally or not, changes in the demand rule empowering special litigation committees to abort meritorious derivative suits coincided with an explosion in executive compensation, and in particular with the large scale practice of compensating executives with options to purchase company stock. In theory, this was meant to align the interests of management with those of shareholders. It was assumed that executives who were paid in part with options to purchase company stock would have financial incentives to ensure the success of the companies they managed.

As a result of the spread of these stock option packages, the 1990s saw a tripling of the median total compensation of CEOs (Murphy (2002), p. 847). Between 1992 and 2000, the average real (inflation-adjusted) pay of CEOs of Standard & Poor's 500 firms jumped from $3.5 million to $14.7 million. A large part of these gains came from increases in option-based compensation, with the value of stock options granted to CEOs skyrocketing nine times during this period (Murphy (2002), p. 847). The rapid rise in executive compensation far outstripped that of compensation for other employees: in 2003, CEOs in the average large company received approximately 500 times the pay of an average worker (Murphy (2002), p. 847). The same ratio in 1999 stood at 419 to 1, some 25 times greater than it was in 1981 (Useem (2002), p. 13). According to the widely used ExecuComp database, compensation paid to the top five executives at each company aggregated of the 1500 companies in the database during 1998–2002 totaled about $100 billion (in 2002 dollars) (Bebchuk and Fried (2004), p. 9).

Executives continued to receive these valuable performance-based bonuses even as the companies they ran headed over a cliff. An analysis conducted in 2008 by the *Wall Street Journal* in collaboration with *ERI Economic Research Institute* showed that the median salary of the top executive of a Standard & Poor's 500 company increased 20.5 per cent from the previous year compared to a median corporate revenue growth of only 2.8 per cent (Tonello (2008)). Moreover, an *Equilar* study found that in 2007, 'while the median value of bonuses tied to performance fell 18.6 per cent, overall CEO total pay grew 1.4 per cent to a median amount of $1.41 million as a result of compensation components that do not depend on corporate results' (Tonello (2008)).

The disconnect between executive compensation and any real measure of company performance stems from governance structures that enable executives to exert considerable – often a controlling – influence over their boards. Our corporate governance system gives boards substantial power and entrusts them with monitoring and supervising company executives. In theory, boards are supposed to engage in arm's-length bargaining with executives in attempting to get the best possible deal for shareholders.

However, directors have various economic as well as social and psychological incentives to support, or at least go along with, arrangements favorable to the company's top executives. Although many directors own shares in their firms, their financial incentives have not been strong enough to deter them from acceding to management's wishes.

When the compensation packages of top executives become disconnected from the value contributed by those executives to their corporations, board members and management alike are vulnerable to claims of corporate waste. While legal definitions of corporate waste vary, Delaware courts have defined 'waste' to mean 'an exchange of corporate assets for consideration so disproportionately small as to lie beyond the range at which any reasonable person might be willing to trade' (*White v. Panic*,[6] p. 554). As a practical matter, a plaintiff shareholder must generally show that the board 'irrationally squander[ed]' corporate assets – for example, in a challenged transaction that served no corporate purpose or in which the corporation received no consideration at all (ibid.).[7]

Two Delaware jurists have observed that Delaware's corporate law did not react quickly or aggressively enough to changes in compensation practices during the past two decades (Chandler III and Strine, Jr., (2003)). However, much of the paralysis in Delaware law is attributable to the slow-down in development of substantive derivative jurisprudence in the wake of Delaware's imposition of the demand requirement. Moreover, there is some sign that the Delaware courts are taking a renewed interest in corporate waste claims predicated on extravagant executive compensation arrangements.

In an insightful 2003 article, Chancellor Chandler and Vice Chancellor Strine noted that in the 20 years preceding their article there has been 'Argentina-like inflation' in executive compensation (Chandler III and Strine, Jr., (2003), p. 1001). Their skepticism about executive pay arrangements seems to be reflected in *In re Citigroup Shareholder Derivative Litigation*.[8] In that case, shareholders of Citigroup brought suit against current and former directors and officers of the company, alleging among other things, that the company's compensation of its former CEO Charles Prince constituted corporate waste. Plaintiffs alleged that the directors of Citigroup breached their fiduciary duties in approving a $68 million compensation package for Prince, whose managerial failures were alleged to have caused billions in losses for Citigroup.

In denying defendants' motion to dismiss the claim, Chancellor Chandler explained that, although directors have broad discretion to make executive compensation decisions, ' "there is an outer limit" to the board's discretion to set executive compensation, "at which point a decision of the directors on executive compensation is so disproportionately large as to be unconscionable and constitute waste"' (*In re Citigroup Shareholder Derivative Litigation*, p. 138).

TOWARDS A NEW DERIVATIVE ACTION

As a result of the recent financial disasters, the public has a great appetite for genuine reform of the markets. A crucial element of any meaningful agenda for reform is to remedy the woeful disconnect between executive compensation and shareholder interests that helped foment a culture where high-risk deals with immediate payoffs were more appealing than lower-risk strategies that would produce profits over the longer term. Even if regulatory proposals to rein in excessive compensation are successful, legislators and courts alike would be wise to return derivative litigation to its rightful place in the arsenal of investor protections. This can only be done by relaxing the demand requirement where the plaintiff shareholder has a real stake in the corporation, and in appropriate cases, requiring a reasonableness standard in determining the culpability of defendant directors in such cases.

NOTES

* Mr. Labaton is a partner with Labaton Sucharow LLP, and Mr. Stocker is Of Counsel to the firm. This article was prepared with the assistance of Yoko Goto, an associate at the firm, and is based on a presentation delivered by Mr. Labaton at The George Washington University Law School's April 3–4, 2008 Symposium 'The Panic of 2008'.

1. 337 U.S. 541 (1949).
2. 466 F.3d 399 (6th Cir. 2006) (applying Tennessee law). Although Federal Rule of Civil Procedure 23.1 does not itself impose any demand requirement, it does require that plaintiffs bringing derivative actions 'state with particularity . . . any effort by the plaintiff to obtain the desired action from the directors or comparable authority, and if necessary, from the shareholders or members'. Fed. R. Civ. P. 23.1.
3. 418 F. Supp. 508 (S.D.N.Y. 1976).
4. 441 U.S. 471 (1979).
5. 404 F.3d 173 (3d Cir. 2005).
6. 783 A2d. 543 (Del. 2001).
7. See also *Grobow v. Perot*, 539 A.2d 180 (Del. 1988) (holding that a waste determination depends on 'whether what the corporation has received is so inadequate in value that no person of ordinary, sound business judgment would deem it worth that which the corporation has paid').
8. 964 A.2d 106, 138 (Del. Ch. 2009).

REFERENCES

15 U.S.C. § 78u-4 (2006).

American Law Institute (1994), *Principles of Corporate Governance,* St. Paul: American Law Institute Publishers.

Bebchuk, Lucian and J. Fried (2004), *Pay Without Performance*, Cambridge: Harvard University Press.

Burks v. Lasker, 441 U.S. 471 (1979).

Chandler III, William B. and L. E. Strine, Jr. (2003), 'The New Federalism of the American Corporate Governance System: Preliminary Reflections of Two Residents of One Small State', *University of Pennsylvania Law Review*, **152**(2), 953–1007.

Cohen v. Beneficial Industrial Loan Corp., 337 U.S. 541 (1949).

Cox, James (1982), 'Searching for the Corporation's Voice in Derivative Suit Litigation: A Critique of *Zapata* and the ALI Project', *Duke Law Journal*, **1982**(6), 959–1012.

Demott, Deborah A. (1987), *Shareholder Derivative Actions: Law and Practice*, Wilmette: Callaghan.

Federal Rules of Civil Procedure (2007).

Gall v. Exxon Corp., 418 F. Supp. 508 (S.D.N.Y.1976).

Grobow v. Perot, 539 A.2d 180 (Del. 1988).

In re Cendant Corp. Securities Litigation, 404 F.3d 173 (3rd Cir. 2005).

In re Citigroup Shareholder Derivative Litigation, 964 A.2d 106, 138 (Del. Ch. 2009).

McCarthy v. Middle Tenn. Electric Membership Corp., 466 F.3d 399 (6th Cir. 2006).

Murphy, Kevin J. (2002), 'Explaining Executive Compensation: Managerial

Power Versus the Perceived Cost of Stock Options', *University of Chicago Law Review* **69**(3), 847–870.
Private Securities Litigation Reform Act of 1995 ('PSLRA'), Pub. L. No. 104–67, 109 Stat. 737 (codified as amended in scattered sections of 15 and 18 U.S.C.).
'Report on the Private Securities Litigation Reform Act of 1995', S. Rep. No. 104–98, reprinted in 1995 U.S.C.C.A.N. 679.
Rostow, Eugene (1959), 'To Whom and For What Ends is Corporate Management Responsible', in Edward S. Mason (ed.), *The Corporation in Modern Society*, Cambridge: Harvard University Press.
Swanson, Carol B. (1993), 'Juggling Shareholder Rights and Strike Suits in Derivative Litigation: The ALI Drops the Ball', *Minnesota Law Review* **77**(6), 1339–1392.
Thompson, Robert B. and R. S. Thomas (2004), 'The Public and Private Faces of Derivative Lawsuits', *Vanderbilt Law Review*, **57**(5), 1747–1794.
Tonello, Mattoe (2008), 'The Role of the Board in Turbulent Times: Overseeing Risk Management and Executive Compensation', *The Conference Board*, Executive Action 292, December.
Useem, Jerry (2002), 'The Winner-Steal-All Society', *American Prospect*, 21 October.
White v. Panic, 783 A2d. 543 (Del. 2001).

12. *Cuomo v. Clearing House*: The Supreme Court responds to the subprime financial crisis and delivers a major victory for the dual banking system and consumer protection

Arthur E. Wilmarth, Jr.*

INTRODUCTION

In *Cuomo v. Clearing House Ass'n, L.L.C.*,[1] the Supreme Court held that the Office of the Comptroller of the Currency (OCC) exceeded its authority when it adopted a regulation (12 C.F.R. § 7.4000) that prohibited state officials from filing lawsuits to enforce applicable state laws against national banks. The Court upheld the OCC's regulation only to the extent that it bars state authorities from bringing administrative enforcement proceedings against national banks. Thus, the Court drew a clear distinction between 'administrative oversight' of national banks by state officials – which the Court viewed as preempted by the National Bank Act (NBA) – and 'judicial enforcement actions' against national banks by state officials, which the Court found to be consistent with the NBA and the Court's prior decisions.[2]

Cuomo arose out of an attempt by the New York Attorney General (NYAG) to enforce New York's fair lending laws against several large national banks that were heavily engaged in nonprime mortgage lending. By affirming New York's authority to enforce its fair lending laws against national banks through the courts, the Supreme Court exhibited a perspective on banking regulation that sharply contrasted with the Court's approach only two years earlier in *Watters v. Wachovia Bank, N.A.*[3] In *Watters*, the Court upheld another OCC regulation (12 C.F.R. § 7.4006), which preempted the application of state laws to nonbank mortgage lending subsidiaries of national banks.

Watters took a broad view of the preemptive reach of the NBA and indicated that national banks would not benefit from supplemental regulation by the states. In *Cuomo*, however, the Court took great pains to limit the scope and precedential force of *Watters*. Moreover, *Cuomo* indicated a renewed appreciation for the historic role of the states in regulating financial institutions and protecting consumers. Three members of the Supreme Court (Justices Ginsburg, Breyer and Souter) switched from supporting the OCC in *Watters* to opposing the OCC in *Cuomo*. Evidently, their positions changed because they modified their views about the merits of the OCC's preemptive regime and the value of state regulation between April 2007, when *Watters* was decided, and June 2009, when *Cuomo* was issued.

The most plausible explanation for the three Justices' change in perspective is that they were influenced by the outbreak of the subprime financial crisis in August 2007 and by subsequent federal bailouts of several major national banks that were deeply involved in nonprime lending. Amicus briefs filed in support of the NYAG included numerous references to the financial crisis. In addition, the briefs sharply criticized the OCC for its sweeping preemption of state law and for its weak record of protecting consumers from abusive lending practices. My hypothesis that the financial crisis and its aftermath influenced the Court's decision in *Cuomo* is necessarily based on inference, because the majority opinion in *Cuomo* did not specifically refer to those events. However, statements made by Justices Ginsburg, Souter and Stevens during oral argument in *Cuomo*, and by Justice Stevens in his dissenting opinion in *Watters*, indicate that the Court was aware of the mortgage crisis and the growing controversy over the OCC's preemptive actions.

Cuomo provides much-needed judicial support for (i) the principles of regulatory federalism inherent in the dual banking system and (ii) the importance of consumer protection in preserving financial stability. *Cuomo* undermines the legal rationale for several of the OCC's other preemption rules, and *Cuomo* reaffirms earlier Supreme Court precedents that upheld the general applicability of state laws to national banks. *Cuomo* also supports legislative proposals recently advanced by the Obama administration, which seek to preserve the states' longstanding role in protecting consumers of financial services.

During the past decade, the states have been far more proactive than the OCC and other federal agencies in enacting laws and bringing enforcement proceedings to protect consumers against predatory lending and other abusive financial practices. The subprime financial crisis has demonstrated that effective consumer protection (including the prevention of predatory lending) is closely linked to the safety and soundness of financial institutions. The states' favorable record of legislation and enforcement over the past decade has confirmed the wisdom of preserving a federalist system of financial regulation, which includes not only a federal component but also a supplemental state role in enacting and enforcing consumer protection laws.

The only disappointing aspect of *Cuomo* for the states is that the Supreme Court failed to resolve a recurring issue about the appropriate level of judicial deference that federal agencies should receive when they claim authority to preempt state law. *Cuomo* did not follow a relatively demanding, four-part framework for judicial review of agency preemption claims that was suggested in Justice Stevens' opinion for the Court in *Wyeth v. Levine*.[4] As explained below, that four-part framework would strike an appropriate balance between (i) the expectation that administrative agencies should receive some deference based on their specialized expertise and (ii) the judiciary's responsibility to ensure that preemption issues are resolved in accordance with the Constitution's allocation of federal and state powers.

Cuomo instead left open the possibility that future preemption claims by federal agencies could receive a higher level of judicial deference under *Chevron U.S.A. Inc. v. National Resources Defense Council*.[5] However, the Supreme Court in *Cuomo* refused to defer to the OCC's preemptive rule, based on the Court's conclusion that Congress did not delegate the preemptive power asserted by the OCC. *Cuomo* may indicate that, even if the Court chooses to apply *Chevron* in future cases involving agency preemption claims, the Court will apply a heightened level of scrutiny under *Chevron*, particularly with regard to the issue of whether Congress has affirmatively delegated the preemptive authority alleged by the agency. While *Cuomo* does not resolve this important question, *Cuomo*'s broader context reveals that the policies of all three branches of the federal government have been deeply implicated by the ongoing financial crisis.

FACTUAL AND LEGAL BACKGROUND OF *CUOMO V. CLEARING HOUSE*

In 2005, NYAG Eliot Spitzer sent informal letters of inquiry to several large national banks that were members of The Clearing House Association, L.L.C. (Clearing House). The recipients of Mr Spitzer's letters included Citigroup, HSBC, JP Morgan Chase and Wells Fargo. Mr Spitzer's letters were based on his office's preliminary analysis of residential mortgage lending data that the banks released to the public pursuant to the federal Home Mortgage Disclosure Act (HMDA). The banks' HMDA data 'appeared to indicate that a significantly higher percentage of high-interest home mortgage loans [were] issued to African-American and Hispanic borrowers than to white borrowers'.[6] Mr Spitzer's letters declared that such disparities 'are troubling on their face, and unless legally justified may violate federal and state antidiscrimination laws such as the Equal Credit Opportunity Act [(ECOA)] and its state counterpart, New York State Executive Law § 296-a'.[7] Like ECOA, § 296-a 'broadly prohibits creditors from discriminating on the basis of sex, national origin, or other protected grounds'.[8] Mr Spitzer stated that he was sending his letters '[i]n lieu of issuing a formal subpoena', and he requested that the recipients voluntarily provide non-public information concerning their residential mortgage lending policies and practices in New York.[9]

The OCC and the Clearing House acknowledged that N.Y. Executive Law § 296-a was not preempted by federal law and therefore applied to national banks.[10] This acknowledgment was consistent with ECOA, which authorizes the states to adopt laws prohibiting discrimination in lending that are equivalent to, or more protective than, the federal statute.[11] The OCC had previously conceded in March 2004 that state antidiscrimination laws were not substantively preempted by regulations issued by the OCC in January of that year. The OCC made its concession in response to an inquiry from Representative Barney Frank, the ranking member of the House Financial Services Committee, who strongly criticized the OCC's preemption rules.[12]

Notwithstanding the conceded applicability of N.Y. Executive Law § 296-a to national banks, the OCC and the Clearing House sued Mr Spitzer and asserted that 12 C.F.R. § 7.4000 preempted his authority to enforce the New York statute against national banks through either administrative or judicial proceedings. Both parties alleged that any investigative or enforcement efforts by Mr Spitzer would constitute 'visitorial' activities and would therefore be preempted by § 7.4000. The district court enjoined Mr Spitzer from pursuing any type of administrative or judicial enforcement proceedings against the Clearing House's member banks. The district court's decision was affirmed by a divided panel of the Second Circuit Court of Appeals.[13] The Supreme Court subsequently granted the petition for certiorari filed by Mr Spitzer's successor, NYAG Andrew Cuomo.

THE OCC'S REGULATION AND THE DEFINITION OF 'VISITORIAL POWERS'

The OCC's regulation at issue in *Cuomo* prohibited state officials from exercising 'visitorial powers' over national banks. The regulation defined 'visitorial powers' to include any attempt by state officials to conduct investigations or enforce state laws with respect to 'activities authorized or permitted [to national banks] pursuant to federal banking law' (12 C.F.R. § 7.4000(a)). In January 2004, the OCC amended the regulation by extending its ban on state enforcement actions to reach judicial as well as administrative proceedings.[14] The OCC thus claimed authority to bar state officials from using any forum – including the courts – to enforce applicable state laws against national banks.

The question presented in *Cuomo* was whether the OCC's expansive definition of 'visitorial powers' was authorized by the NBA. In answering that question, the Supreme Court applied 'the familiar *Chevron* framework' to determine whether the Court should defer to the OCC's regulation as a lawful interpretation of the NBA.[15] The Court held, in a 5–4 decision authored by Justice Scalia, that the OCC's regulation exceeded the agency's authority to the extent that it barred state officials from filing lawsuits to enforce valid, non-preempted state laws against national banks.

The relevant provision of the NBA, 12 U.S.C. § 484(a), states that '[n]o national bank shall be subject to any visitorial powers except as authorized by Federal law, vested in the courts of justice or . . . exercised or directed by Congress or by either House thereof or by [an authorized congressional committee]'. The NBA has included a provision similar to § 484(a) since its original enactment in 1864.[16] Neither § 484(a) nor any other section of the NBA defines the term 'visitorial powers'. The majority opinion in *Cuomo* acknowledged that '[t]here is necessarily some ambiguity as to the meaning of the statutory term "visitorial powers", especially since we are working in an era when the prerogative writs – through which visitorial powers were traditionally enforced – are not in vogue'.[17] However, Justice Scalia concluded that '[w]e can discern the outer limits of the term "visitorial powers" even through the clouded lens of history', based on '[e]vidence from the time of the statute's enactment, a long line of our own cases, and application of normal principles of construction to the [NBA]'.[18]

The majority and dissenting opinions in *Cuomo* strongly disagreed over the historical understanding of the term 'visitorial powers'. In the majority's view, '[o]ur cases have always understood "visitation" as [the] right to oversee corporate affairs, quite separate from the power to enforce the law'.[19] As support for this historical distinction, the majority cited Justice Story's concurring opinion in the Supreme Court's 1819 decision in *Dartmouth College*. In that case, Justice Story observed that chancery courts possessed 'a general jurisdiction . . . to redress grievances and fraud' committed by a corporation, but Story explained that the jurisdiction of chancery courts was not a 'visitorial power' and was separate from the 'controlling authority of [the corporation's] legal visitor'.[20]

In his dissenting opinion in *Cuomo*, Justice Thomas attempted to distinguish *Dartmouth College* on the ground that the college was a charitable rather than a civil (for profit) corporation. Justice Thomas argued that visitors of charitable corporations historically did not have law enforcement powers, while visitors of civil corporations did possess such powers. Therefore, he contended, Justice Story's opinion in *Dartmouth College* did not contradict the OCC's position that all law enforcement activities directed at for profit corporations (including national banks) should be viewed as 'visitorial'.[21] Justice Scalia responded to this argument by denying the significance of any difference between visitors of charitable and for profit corporations. He concluded that 'whether or not visitors of charitable corporations had law-enforcement powers, the powers that they *did* possess demonstrate that visitation is different from ordinary law enforcement'.[22]

In a 1936 law review article, Dean Roscoe Pound pointed out that there was a division of opinion in both England and the United States on the question of whether courts of equity possessed a power to enforce laws against corporations that was independent of the 'visitorial' powers held by the sovereign chartering authority (namely, the British monarch or the national and state governments of the United States). As Dean Pound explained, the sovereign chartering authority had the unquestioned right to exercise 'visitorial' powers either administratively or by invoking the jurisdiction of common law courts through the prerogative writs of mandamus, *scire facias* and *quo warranto*. In contrast, the law enforcement jurisdiction of equity courts over corporations was not universally recognized. Nevertheless, a number of authorities in both England and America held that equity courts did have an independent power to enforce applicable laws against corporations, as indicated by Justice Story's concurring opinion in *Dartmouth College*.[23] Dean Pound noted that the NBA appeared to recognize the independent enforcement power of equity courts by providing that the limitation on 'visitorial powers' under § 484(a) would not extinguish powers 'vested in the courts of justice'.[24]

The majority opinion in *Cuomo* agreed that a decision in favor of allowing state officials to sue national banks was 'suggested' by the 'vested in the courts of justice' clause in § 484(a).[25] In Justice Scalia's view, that provision's 'only conceivable purpose is to preserve normal civil and criminal lawsuits . . . [I]t is explicable only as an attempt to make clear that the court's ordinary powers of enforcing the law are not affected'.[26]

The majority opinion in *Cuomo* relied heavily on two Supreme Court decisions from the first quarter of the twentieth century – *Guthrie v. Harkness*[27] and *First National Bank in St. Louis v. Missouri*.[28] *Guthrie* held that a shareholder's suit against a national bank to enforce his right to inspect corporate records did not involve a prohibited exercise of 'visitorial' powers. In *Cuomo*, Justice Scalia pointed out that *Guthrie* 'drew a contrast between the nonvisitorial act of "su[ing] in the courts of the State" and the visitorial "supervision of the [OCC]"'.[29] The Court in *Guthrie* placed substantial weight on the 'courts of justice' clause, observing that 'powers . . . "vested in the courts of justice" . . . are expressly excepted from the inhibition of [§ 484(a)]'.[30]

St. Louis upheld the right of Missouri (through its attorney general) to bring a *quo warranto* action in state court against a national bank for violating Missouri's anti-branching law.[31] The Court determined in *St. Louis* that the NBA (as of 1924) did not authorize national banks to establish branches, except in narrowly limited circumstances that were not relevant to the case. Accordingly, the Court held that since 'the power sought to be exercised by the bank finds no justification in any law or authority of the United States, the way is open for the enforcement of the state statute'.[32] The Court rejected the national bank's claim (supported by the United States) that the federal government had exclusive authority to bring a *quo warranto* action to enforce Missouri's law against the bank. As Justice Scalia explained in *Cuomo*, the Court in *St. Louis* affirmed that 'only the United States may perform visitorial administrative oversight' over national banks, but 'if a state statute of general applicability is not substantively pre-empted, then "the power of enforcement must rest with the [State] and not with" the National Government'.[33] Justice Scalia concluded that '*St. Louis* is one of a long and unbroken line of cases distinguishing visitation from law enforcement'.[34]

Dean Pound observed that the decision in *St. Louis* was highly significant in upholding the authority of a state to maintain a *quo warranto* action against a national bank that the state did not charter.[35] *St. Louis* cited, and was consistent with, the Supreme Court's earlier decision in *Standard Oil Co. v. Missouri*.[36] In *Standard Oil*, the Court affirmed the right of Missouri (through its attorney general) to prosecute a *quo warranto* proceeding in state court against two out-of-state corporations that violated Missouri's antitrust statute.[37] As Dean Pound pointed out, Missouri's independent authority to sue the national bank in *St. Louis* was analogous to Missouri's power to sue the two foreign corporations in *Standard Oil*, because Missouri was not the chartering authority for any of the three corporations and therefore did not possess visitorial powers over them.[38]

The majority opinion in *Cuomo* next turned to the Supreme Court's 2007 decision in *Watters*. *Watters* held that the NBA preempted the application of Michigan's laws governing nonbank mortgage lenders to operating subsidiaries of national banks.[39] In *Cuomo*, Justice Scalia maintained that

Watters 'is fully in accord with the well established distinction between supervision and law enforcement. . . . All parties to the case agreed that Michigan's general oversight regime could not be imposed on national banks; the sole question was whether operating subsidiaries of national banks enjoyed the same immunity from state visitation'.[40] Justice Scalia emphasized that *Watters* 'addresses and answers no other question'.[41]

Based upon its review of the Court's previous cases dealing with 'visitorial' powers, the majority opinion in *Cuomo* concluded that 'the unmistakable and utterly consistent teaching of our jurisprudence, both before and after enactment of the [NBA], is that a sovereign's "visitorial powers" and its power to enforce the law are two different things. . . . [C]ontrary to what the [OCC's] regulation says, the [NBA] pre-empts only the former'.[42]

Accordingly, *Cuomo* held that 'visitorial powers . . . include any form of administrative oversight that allows a sovereign to inspect books and records on demand'.[43] In contrast, a lawsuit by a state attorney general to enforce state law 'is not an exercise of "visitorial powers" and thus the [OCC] erred by extending the definition of "visitorial powers" to include "prosecuting enforcement actions" in state courts'.[44] The Supreme Court upheld the Second Circuit's judgment 'as applied to the threatened issuance of executive subpoenas' by the NYAG, but the Supreme Court reversed the lower court's judgment 'insofar as it prohibits the [NYAG] from bringing judicial enforcement actions'.[45]

Justice Scalia emphasized the 'pragmatic' significance of the majority opinion's distinction between visitation and judicial enforcement. The OCC as visitor 'may inspect books and records at any time for any or no reason'.[46] In contrast, a state 'attorney general acting as a civil litigant must file a lawsuit, survive a motion to dismiss, endure the rules of procedure and discovery, and risk sanctions if his claims are frivolous or his discovery tactics abusive'.[47] Courts could also enter protective orders to prevent unreasonable expense or prejudice to national banks. In Justice Scalia's view, courts could be 'trusted to prevent "fishing expeditions" or an undirected rummaging through bank books' by state officials.[48]

THE DRAMATIC CONTRAST BETWEEN *CUOMO* AND *WATTERS*

The majority opinion in *Cuomo* sharply limited the scope and precedential effect of the Court's previous opinion in *Watters*. As noted above, *Cuomo* declared that the 'sole question' decided in *Watters* was 'whether operating subsidiaries of national banks enjoyed the same immunity from state visitation' as national banks possessed, and *Cuomo* reiterated that *Watters* 'addresses and answers no other question'.[49]

Cuomo's emphatic pronouncement concerning the narrow scope of *Watters* echoed statements made by Justice Ginsburg during the oral argument in *Cuomo*. Justice Ginsburg wrote the majority opinion supporting the OCC's position in *Watters*, but she joined the majority opinion striking down the OCC's regulation in *Cuomo*. During oral argument in *Cuomo*, Justice Ginsburg advised counsel for the Clearing House that '[t]he sole question [in *Watters*] was whether . . . the national bank's operating subsidiary was to be equated with a division of the national bank. That was the only question provided the Court'.[50] She also admonished counsel that 'I do not think that excerpts from [the *Watters*] opinion should be taken out of that context'.[51]

The majority opinion in *Cuomo* and Justice Ginsburg's comments at oral argument appear to have been consciously designed to limit the precedential force of *Watters* in future cases raising preemption issues under the NBA. The *Cuomo* majority might have been concerned about certain statements in *Watters* that indicated an expansive view of the NBA's preemptive effect.[52] Not surprisingly, the Clearing House quoted those statements in its brief in *Cuomo*.[53] During oral argument in *Cuomo*, Justice Ginsburg stated that she viewed the Clearing House's discussion of *Watters* in its brief as 'an inaccurate description of what that opinion held'.[54]

During oral argument, Justice Souter similarly questioned the OCC's assertion that a 1994 statute, 12 U.S.C. § 36(f)(1)(B), granted the OCC exclusive authority to enforce state laws against interstate branches of national banks. Justice Souter suggested that the text and legislative history of the 1994 statute did not clearly manifest a congressional purpose to bar state officials from enforcing valid, non-preempted state laws against interstate branches of national banks. If Congress had plainly stated that intent, Justice Souter said that he would have expected such an 'extraordinary' displacement of state enforcement authority to produce 'rather a dust-up'. The fact that Section 36(f)(1)(B) failed to trigger any substantial controversy created what Justice Souter described as 'kind of a "dog that didn't bark" argument' and, therefore, led him to doubt the OCC's exclusivity claim.[55]

Justice Ginsburg also indicated her apprehension about the potentially far-reaching scope of the OCC's claim of exclusive enforcement authority over national banks. During the oral argument in *Cuomo*, she asked counsel for the Clearing House whether the OCC's exclusivity claim applied not only to 'core banking activities' but also to 'matters incidental to banking'.[56] Counsel responded that the OCC's exclusivity claim 'would [apply] if those incidental authorities are in fact authorized, approved and regulated by the OCC'.[57]

Justice Ginsburg's inquiry was apparently prompted by her concern that the OCC might assert exclusive enforcement authority over the full range of national bank activities that the OCC deemed to fall within the 'incidental powers . . . necessary to carry on the business of banking' under 12 U.S.C. § 24 (Seventh). Justice Ginsburg wrote the Supreme Court's 1995 decision in *NationsBank of N.C., N.A. v. Variable Annuity Life Ins. Co.* (*VALIC*).[58] In *VALIC*, the Court held that an OCC opinion letter, which approved a bank activity as falling within the 'incidental powers' of national banks, was entitled to judicial deference under *Chevron*.[59] However, the Court cautioned the OCC that '[t]he exercise of the [agency's] discretion . . . must be kept within reasonable bounds' and should not include '[v]entures distant from dealing in financial investment instruments'.[60]

Amicus briefs filed in *Cuomo* by a realtors' association and by consumer groups informed the Court that, notwithstanding the cautionary language in *VALIC,* the OCC had expansively construed the 'incidental powers' of national banks. For example, the OCC issued rulings that approved such far-flung activities as 'providing counseling to Medicare and Medicaid recipients, selling long-term care and disability insurance, operating roadside assistance programs, finding customers for automobile sales, developing commercial buildings and managing residential condominiums in those buildings, dispensing various prepaid products . . . through their ATM machines, operating a "virtual mall" where bank customers "can shop for a range of financial and non-financial products and services", and providing "Web design and development services"'.[61]

As the consumer groups' brief pointed out, the OCC had published a compilation of national bank powers in which the OCC declared that '[t]he business of banking is an evolving concept and the permissible activities of national banks similarly evolve over time'.[62] At oral argument in *Cuomo*, Justice Ginsburg noted that 'today national banks have a lot of . . . authority to do things incidental to banking'.[63] Justice Ginsburg evidently understood that the OCC was continually expanding the scope of 'incidental powers' for national banks under the NBA.

Thus, comments by Justice Ginsburg and Justice Souter during oral argument in *Cuomo* foreshadowed their shift from a pro-OCC position in *Watters* to an anti-OCC position in *Cuomo*. Justice Breyer was the only member of the *Cuomo* majority who did not indicate any doubts about the OCC's position during the oral argument. Like Justice Ginsburg and Justice Souter, Justice Breyer supported the OCC in *Watters*. In addition, Justice Breyer expressed misgivings during oral argument in *Cuomo* about the potential disadvantages of allowing state attorneys general to second-guess the enforcement decisions of the OCC.[64] His decision to join the majority opinion in *Cuomo* was therefore somewhat surprising.

The majority opinion in *Cuomo* criticized the OCC for adopting an aggressive theory of preemption that 'attempts to do what Congress declined to do: exempt national banks from all state banking laws, or at least state enforcement of those laws'.[65] In view of the virtually unbounded theories of 'incidental powers' and preemption advanced by the OCC, the *Cuomo* majority may have decided to include in *Cuomo* a narrowly circumscribed reading of *Watters* in order to curtail the OCC's ability to assert similar preemption claims in the future. As discussed in the next section of this chapter, it also seems likely that the *Cuomo* majority was responding to the subprime financial crisis and federal bailouts of several leading national banks. Those developments may have caused the majority to lose confidence in the OCC's policy judgments, particularly with regard to the desirability of preempting state enforcement of mortgage lending laws, an issue that was central to both *Watters* and *Cuomo*.

In sharp contrast to the broad preemptive language used by the Court in *Watters*, the majority opinion in *Cuomo* indicated a renewed appreciation for federalism and the potentially beneficial effects of a supplemental state role in regulating financial institutions. Justice Scalia pointed out that '[n]o one denies that the [NBA] leaves in place some state substantive law affecting banks'.[66] He further observed that 'States . . . have always enforced their general laws against national banks – and have enforced their banking-related laws against national banks for at least 85 years, as evidenced by *St. Louis*'.[67] The foregoing statements in *Cuomo* are consistent with the Supreme Court's 1997 decision in *Atherton v. FDIC*,[68] where the Court declared that 'federally chartered banks are subject to state law'.[69] As support for that principle, *Atherton* quoted decisions reaching back to an 1870 case – decided only six years after the NBA's enactment – where the Court held that national banks:

> are subject to the laws of the State, and are governed in their daily course of business far more by the laws of the State than of the nation. All their contracts are governed and construed by State laws. Their acquisition and transfer of property, their right to collect their debts, and their liability to be sued for debts, are all based on State law. It is only when State law incapacitates the [national] banks from discharging their duties to the federal government that it becomes unconstitutional.[70]

In *St. Louis*, the Supreme Court explained that 'the operation of general state laws upon the dealings and contracts of national banks' is the 'rule', while preemption is an 'exception' that applies only when state laws 'expressly conflict with the laws of the United States or frustrate the purpose for which national banks were created, or impair their efficiency to discharge the duties imposed upon them by the law of the United States'.[71] Similarly, in *Anderson National Bank v. Luckett*,[72] the Court held that 'national banks are subject to state laws, unless those laws infringe the national banking laws or impose an undue burden on the performance of the banks' functions'.[73] In *Cuomo*, the Court cited *St. Louis* and *Luckett* with approval,[74] and both decisions therefore retain strong precedential value with respect to future preemption cases under the NBA.

In *Lewis v. Fidelity & Deposit Co.*,[75] the Court held that the NBA embodies a congressional 'policy of equalization' between the national and state banking systems.[76] Congress has long sought to preserve the vitality of the dual banking system by maintaining a basic parity of competitive opportunities between state and national banks.[77] This congressional policy of equalization has been carried out in two ways – first, by 'expressly incorporat[ing] state-law standards into several federal statutes', and second, 'through statutory silence [that] permits state laws to govern other aspects of the operations of national banks *except* in situations where a state law creates an irreconcilable conflict with federal law'.[78] *Cuomo* did not cite *Lewis*, but Justice Stevens quoted *Lewis* with approval in his dissenting opinion in *Watters*.[79]

The *Cuomo* majority held that the OCC erred in asserting that 'the State may not *enforce* its valid, non-preempted laws against national banks. The bark remains, but the bite does not'.[80] The *Cuomo* majority described this result as '[b]izarre', particularly in view of the Court's statement in *St. Louis* that it would be a 'fallacy' to acknowledge 'the binding quality of a statute but deny the power of enforcement'.[81] Indeed, *St. Louis* declared that the 'power [of enforcement] is essentially inherent in the very conception of law'.[82]

During oral argument in *Cuomo*, Justice Ginsburg similarly found it 'passing strange' for the OCC to maintain that 'State . . . substantive law [is] applicable to [national] banks but only the Federal authority can enforce it'.[83] Justice Ginsburg asked counsel for the OCC if there were any comparable federal statutes in which Congress recognized the applicability of state laws but gave federal officials exclusive authority to enforce those laws. Counsel was unable to identify any such federal statute.[84]

In contrast to the '[b]izarre' outcome created by the OCC's regulation, Justice Scalia maintained that an 'entirely commonplace result' would be produced by interpreting § 484(a) as '[c]hanneling state attorneys general into judicial law enforcement proceedings . . . [while] preserv[ing] a regime of exclusive administrative oversight by the [OCC]'.[85] Justice Scalia explained that such an outcome 'echoes many other mixed state/federal regimes in which the Federal Government exercises general oversight while leaving state substantive law in place'.[86] In this regard, the *Cuomo* majority cited the Court's recent decision in *Wyeth v. Levine*,[87] discussed below, in which the Court held that the federal statutory regime governing labeling of prescription drugs did not preempt failure-to-warn claims based on state tort law. Thus, in marked contrast to *Watters*, the majority opinion in *Cuomo* interpreted the NBA in light of the strong federalism principles applied in cases such as *St. Louis, Lewis*, *Luckett*, *Atherton* and *Wyeth*.

THE IMPACT OF THE SUBPRIME FINANCIAL CRISIS AND THE OCC'S WEAK RECORD OF ENFORCING CONSUMER PROTECTION LAWS

The outbreak of the subprime financial crisis in August 2007 and subsequent federal bailouts of several leading national banks apparently changed the Supreme Court's assessment of the desirability of OCC preemption between the dates of the Court's decisions in *Watters* (17 April 2007) and *Cuomo* (29 June 2009). Amicus briefs filed in support of NYAG Cuomo contained numerous references to the financial crisis. In addition, those briefs sharply attacked the OCC for its sweeping preemption of state law and its alleged failure to protect consumers from predatory lending. Although the majority opinion in *Cuomo* did not directly refer to the financial crisis, other evidence indicates that the Court was aware of the crisis and the controversy surrounding the OCC's preemption efforts.

Criticisms of the OCC's Preemptive Actions and Supervisory Record

Amicus briefs filed in support of NYAG Cuomo strongly criticized the OCC for (i) failing to protect consumers against abusive mortgage lending practices by national banks and (ii) preempting the states' efforts to protect consumers. *Amici* – who included members of Congress, state officials, civil rights organizations and consumer groups – contended that the OCC's preemptive actions and supervisory failures were a significant factor leading to the subprime financial crisis.[88]

As *amici* pointed out, the OCC issued a series of preemptive rules and orders that barred the states from enforcing a wide range of state laws – including state anti-predatory lending laws and other consumer protection laws – against national banks and their operating subsidiaries.[89] The OCC's rulings had the cumulative effect of 'cancel[ing] out much state-level consumer protection law'.[90]

Amici cited studies showing that the OCC had powerful budgetary incentives to use preemption as a marketing tool to persuade the largest banks to operate under national charters. The OCC's budget is funded almost entirely by assessments paid by national banks, and the biggest banks pay the highest assessments.[91] A former head of the OCC described preemption as 'a significant benefit of the national [bank] charter – a benefit that the OCC has fought hard over the years to preserve'.[92] In response to the OCC's preemption campaign, several large, multistate banks converted from state to national charters, thereby producing a significant increase in the OCC's assessment revenues.[93]

In addition, studies cited by *amici* described the OCC's record of enforcing consumer protection laws as a 'long history of inaction', 'relatively lax', 'weak' and 'unimpressive'.[94] Publicly available information indicated that, during 1995–2007, the OCC issued only 13 public enforcement orders against national banks for violations of consumer protection laws.[95] Most of those enforcement orders were issued against small national banks, and only one order included a charge that the bank violated state laws.[96] In that one case, the OCC took action only after the public became aware that a California prosecutor was investigating the offending bank.[97]

The states' record of protecting consumers presented a dramatic contrast with the OCC. Between 1999 and 2006, more than 30 states enacted laws to combat predatory lending.[98] A recent study found that state anti-predatory laws reduced the number of mortgages with unsound or abusive features such as prepayment penalties, balloon payments, and no- and low-documentation terms.[99] In addition, state officials vigorously used their enforcement powers to prosecute financial service providers for a wide range of unlawful practices.[100] In 2003 alone, 'state bank supervisory agencies performed more than 20,000 investigations in response to consumer complaints about abusive lending practices, and those investigations produced more than 4,000 enforcement actions'.[101]

Despite these initiatives by the states, the OCC's actions seriously obstructed the states' ability to protect consumers from predatory lending practices. In addition to adopting preemptive regulations, the OCC filed amicus briefs in many other cases to support efforts by national banks to obtain judicial decisions preempting state consumer protection laws. The OCC's decision to sue NYAG Spitzer, in concert with the Clearing House (whose members included most of the largest national banks), provided a striking example of the OCC's unrelenting efforts to support its regulated constituents and to block efforts by state officials to enforce state laws against those constituents.[102]

By preempting state laws and state enforcement proceedings, the OCC (i) undermined the effectiveness of state predatory lending laws,[103] and

(ii) contributed to the severity of the current credit crisis by 'stifling . . . prescient state enforcers and legislators' who tried to prevent irresponsible lending.[104] For example, the OCC issued rulings declaring that Georgia officials were preempted from applying the Georgia Fair Lending Act not only to national banks and their operating subsidiaries, but also to mortgage brokers who arranged loans funded at closing by national banks or their subsidiaries.[105] Similarly, after state officials brought enforcement actions and imposed heavy penalties against two major nonbank mortgage lenders (Household and Ameriquest), those organizations sold themselves to large national banks (HSBC and Citigroup) and thereby obtained substantial protection from further state regulation. A comparable incident occurred in 2006, when the Iowa Division of Banking sued Okoboji Mortgage for refusing to cooperate with the state's investigation of suspected illegal lending practices. Okoboji promptly sold itself to a large national bank (Wells Fargo) and then claimed immunity from any further state enforcement proceedings.[106]

The OCC's preemption rules closely paralleled regulations that the Office of Thrift Supervision ('OTS') issued between 1983 and 1996. The OTS regulations preempted a broad range of state laws from applying to federal thrifts and their operating subsidiaries. Like the OCC, the OTS issued additional rulings that specifically preempted the application of state predatory lending laws to federal thrifts and their subsidiaries and agents. Again like the OCC, the OTS has strong financial incentives to use preemption as a means of attracting large, multistate institutions to its chartering regime, because virtually all of the OTS's budget is financed by assessments and fees paid by federal thrifts. Given those incentives, it is not surprising that the OTS's record of initiating public enforcement actions against its regulated constituents for violating consumer protection laws is as sparse as the OCC's score sheet.[107]

The preemptive actions of the OCC and OTS prevented state officials from responding to predatory lending problems with the same effectiveness they displayed in exposing a series of scandals on Wall Street between 2002 and 2006. State authorities took the lead in prosecuting securities firms (including securities affiliates of major banks) for pressuring their research analysts to produce biased reports to investors, for engaging in corrupt practices related to initial public offerings, and for permitting hedge funds to carry out abusive market timing and late trading strategies that exploited mutual funds sponsored by securities firms. The Securities and Exchange Commission (SEC) cooperated with the states' enforcement measures against Wall Street firms.[108] In contrast, as shown above, the OCC and OTS repeatedly issued preemptive rulings and intervened in lawsuits to block efforts by state officials to enforce state anti-predatory lending laws against federally-chartered depository institutions and their subsidiaries and agents.

The Supreme Court was evidently aware of the public controversy over the OCC's aggressive preemptive actions and its questionable commitment to protecting consumers when the Court considered both *Watters* and *Cuomo*. As indicated above, remarks by Justices Ginsburg and Souter at the *Cuomo* oral argument indicated that they had serious misgivings about the OCC's far-reaching assertions of preemptive authority.[109] In addition, at the oral arguments in both *Watters* and *Cuomo*, Justice Stevens asked pointed questions about the number of personnel that the OCC assigned to its enforcement and compliance functions. Those questions suggested that Justice Stevens had significant doubts about the OCC's commitment to consumer protection.[110]

In addition, Justice Stevens' dissenting opinion in *Watters* strongly criticized the Court for upholding an OCC regulation, 12 C.F.R. § 7.4006, that barred the states from regulating state-chartered mortgage lending companies that were operating subsidiaries of national banks. Justice Stevens declared that '[i]t is especially troubling that the Court so blithely preempts Michigan laws designed to protect consumers. Consumer protection is quintessentially a "field which the States have traditionally occupied".'[111] In addition, Justice Stevens warned that 'the OCC's regulation may drive companies seeking refuge from state regulation into the arms of federal parents, harm those state competitors who are not lucky enough to find a federal benefactor, and hamstring States' ability to regulate the affairs of state corporations'.[112]

The OCC's Unfounded Attack on the States

In response to the strong attacks on its preemptive actions and its consumer protection record, the OCC attempted to shift the blame for the subprime mortgage debacle to the states. In *Cuomo*, six former Comptrollers of the Currency filed an amicus brief in support of the OCC and the Clearing House. The former Comptrollers alleged that (i) nonbank mortgage lenders and brokers bore most of the blame for the subprime financial crisis, and (ii) nonbank lenders and brokers 'are – and always have been – subject to the oversight and enforcement jurisdiction of state officials'. The former Comptrollers further claimed that 'the OCC provided early and unmatched leadership on subprime lending'.[113] Similarly, in congressional testimony presented in March 2009, the incumbent Comptroller of the Currency declared that nonbank lenders and brokers 'have been widely recognized as the overwhelming source of abusive subprime mortgages'. He also contended that 'national banks were not significant originators of subprime loans'.[114]

The OCC's attempt to blame the states for the current financial crisis is unpersuasive. Nonbank lenders and brokers did play a significant role in originating subprime and Alt-A mortgages. However, as discussed above, the OCC and OTS barred the states from regulating nonbank lenders and brokers that were affiliated with national banks. In addition, national banks and federal thrifts acquired several of the largest nonbank mortgage lenders between 1999 and 2007. For example, HSBC bought Household, Citigroup purchased Associates First Capital and Argent (the parent of Ameriquest), Washington Mutual (Wamu) bought Long Beach Mortgage and National City purchased First Franklin.[115]

A recent Federal Reserve study found that depository institutions (together with their subsidiaries and other affiliates) accounted for about half of nonprime (subprime and Alt-A) mortgages originated in 2004 and 2005, 54 per cent of nonprime mortgages in 2006, and 79 per cent of nonprime mortgages in 2007.[116] This accelerating shift in nonprime loan originations toward national banks and federal thrifts and their affiliates reflected the growing impact of the OCC's and OTS' preemption rules. Those preemption rules shielded federally-chartered institutions and their operating subsidiaries from state predatory lending laws, while unaffiliated nonbank lenders remained subject to state laws.[117]

A study by the National Consumer Law Center found that national banks, federal thrifts and their operating subsidiaries accounted for 31.5 per cent of subprime mortgage loans, 40.1 per cent of Alt-A loans, and 51.0 per cent of payment-option and interest-only adjustable-rate mortgages (ARMs) originated in 2006.[118] A second study, by the Center for Public Integrity, confirmed that large national banks and federal thrifts (along with their affiliates) ranked among the biggest funding sources for subprime mortgages between 2005 and 2007. The largest subprime lender during that period was Countrywide. Countrywide operated as a national bank from 2001 to 2007 and as a federal thrift from 2007 to 2008, at which point it was forced – on the brink of insolvency – to enter into an emergency merger with Bank of America (BofA).[119]

In addition to Countrywide, the top 25 sources of funding for subprime mortgages between 2005 and 2007 included seven big national banks (Citigroup, JP Morgan Chase, HSBC, Wachovia, Wells Fargo, National City and Capital One), two large federal thrifts (Wamu and IndyMac), three major Wall Street firms, which each controlled a federal thrift (Merrill Lynch, Lehman Brothers and Bear Stearns), and a big insurance company that also controlled a federal thrift (American International Group (AIG)).[120] Those three Wall Street firms and AIG were subject to consolidated supervision by the OTS because of their ownership of federal thrifts.[121]

Many of the same financial institutions were heavily involved in Alt-A lending, as was BofA. Alt-A mortgages included some of the most risky loans, including low- and no-documentation mortgages (frequently called 'liars' loans') and payment option ARMs.[122] In addition to their direct nonprime lending activities, national banks, federal thrifts and Wall Street firms provided indirect funding for subprime and Alt-A loans by furnishing wholesale lines of credit to nonbank lenders such as Ameriquest, New Century and Option One. When the major wholesale lenders cut off their lines of credit in 2007, many nonbank mortgage lenders and mortgage brokers quickly went out of business. The rapid disappearance of nonbank lenders and brokers confirmed that they were acting as conduits for the big national banks, federal thrifts and Wall Street firms.[123]

The largest federally-regulated financial institutions also created and marketed complex financial instruments whose performance was linked to nonprime mortgages, including residential mortgage-backed securities (RMBS), collateralized debt obligations (CDOs) and credit default swaps (CDS). Financial giants used CDOs and CDS to place multiple bets on nonprime mortgages and to facilitate the worldwide marketing of investment-grade securities derived from pools of nonprime mortgages. RMBS, CDOs and CDS magnified the impact of defaults on nonprime mortgages and triggered a global contagion of losses when the US housing market collapsed. The OCC and the OTS, along with other federal regulators (including the Federal Reserve Board (FRB) and the SEC) failed to control the risks inherent in nonprime mortgages as well as the aggravation of those risks in RMBS, CDOs and CDS.[124]

The failures and federal bailouts of several large national banks, federal thrifts and Wall Street firms revealed (i) the deep involvement of those institutions in the nonprime mortgage debacle and (ii) serious regulatory failures by the OCC, the OTS and other federal regulators. On the OCC's side of the regulatory ledger, four of the 16 largest national banks would have failed absent costly federal bailouts. The largest and third-largest national banks (BofA and Citigroup) suffered huge losses from nonprime-related activities and received mammoth bailout packages from the federal government, including $90 billion of capital infusions and more than $400 billion of asset price guarantees.[125]

In addition, the fourth-largest and sixteenth-largest national banks (Wachovia and National City) were pushed to the brink of failure by heavy losses resulting from risky nonprime lending. Federal regulators arranged a 'hasty sale' of Wachovia to Wells Fargo and supported the transaction by infusing $25 billion of capital into Wells Fargo. Federal regulators forced National City into a similar 'shotgun marriage' with PNC, which was assisted by a federal infusion of $7.7 billion of capital into PNC.[126] It was ironic – but almost certainly not coincidental – that Wachovia and National City filed the lawsuits that ultimately led to the Supreme Court's decision in *Watters*, because both banks wanted to stop the states from regulating their mortgage operating subsidiaries.[127] The foregoing disasters occurred despite the fact that the OCC maintained permanent teams of on-site examiners at each of the 17 largest national banks.[128]

On the OTS' side of the regulatory ledger, two of the largest thrifts (Wamu and IndyMac) failed after suffering devastating losses from reckless nonprime lending. Similar debacles occurred at AIG and three big Wall Street firms, all of which owned thrifts and were subject to oversight by the OTS. AIG was saved from bankruptcy by a huge federal bailout that grew to $182.5 billion by March 2009. Lehman Brothers collapsed and filed for bankruptcy. To avoid a similar fate, Bear Stearns and Merrill Lynch entered into emergency, federally-assisted mergers with JP Morgan Chase and BofA. The OTS received heavy criticism for its shortcomings in regulating all six of the foregoing entities. The SEC was also at fault for failing to provide effective supervision of Bear Stearns, Lehman Brothers and Merrill Lynch.[129]

A recent study by Patricia McCoy, Andrey Pavlov and Susan Wachter analyzed delinquency rates on residential mortgage loans made by four categories of depository institutions between 2006 and 2008. The study found that loans made by federal thrifts had the highest delinquency rate and loans made by national banks had the second highest delinquency rate. In contrast, state banks had the lowest mortgage delinquency rate and state thrifts had the second lowest rate.[130] In view of the substantially inferior lending performance of federally-chartered depository institutions, the study's authors rejected arguments by federal regulators that state authorities bore most of the blame for the subprime lending crisis. Instead, the authors concluded that the OCC, OTS and FRB were guilty of more serious regulatory lapses:

> After the magnitude of the subprime debacle became known, federal regulators became adept at blaming the states for not regulating independent mortgage lenders and brokers effectively. Certainly, some states regulated these actors more heavily than others, and some states failed to regulate them at all. But the attack on the states obscures two essential facts. First, by the end of 2005, the majority of states *had* enacted comprehensive laws of varying strengths to address improvident subprime loans. Indeed, proactive states adopted their laws years before the OCC, OTS, and the Federal Reserve Board took any meaningful action. Second, through their preemption rules, the OCC and OTS blocked enforcement of the most meaningful body of laws regulating reckless loan products – the state mini-HOEPA laws – for federal savings associations, national banks, and their mortgage lending subsidiaries. The Federal Reserve Board meanwhile refused to exercise its authority under HOEPA to correct the

> unlevel playing field by promulgating binding rules against unfair and deceptive acts and practices that [would have] applied to virtually all lenders nationwide. As a result, meaningful regulation was non-existent at worst and ineffective at best for lenders cloaked with federal preemption and for lenders in unregulated states.[131]

As noted above, the briefs filed by NYAG Cuomo and supporting *amici* contained extensive allegations that the OCC's preemption rules and regulatory failings contributed to the severity of the subprime financial crisis.[132] It seems likely that the Supreme Court's decision in *Cuomo* was influenced by those arguments. The comments made by Justices Ginsburg, Stevens and Souter during the *Cuomo* oral argument provide suggestive evidence of that influence.

UNRESOLVED QUESTIONS CONCERNING THE APPLICABILITY OF *CHEVRON* DEFERENCE TO PREEMPTION CLAIMS BY FEDERAL AGENCIES

Cuomo addressed, but did not resolve, two recurring questions concerning the appropriate judicial treatment of preemptive rulings by federal agencies. First, should courts give *Chevron* deference or a lower degree of deference to an agency regulation or order that includes a declaration of preemption? Second, should courts apply a presumption against preemption in evaluating agency claims of authority to override state laws in areas that the states have traditionally regulated?

Justice Stevens, who authored *Chevron*, addressed both of the foregoing questions in his dissenting opinion in *Watters* and again in his majority opinion in *Wyeth*. In those opinions, Justice Stevens indicated that *Chevron* deference should not be given to a federal agency's declaration of preemption unless Congress has made an explicit delegation of preemptive rulemaking authority to the agency. In place of *Chevron*, Justice Stevens' opinions provide the basis for a more demanding, four-part test to determine the appropriate degree of deference that courts should apply in reviewing preemption claims by federal agencies. As part of that framework, the presumption against preemption would require a federal agency to present persuasive evidence showing that Congress intended to delegate authority permitting the agency to issue preemptive rules overriding state law in fields of traditional state regulation.

Justice Scalia took a significantly different approach to the question of judicial deference in his majority opinion in *Cuomo*. Justice Scalia said that he was applying *Chevron* in reviewing the validity of the OCC's 'visitorial powers' rule. However, he applied a much less deferential version of *Chevron* than the approach advocated by Justice Thomas in his dissenting opinion. After making a careful evaluation of the OCC's claim of delegated authority, Justice Scalia concluded that the OCC's preemptive rule exceeded the limits of the OCC's power under the NBA. Thus, after *Cuomo* there is continuing uncertainty regarding the appropriate level of judicial deference for agency preemption claims.

Justice Stevens' Treatment of *Chevron* in *Watters* and *Wyeth*

In his dissenting opinion in *Watters,* Justice Stevens maintained that 'the most pressing questions in this case are whether Congress delegated to the [OCC] the authority to preempt the laws of a sovereign State as they apply to operating subsidiaries [of national banks], and if so, whether that authority was properly exercised here'.[133] Justice Stevens' framing of those questions in *Watters* was consistent with his opinion for the Court in *Louisiana Public Service Comm'n v. FCC.*[134] In that case, the Court declared that 'an agency literally has no power to act, let alone . . . preempt the validly enacted legislation of a sovereign State, unless and until Congress confers power upon it'.[135]

In *Watters*, Justice Stevens argued that *Chevron* did not provide the appropriate framework for reviewing the OCC's preemptive regulation. In his view, 'when an agency purports to decide the scope of federal preemption, a healthy respect for state sovereignty calls for something less than *Chevron* deference'.[136] He concluded that an agency's views on preemption should be entitled to 'some weight' but only to the extent that the agency provided an 'expert' opinion about the ways in which state law conflicted with the federal statutory scheme.[137]

In addition, Justice Stevens maintained that the Court should have applied a presumption against preemption in *Watters,* because the state mortgage lending laws in question were 'designed to protect consumers' and '[c]onsumer protection is quintessentially "a field which the States have traditionally occupied"'.[138] Based on that presumption, Justice Stevens contended that the OCC's preemptive regulation should have been struck down in the absence of any 'clear and manifest purpose of Congress' to preempt the states' authority to regulate state-chartered operating subsidiaries of national banks.[139]

Justice Ginsburg's majority opinion in *Watters* carefully avoided the issue of *Chevron* deference and instead based its finding of preemption solely on the statutory provisions of the NBA. Justice Ginsburg declared that 'the level of deference owed to the [OCC's] regulation is an academic question', because 'the NBA itself – independent of the OCC's regulation – preempts the application of the pertinent Michigan laws to national bank operating subsidiaries'.[140] She maintained that any argument concerning the propriety of *Chevron* deference 'is beside the point' because the OCC's regulation 'merely clarifies and confirms what the NBA already conveys'.[141]

In his majority opinion in *Wyeth*, Justice Stevens returned to the question of whether a federal agency's claim of preemption should receive *Chevron* deference. Once again, he indicated that *Chevron* does not provide the appropriate framework for reviewing agency assertions of preemption, except in situations where Congress has explicitly granted preemptive rulemaking authority to an agency. In that context, Justice Stevens declared that 'agencies have no special authority to pronounce on preemption absent delegation by Congress'.[142]

Justice Stevens explained in *Wyeth* that the Supreme Court had previously reviewed agency claims of preemption by 'perform[ing] its own conflict determination, relying on the substance of state and federal law and not on agency proclamations of pre-emption'.[143] In such cases, Justice Stevens emphasized that 'we have not deferred to the agency's *conclusion* that state law is pre-empted'. Instead, 'we have given "some weight" to an agency's views . . . . about how state requirements may pose an "obstacle to the accomplishment of the full purposes and objectives of Congress"'.[144] In Justice Stevens' view, '[t]he weight we accord to the agency's explanation of state law's impact on the federal scheme depends on its thoroughness, consistency, and persuasiveness'.[145]

Justice Stevens' majority opinion in *Wyeth* did not define the precise degree of 'weight' that courts should give to agency claims of preemption. However, his citation to *Skidmore* and his reference to the *Skidmore* factors of 'thoroughness, consistency, and persuasiveness' indicated that agency preemptive determinations should receive the relatively low level of deference described in *Skidmore*.[146] In addition, Justice Stevens maintained in *Wyeth* that a presumption against preemption should apply '[i]n all preemption cases, and particularly those in which Congress has "legislated in a field which the States have traditionally occupied"'.[147] As he had previously indicated in his dissent in *Watters*, Justice Stevens did not believe that the presumption against preemption should be set aside simply because a federal agency had issued a finding of preemption.

In *Wyeth*, the Food and Drug Administration ('FDA') declared in a preamble to a final regulation that tort claims under state law were preempted by federal statutes regulating the labeling of prescription drugs. For two reasons, the Supreme Court refused to give any deference to the FDA's preemption claim. First, when the FDA issued the proposed regulation for public comment, the FDA said that the regulation would not preempt state law. The FDA did not notify the public of any change in its position until the agency published its final rule. At that point, the FDA suddenly inserted a declaration of preemption into the preamble without any advance notice or any opportunity for public comment on the preemption issue. The Court concluded that the FDA's preemption claim was 'inherently suspect in light of this procedural failure'.[148]

Second, the Court determined that the FDA's assertion of preemption 'is at odds with what evidence we have of Congress' purposes, and it reverses the FDA's own longstanding position [of non-preemption] without providing a reasoned explanation, including any discussion of how state [tort] law has interfered with the FDA's regulation of drug labeling during decades of coexistence'.[149] In view of the fact that 'Congress has repeatedly declined to pre-empt state [tort] law' with respect to prescription drugs, the Court held that the FDA's claim of preemption was 'entitled to no weight'.[150]

Justice Stevens' Four-Part Framework for Determining the Appropriate Level of Judicial Deference for Agency Preemption Claims

Justice Stevens did not articulate a precise formula for reviewing agency assertions of preemptive authority in his dissenting opinion in *Watters* or his majority opinion in *Wyeth*. However, a four-part framework for determining the appropriate level of judicial deference for agency preemption claims can be derived from those opinions. As explained below, that four-part test would strike an appropriate balance between (i) the granting of some deference to the specialized expertise of administrative agencies and (ii) the judiciary's responsibility to ensure that preemption issues are resolved in accordance with constitutional and statutory limits on federal power.

First, Chevron *deference is inapplicable absent an explicit delegation of preemptive rulemaking authority to the agency*. In his opinions in *Watters* and *Wyeth*, Justice Stevens indicated that a federal agency's preemptive regulation should not receive *Chevron* deference unless Congress has expressly granted preemptive rulemaking power to the agency.[151] This requirement would ensure that a federal agency cannot appeal to *Chevron* unless its preemption claim is based on an explicit statutory grant of preemptive authority rather than merely the agency's 'interpretation' of an ambiguous statute. As Justice Stevens explained in *Watters*, granting *Chevron* deference to preemptive agency rulings based on ambiguous statutes would grant federal agencies a far-reaching power to override state law, except in those rare situations where Congress has unambiguously barred an agency from acting.[152]

The opinions of the Second Circuit Court of Appeals and Justice

Thomas in *Cuomo* reveal the inadequacy of highly deferential review in the preemption context. The Second Circuit stated that '[a]lthough the precise scope of "visitorial" powers is not entirely clear from the text of [12 U.S.C.] § 484(a), . . . we cannot agree . . . that the statute clearly precludes the interpretation the OCC has adopted'.[153] Similarly, Justice Thomas argued in his dissenting opinion in *Cuomo* that, under *Chevron*, the Court was required to 'decide only whether the construction adopted by the [OCC] is unambiguously foreclosed by the statute's text'.[154] As a practical matter, the approach followed by the Second Circuit and Justice Thomas in *Cuomo* would have created a virtually conclusive presumption in favor of the OCC's authority to preempt the states' sovereign law enforcement powers, even though the OCC was relying on an admittedly ambiguous statute.[155]

In *Gregory v. Ashcroft*,[156] the Supreme Court declared that the power of Congress to adopt legislation preempting 'areas traditionally regulated by the States . . . is an extraordinary power in a federalist system. It is a power that we must assume Congress does not exercise lightly.'[157] The Court therefore held that Congress must 'make its intention "clear and manifest" if intends to pre-empt the historic powers of the States'.[158]

Because *Gregory* involved a claim of statutory rather than regulatory preemption, *Gregory* did not consider the issue of whether courts should apply *Chevron* in reviewing agency preemptive rulings. However, *Gregory*'s reasoning strongly supports the view that *Chevron* should not apply when a federal agency's claim of preemptive authority rests on an ambiguous statute. *Gregory* held that the courts may not conclude that a statute alters 'the state-federal balance' in the absence of a 'plain statement' of Congress' intent to change that balance. The Court explained that this 'plain statement rule' helps to ensure that 'the political process' has given appropriate consideration to the states' interest in being protected 'against intrusive exercises of Congress' Commerce Clause powers'.[159] In addition, as the Court observed, to 'give the state-displacing weight of federal law to mere congressional *ambiguity* would evade the very procedure for law-making on which *Garcia* relied to protect states' interests'.[160]

Granting *Chevron* deference to preemptive agency rulings based on ambiguous statutes would clearly undermine the federalism-based canons articulated in *Gregory*. *Gregory* bars courts from relying on ambiguous statutes to infer a congressional intent to preempt traditional state functions. Similarly, courts should not allow a federal agency to infer a preemptive congressional purpose based solely on the agency's 'interpretation' of a statute that is silent or ambiguous with regard to any such purpose.

To preserve our federal structure, *Gregory*'s ban on judicial inference of preemptive intent from ambiguous statutes should apply with at least equal force when federal agencies claim to speak for Congress in asserting preemption based on statutory ambiguity. Unlike Congress, federal agencies are less vulnerable to discipline from 'the political process' and do not provide the states with any constitutionally-guaranteed structure of representation that would promote a vigorous and thorough discussion of the states' interests and concerns before a preemptive regulation is adopted. Justice Stevens declared in *Watters* that federal agencies should not receive *Chevron* deference when they issue preemptive rulings because such agencies 'are clearly not designed to represent the interests of States'.[161] For similar reasons, Nina Mendelson contends that courts should not defer to an agency's assertion of preemptive authority over an area in which Congress has not clearly expressed its intent to displace state law:

> [R]equiring a showing that Congress clearly wishes to preempt state law . . . gives some protection to state regulatory autonomy. . . . [A] presumption [against preemption] also helps assure that legislative decisions to preempt are thoughtful and deliberate rather than simply 'incidental.' . . .
>
> . . .
>
> Although state institutions have the opportunity to comment on rulemaking through the notice-and-comment process, those comments are likely to be lower-visibility, both to decisionmakers and to the public, than objections raised by a member of Congress to a legislative proposal . . .
>
> [A]gencies, unlike Congress and the courts, are specialized institutions that are not set up to consider state autonomy concerns.[162]

Professor Mendelson and Thomas Merrill contend that federal agencies are subject to additional institutional limitations (including a tendency toward 'empire building' and a bias against allowing regulatory 'competition' from the states) that undermine the agencies' ability to resolve preemption issues in a manner that gives appropriate weight to the interests of state autonomy within our federal system.[163] After considering similar factors based on institutional competence and motivation, Professor Merrill concludes that courts are better suited to resolve preemption issues that arise out of ambiguous federal statutes. Accordingly, he contends that courts should not give *Chevron* deference to agency preemption claims based on statutory ambiguity:

> [A]lthough preemption entails the resolution of policy disputes, those disputes have significant dimensions along which courts are likely to perform better than agencies – dimensions such as preserving fidelity to the Constitution's division of powers, the need for preserving stability in that division, the desirability of preserving an overall balance between federal and state authority, and the need to discern accurately the nature and content of state law alleged to be in tension with federal law.[164]

Second, no deference should be given to agency interpretations of statutes, judicial precedents and other legal authorities that do not require specialized agency expertise. Justice Stevens' opinion in *Wyeth* supports the view that courts should not defer to an agency's legal conclusions about preemption based on the agency's interpretations of statutes, Supreme Court precedents or other legal authorities that do not require the agency to apply its specialized expertise.[165] Moreover, in a 2004 decision authored by Justice Stevens, the Supreme Court held that 'pure question[s] of statutory construction . . . well within the province of the Judiciary . . . merit no special deference', and the Court further explained that an agency's 'views on questions within its area of expertise merit greater deference than its opinions regarding the scope of a congressional enactment'.[166] Similarly, the Court recently declared that '[a]gencies have no special claim to deference in their interpretation of our decisions'.[167]

Third, 'some weight' may be given to an agency's expert analysis of the ways in which state laws conflict with the statutory scheme administered by the agency, but courts should carefully scrutinize agency claims of 'obstacle' preemption. Justice Stevens' opinion in *Wyeth* indicates that courts should give 'some weight' to an agency's analysis of alleged conflicts between state laws and the governing federal statute, provided the agency's analysis is based on matters within the agency's special expertise and otherwise has 'power to persuade' under *Skidmore*. Thus, courts should consider evidence showing that the agency has made 'informed determinations about how state requirements may pose an "obstacle to the accomplishment and execution of the full purposes and objectives of Congress"'.[168]

Even here, Professor Mendelson warns that courts should closely scrutinize an agency's claim that state law presents an 'obstacle' to the accomplishment of congressional purposes. In her view, courts should carefully evaluate the content and strength of legislative policies inherent in federal statutes and should determine whether state laws actually create significant conflicts with those policies. Otherwise, 'federal agencies would have the power to preempt nearly any state law . . . as long as the agency can explain how the state law strikes a different balance of statutory objectives than the federal [agency's] approach does'.[169]

Similarly, William Buzbee contends that federal agency claims of 'obstacle' preemption should be subject to 'hard look review', including (i) 'close scrutiny of agency factual and policy conclusions', and (ii) a careful evaluation of the agency's decision-making process to ensure that the 'agency engaged the views of affected stakeholders, considered underlying facts or data in dispute, and addressed them in a reasonable way'.[170] Professor Buzbee notes that agency claims of conflict preemption frequently turn on the agency's 'assertions about benefits and harms of allowing multiple [state and federal] regulatory voices or displacing all but a single, federal regulatory actor'.[171] Unless courts engage in 'hard look' review that insists upon an 'open and deliberative agency process', he fears that federal agencies will often discount or ignore the benefits of preserving a federalist system with multiple regulators. In this regard, he believes that overlapping federal-state regulatory systems 'improve the odds of superior regulatory outcomes' by (i) reducing the risk of policy mistakes by a single, all-powerful regulator whose decisions are difficult to challenge or correct, (ii) increasing 'opportunities for mutual adjustment and learning' by multiple regulators with concurrent jurisdictions, and (iii) preserving the 'states as laboratories of [experimentation and] democracy'.[172]

Fourth, a presumption against preemption applies whenever an agency seeks to preempt a traditional state function. Justice Stevens' opinion in *Wyeth* indicates that courts should not defer to an agency's preemption claim under *Skidmore* unless the agency's case for preemption is sufficiently strong to overcome the presumption that Congress does not intend to preempt state law in areas of traditional state regulation. In *Wyeth,* Justice Stevens rejected the FDA's claim that state tort suits presented an 'obstacle' to congressional objectives regarding the labeling of prescription drugs. Justice Stevens noted that Congress adopted an express preemption statute covering medical devices in 1976 but failed to do so with respect to prescription drugs. In view of the presumption against preemption of state laws in the field of consumer protection, Justice Stevens determined that the 'silence [of Congress] on the issue, coupled with its certain awareness of the prevalence of state tort litigation, is powerful evidence that Congress did not intend FDA oversight to be the exclusive means of ensuring drug safety and effectiveness'.[173]

Four justices joined Justice Stevens' majority opinion in *Wyeth*.[174] However, it is debatable whether a majority of the Court fully supported Justice Stevens' suggested framework for judicial deference. In addition to joining the majority opinion in *Wyeth*, Justice Breyer filed a concurring opinion indicating that he might have given the FDA's preemption claim greater deference if it had been adopted through notice-and-comment rulemaking.[175] Justice Thomas did not join the majority opinion in *Wyeth* and instead filed an opinion concurring only in the judgment.[176]

The Application of *Chevron* in *Cuomo* and the Relevance of *Gonzales* and *Brand X*

As previously noted, Justice Scalia cited *Wyeth* with approval in his majority opinion in *Cuomo*.[177] However, Justice Scalia did not adopt the analytical approach for reviewing agency preemption claims that Justice

Stevens suggested in *Wyeth*. Justice Scalia instead explained that he was applying 'the familiar *Chevron* framework'.[178] Even so, Justice Scalia's application of *Chevron* gave little deference to the OCC and instead carefully scrutinized the OCC's claim of preemptive authority.

Cuomo* and *Gonzales v. Oregon

With regard to the first step of *Chevron* – determining whether 'the intent of Congress is clear'[179] – Justice Scalia declared that the existence of 'some ambiguity' in 12 U.S.C. § 484(a) 'does not expand *Chevron* deference to cover virtually any interpretation of the [NBA]'.[180] Justice Scalia's refusal in *Cuomo* to grant *Chevron* deference, based simply on statutory ambiguity, was similar to the Supreme Court's approach in *Gonzales v. Oregon*.[181] In *Gonzales*, the Court held that '*Chevron* deference . . . is not accorded merely because the statute is ambiguous and an administrative official is involved. [Rather,] the rule must be promulgated pursuant to authority Congress has delegated to the official.'[182] Additionally, the Court warned in *Gonzales* that if an agency claims 'broad and unusual authority through an implicit delegation' based on 'vague terms' in the governing statute, the Court may well conclude that 'Congress could not have intended to delegate a decision of such economic and political significance to an agency in so cryptic a fashion'.[183]

In *Gonzales*, the US Attorney General issued an interpretive rule barring doctors from prescribing drugs to be used in assisted suicides. The Attorney General's rule specifically preempted any state law authorizing state-licensed physicians to prescribe drugs for that purpose. The Supreme Court struck down the rule because (i) the Attorney General's claim of preemptive authority would 'effect a radical shift of authority from the States to the Federal Government to define general standards of medical practice in every locality', and (ii) the 'text and structure of the [governing federal statute] show that Congress did not have this far-reaching intent to alter the federal-state balance'.[184] Justice Scalia's refusal in *Cuomo* to give the OCC wide leeway in inferring preemptive authority from statutory ambiguity was consistent with the limitations on *Chevron* deference expressed in *Gonzales*.

With regard to the second step of *Chevron* – determining whether the OCC made a 'reasonable interpretation' of the NBA[185] – Justice Scalia concluded in *Cuomo* that historical evidence and judicial precedents enabled the Court (i) to 'discern the outer limits' of § 484(a) and (ii) to determine that the OCC exceeded its authority in defining 'visitorial powers' to include 'ordinary enforcement of the law'.[186] As previously discussed, Justice Scalia held that applicable federal statutes did not contemplate the 'bizarre' result produced by the OCC's regulation – namely, a preemptive bar that would override 'traditional state powers' to enforce valid state laws against national banks through judicial proceedings.[187]

Justice Scalia's careful analysis of whether Congress affirmatively delegated the preemptive authority claimed by the OCC could be viewed as supporting either of two possible approaches to the application of *Chevron* in similar agency preemption cases. Each of those approaches would strengthen judicial scrutiny of preemptive agency rulings under *Chevron*. The first possibility is that the question of whether the agency has received an adequate delegation of statutory preemptive authority should be made at 'step zero', before a reviewing court even begins to apply the two-step *Chevron* analysis.[188]

The second possibility is that a reviewing court should examine the question of congressionally delegated authority at 'step 2.1' of the *Chevron* analysis. Under this approach, if a reviewing court finds at 'step one' that the agency has based its preemptive ruling on an ambiguous statute, the court should then decide at the *beginning* of 'step two' whether Congress has affirmatively delegated preemptive authority to the agency, *before* the court proceeds to determine whether the agency has made a 'reasonable' interpretation of the ambiguous statute. Thus, under a 'step 2.1' approach,

> the court must carefully consider whether Congress has authorized the agency to adopt a preemptive regulation to clarify the ambiguity or to fill the 'gap' that the agency has identified in the governing statute.
>
> Only if the court answers 'yes' at 'step 2.1' may the court then proceed to a more deferential analysis of whether the agency has made a 'reasonable' interpretation of the statute. . . . [I]f the agency adopts an 'interpretation' of a statute that . . . encroaches upon an area traditionally regulated by the states, the reviewing court should require a clear showing that the agency's 'interpretation' is consistent with the available evidence of Congress' intent.[189]

Gonzales and *Cuomo* followed an analytical approach that could be viewed as fitting within the 'step 2.1' formulation. In each case, the Court first determined that there was some degree of ambiguity in the governing federal statute.[190] In each case, the Court proceeded to make a careful analysis of whether the federal agency's preemptive ruling was supported by a sufficient congressional delegation of preemptive authority. Finding that the available evidence of congressional intent did not support such a delegation, the Court concluded in each case that the agency's preemptive ruling was invalid and not entitled to deference.[191]

In *Gonzales*, the Court shifted from a *Chevron* analysis to the less deferential standard of *Skidmore* after the Court concluded that the challenged ruling 'was not promulgated pursuant to the Attorney General's [statutory] authority'.[192] In *Cuomo*, the Court did not make an explicit shift from *Chevron* to *Skidmore*. However, Justice Scalia closely scrutinized the OCC's claims of authority in a manner that suggested a less deferential, *Skidmore* type of inquiry.

In my view, the four-part framework for judicial deference derived from Justice Stevens' opinions in *Watters* and *Wyeth* would provide a superior methodology for analyzing agency preemption claims based on ambiguous statutes. By completely avoiding the *Chevron* mode of analysis, the four-part framework would encourage reviewing courts to perform an independent and thorough consideration of the federalism-related factors discussed in *Gregory*. If, however, the Supreme Court ultimately decides to choose *Chevron* as the governing standard for evaluating preemptive agency rulings, the Court should make clear – as it indicated in *Gonzales* and *Cuomo* – that preemptive rulings are subject to heightened judicial scrutiny on the issue of whether Congress has affirmatively delegated the preemptive authority asserted by the agency. Such enhanced scrutiny could be applied in accordance with either of the 'step zero' or 'step 2.1' approaches discussed above.

In contrast to Justice Scalia's searching analysis of the OCC's delegated authority in *Cuomo*, Justice Thomas' dissenting opinion illustrates the pitfalls of applying a highly deferential version of *Chevron* in a case where the agency's preemptive ruling is based on an ambiguous statute. Justice Thomas maintained that the OCC was entitled to *Chevron* deference because the agency had 'selected a permissible construction of a statutory term that was susceptible to multiple interpretations'.[193] In addition, as previously noted, he argued that under *Chevron* '[t]he Court must decide only whether the construction adopted by the agency is unambiguously foreclosed by the statute's text'.[194]

As a practical matter, Justice Thomas' implementation of *Chevron* would create a nearly uncontestable presumption in favor of an agency's authority to adopt preemptive interpretations of ambiguous statutes. In most cases, the very existence of statutory ambiguity would make it almost impossible for the states to show that Congress had 'unambiguously foreclosed' the agency's preemptive ruling. As a federal appellate court explained in a comparable preemption case, such an application of *Chevron* would be 'flatly unfaithful to the principles of administrative law' because 'if we were to *presume* a delegation of power from the absence of an express *withholding* of such power, agencies would enjoy virtually limitless hegemony'.[195] Accordingly, the heightened scrutiny applied by the Court in *Gonzales* and *Cuomo* should become the governing approach if the Court ultimately selects *Chevron* as the applicable standard for judicial review of agency preemption claims.

Cuomo* and *Brand X

Justice Scalia and Justice Thomas also sharply differed in *Cuomo* as to the binding impact of prior Supreme Court decisions on federal agencies under *Chevron*. Relying on *National Cable & Telecommunications Ass'n v. Brand X Internet Services*,[196] Justice Thomas contended that the OCC was free under *Chevron* to adopt its own interpretation of 'visitorial powers' and to disregard *St. Louis* and several other Supreme Court decisions that had previously upheld the authority of state officials to file lawsuits against national banks. Justice Thomas maintained that *Brand X* made those earlier decisions irrelevant because they did not adopt an 'authoritative' construction of 12 U.S.C. § 484(a) that explicitly preserved the states' power of judicial enforcement as an exception to the limitation on 'visitorial powers' under § 484(a). Justice Thomas concluded that none of the cited decisions 'addressed the meaning of "visitorial powers" for purposes of § 484(a), let alone provided a definitive construction of the statute'.[197] In his view, '[i]f the *Chevron* doctrine is to have any interpretive value, an agency's construction of a statute cannot be foreclosed by a prior decision in which the [statutory] provision in question was neither raised by the parties nor passed upon by the court'.[198]

Justice Scalia rejected Justice Thomas' argument based on *Brand X*. In Justice Scalia's view, '*St. Louis* is relevant to the proper interpretation of 12 U.S.C. § 484(a) . . . because it is one in a long and unbroken line of cases distinguishing visitation from law enforcement'.[199] Although Justice Scalia did not contest the point, it appears that Justice Thomas was mistaken in concluding that the federal statutory limitation on 'visitorial powers' was not invoked by the litigants in *St. Louis*. The summaries of arguments presented by counsel in *St. Louis*, as published in *United States Reports*, indicate that both the national bank and the United States as *amici curiae* argued that Missouri's *quo warranto* action against the national bank was a violation of the NBA's limitation on the exercise of 'visitorial powers'.[200] Thus, *St. Louis* could reasonably be viewed as adopting, by necessary implication, a position that Section 484's limitation on 'visitorial powers' did not preempt the states' authority to enforce valid, non-preempted state laws by filing lawsuits against national banks.

The debate in *Cuomo* between Justice Thomas and Justice Scalia over the binding effect of *St. Louis* was effectively a replay of their dueling opinions in *Brand X*. Justice Thomas wrote the majority opinion in *Brand X* while Justice Scalia authored a vigorous dissent. Justice Thomas' majority opinion held that '[b]efore a judicial construction of a statute . . . may trump an agency's [interpretation], the court must hold that the statute unambiguously requires the court's construction'.[201] In his dissent, Justice Scalia declared that *Brand X*'s concept of 'judicial decisions subject to reversal by executive officers' was 'bizarre' and 'probably unconstitutional' as a violation of separation of powers.[202] In Justice Scalia's view, 'Article III courts do not sit to render decisions that can be reversed or ignored by executive officers'.[203]

Justice Scalia's dissent in *Brand X* was consistent with his subsequent refusal in *Cuomo* to allow the OCC to disregard *St. Louis* and other Supreme Court decisions that had previously upheld the right of state officials to file lawsuits to enforce state laws against national banks. While the majority opinion in *Cuomo* did not expressly overrule or limit *Brand X*, the two opinions cannot easily be reconciled except on the ground that the agency in *Brand X* overruled the decision of a court of appeals while the agency in *Cuomo* disregarded a Supreme Court precedent. It therefore remains to be seen whether *Cuomo* will be interpreted in the future as barring federal agencies from adopting interpretations of 'ambiguous' statutes that conflict with previous Supreme Court (as opposed to appellate court) decisions.[204]

The Presumption against Preemption and the Doubtful Relevance of *Locke* and *Smiley*

Another recurring issue in agency preemption cases is whether an agency's claim to judicial deference under *Chevron* must overcome a presumption against preemption. As discussed above, Justice Stevens strongly endorsed the applicability of a presumption against preemption in both his dissenting opinion in *Watters* and his majority opinion in *Wyeth*.[205]

In *Cuomo*, Justice Scalia found it 'unnecessary' to invoke a presumption against preemption in order to strike down the OCC's regulation.[206] However, he emphasized that 'the incursion that the [OCC's] regulation makes upon traditional state powers [should not] be minimized'.[207] He pointed out that 'the [OCC] was not given authority to enforce nonpreempted state laws [against national banks] until 1966', and he therefore rejected Justice Thomas' claim that the 'historic police powers of the States' were unaffected by the OCC's regulation.[208]

Similarly, in *Gonzales* the Supreme Court found it 'unnecessary even to consider the application of . . . presumptions against pre-emption' in concluding that Congress '[did] not authorize the Attorney General to bar dispensing controlled substances for assisted suicide in the face of a state medical regime permitting such conduct'.[209] The Court rejected the Attorney General's claim that the governing federal statue 'impliedly authorizes . . . an expansive federal authority to regulate medicine', in view of the statute's 'silence on the practice of medicine generally and its recognition of state regulation of the medical profession'.[210] Thus, in both *Cuomo* and *Gonzales*, the Court recognized the potential applicability of a presumption against preemption in determining whether to defer to a federal agency's preemptive ruling under *Chevron*. However, the Court did not consider it necessary in either case to invoke the presumption, because the evidence of congressional intent was sufficiently persuasive on its own to defeat the agency's claim of preemptive authority.

The inapplicability of *Locke* to fields of dual federal-state regulation

In his dissenting opinion in *Cuomo*, Justice Thomas contended, based on *United States v. Locke*,[211] that a presumption against preemption should never be applied in construing the preemptive effect of the NBA.[212] However, Justice Thomas' reliance on *Locke* was misplaced. In *Locke* the Supreme Court struck down state laws that imposed requirements and restrictions on oil tankers operating in navigable waterways. The Court refused to apply 'an "assumption"' of 'nonpre-emption' in *Locke* with respect to the field of 'national and international maritime commerce', because 'Congress has legislated in the field from the earliest days of the Republic' and has consistently expressed its desire to establish a 'uniformity of regulation for maritime commerce'.[213] Thus, *Locke* involved a field of commerce in which the federal government exercised near-monolithic control and left little room for state involvement. In contrast, the Court held in *Atherton* that federal policy did *not* require any 'uniformity' of treatment for federally-chartered banks, in view of the long history of supplemental state regulation of national banks. Accordingly, *Atherton* refused to adopt a federal common-law rule for federally-chartered banks that would override state-law standards governing fiduciary duties of bank directors.[214]

Congress expressed its strong support for the continuing application of state laws to national banks when it passed the Riegle-Neal Interstate Banking and Branching Efficiency Act of 1994, 108 Stat. 2338 (Riegle-Neal Act). The Riegle-Neal Act requires interstate branches of national banks to comply with host state laws in four broadly-defined areas – community reinvestment, consumer protection, fair lending and intrastate branching – unless such laws discriminate against national banks or are otherwise preempted by federal law, 12 U.S.C. § 36(f)(1)(A). In explaining why state laws should generally apply to national banks, the conference report on the Riegle-Neal Act declared:

> States have a strong interest in the activities and operations of depository institutions doing business within their jurisdictions, regardless of the type of the charter an institution holds. In particular, States have a legitimate interest in protecting the rights of their consumers, businesses and communities. . . .

> Under well-established judicial principles, national banks are subject to State law in many significant respects. . . . Courts generally use a rule of construction that avoids finding a conflict between the Federal and State law where possible. The [Riegle-Neal Act] does not change these judicially established principles.[215]

The Riegle-Neal conference report thus endorsed a judicial 'rule of construction' that closely resembles a presumption against preemption. The Riegle-Neal conference report – read in context with *Atherton* and previous Supreme Court decisions (including *St. Louis*, *Lewis* and *Luckett*) – demonstrates that Congress has preserved a significant, supplemental role for the states in regulating national banks. The history of dual federal-state regulation of national banks stands in sharp contrast to Congress' preclusion of any substantial role for the states in regulating maritime commerce. Accordingly, the reasoning in *Locke* is clearly inapplicable to preemption cases arising under the NBA.[216]

Similarly, in *Wyeth* Justice Stevens rejected the argument that 'the presumption against pre-emption should not apply to this case because the Federal Government has regulated drug labeling for more than a century'.[217] Justice Stevens explained that 'the presumption [against preemption] accounts for the historic presence of state law' in a particular field and 'does not rely on the absence of federal regulation'. He further maintained that a presumption against preemption was warranted in *Wyeth* because 'Congress has indicated its awareness of the operation of state law in a field of federal interest, and has nonetheless decided to stand by both concepts and to tolerate whatever tension there [is] between them'.[218] Thus, *Wyeth* confirms that *Locke* does not apply to a field of activity with a strong tradition of concurrent state regulation, even if the federal government has a major presence or even the predominant role in regulating that field. In view of Congress' continuing support for the states' supplemental role in regulating national banks, a presumption against preemption should be applied in future cases raising preemption claims under the NBA.

The questionable relevance of *Smiley* after *Cuomo*

In *Cuomo*, Justice Thomas and Justice Scalia also disagreed about whether the OCC's challenged regulation should be viewed as preemptive in the first place. In *Smiley v. Citibank (South Dakota), N.A.*,[219] the Supreme Court held (in an opinion written by Justice Scalia) that an OCC regulation defining the term 'interest' for purposes of 12 U.S.C. § 85 did not preempt state law. As noted in *Smiley*, a 1978 decision of the Supreme Court had previously held that § 85 preempted state usury laws as a statutory matter. *Smiley* therefore concluded that the OCC's regulation merely defined 'the substantive (as opposed to pre-emptive) *meaning* of [§ 85]'.[220] Accordingly, *Smiley* concluded that the OCC's regulation was not preemptive and did not need to overcome any presumption against preemption in order to receive deference under *Chevron*.

Relying on *Smiley*, Justice Thomas argued in *Cuomo* that 12 C.F.R. § 7.4000 was not preemptive because the rule merely interpreted 'an ambiguous statutory term' (namely, 'visitorial powers') in order to 'clarify the preemptive scope of enacted federal law'.[221] However, as Nina Mendelson has pointed out, the reasoning in *Smiley* is open to serious question, because the OCC's expansive 'interpretation' of the statutory term 'interest' for purposes of § 85 'effectively broadened the statute's preemption of state [usury] law'.[222]

Justice Scalia insisted in *Cuomo* that the OCC's regulation was indeed preemptive. As he pointed out, '[a]ny interpretation of "visitorial powers" necessarily "declares the pre-emptive scope of the NBA", . . . If that is not pre-emption, nothing is.'[223] Thus, Justice Scalia essentially repudiated his prior reasoning in *Smiley*. Based on *Cuomo*, litigants can now argue that an agency regulation that defines the 'meaning' of a preemptive statute in a way that expands the statute's reach should itself be viewed as preemptive. Accordingly, for the reasons discussed above, such a rule should receive a lower level of judicial deference and should be subject to the presumption against preemption.

CUOMO'S IMPLICATIONS FOR THE FUTURE OF THE DUAL BANKING SYSTEM AND CONSUMER PROTECTION

For at least three reasons, *Cuomo* is likely to have a significant impact on future court cases and legislative proposals dealing with the dual banking system and consumer protection. First, the decision affirms the right of state officials to seek judicial enforcement of valid, non-preempted state laws against national banks. *Cuomo* provides a significant boost to the dual banking system and consumer protection by ensuring that national banks, like other lenders, are subject to judicial enforcement of applicable state laws by state officials. In contrast, a victory by the OCC and the Clearing House in *Cuomo* (i) would have encouraged state banks to convert to national charters to avoid exposure to state enforcement proceedings, and (ii) would have made it much more difficult politically for states to enact and implement new laws protecting consumers of financial services, because state officials would have been barred from enforcing such laws against national banks and their operating subsidiaries.

Second, *Cuomo* will shift the focus of future preemption cases involving national banks to the question of *which* state laws apply to national banks, and it will also encourage legal challenges to the validity of the OCC's substantive preemption rules. In 2004, the OCC adopted sweeping regulations that purport to preempt state laws in four broadly-defined areas – real estate lending, other lending, deposit-taking, and other federally-authorized 'activities'. In all four areas, the OCC's rules (i) preempt state laws if they 'obstruct, impair, or condition a national bank's ability to fully exercise its powers to conduct activities authorized under Federal law', and (ii) allow state laws to apply to national banks only if such laws 'establish the legal infrastructure that makes [it] practicable' for national banks to conduct their federally-authorized activities.[224] The practical effect of the OCC's 'infrastructure' theory, as embodied in the 2004 preemption rules, is to establish a regime of 'de facto field preemption', in which 'only those state laws that *promote* the ability of national banks to [conduct a banking business] will remain applicable'.[225]

Cuomo strikes a significant blow at the OCC's claim of exclusive preemptive authority over the banking activities of national banks. As previously discussed, *Cuomo* declared that 'States . . . have always enforced their general laws against national banks – and have enforced their banking-related laws against national banks for at least 85 years, as evidenced in *St. Louis*'.[226] *Cuomo* thus reaffirmed the presumptive applicability of state laws to national banks, and *Cuomo* also vitiated the precedential force of *Watters*' arguably broader view of NBA preemption.

In addition, *Cuomo* addressed and rejected the OCC's assertions that (i) the NBA generally preempts state laws that 'affect the content or extent of the Federally-authorized business of banking', and (ii) the NBA permits the application of state law only if it 'establishes the legal infrastructure that surrounds and supports the ability of national banks . . . to do business'.[227] In *Cuomo*, the Court declared that the OCC's asserted 'distinction between "implementation" of "infrastructure" and judicial enforcement of other [state] laws can be found nowhere within the text of the [NBA]. This passage . . . attempts to do what Congress declined to do: exempt national banks from all state banking laws, or at least enforcement of those laws.'[228] *Cuomo* creates serious doubts about the validity of the OCC's substantive preemption rules, because those rules rely on the same purported distinction between non-preempted state 'infrastructure' laws and other state laws that the OCC claims are preempted if they place any 'condition' on authorized national bank activities.[229]

Third, *Cuomo* dramatically changes the legal status quo for debates about the adoption of new federal legislation to provide greater protection for consumers of financial services. In June 2009, the Treasury Department published a comprehensive plan for financial regulatory reform.[230] One of the key elements of the Treasury plan is its proposal for a new 'Consumer Financial Protection Agency' (CFPA). The proposed CFPA would have broad authority to issue and enforce consumer protection regulations applicable to all providers of financial services, including national banks and federal thrifts.[231]

In July 2009, Representative Barney Frank, Chairman of the House Financial Services Committee, introduced a proposed bill (H.R. 3126) to create the CFPA. Like the Treasury plan, Subtitle D of H.R. 3126 would preserve the states' authority to enact laws that give additional protections to consumers beyond those established by the CFPA's regulations. Such supplemental state laws would be applicable on a nondiscriminatory basis to all financial service providers, including national banks, federal thrifts and their subsidiaries and agents.[232] In addition, Subtitle D would empower state attorneys general, after consulting with the CFPA, to bring judicial proceedings to enforce applicable state laws against all financial service providers.[233]

Prior to the Supreme Court's decision in *Cuomo*, the OCC and national banks might have claimed – with some arguable support from *Watters* – that Subtitle D of H.R. 3126 would constitute a significant departure from the legal status quo governing the dual banking system. After *Cuomo*, however, state officials and consumer groups have a persuasive basis for their position that Subtitle D represents an appropriate congressional endorsement of the states' legitimate role in regulating financial institutions and protecting consumers.

NOTES

* Professor of Law, George Washington University Law School. I wish to thank the Law School and Dean Fred Lawrence for a summer research grant that supported my work on this book chapter. I also wish to express my appreciation for the excellent research assistance provided by Christopher Scott Pollock, a member of our Law School's Class of 2010, and by Germaine Leahy, Head of Reference for the Jacob Burns Law Library. I was the principal author of an amicus brief that was filed in the *Cuomo* case by an association of state financial regulators in support of New York Attorney General Andrew Cuomo.

1. 129 S. Ct. 2710 (2009).
2. Ibid at 2721–22.
3. 550 U.S. 1 (2007).
4. 129 S. Ct. 1187 (2009).
5. 467 U.S. 837 (1984).
6. *Clearing House Ass'n, L.L.C. v. Cuomo*, 510 F.3d 105, 109 (2d Cir. 2007), *aff'd in part, rev'd in part,* 129 S. Ct. 2710 (2009).
7. Ibid.
8. Ibid at 109 n.3.

9. Ibid at 109.
10. See ibid at 114, 120.
11. ECOA prohibits all 'creditors' – a category that includes national banks – from discriminating in credit transactions on the basis of several characteristics, including race and national origin. 15 U.S.C. §§ 1691(a), 1691a(e). ECOA expressly preserves the states' authority to enact laws prohibiting lending discrimination that are consistent with the federal statute. In this regard, ECOA specifically affirms the states' power to adopt laws that give 'greater protection' to borrowers than is afforded under ECOA. Ibid § 1691d(f).
12. OCC Interpretive Letter No. 998 (letter from OCC Chief Counsel Julie L. Williams to Rep. Barney Frank dated 9 March 2004). For an analysis and critique of the OCC's 2004 preemption rules, see Arthur E. Wilmarth, Jr., 'The OCC's Preemption Rules Exceed the Agency's Authority and Present a Serious Threat to the Dual Banking System and Consumer Protection', 23 *Annual Review of Banking and Financial Law* 225 (2004), available at http://ssrn.com/abstract=577863. See also *infra* notes 89–90, 224–29 and accompanying text (discussing the OCC's preemption rules); Karen L. Werner, 'Preemption: Frank, House Democrats Urge OCC to Delay Effective Date of Rulemaking', 92 *Banking Report (BNA)* 283 (16 February 2004) (describing Rep. Frank's opposition to the OCC's preemption rules).
13. *Cuomo*, 510 F.3d at 109–10. The district court also enjoined NYAG Spitzer from suing national banks under the Federal Housing Act ('FHA') in the state's capacity as *parens patriae* on behalf of New York citizens. The Second Circuit vacated that portion of the district court's decision, concluding that the district court did not have jurisdiction to decide the FHA issues due to lack of ripeness. Ibid at 110, 121–26.
14. 69 *Federal Register* 1895, 1904 (2004) (amending 12 C.F.R. § 7.4000); see ibid at 1895 (declaring that 'state authorities may not achieve indirectly by resort to judicial actions what [the NBA] prohibits them from achieving directly through state regulatory or supervisory mechanisms').
15. *Cuomo*, 129 S. Ct. at 2715.
16. See Act of June 3, 1864, c. 78, § 54, 13 Stat. 116.
17. *Cuomo*, 129 S. Ct. at 2715. In his dissenting opinion in *Cuomo*, Justice Thomas agreed that the term 'visitorial powers' was 'ambiguous'. However, he argued that, under *Chevron*, the ambiguity of the statute required the Court to defer to the OCC's 'reasonable' interpretation of the term. Ibid at 2723, 2732–33 (Thomas, J., concurring in part and dissenting in part).
18. Ibid at 2715.
19. Ibid at 2716.
20. Ibid at 2716 (quoting *Trustees of Dartmouth College v. Woodward*, 17 U.S. (4 Wheat.) 518, 676 (1819) (Story J., concurring)).
21. Ibid at 2724–25 and n.1 (Thomas, J., concurring in part and dissenting in part).
22. Ibid at 2716 n.1 (majority opinion).
23. Roscoe Pound (1936), 'Visitatorial Jurisdiction over Corporations in Equity', 49 *Harvard Law Review* 369. Surprisingly, Dean Pound's article did not discuss or even cite Justice Story's opinion in *Dartmouth College*.
24. Ibid at 389 (citing Rev. Stat. § 5241 (codified as amended at 12 U.S.C. § 484(a)). An antecedent of the 'vested in the courts of justice' clause appeared in § 54 of the original NBA of 1864. Section 54 provided that the powers 'vested in the several courts of law and chancery' would not be disturbed by the general restriction on the exercise of 'visitorial powers' over national banks. Act of June 3, 1864, c. 78, § 54, 13 Stat. 116.
25. *Cuomo*, 129 S. Ct. at 2718.
26. Ibid.
27. 199 U.S. 148 (1905).
28. 263 U.S. 640 (1924).
29. *Cuomo*, 129 S. Ct. at 2717 (quoting *Guthrie*, 199 U.S. at 159).
30. *Guthrie*, 199 U.S. at 159.

31. *St. Louis,* 263 U.S. at 655 (explaining that 'the State of Missouri brought this proceeding in the nature of *quo warranto* in the State Supreme Court against the [national bank] to determine its authority to establish and conduct a branch bank in the City of St. Louis. . . . The prayer is that, upon final hearing, the bank be ousted from the privilege of operating this branch bank or any other').
32. Ibid at 660.
33. *Cuomo*, 129 S. Ct. at 2717 (quoting *St. Louis*, 263 U.S. at 660).
34. Ibid at 2717 n.2.
35. Pound, *supra* note 23, at 389.
36. 224 U.S. 270 (1912).
37. Ibid at 272 (explaining that Missouri's *quo warranto* action requested that 'each of the defendants be ousted of their corporate franchises and license to do business under the laws of [Missouri]' because they entered into a combination that illegally sought to restrain trade in Missouri). In *St. Louis*, the Supreme Court cited *Standard Oil* to support its conclusion that a *quo warranto* proceeding was consistent with Missouri law and did not result in a denial of due process. *St. Louis*, 263 U.S. at 661 (citing *Standard Oil*).
38. Pound, *supra* note 23, at 389.
39. *Watters*, 550 U.S. at 15–21.
40. *Cuomo*, 129 S. Ct. at 2717.
41. Ibid.
42. Ibid In this regard, the majority cited cases finding that 'law enforcement by federal agencies' against national banks did not constitute a prohibited exercise of 'visitorial' powers. Ibid (citing two lower court opinions). The majority subsequently cited additional cases to show that 'States . . . have always enforced their general laws against national banks – and have enforced their banking-related laws against national banks for at least 85 years, as evidenced by *St. Louis*'. Ibid at 2720–21 (citing, inter alia, *Anderson National Bank v. Luckett,* 321 U.S. 233, 237, 248–49 (1944)).
43. Ibid at 2721.
44. Ibid.
45. Ibid at 2722.
46. Ibid at 2718.
47. Ibid at 2718–19.
48. Ibid at 2719.
49. Ibid at 2717.
50. Transcript of Oral Argument in *Cuomo*, at 37 (statement by Justice Ginsburg to Seth P. Waxman, counsel for the Clearing House), available at http://www.supremecourtus.gov/oral_arguments/argument_transcripts/08-453.pdf.
51. Ibid at 38 (same).
52. See *Watters*, 550 U.S. at 11 ('federal control [under the NBA] shields national banking from unduly burdensome and duplicative state regulation'); Ibid at 13 ('state law may not significantly burden a national bank's own exercise of its real estate lending powers, just as it may not curtail or hinder a national bank's efficient exercise of any other power, incidental or enumerated under the NBA').
53. See Brief of Respondent Clearing House Ass'n in *Cuomo*, at 29 and n.5 (quoting *Watters*, 550 U.S. at 11, 13).
54. Transcript of Oral Argument in *Cuomo*, *supra* note 50, at 37 (statement by Justice Ginsburg to Mr. Waxman).
55. Ibid at 31–32 (colloquy between Justice Souter and Malcolm L. Stewart, counsel for the OCC). Section 36(f)(1)(B) provides that four specific categories of state laws applicable to interstate branches of national banks 'shall be enforced' by the OCC. 12 U.S.C. § 36(f)(1)(B). The OCC argued that the words 'shall be enforced' were intended to give the OCC *exclusive* power to enforce those state laws against national bank branches. Ibid at 25–26 (argument of Mr. Stewart). NYAG Cuomo contended that the purpose of the clause was to direct the OCC to exercise its *concurrent* authority

to enforce applicable state laws against national bank branches, because Congress believed that the OCC was improperly ignoring those laws. Ibid at 13 (argument of Barbara D. Underwood, counsel for Mr. Cuomo). The majority opinion in *Cuomo* concluded that the terms of Section 36(f)(1)(B) 'shed no light on the meaning of "visitorial powers" in the National Bank Act, a statute that it does not refer to and that was enacted more than a century earlier'. *Cuomo*, 129 S. Ct. at 2718 n.3. In contrast, the dissenting opinion in *Cuomo* maintained that Section 36(f)(1)(B) 'reinforces OCC's interpretation of § 484(a)'. Ibid at 2728 n.2. (Thomas J., dissenting in part).

56. Transcript of Oral Argument in *Cuomo*, *supra* note 50, at 48 (question by Justice Ginsburg to Mr. Waxman).
57. Ibid (statement by Mr. Waxman). Counsel added that 'this case doesn't require [the Court] to address' the issue of incidental activities, because *Cuomo* involved real estate lending, 'an express power [of national banks] under [12 U.S.C.] section 371(a)'. Ibid at 48–49.
58. 513 U.S. 251 (1995) ('*VALIC*').
59. Ibid at 257.
60. Ibid at 259 n.2.
61. Brief of *Amicus Curiae* Nat'l Ass'n of Realtors in Support of Petitioner in *Cuomo*, at at 17–18 (citing and quoting OCC, *Activities Permissible for a National Bank, 2007* (2008)); see also Brief of *Amici Curiae* Center for Responsible Lending et al. in Support of Petitioner in *Cuomo*, at 12 (same).
62. Brief of *Amici Curiae* Center for Responsible Lending et al., *supra* note 61, at 13 (quoting OCC, *Activities Permissible for a National Bank, 2007* (2008), at 1). Similarly, the OCC's Chief Counsel and Assistant Chief Counsel proclaimed in a 1997 article that 'the business of banking is in a constant state of evolution'. Julie L. Williams & James F.E. Gillespie, Jr. (1997), 'The Business of Banking: Looking to the Future – Part II', 52 *Business Lawyer* 1279, 1299. They further contended that OCC decisions defining the 'incidental powers' of national banks 'provide key authority for national banks to transform their banking franchises in ways that will be necessary to enable them to compete and effectively serve customers in the financial arena of the future'. Ibid at 1331.
63. Transcript of Oral Argument in *Cuomo*, *supra* note 50, at 48 (statement by Justice Ginsburg).
64. Ibid at 6–11 (colloquies between Justice Breyer and Barbara D. Underwood, counsel for Mr. Cuomo).
65. *Cuomo*, 129 S. Ct. at 2720.
66. Ibid at 2717–18.
67. Ibid at 2720.
68. 519 U.S. 213 (1997).
69. Ibid at 222.
70. Ibid at 222–23 (quoting *National Bank v. Commonwealth,* 76 U.S. (9 Wall.) 353, 362 (1870)). In a 1996 decision, the Supreme Court similarly held that 'States [retain] the power to regulate national banks, where . . . doing so does not prevent or significantly interfere with the national bank's exercise of its powers.' *Barnett Bank of Marion County, N.A. v. Nelson,* 517 U.S. 25, 33 (1996).
71. *St. Louis*, 263 U.S. at 656 (quoting *McClellan v. Chipman,* 164 U.S. 347, 357 (1896)).
72. 321 U.S. 233 (1944).
73. Ibid at 248.
74. See *Cuomo*, 129 S. Ct. at 2717, 2718, 2720–21.
75. 292 U.S. 559 (1934).
76. Ibid at 564–65.
77. See Wilmarth, *supra* note 12, at 253–65.
78. Ibid at 266. See *Lewis,* 292 U.S. at 564–65, 566 (describing both methods for applying state laws to national banks).
79. *Watters*, 550 U.S. at 25 (Stevens J., dissenting, joined by Roberts C.J., and Scalia J.).

80. *Cuomo*, 129 S. Ct.. at 2718.
81. Ibid at 2718 (quoting *St. Louis*, 263 U.S. at 660).
82. *St. Louis*, 263 U.S. at 660, quoted in *Cuomo*, 129 S. Ct. at 2718.
83. Transcript of Oral Argument in *Cuomo*, *supra* note 50, at 27.
84. Ibid at 27–28 (colloquy among Justice Ginsburg, Malcolm L. Stewart and Justice Scalia).
85. *Cuomo*, 129 S. Ct. at 2718.
86. Ibid.
87. 129 S. Ct. 1187 (2009).
88. See, for example, the following amicus briefs filed in *Cuomo* to support NYAG Cuomo: Brief of Members of Congress as *Amici Curiae* in Support of Petitioner, at 3–8 (filed by six members of Congress, including Rep. Barney Frank); Brief for the States of North Carolina et al. as *Amici Curiae* in Support of Petitioner, at 8–14, 22–25, 33–39 (filed by the attorneys general of 49 states and the District of Columbia); Brief of the American Ass'n of Residential Mortgage Regulators as *Amicus Curiae* in Support of Petitioner, at 1–2, 17–21 (filed by an organization of state officials who regulate mortgage lenders, servicers and brokers); Brief of the Conference of State Bank Supervisors as *Amicus Curiae* in Support of Petitioner, at 3–4, 17–21, 28–32 (filed by an organization of state officials who regulate state-chartered banks); Brief of Lawyers' Committee for Civil Rights under Law et al. as *Amici Curiae* in Support of Petitioner, at 1–4, 20–22, 26–38 (brief filed by three civil rights groups); Brief *Amici Curiae* of Center for Responsible Lending et al., *supra* note 61 (amicus brief filed by nine consumer groups and New York City's Department of Consumer Affairs).
89. See, for example, 66 Fed. Reg. 28,593 (2001) (order declaring that Michigan laws, which required car dealers to obtain lending licenses and comply with Michigan consumer protection laws if they arranged auto loans, were preempted by the NBA with respect to those car dealers who acted as agents of national banks in arranging car loans); 66 *Federal Register* 34,784 (2001) (adopting 12 C.F.R. § 7.4006, which preempted the application of state laws to operating subsidiaries of national banks); 68 *Federal Register* 46,264 (2003) (preemption determination declaring that the Georgia Fair Lending Act was completely preempted by federal law as to national banks and their operating subsidiaries); 69 *Federal Register* 1904 (2004) (adopting 12 C.F.R. §§ 7.4007–7.4009 and 34.4, which preempted all state laws that 'obstruct, impair, or condition a national bank's ability to fully exercise its Federally authorized powers' in four broadly-defined areas – real estate lending, lending not secured by real estate, deposit-taking, and other 'operations').
90. Oren Bar-Gill and Elizabeth Warren (2008), 'Making Credit Safer', 157 *University of Pennsylvania Law Review* 1, 82.
91. Ibid at 93–94; Wilmarth, *supra* note 12, at 276.
92. Speech by Comptroller of the Currency John D. Hawke, Jr., 12 February 2002, quoted in Wilmarth, *supra* note 12, at 236, 274.
93. Bar-Gill and Warren, *supra* note 90, at 81–83, 93–94 (citing charter conversions by three large banks in 2004 and 2005, which moved $1 trillion of assets from the state banking system to the national banking system and produced a 15% increase in the OCC's budget); Wilmarth, *supra* note 12, at 233–36, 274–79, 289–93.
94. Bar-Gill and Warren, *supra* note 90, at 90–95 (quote at 94); Christopher L. Peterson (2005), 'Federalism and Predatory Lending: Unmasking the Deregulatory Agenda', 78 *Temple Law Review* 1, 70–74, 77–81 (quote at 81); Amy Quester and Kathleen Keest (2008), 'Looking Ahead After *Watters v. Wachovia Bank*: Challenges for the Lower Courts, Congress, and the Comptroller of the Currency', 27 *Review of Banking & Financial Law* 187, 195–97 (quote at 195); Wilmarth, *supra* note 12, at 232 (quote), 274–77, 289–93, 310–16, 351–56.
95. See Bar-Gill and Warren, *supra* note 90, at 92–93; Wilmarth, *supra* note 12, at 353, 355–56; Stephanie Mencimer, 'No Account' (2007), *New Republic*, 27 August, at 14.

96. *In re Providian National Bank,* 28 June 2000, 2000 OCC Enf. Dec. LEXIS 55, at *1 (alleging violations of California statutes prohibiting unfair business practices); see also Wilmarth, *supra* note 12, at 353–56.
97. Wilmarth, *supra* note 12, at 316 and n.357; 'Correspondence', *New Republic*, 8 October 2007, at 7 (response by Stephanie Mencimer to letter from Comptroller of the Currency John C. Dugan).
98. Julia Patterson Forrester (2006), 'Still Mortgaging the American Dream: Predatory Lending, Preemption, and Federally Supported Lenders', 74 *University of Cincinnati Law Review* 1303, 1308–10, 1319–22, 1359–68; Patricia A. McCoy et al. (2009), 'Systemic Risk Through Securitization: The Result of Deregulation and Regulatory Failure', 41 *Connecticut Law Review* 1327, 1348.
99. Raphael W. Bostic et al., 'Mortgage Product Substitution and State Anti-Predatory Lending Laws: Better Loans and Better Borrowers?' (12 May 2009), Univ. of Pa. Instit. for Law & Econ. Res. Paper 09–27, at 19–24, available at http://ssrn.com/abstract=1460871.
100. Wilmarth, *supra* note 12, at 316, 348–52, 354–55; Amir Efrati and Aaron Lucchetti (2008), 'U.S. News: Cuomo Blazes Own Trail as Wall Street Cop', *Wall Street Journal,* 11 August, at A3; Brooke Masters (2007), 'In Spitzer's footsteps: Cuomo trains his sights on financial services', *Financial Times*, 5 June, at 1.
101. Wilmarth, *supra* note 12, at 316 (quoting 2004 House budget committee document); see also Eric Nalder (2008), 'Mortgage System Crumbled While Regulators Jousted', *Seattle Post-Intelligencer*, 11 October, at A1 (reporting that 'States . . . took 3,694 enforcement actions against mortgage lenders and brokers in 2006 alone, according to congressional testimony').
102. Bar-Gill and Warren, *supra* note 90, at 91; Quester and Keest, *supra* note 94, at 199; Wilmarth, *supra* note 12, at 289–93, 353–55; Mencimer, *supra* note 95 (citing an informal survey indicating that the OCC filed 60 amicus briefs in court cases from 1994 to 2006, 'at least 58 of which were in support of [national] banks'); *supra* notes 6–13 and accompanying text (discussing the decision by the OCC and the Clearing House to sue Mr Spitzer).
103. Bar-Gill and Warren, *supra* note 90, at 81–82, 90–95; Forrester, *supra* note 98, at 1339–42, 1349–53; Quester and Keest, *supra* note 94, at 223–37; Wilmarth, *supra* note 12, at 306–16, 348–52.
104. Robert Berner and Brian Grow (2008), 'They Warned Us: The Watchdogs Who Saw the Subprime Disaster Coming – and How They Were Thwarted by the Banks and Washington', *Business Week*, 20 October, at 36, 38; see also Nicholas Bagley (2008), 'Subprime Safeguards We Needed', *Washington Post*, 25 January, at A19; Nalder, *supra* note 101.
105. OCC Preemption Determination and Order, 68 Fed. Reg. 46,264 (5 August 2003); OCC Interpretive Letter No. 1002, 13 May 2004, from Comptroller of the Currency John D. Hawke, Jr. to Georgia Banking Commissioner David G. Sorrell.
106. Brief of North Carolina et al. in *Cuomo, supra* note 88, at 11–12; Erick Portanger et al. (2002), 'Buying American: HSBC to Acquire Lender in Big Bet on U.S. Economy', *Wall Street Journal*, 15 November, at A1; Harry Terris (2007), 'Citi-ACC: A Bet Vertical Integration Still Has Legs', *American Banker*, 13 September, at 1; Berner and Grow, *supra* note 104, at 41–42 (describing incident involving Okoboji Mortgage).
107. Wilmarth, *supra* note 12, at 228, 233–35, 280–87 (discussing the OTS' preemption initiatives, and their similarity to the OCC's preemptive actions); *State Farm Bank, FSB v. Reardon*, 539 F.3d 336 (2008) (upholding an OTS ruling that permitted agents of a federal thrift to offer mortgage loans in Ohio without complying with Ohio's laws governing mortgage brokers); Office of Thrift Supervision, *Annual Report, Fiscal Year 2008,* at 43, available at http://files.ots.treas.gov/482008.pdf (showing that 95% of the OTS' budget is funded by assessments and fees paid by federal thrifts). For discussions of the OTS' weak record of enforcing consumer protection laws against federal thrifts,

see McCoy, *supra* note 98, at 1348–57; Nalder, *supra* note 101 (reporting that the OTS initiated only 'five to six' enforcement actions against federal thrifts for unfair and deceptive practices between 2000 and 2008).

108. Wilmarth, *supra* note 12, at 348–52; Arthur E. Wilmarth, Jr. (2009), 'The Dark Side of Universal Banking: Financial Conglomerates and the Origins of the Subprime Lending Crisis', 41 *Connecticut Law Review* 963, 1000–02, available at http://ssrn.com/abstract=1403973.

109. See *supra* notes 50–63 and accompanying text.

110. Transcript of Oral Argument in *Watters v. Wachovia Bank, N.A.*, at 45–46 (colloquy between Justice Stevens and Sri Srinivasan, counsel for the United States), available at http://www.supremecourtus.gov/oral_arguments/argument_transcripts/05-1342.pdf; Transcript of Oral Argument in *Cuomo*, *supra* 50, at 25–26 (colloquy between Justice Stevens and Malcolm L. Stewart, counsel for the OCC).

111. *Watters*, 550 U.S. at 35–36 (Stevens J., dissenting) (quoting *Rice v. Santa Fe Elevator Corp.*, 330 U.S. 218, 230 (1947)). Chief Justice Roberts and Justice Scalia joined the dissenting opinion in *Watters*. Justice Stevens and Justice Scalia were members of the majority in *Cuomo*. However, as discussed *infra* in note 136, Chief Justice Roberts joined the dissenting opinion in *Cuomo*.

112. Ibid at 43.

113. Brief of All Former Comptrollers of the Currency since 1973 as *Amici Curiae* in Support of Respondents in *Cuomo*, at 32–34 (quotes at 34).

114. Testimony of Comptroller of the Currency John C. Dugan before the House Committee on Financial Services, 20 March 2009, at 15, available at http://www.occ.treas.gov/ftp/release/2009-26a.pdf. Mr. Dugan's testimony was cited in the amicus brief filed in *Cuomo* by six former Comptrollers of the Currency. Brief of All Former Comptrollers of the Currency since 1973, *supra* note 113, at 32–33.

115. Wilmarth, *supra* note 108, at 1013–15, 1017–18; see also *supra* note 106 and accompanying text.

116. Robert B. Avery et al. (2008), 'The 2007 HMDA Data', *Federal Reserve Bulletin.*, December, at A107, 124–25, 124 (tbl. 11) (showing percentages of '[h]igher-priced loans' made in each year by depository institutions and their subsidiaries and other affiliates, and by independent mortgage companies); see also ibid at A107 n.7 (explaining that the 'higher-priced loans' covered by the study generally fell into the subprime and Alt-A categories).

117. McCoy et al., *supra* note 98, at 1348–55; Wilmarth, *supra* note 108, at 1013–19.

118. National Consumer Law Center (NCLC) (2009), 'Preemption and Regulatory Reform: Restore the States' Traditional Role as "First Responder"', September, at 11–13 & tbls. 1–3, available at http://www.nclc.org/issues/legislative/content/PR-Preemption091609.pdf (last visited on 28 September 2009). The NCLC's study showed that, in 2006, national banks and their operating subsidiaries accounted for 19.2% of subprime loans, 11.3% of Alt-A loans and 31.2% of payment-option and interest-only ARMs. Ibid.

119. Paul Muolo and Mathew Padilla (2008), *Chain of Blame: How Wall Street Caused the Mortgage and Credit Crisis* 18–21, 111–25, 249–70, 300–03, Hoboken, NJ: John Wiley & Sons, Inc.; McCoy et al., *supra* note 98, at 1351 and n.60; Wilmarth, *supra* note 108, at 1018–19, 1045.

120. Center for Public Integrity, 'The Subprime 25', available at http://www.publicintegrity.org/investigations/economic_meltdown/the_subprime_25/full_list/ (last visited on 28 September 2009); John Dunbar & David Donald (2009), 'The Roots of the Financial Crisis: Who Is to Blame?', Center for Public Integrity, 6 May 2009, available at http://www.publicintegrity.org/investigations/economic_meltdown/articles/entry/1286/ (last visited on 28 September 2009); see also McCoy et al., *supra* note 98, at 1351–56 (describing leading roles of large federal thrifts and national banks in the subprime mortgage market); Wilmarth, *supra* note 108, at 1017–19 (describing growing presence of national banks and federal thrifts in the subprime mortgage market, and stating

that '[a]fter 2000, large national banks and federal thrifts represented half or more of the top ten subprime lenders').

121. U.S. General Accountability Office (2007), *Financial Market Regulation: Agencies Engaged in Consolidated Supervision Can Strengthen Performance Measurement and Collaboration*, GAO-07-154, March, at 12–14, 27–29, 40–41; Remarks by OTS Director John M. Reich at a Special Seminar on International Banking and Finance (Tokyo, Japan) (2006), 15 November 2006, at 1–2, available at http://files.ots.treas.gov/87127.pdf.
122. McCoy et al., *supra* note 98, at 1351–57; 'Top Alt-A Lenders in 4Q 07', *Mortgage Line*, 30 April 2008, at 1 (listing HSBC, JP Morgan Chase (Chase), Flagstar, BB&T, Lehman Brothers (Aurora), First Horizon, SunTrust, Wells Fargo, M&T, Bear Stearns (EMC) and Fifth Third among the top 15 providers of Alt-A loans in the fourth quarter of 2007); 'Top Alt-A Lenders in 3Q 07', *National Mortgage News*, 17 December 2007, at 1 (listing Lehman Brothers (Aurora), Chase, Wamu, BofA, Bear Stearns (EMC), Flagstar, Wells Fargo, National City, First Horizon, Wachovia and BB&T among the top 15 providers of Alt-A loans in the third quarter of 2007); 'Top Alt-A Lenders in First Half of 2007', *National Mortgage News*, 17 September 2007, at 1 (listing IndyMac, Countrywide, Lehman Brothers (Aurora), Wamu, Bear Stearns (EMC), Chase, Wells Fargo, Wachovia and National City among the top 15 Alt-A lenders in the first half of 2007); 'Top Alt-A Lenders in Q4 2005', *National Mortgage News*, 10 April 2006, at 1 (listing Bear Stearns (EMC), IndyMac, Lehman Brothers (Aurora), Wells Fargo, SunTrust, First Horizon, Wachovia, BB&T and Chase among the top 15 Alt-A lenders in the fourth quarter of 2005). Payment option ARMs gave borrowers several payment choices, including a negative amortization option that allowed borrowers to pay less than the accrued interest until the principal amount of their loans reached 110% or 120% of the original face amount, at which point the borrowers would be obligated to make much larger payments. Wilmarth, *supra* note 108, at 1022 n.300.
123. Dunbar & Donald, *supra* note 120; see also Wilmarth, *supra* note 108, at 1018–20. For example, Citigroup, BofA and four Wall Street firms were the largest providers of warehouse loans to New Century, which ranked as the third largest subprime lender between 2005 and 2007. Ibid.
124. McCoy et al., *supra* note 98, at 1344–66; Wilmarth, *supra* note 108, at 968–71, 1011–35, 1046–48.
125. McCoy et al., *supra* note 98, at 1354; Wilmarth, *supra* note 108, at 1032–35, 1044.
126. McCoy et al., *supra* note 98, at 1353–55; see also Wilmarth *supra* note 108, at 1044–45; Ari Levy (2008), 'Wells Fargo Chairman Prefers U.S. Plan to Buy Stakes (Update 2)', *Bloomberg.com*, 22 October; Dan Fitzpatrick et al. (2008), 'PNC Buys National City in Bank Shakeout', *Wall Street Journal*, 25 October, at B1; 'The PNC Financial Services Group, Inc.', *Federal Reserve Bulletin*, March 2009, at B1, B7.
127. Wachovia and its mortgage lending subsidiary were the plaintiffs in *Watters* and also in a Second Circuit case that came before the Supreme Court while *Watters* was pending. *Wachovia Bank, N.A. v. Burke,* 414 F.3d 305 (2d Cir. 2005), *cert. denied*, 550 U.S. 913 (2007). National City and its mortgage lending subsidiary were the plaintiffs in a Fourth Circuit case that reached the Supreme Court while *Watters* was pending. *National City Bank of Indiana v. Turnbaugh,* 463 F.3d 325 (4th Cir. 2006), *cert. denied,* 550 U.S. 913 (2007).
128. Office of the Comptroller of the Currency, *Annual Report, Fiscal Year 2008*, at 13, available at http://www.occ.treas.gov/annrpt/1-2008AnnualReport.pdf.
129. McCoy et al., *supra* note 98, at 1352–53, 1358–66; William K. Sjostrom, Jr. (2009), 'The AIG Bailout', 66 *Washington and Lee Law Review* (forthcoming) (working paper version at 2–3, 26–29, 41), available at http://ssrn.com/abstract=1346552; Wilmarth, *supra* note 108, at 1045.
130. McCoy et al., *supra* note 98, at 1356 and fig. 6.
131. Ibid at 1357; see also ibid at 1344–56 (presenting a detailed analysis of regulatory

failings by the FRB, OTS and OCC); Binyamin Appelbaum (2009), 'As Subprime Lending Crisis Unfolded, Watchdog Fed Didn't Bother Barking', *Washington Post*, 27 September 2009, at A1 (criticizing the FRB's failure to take effective action to control the risks of subprime lending by bank holding companies).

132. See *supra* note 88 (citing amicus briefs filed in support of Mr. Cuomo). A preliminary version of the study by McCoy et al., *supra* note 98, was contained in congressional testimony presented by Professor McCoy on 3 March 2009. NYAG Cuomo's reply brief cited Professor McCoy's testimony. See Prepared Statement of Patricia A. McCoy before the US Senate Committee on Banking, Housing, and Urban Affairs, Hearing on 'Consumer Protections in Financial Services', 3 March 2009, available at http://ssrn.com/abstract=1367977 (cited in Reply Brief of Petitioner in *Cuomo*, at 28 n.12).
133. *Watters*, 550 U.S. at 38 (Stevens J., dissenting).
134. 476 U.S. 355 (1986).
135. Ibid at 374.
136. *Watters*, 550 U.S. at 41 (Stevens J., dissenting). Justice Stevens' dissent in *Watters* was joined by Justice Scalia, who wrote the majority opinion in *Cuomo*, and also by Chief Justice Roberts, who joined the dissenting opinion in *Cuomo*. Thus, Justices Stevens and Scalia opposed the OCC's position in both cases, while Chief Justice Roberts switched from opposing the OCC in *Watters* to supporting the OCC in *Cuomo*. It appears that the decisive difference between the two cases for Chief Justice Roberts was that *Watters* considered the applicability of state laws to state-chartered operating subsidiaries of national banks, while *Cuomo* dealt with the authority of a state to enforce its laws directly against national banks. See Transcript of Oral Argument in *Watters*, *supra* note 110, at 28 (question by Chief Justice Roberts, asking why 'a separate subsidiary that is not a national bank . . . is immune from [state] regulation'); ibid at 51–52 (inquiry by Chief Justice Roberts, questioning why a national bank can 'take advantage of [state limited liability protection] by establishing a subsidiary chartered under State law . . . and yet they're claiming immunity from all other State regulations?'). Chief Justice Roberts exhibited a very different attitude toward state authority during the oral argument in *Cuomo*. In response to New York's claim of authority to enforce its fair lending law against national banks, the Chief Justice cited *McCulloch v. Maryland*, 17 U.S. (4 Wheat.) 316 (1819), and he suggested that Congress had 'an historical reason' to be concerned that '[n]ational banks were always targeted by the States' and therefore needed special protection from state enforcement. Transcript of Oral Argument in *Cuomo*, *supra* note 50, at 16. The Chief Justice also indicated that he viewed 'Federal policy' as favoring a uniform regulatory regime governing national banks throughout the nation. Ibid at 9.
137. *Watters*, 550 U.S. at 41 (Stevens J., dissenting) (quoting *Geier v. American Honda Motor Co.*, 529 U.S. 861, 883 (2000)).
138. Ibid (quoting *Rice v. Santa Fe Elevator Corp.*, 331 U.S. 218, 230 (1947)).
139. Ibid at 35–36 (quoting *Rice,* 331 U.S. at 230).
140. Ibid at 20, 21 n.13.
141. Ibid at 20–21.
142. *Wyeth*, 129 S. Ct. at 1201; see also ibid at 1201 and n.9 (stating that 'Congress has not authorized the FDA to preempt state law directly', and giving examples of other federal statutes that expressly authorized agencies to adopt regulations preempting state law); *Watters*, 550 U.S. at 38 and n.21 (Stevens J., dissenting) (stating that 'Congress knows how to authorize executive agencies to preempt state laws' and giving similar examples of federal statutes that expressly delegated preemptive rulemaking authority to agencies). Unlike his dissenting opinion in *Watters*, Justice Stevens' majority opinion in *Wyeth* did not explicitly reject the applicability of *Chevron*. However, as discussed *infra* at notes 145–47 and accompanying text, Justice Stevens' opinion in *Wyeth* strongly indicated that *Skidmore* rather than *Chevron* provided the appropriate level of judicial deference for agency claims of preemption.

143. *Wyeth*, 129 S. Ct. at 1201.
144. Ibid (quoting *Geier,* 529 U.S at 883, and *Hines v. Davidowitz*, 312 U.S. 52, 67 (1941)).
145. Ibid (citing *United States v. Mead Corp.*, 533 U.S. 218, 234–35 (2001), and *Skidmore v. Swift & Co.*, 323 U.S. 134, 140 (1944)).
146. Ibid; see also *Skidmore,* 323 U.S. at 140 (stating that '[t]he weight of [the agency's] judgment in a particular case will depend upon the thoroughness evident in its consideration, the validity of its reasoning, its consistency with earlier and later pronouncements, and all those factors which give it power to persuade, if lacking power to control').
147. *Wyeth,* 129 S. Ct. at 1194 (quoting *Metronic v. Lohr*. 518 U.S. 470, 485 (1996) (quoting *Rice,* 331 U.S. at 230)).
148. Ibid at 1201.
149. Ibid The three dissenters in *Wyeth* did not contend that the FDA's preemption claim should receive *Chevron* deference. Instead, they argued that the FDA's position was entitled to 'some weight' under *Geier* and should have been upheld. They also contended that it was irrelevant that the FDA's preemption claim was not adopted through notice-and-comment rulemaking or that it represented a change in the agency's position. Ibid at 1227–29 (Alito J., dissenting).
150. Ibid at 1201–04 (quotes at 1204).
151. *Watters,* 550 U.S. at 38–39, 41 (Stevens, J., dissenting); see also *Wyeth*, 129 S. Ct. at 1201 and n.9. Justice Stevens emphasized in *Watters* that Congress had *not* made an explicit grant of preemptive rulemaking authority to the OCC. He described the OCC's rulemaking powers under 12 U.S.C. §§ 93a and 371(a) as 'generic authorizations of rulemaking authority . . . and neither says a word about preemption. . . . Needless to say, they provide no textual foundation for the OCC's assertion of preemption authority'. *Watters,* 550 U.S. at 39 and nn.22–23 (Stevens J., dissenting).
152. Ibid at 41 ('No case from this Court has ever applied such a deferential standard to an agency decision that could so easily disrupt the federal-state balance. . . . [W]ith relative ease [federal agencies] can promulgate comprehensive and detailed regulations that have broad preemption ramifications for state law. . . . For that reason, when an agency purports to decide the scope of federal preemption, a healthy respect for state sovereignty calls for something less than *Chevron* deference'.) (internal quotation marks and citations omitted); see also ibid at 39 and n. 23 (maintaining that Congress had not delegated any preemptive rulemaking authority to the OCC).
153. *Cuomo*, 510 F.3d at 117.
154. *Cuomo,* 129 S. Ct. at 2733 (Thomas J., dissenting in part).
155. As previously noted, both the majority and dissenting opinions in *Cuomo* determined that the term 'visitorial powers' in 12 U.S.C. § 484 contained at least 'some ambiguity' with respect to the question of whether § 484 barred judicial enforcement actions by state officials against national banks. See *supra* note 17 and accompanying text. Prior to *Cuomo*, the Supreme Court affirmed the sovereign nature of the states' law enforcement powers in several cases, including *Calderon v. Thompson,* 523 U.S. 538, 556 (1998); *Diamond v. Charles,* 476 U.S. 54, 65 (1986); *Heath v. Alabama,* 474 U.S. 82, 89, 93 (1985); and *Bartkus v. Illinois*, 359 U.S. 121, 137 (1959). In his dissent from the Second Circuit's decision in *Cuomo*, Judge Cardamone argued that '[i]t is difficult to imagine a more core aspect of state sovereignty than the authority to pass and enforce valid nonpreempted state laws'. *Cuomo*, 510 F.3d at 131 (Cardamone J., dissenting).
156. 501 U.S. 452 (1991).
157. Ibid at 460.
158. Ibid (quoting *Rice v. Santa Fe Elevator Corp.*, 331 U.S. 218, 230 (1947)).
159. Ibid at 460–61, 464–67 (quotes at 461, 464).
160. Ibid at 464 (quoting Laurence H. Tribe (1988), *American Constitutional Law* (2nd edn), § 6–25 at 480, Mineola, NY: Foundation Press, and citing *Garcia v. San Antonio Metropolitan Transit Auth.*, 469 U.S. 528 (1985)). Thus, *Gregory* reflects the Supreme Court's view that 'a clear statement requirement is necessary in order to ensure

compliance with federal lawmaking procedures and to protect the residual authority of the states under the Supremacy Clause'. Bradford R. Clark (2009), 'Process-Based Preemption', in William W. Buzbee (ed.), *Preemption Choice: The Theory, Law, and Reality of Federalism's Core Question*, Cambridge, UK: Cambridge University Press, at 191, 204. Professor Clark has explained that the Supremacy Clause (the constitutional source of the preemption doctrine) and other provisions of the Constitution are 'carefully structured to restrict both who may exercise lawmaking power on behalf of the United States (actors subject to the political safeguards of federalism) and how they may exercise it (only in accordance with precise procedures that require the participation and assent of the states or their representatives in the Senate)'. Ibid at 195–97 (quote at 197). Accordingly, '[i]f judges permit an ambiguous provision of a federal statute to preempt state law, they risk circumventing federal lawmaking procedures and the political safeguards [of federalism] they incorporate'. Ibid at 204–05.

161. *Watters,* 550 U.S. at 41 (Stevens J., dissenting) (quoting *Geier,* 529 U.S. at 883 (Stevens J., dissenting)); see also Cass R. Sunstein (2000), 'Nondelegation Canons', 67 *University of Chicago Law Review* 315, 331 (explaining that 'the idea that administrative agencies will not be allowed to interpret ambiguous [statutory] provisions so as to preempt state law . . . [is] an important requirement in light of the various safeguards against cavalier disregard of state interests created by the system of state representation in Congress'); Clark, *supra* note 160, at 213 (agreeing with Professor Sunstein's suggestion that 'the preemption decision must be made legislatively, not bureaucratically' in view of the 'constitutional commitment to a federal structure') (quoting Sunstein, *supra*, at 331).

162. Nina A. Mendelson (2008), 'A Presumption Against Agency Preemption', 102 *Northwestern Law Review* 695, 710, 717.

163. Ibid at 717–22; Thomas W. Merrill (2008), 'Preemption and Institutional Choice', 102 *Northwestern Law Review* 727, 755–57, 772–73 (quotes at 756). In contrast, Brian Galle and Mark Seidenfeld contend, based on a 'realist approach to administrative law' and a 'functional analysis of . . . the relative institutional competence of the three branches' of federal government, that 'agencies are in many contexts better suited to consider federalism concerns than are Congress or the federal judiciary'. Brian Galle and Mark Seidenfeld (2008), 'Administrative Law's Federalism: Preemption, Delegation, and Agencies at the Edge of Federal Power', 57 *Duke Law Review* 1933, 1938–39, 1948–49. Professors Galle and Seidenfeld explain that their 'functional' analysis is directed at 'improving the regulatory process, not the preservation of state regulatory prerogatives per se'. Ibid, at 1949. Thus, their 'realist approach' does not seek to justify or defend any 'formalistic preference for protection of dual sovereignty'. Ibid at 1938, 1949.

164. Merrill, *supra* note 163, at 772; see also ibid at 757–59 (concluding that, '[t]aking all these factors into consideration, . . . courts should continue to function as the institution that has the last word on whether to displace state law through preemption', ibid at 759). In contrast, Professors Galle and Seidenfeld maintain that 'any doctrinal trend toward requiring in all cases clear congressional authorization for [agency] preemption . . . is mistaken'. Galle and Seidenfeld, *supra* note 163, at 1940. They conclude, based on institutional considerations of 'accountability, transparency, and deliberativeness', that 'federal agencies should often be the preferred institutions in which to vest the authority to allocate power between the states and federal government'. Ibid at 1948, 1936.

165. *Wyeth*, 129 S. Ct. at 1200–01.

166. *Republic of Austria v. Altmann*, 541 U.S. 677, 701, 702 n.23 (2004) (opinion for the Court by Stevens J.) (quoting *INS v. Cardoza-Fonseca*, 480 U.S. 421, 466, 468 (1987) (same). Similarly, in *Cuomo* the Second Circuit found it 'troublesome' that the 'administrative record [supporting the OCC's claim of exclusive enforcement powers over national banks] consists almost entirely of the agency's interpretations of case law, legislative history, and statutory text. . . . These are not subjects on which the OCC

holds any special expertise'. *Cuomo*, 510 F.3d at 118. The Second Circuit also observed that 'the OCC does not appear to have found any facts at all in promulgating its visitorial powers regulation. It accretes a great deal of regulatory authority to itself at the expense of the states through rulemaking lacking any real intellectual rigor or depth'. Ibid.

167. *Ledbetter v. Goodyear Tire & Rubber Co.*, 550 U.S. 618, 642 n.11 (2007), *superseded by statute on other grounds*, Pub. L. No. 111–2, 123 Stat. 5 (codified at 42 U.S.C. § 2000e-5(e)).
168. *Wyeth*, 129 S. Ct. at 1202 (quoting *Hines*, 312 U.S. at 67).
169. Mendelson, *supra* note 162, at 714.
170. William W. Buzbee (2009), 'Preemption Hard Look Review, Regulatory Interaction, and the Quest for Stewardship and Intergenerational Equity', 77 *George Washington Law Review* 1521, 1557–69 (quote at 1569).
171. Ibid at 1556.
172. Ibid at 1576–78.
173. *Wyeth*, 129 S. Ct. at 1194–95, 1200 (quote). Professor Buzbee agrees that courts should apply a presumption against preemption when they review agency claims of preemptive authority. As he points out, '[i]f preemption is ultimately a question of congressional intent, shaped against a constitutional norm of retained state concurrent power, then agencies [like Congress] should have to overcome the presumption against preemption'. Ibid at 1564.
174. The group of Justices joining the majority opinion in *Wyeth* was the same as in *Cuomo*, except that Justice Kennedy joined the majority opinion in *Wyeth* but not in *Cuomo*, while Justice Scalia took the opposite position in both cases.
175. *Wyeth*, 129 S. Ct. at 1204 (Breyer J., concurring).
176. Ibid (Thomas, J., concurring in the judgment). Justice Thomas contended that the FDA's preemption claim should be struck down because it relied on a theory of implied preemption (which he rejected as unconstitutional) instead of express statutory preemption. Ibid at 1205, 1207 (arguing that the Supremacy Clause 'requires that pre-emptive effect be given only to those federal standards and policies that are set forth in, or necessarily follow from, the statutory text that was produced through the constitutionally required bicameral and presentment procedures'). Justice Thomas evidently did not have the same problem with the OCC's preemptive rule in *Cuomo* because the OCC relied on a statute – 12 U.S.C. § 484(a) – that expressly preempted state law, even though the statute did not explicitly grant preemptive rulemaking authority to the OCC. See *Cuomo*, 129 S. Ct. at 2722–23, 2732–33 (Thomas J., dissenting in part).
177. *Cuomo*, 129 S. Ct. at 2718.
178. Ibid at 2715.
179. *Chevron*, 467 U.S. at 842.
180. *Cuomo*, 129 S. Ct. at 2715.
181. 546 U.S. 243 (2006).
182. Ibid at 258; see also *Adams Fruit Co. v. Barrett*, 494 U.S. 638, 649 (1990) ('A precondition to deference under *Chevron* is a congressional delegation of administrative authority').
183. *Gonzales*, 546 U.S. at 267 (internal quotation marks and citations omitted).
184. Ibid at 253–54, 275. On similar grounds, a federal appellate court invalidated a ruling issued by the Federal Trade Commission (FTC) that sought to impose federal privacy requirements on attorneys by classifying them as 'financial institutions'. *American Bar Ass'n v. FTC*, 430 F.3d 457 (D.C. Cir. 2005). The court held that 'Congress has not made an intention to regulate the practice of law "unmistakably clear" in the language of the [governing federal statute]'. Ibid at 472. Accordingly, the court rejected the FTC's attempt to rely on an ambiguous statute to regulate 'the practice of law [which] is traditionally the province of the states'. Ibid at 471.
185. *Chevron*, 467 U.S. at 843–44.

186. *Cuomo*, 129 S. Ct. at 2715.
187. Ibid at 2718, 2720.
188. See Thomas W. Merrill and Kristin E. Hickman (2001), '*Chevron*'s Domain', 89 *Georgetown Law Review* 833, 910–13 (contending that (i) the courts should decide at 'step zero' the comparable question of whether *Chevron* deference should be granted to an agency's interpretation of the scope of its delegated authority, and (ii) the courts should decide that question by asking 'whether Congress would want the particular question about the scope of agency authority to be resolved' by the agency acting as 'the primary interpreter of the agency's jurisdiction'); but see Cass R. Sunstein (2006), '*Chevron* Step Zero', 92 *Virginia Law Review* 187, 248 (arguing that '[c]onstraints on administrative discretion, rooted in the rule of law, . . . should be supplied not through Step Zero but through other means, above all through an emphasis on the limitations recognized in *Chevron* itself').
189. Arthur E. Wilmarth, Jr. (2006), '*OCC v. Spitzer*: An Erroneous Application of *Chevron* That Should Be Reversed', 86 *Banking Report (BNA)* 379, 386, available at http://ssrn.com/abstract=886380.
190. *Gonzales,* 546 U.S. at 258; *Cuomo*, 129 S. Ct. at 2715.
191. *Gonzales*, 546 U.S. at 258–75; *Cuomo*, 129 S. Ct. at 2716–22.
192. *Gonzales*, 546 U.S. at 269.
193. *Cuomo*, 129 S. Ct. at 2727 (Thomas J., dissenting in part).
194. Ibid at 2733.
195. *American Bar Ass'n v. FTC*, 430 F.3d 457, 468 (D.C. Cir. 2005) (internal quotation marks and citation omitted). See *supra* note 184 (discussing the appellate court's rejection of the FTC's preemption claim).
196. 545 U.S. 967 (2005).
197. *Cuomo*, 129 S. Ct. 2730 (Thomas, J., dissenting in part).
198. Ibid at 2730 n.3.
199. *Cuomo*, 129 S. Ct. at 2717 n.2 (majority opinion).
200. See *St. Louis*, 263 U.S. at 641–47 (summaries of arguments for the national bank and the United States). In his dissenting opinion in *Cuomo*, Justice Thomas cited NYAG Cuomo's reply brief for the proposition that 'the [national] bank never raised the "visitorial powers" defense in [*St. Louis*]'. *Cuomo*, 129 S. Ct. at 2730 n.3 (citing Reply Brief for Petitioner at 6). There appears to be a conflict between the national bank's argument as described by Justice Thomas and the summary of the bank's arguments published in *United States Reports.* In the published summary, the national bank maintained that Missouri was attempting to exercise a 'visitatorial power' which was 'forbidden', and the bank cited Rev. Stat. § 5241, the predecessor of 12 U.S.C. § 484(a). See *St. Louis*, 263 U.S. at 643 (summary of argument for the bank). The summary of argument for the United States published in *United States Reports* included an assertion that Missouri's *quo warranto* proceedings were 'an obvious attempt to exercise visitatorial powers' that 'our system of government forbids'. See ibid at 645 (summary of argument for the United States). The summary of the United States' argument also included citations to (i) *Guthrie v. Harkness*, 199 U.S. 148 (1905), in which the Supreme Court construed the meaning of the prohibition on 'visitorial powers' in Rev. Stat. § 5241, and (ii) Rev. Stat. §§ 5239 & 5240, the predecessors of 12 U.S.C. 93(a) & 481, which define the visitorial powers of the OCC. See *St. Louis*, 263 U.S. at 645, 647 (summary of argument for the United States). Thus, the published summaries of arguments for the national bank and the United States in *St. Louis* strongly indicate that both parties raised the issue of whether Missouri's judicial enforcement proceedings were barred by the NBA's limitation on 'visitorial powers'.
201. *Brand X*, 545 U.S. at 985.
202. Ibid at 1016–17 (Scalia J., dissenting).
203. Ibid at 1017 (citing *Southern Air Lines, Inc. v. Waterman*, 333 U.S. 103 (1948)).
204. Justice Stevens filed a concurring opinion in *Brand X*, in which he agreed that 'a court of appeals' interpretation of an ambiguous statute does not foreclose a contrary

reading by the agency'. However, Justice Stevens stated that the same result 'would not necessarily be applicable to a decision by this Court that would presumably remove any preexisting ambiguity'. Ibid at 1004 (Stevens J., concurring). Justice Stevens' concurrence suggests that he might not have supported the outcome in *Brand X* if the agency had disregarded a construction of the applicable statute by the Supreme Court instead of a court of appeals.

205. See *supra* notes 138–39, 147, 173 and accompanying text.
206. *Cuomo*, 129 S. Ct. at 2720 (majority opinion).
207. Ibid.
208. Ibid (quoting *Rice*, 331 U.S. at 230).
209. *Gonzales*, 546 U.S. at 274–75.
210. Ibid at 273, 272.
211. 529 U.S. 89 (2000).
212. Justice Thomas pointed out that Congress has legislated with regard to national banks since 'the earliest days of the Republic', and he therefore argued that a presumption against preemption should be rejected in interpreting the NBA for the same reason that *Locke* held such a presumption to be inapplicable in construing federal maritime law. Ibid at 2732 (Thomas J., dissenting in part) (quoting *Locke*, 529 U.S. at 108).
213. *Locke*, 529 U.S. at 108; see also ibid at 109 (explaining that the governing federal statutes mandated 'uniform, national rules regarding general tanker design, operation, and seaworthiness').
214. *Atherton*, 519 U.S. at 219–26.
215. H.R. Rep. No. 103–651, at 53 (1994) (Conf. Rep.), reprinted in 1994 *U.S. Code Congressional and Administrative News* 2068, 2074.
216. Wilmarth, *supra* note 12, at 288–89, 245–71. As previously noted, Justice Scalia observed in *Cuomo* that the OCC 'was not given authority to enforce nonpre-empted state laws [against national banks] until 1966', while 'States . . . have always enforced their general laws against national banks – and have enforced their banking-related laws against national banks for at least 85 years'. *Cuomo*, 129 S. Ct. at 2720. In response to Justice Thomas' invocation of *Locke*, Justice Scalia remarked that '[a] power first exercised [by the OCC] during the lifetime of every current Justice is hardly involvement "from the earliest days of the Republic"'. Ibid (quoting *Locke*, 529 U.S. at 108).
217. *Wyeth*, 129 S. Ct. at 1195 n.3.
218. Ibid at 1200 (quoting *Bonita Boats, Inc. v. Thunder Craft Boats, Inc.*, 489 U.S. 141, 166–67 (1989) (internal quotation marks omitted)). Justice Stevens did not mention *Locke* in his opinion for the Court in *Wyeth*. However, Justice Alito invoked *Locke* in his dissenting opinion to support his contention that the Court should not have applied a presumption against preemption in *Wyeth*. Ibid at 1229 n.14 (Alito J., dissenting) (quoting *Locke*). Thus, it could be argued that Justice Stevens' opinion in *Wyeth* implicitly rejected the applicability of *Locke* to the labeling of prescription drugs because that was a field in which Justice Stevens found a 'historic presence of state law' as well as evidence of 'Congress' decision not to pre-empt [state] common-law tort suits'. Ibid at 1195 n.3, 1202 (majority opinion).
219. 517 U.S. 735 (1996).
220. Ibid at 744 (citing and quoting *Marquette National Bank of Minneapolis v. First of Omaha Service Corp.*, 439 U.S. 299, 318–19 (1978)).
221. *Cuomo*, 129 S. Ct. at 2732–33 (Thomas J., dissenting in part).
222. Nina A. Mendelson (2004), '*Chevron* and Preemption', 102 *Michigan Law Review* 737, 739–40.
223. *Cuomo*, 129 S. Ct. at 2721 (majority opinion) (quoting *id* at 2732 (Thomas, J., dissenting in part)).
224. 12 C.F.R. §§ 7.4007–7.4009 & 34.4; 69 Fed. Reg. 1904, 1912–13 (2004); see Wilmarth, *supra* note 12, at 233–36 (describing the OCC's 2004 preemption rules). For a

comprehensive critique of the legal rationale for the OCC's 2004 preemption rules, see generally Wilmarth, *supra* note 12.

225. Wilmarth, *supra* note 12, at 235–37, 298–99.
226. *Cuomo*, 129 S. Ct. at 2720.
227. 69 Fed. Reg. 1895, 1896 (2004), quoted in *Cuomo*, 129 S. Ct. at 2719.
228. *Cuomo*, 129 S. Ct. at 2720.
229. See 69 Fed. Reg. at 1912–13 (asserting that (i) 'state laws do not apply to national banks if they obstruct, impair, or condition a national bank's ability to fully exercise [its] powers', and (ii) state laws may apply to national banks if they 'do not regulate the manner or content of the banking business authorized for national banks, but rather establish the legal infrastructure that makes practicable the conduct of that business').
230. U.S. Dept. of the Treasury, *Financial Regulatory Reform: A New Foundation* (June 2009).
231. Ibid at 55–70.
232. Ibid at 60–61; H.R. 3126, 111th Congress, 1st Session, §§ 141–48 (original bill as introduced on 8 July 2009).
233. H.R. 3126, *supra* note 232, §§ 142–48.

Index